THE NORSE-FOLK;

OR,

A VISIT TO THE

Homes of Norway and Sweden.

BY

Charles Loring Brace,

AUTHOR OF "HUNGARY IN 1851," AND "HOME-LIFE IN GERMANY."

NEW YORK:
CHARLES SCRIBNER.
377 AND 379 BROADWAY.
1859.

W. H. TINSON, STEREOTYPER, 43 CENTRE ST.

GEORGE RUSSELL & CO., PRINTERS.

PREFACE.

To an American, a visit to the home of the old Northmen is a visit back to his forefathers' house. A thousand signs tell him he is at the cradle of the race which leads modern enterprise, and whose Viking-power on both hemispheres has not yet ceased to be felt. In giving a sketch of a journey among the Norse-Folk, it has seemed to me that there were two sides which should most of all interest their descendants and kinsmen in the New World: one, the associations and memorials which connect them with the age when the wild energy of the race was transplanted to the British Islands, and even touched briefly in its enterprises the coasts of America; and the other, the life of to-day.

When one puts his mind into the position of reading a book of travels, an author should not give him instead, dry historical details; still, glimpses and scenes of the past, side-views into the misty perspectives of early history, suggestions, quaint superstitions, relics which keep the busy present in connection with a far-away time, can surely be properly presented in the traveller's journal. In this view, while I have given free play to the memories which constantly and naturally, through various associations, bring back the saga-period and the days of the early Norsemen, I have left out of view the modern history, glorious as it is, of the Scandinavian States.

The main object of this book, however, is not historical, but simply to picture the life of to-day. It has seemed to me possible to present a country and its people with something of the *personal* and living interest with which they come before a traveller. When we hear general statements on the polity or institutions of a nation, they make, even on the most reflective of us, only a faint impression; but when we are brought into intercourse with its persons, when we hear their words, see their manner, and study their habits; when we sit at their tables, and mingle in their households, and become familiar with their current of thought, we learn, in a way not easily forgotten, the main features of the society and the essential life of such a people. I have in this book attempted to give at least faithfully what I saw in my sojourn in Norway and Sweden, and I hope so faithfully that the reader can often form his conclusion in regard to these countries independently of my conclusion.

It is often a difficulty in a traveller's description, to draw a line between the strict privacies of life to which he is frankly introduced, and which are for him alone, and those customs and habits which illustrate the general life of a people. I trust I have never invaded the former. The names and estates of individuals are usually so disguised that they would be recognized with difficulty even in Norway or Sweden. Of public men I have given no details which are not known to all their countrymen. The conversations related are merely those which chanced on characteristic and public topics.

Norway has been so thoroughly travelled and described of late years by English tourists, that I have bestowed much less space and investigation on its peculiarities than on those of Sweden, which is yet a somewhat fresh field.

Possibly, in some respects, I have spoken too favorably of the atter country, yet I would rather err on that side than on the other. No one can behold a national any more than an individual character accurately who does not behold it with a genial eye. Certainly in respect to its alleged popular vices, intemperance and licentiousness, there must have been in later years a vast improvement. With the present advance of education, the development of agriculture, the increase of trade, the building of railroads and telegraphs, and the proposed liberal measures with respect to freedom of conscience, what may not be accomplished yet by the modern Norsemen? The American kinsmen cannot but wish them God-speed.

CHARLES L. BRACE.

New York, April, 1857.

CONTENTS.

I.—Norway.

CHAPTER XVI.

RETURN JOURNEY TO CHRISTIANIA.

II.—Sweden.

CHAPTER XVII.

GOTTENBURG.

CHAPTER XVIII.

COTTON SPINNERS.

CHAPTER XIX.

HOME MANUFACTURES.

CHAPTER XX.

GÖTHA CANAL AND STOCKHOLM.

CHAPTER XXI.

SUNDAY IN STOCKHOLM.

CHAPTER XXII.

UPSALA—DALECARLIA.

CHAPTER XXXII.

GOTTLAND.

CHAPTER XXXIII.

KALMAR AND SMÅLAND.

CHAPTER XXXIV.

A COUNTRY HOME.

CHAPTER XXXV.

THE FLEET.

CHAPTER XXXVI.

CASTLE L——.

CHAPTER XXXVII.

TABLE-TALK.

CHAPTER XXXVIII.

SOUTH SWEDEN.

CHAPTER XXXIX.

CONSTITUTION OF SWEDISH CHURCH.

CHAPTER XL.

SWEDISH PARLIAMENT.

CHAPTER XLI.

RACES IN SWEDEN.

III.—Denmark.

CHAPTER XLII.

COPENHAGEN.

CHAPTER XLIII.

SCANDINAVIAN MYTHOLOGY.

I.

Norway.

THE NORSE-FOLK.

CHAPTER I.

CHRISTIANIA.

June twenty-first !—the long summer-day, celebrated by the old Norse-people and the Vikings, equally with the shortest day, *Yule*, or Christmas : it is a holiday here. Arbors of branches are in the gardens, flowers on the tables, and last night bonfires were burning. To-day, business is abandoned ; my carriole, which was preparing for the journey over the mountains, must wait another day ; people are taking excursions, some on the water in boats, and some in carriages to the country. It is a beautiful sight, this cool fresh day, to watch the parties on the Fiord, from the bastions of the old fort (Aggershuus). There is an endless sparkle of the waters, and the gaily-dressed parties cross and re-cross to the little islets which break in picturesquely on the distant reach of the bay. You look down, some seven miles, through what seems a chain of lakes, but which is the broken outline of the Fiord, until the eye turns away from the bright glimmer to the shaded valleys and wooded hills that make the horizon on every side.

The market-place is full of women, with bright kerchiefs on their heads, selling flowers and vegetables, and of little four-wheeled carts, with cloths and stuffs for sale. Every one is neatly dressed, and I have met no one intoxicated.

The city is a neat, cheerful-looking place, with stuccoed houses, two stories high, placed directly on the street, as in the German and French villages.

In the quarter near the Palace, there are some large, handsome buildings, inhabited by the wealthiest people, in *flats*, like the Berlin and Paris houses. The streets are lighted with gas. There is nothing in the city to especially distinguish it from other European cities, except the appearance of the peasants. These are marked-looking men and women—usually blonde, with ruddy complexion, regular Norman features, light hair, and faces expressing a certain reserved and sober strength of feeling. They have, most of them, powerful frames. I notice some of darker complexion, with an obliquity of eyelids, almost Mongolian—the same feature which struck me in the Norwegian waiters on our boat from Copenhagen. Probably they have a slight mixture of Finnish blood.

The town is evidently a great resort for travellers. All the principal shops are for strangers—filled with prints, or characteristic Norwegian objects; others are crowded with accoutrements for carriole-travelling, and salmon-fishing.

English is spoken everywhere, and Englishmen throng in every hotel. Our landlord (in the *Hotel du Nord*) says he sent off fifteen English sportsmen yesterday up the country, each in his carriole.

The outskirts of the city are beautiful—a broken, hilly, green country, with wooded roads running near the Fiord, and catching the most picturesque glimpses, as of mountain-lakes. The country-seats are very neat and comfortable in aspect, and the soil does not seem inferior. I see fields of all our Northern productions in America, except of the Indian corn.

One of the sights without the city, which gives a pleasant ride, is the villa of Prince Oscar, the crown prince; a pretty little country-seat on a rocky-point, looking out over the Fiord. It seemed to me the most tasteful and really enjoyable royal residence to be seen in Europe. A gem of a house. If any of our wealthy gentlemen would like a model for a rich little villa, they should see this. The furniture is all of Norwegian materials—the tables and chairs of exquisite polished Norwegian maple, giving a most original and pretty effect. The floors are parquette of inlaid polished woods of the country. The pictures illustrate the Norwegian life and scenery.

Tiedemann has there his series, representing the "Life of a Norwegian Peasant." Such narrative-paintings are usually too palpable to be interesting artistically. But this is so simply and skillfully managed that it is very effective. You are interested in the characteristic scenes of Norwegian peasant-life, but you are led on to the greater mysteries of human life ;—the memories of childhood, seen through tears, the sunny glow, the ideal hope and passion, the sorrow and blank disappointment, the maturity and decay.

I visited afterwards several studios and galleries in the city. There are some very pretty landscapes in these collections ; and works of a good quality can be got quite cheaply.

INSTITUTIONS.

The schools in Christiania seem in an advanced condition. There are one hundred and ninety-seven stationary schools in this diocese, beside high schools, a school of drawing for workmen, and a normal school for teachers. I have visited one Institution for vagrant and homeless girls, which seems excellently managed—the *Eugenia Stift.* An old spacious house is occupied by the school, with the dormitories, and various work-rooms.

The girls work at spinning, sewing, embroidery, and straw-weaving within doors, and have a large garden in which to labor in the mild months. When they have been here a certain time, they are commonly sent away to families as servants.

Among other institutions, I drove out to see the new Insane Asylum. It is a large building, and arranged on the best modern principles. As is usual, there are apartments for all degrees of insanity, and for different conditions of wealth among the patients. There is no wall about the asylum, and the view, at this season, is exquisite enough in itself to be a cure for the diseased mind. We found in one sitting-room a very well dressed party of gentlemen, with billiard-table, books, piano, and various luxuries. They received us politely, and at our request, one played very prettily a modern German waltz.

Nothing betrayed them as a company of lunatics. In another ward, the superintendent pointed us out a mild old man, bent with some previous suffering, who, he said, had been kept in one of the villages for fifteen years in chains! —so little understanding was there among the people of the proper treatment of this disease. I was surprised to see *wooden* bedsteads used in so complete an establishment. The asylum has no idiots within it, and the superintendent tells me that there is no institution in Norway for this most unfortunate class—though he estimated their number at three thousand in the whole country! It was a very significant fact, and characteristic of Norway, that among this great company of insane, not love, or licentiousness, or intemperance, or disappointment, was the preponderant cause, but *solitude*—its gloom and moroseness, and above all, its unnatural self-consuming lusts.

I did not understand this effect of the mountain life clearly at the time—but now, after being in those vast, melancholy solitudes, and seeing how utterly lonely, on the great mountain-sides and by the rock-bounded Fiords of the North, thousands must live year after year in Norway, I can well believe that the soul may become diseased or poisoned for want of its atmosphere—the society of other beings.

I hear here, as in all the hospitals, of a new cure of a fearful disease, which, while it scourges the guilty, often does not spare the innocent. It attracts great attention, and is practised by the University physician, Dr. BOECK, though discovered first in France. If the results of the last five years be continued in this gentleman's practice, the cure will form an era with the original discovery which checked the small-pox. It seems a treatment somewhat on the same principle ; and if I understand the subject, it is the most thorough application yet made of homœopathic principles, though by olopathic physicians.

Medical readers will know what I mean, when I give the title of the pamphlet, which has already reached the Smithsonian Institute, on the subject, "*Die Syphilization der Kinder*."*

As this is the summer vacation, I have been able to see but little of either the professors or students of the University. The buildings are tasteful and well situated, and the collections, both of natural history and antiquities, seemed valuable. It has thirty-one professors : sixty thousand dollars per annum is the amount devoted to it by the state.

At the present time, the students are away on an invited visit, with the Danish students from Copenhagen, to the Universities of Lund and Upsala, in Sweden. The papers are filled with accounts of their speeches, the reception by the king in his palace, and the various festivities. Though principally a youthful frolic, there is no doubt that the excursion is encouraged by thousands, who are seriously hoping

* This pamphlet will also be found in the Mercantile Library, New York.

such mutual associations among the young men of the three countries, may tend to the great result so long prayed for—a SCANDINAVIAN UNION.

June 1856. A procession of the Fathers of the city went down to-day to the dock, to meet the returning students. I took the arm of a friend, and we made our way to the same point.

We found already a crowd of thousands assembled. Not a man was intoxicated. There were no soldiers or policemen to preserve order, and my friend assured me that in such crowds, picking pockets was almost unknown. Every one was decently dressed, and the faces wore a superior, intelligent expression. The crowd lined the pier, and at length as the guns announced that the *Ganger Rolf* was coming up the Fiord, they swarmed over the schooners and small craft lying near, while little boats moved about to catch a good view of the returning steamer.

One boy excited great admiration on my part by his skillful motions with the "Water Shoes." These are long wooden shoes, appearing precisely like snow shoes, except that they are somewhat longer, and are fastened together by an iron bar, about a foot apart. The boy's feet were kept steady on them by little iron clamps, under which he put his toes. His oar was a light paddle, with a blade at each end, so that he could whirl and strike the water, backing, turning, or swinging with the most beautiful ease. With this ingenious apparatus, he glided over the water faster than the fastest row-boats near him.

My friend, with whom I had been speaking of the remarkable sobriety of the crowd, said that the new Sunday law had made a great difference. Now, no one is allowed to sell spirits from five o'clock Saturday evening till nine o'clock Monday morning. The first offense was a fine of ten dollars ; second, twenty, and so on, with a final chance of imprisonment. The informant received half. Our own landlord, he said, of the *Hotel du Nord*, had been fined twice, merely for sending toddy up to gentlemen's rooms on Sunday. The beer of the country—a beverage much like *Lager Bier*—is wisely excepted.

At length our steamer drew up to the wharf, gay with flags, and crowded with the hundreds of students. Cheers echoed on both sides, and handkerchiefs waved. The bands on shore struck up spirited music, and the students in procession, welcomed by the guilds and the societies of the city, marched animatedly into the town. It was a very lively scene.

As we walked home, passing a few soldiers, my companion said that a new Law would soon be in operation, which would make every man a soldier, and he should have to pay a hundred species (dollars) to get rid of it! It appears this is a militia law, much like our own, requiring service from every man, but accepting a substitute—though here the service would often be much heavier ; as, for instance, standing guard in the city, and drilling every day—while the fines are heavier.

The law is probably intended to throw more of the burdens of State, especially of the army, on Norway, which has not yet borne a proportional part to Sweden.

CHAPTER II.

A NORWEGIAN DINNER.

A GENIAL friend gave us, with some other strangers, a most agreeable dinner-party to-day. Some eighteen or twenty gentlemen and ladies were present, and the table was truly splendid. The language spoken was mostly English, (I have but one acquaintance in Christiania who does not speak English.) The talk was very lively. Several students were present, who had just returned from the great Excursion, one or two Norwegian gentlemen of distinction, a rough, blunt English naturalist, a distinguished Swedish Professor, an English salmon-fisher, and several ladies.

"You should have seen our festiveness in Stockholm," said an enthusiastic young student near me. "We had the splendid dining-hall of the Palace, and the king hospitiated us. Nearly a thousand sat down at once. But those stupids—those Swedes—they seem as they had never seen a lady! Ah, the ladies! Mr. B.,—they really covered us with flower! We had bouquets each moment!" I asked whether these excursions had been tried before. He replied that they had; and that they had already all visited Copenhagen. "Do people really have much hope for a Union?" I asked. "No," said he, "to tell you the truth, I do not think they have. It is a good thing to write poems about, and make oratories, but for a *fact*, I must confess," and he shrugged his shoulders, "we have no very high respects for either Sweden or Denmark."

"He has reason;" said an old gentleman near me—a politician. "We are a democratic country, and we could never unite with any other country, except on the freest Constitution. Besides, there would be practical hindrances—where the capital to put, and how raise the common revenues? The benefits would by no means be so great to us as to Denmark:—she needs Union to save her. She must in years fall to pieces—losing Holstein, and having the Sound-dues capitalized, and becoming into quarrels through the change of succession."

"But you speak of Union—you have one now with a monarchy."

"Yes, that is true—but it is really only a union in name. We have our own Storthing, and our laws, and our soldiery—and not a King of Sweden ever will dare to lay fingers on them. We were obliged to unite under Carl Johan, when all Europe was against us; but even he never dared to attack long our liberties—but listen—there is a toast for you!"

Our host, though we were only on the second course, rose for a toast, and in a neat little English speech, proposed the health of the "American guest," and deprecated the unnatural and horrible contest into which the two countries of England and America seemed about to enter.

The company drank, and bowed to me, and I replied. After this, a succession of toasts was kept up in a much more formal manner, than would be customary with us, or on the Continent. The English and Norwegian habits in this seems to express a more dignified hospitality than ours.

The dishes were peculiar. The second course after soup was ham cut up, and peas, passed about, and tongue with *kraut;* the third, lobsters boiled; the fourth asparagus; the fifth, salmon; sixth, chickens and mutton cut up and handed to each by the servants; then custards, fruit and cakes, with claret, hock, champagne, sherry, port, etc., etc.

In the drinking of healths, my neighbor whispered that he never filled his glass, and so escaped too much wine. The old custom was for each to empty his glass, which is fast going into disuse. The Norwegian cookery seems excellent, with much use of cream in the dishes.

In the course of the conversation, the subject of America came up, and our Swedish Professor said a very good thing.

They were speaking of the State-Church—and of the experiment of separation in our country. "The truth is," said one gentleman, "nothing can be learnt from the American Free Church System—America is too young. What is her whole age against two thousand years? it is a mere day!" "But," said the Swede with a fine expression, "how do we know that these two thousand years are not a mere day, compared with the whole coming human history! America has little to learn from the past."

After a little, the talk turned to the subject of Slavery, and the recent disgraceful and cowardly assault by Brooks upon Senator Sumner. The words spoken were such as would be good for our people to hear—scathing, indignant words at such ruffianly brutality. Much further interesting conversation was kept up on American affairs, showing a thorough understanding of our difficulties and struggles.

At length we arose and took our ladies to the drawing-room, each bowing to his companion, and then shaking hands with the host, with the words "*Tak for mad!*"—(thanks for the meal!) The gentlemen then retreated to the library to smoke, while coffee was brought.

It is very evident, as I converse with people here, and in other parts of Northern Europe, that a great change has come over the popular feeling towards America, since I was last on the Continent, five years ago. Then America was the ideal everywhere to free-thinking and aspiring men. The oppressed looked hopefully to it; the philosopher found the confirmation of his theories of human liberty there; the hard-working, the politically degraded, the idealists, the struggling masses, felt that the Western Republic was especially for them, and even if they could never share its privileges, they were happy that humanity had at length looked on such a glorious effort. The reports of the common freedom, of the education of the masses, of the high morality prevailing, came over even exaggerated, and silenced the enemies of popular rights, and converted many doubtful. One felt the effect of all this, as a traveller. You were not alone; you were the representative of the best thoughts and aspirations of mankind. The warm hand grasping yours, welcomed not you, but a nation of freemen. The rich did not condemn, because property and person had been better shielded under the Republic, than under European monarchies. The poor, the laborers, were especially your friends, for was not your land the very land which elevated labor?

All this is quite different now. You are treated politely as a stranger; or you are welcomed more or less for what you personally are, but for your country, among the populace you get no welcome. The glory has departed.

Within five years, various circumstances have opened the eyes of Europe to our real situation, and, as often happens, the people see nothing but our sins. We are simply now a tricky, jobbing, half-barbaric people, where the worst political corruption of the Old World exists without its refinement; and where brutality, rowdyism, and unlimited despotism have in certain quarters free play. Our politicians and diplomats are despised; our Constitution is sneered at, as inflicting upon us the most disgraceful legislators; and the laboring class and the democrats know that within our limits, a more abominable tyranny over labor and free speech and thought exists, than the worst despotisms of the Continent ever exhibited. There is nothing now in our situation to dazzle the world. They see with clear eye our blackest sins and our miserable political jobbing.

To-day a leader appears of some length in the Christiania "*Aften Bladet*," with the following mild opening—"The scandal in the North American Senate, which has roused such feelings of excitement, it appears to us, in its treatment by the Senate, the press, and the public meetings, shows a greater degree of general brutality, even than the scene itself between Brooks and Sumner."

Then it gives us the scene between Mr. Wilson and Mr. Butler, where the latter says, "You are a liar," and follows this by quoting at length two atrocious articles, disgraceful to South Sea Islanders, from the *Richmond Whig* and the *Examiner*, approving of the assault. It closes with a sarcastic remark, on the respect due to American institutions.

For my own part, unpleasant as the change is in the public sympathy and respect for us, I am glad of it. We have had the world's applause too long. We need the frown. Besides, how can men in distant countries and engaged in petty questions of state or commerce, judge on those mighty struggles, whose scum only appears on the surface of American affairs!

Yet never does one love his country so as in hearing this universal voice of condemnation. At home, you do not think much of patriotism. But when you see from a distance the grand nature of the experiment made in your country, and when you behold the dark storms that threaten, you say, as you never could say before, "I belong to her, and with her fall, will I fall."

We went out from our dinner-party, about 8 o'clock, to see a meeting of the students in the little park, to celebrate their return. A considerable crowd of the young men and the professors were assembled, nearly all smoking vigorously. Just outside the slight palings and hedge, a great concourse of the town's people had gathered, watching the proceedings. It was characteristic that these never once offered to intrude, though there was nothing to prevent them, except a few students' marshals. The first exercises were some spirited chorus-songs from the crowd of young men ; then one of the professors followed, with an extemporaneous oration. It was delivered with a great deal of fire and enthusiasm—recounting the interesting points of their visit, and glorifying the idea of Scandinavian Union—picturing the possible future, when the three nations, even more than in the old Kalmar Union, would form a united whole, and become the great barrier to Russian invasion, and a State of influence in the world. These sentiments were received with great applause.

Other speeches followed, to the same effect, with more songs. I met a Danish gentleman in the crowd, and we spoke of the oration. He admitted that the idea of union was very popular, but thought, as do all, that practical difficulties were in the way—there were now such great dissimilarities in the characters of the peoples, and in the forms of their government—each had so much jealousy and dislike of the other—the Norwegians were democratic, rough, and practical ; the Danes more reserved, refined, and ideal. Still, he confessed, a union was almost indispensable to Denmark.

June —th.—One of my friends drove me out to-day, to see the beautiful environs of Christiania. There is something in the aspect of the country which reminds me of scenery in Maine : the broken coast of the Fiord, with little wooded islets—the pine-covered hills in the distance, and the warm, green valleys by the streams. It is a warmer and more genial scenery than I should have expected in Norway.

A gentleman whom my friend knew, overtook us on our ride, mounted on a beautiful blood-horse.

They saluted formally, and at his hearty invitation, we turned to pay him a visit. We entered his place through a pleasant avenue, and came in on a little square of low, neat buildings, with a bell-tower over one, giving a pleasant effect of grouping about it to the cluster of houses. We were shown to a comfortable sitting-room, and after a short chat, our host most kindly gave us a glimpse of his house. There were numbers of fine rooms opening into each other—the bed-rooms being usually on the ground floor. The guest-chamber had its own sitting-rooms adjoining. There was one large dancing-saloon. Scarcely any of the rooms were carpeted, but the furniture was tasteful and comfortable. The kitchen was below, a good spacious room, as it should be. The only Norwegian peculiarity was a great covering, like a roof, reaching out over the brick-range, serving as a funnel or ventilator to carry off smoke and smells—not a useless invention for our American kitchens.

The most marked thing about the house was the great extent of it, through building on laterally rather than perpendicularly, as an American would do.

The gentleman took us also out to his grounds, and his barns and farm-houses, which were large brick buildings with pointed gables. In a pretty arbor of beech he sat us at a table, and a servant brought champagne. At parting, a servant opened the carriage-door, and he himself stood with head uncovered, bowing repeatedly to us. Norway is certainly opening in Christiania, most courteously and agreeably.

AN ICELANDER.

June —th.—I called to-day on a student, from Iceland, a thorough scholar in the old Norse Literature. After a few words, he said, with a fine enthusiasm, speaking English. " Ah, sir,—I love your country and your folk. You are the true descendants of the Norsemen. I see more of the qualities of our old Vikings in your country than I do anywhere in Scandinavia, or England. Even your vices are the vices of the Vikings—how like !—you love so the adventure, and the sea-water life, and to be uncontrolled. The filibusters, as you do call them, they are modern vikinger !"

I agreed, but hoped we should imitate the descendants of the Vikings, and free our villains and serfs.

His face had a beautiful spiritual, enthusiastic expression, and he said sadly, " Yes ! it is to hope ! God will surely so guide you. The Northmen were, it is true, sea-pirates, but they always planted free institutions wherever they settled, and left things better than they found. You have a horrible—I know not if you have the Icelandic word—*thralldom* there ; but the blood of the Northmen leads to freedom.

You and the Norse-folk are the only ones in history, where the individual does so venture every thing. Look at your first settlers and at your sea-captains and discoverers, and now at Walker! It is, sir, the old blood. Do you remember the description of the Vikings and of Gauka Thorer, in the Heimskringla.* You do have a translation, I believe. Yours are the men, who have the faith above all in themselves."

I inquired about Iceland and its present condition. He

* THE SEA-KING.

The hero who knows well to ride
The sea-horse o'er the foaming tide,—
He who in boyhood wild rode o'er
The seaman's horse to Scania's shore,
And showed the Danes his galley's bow,
Right nobly scours the ocean now.
On Scotland's coast he lights the brand
Of flaming war; with conquering hand
Drives many a Scottish warrior tall
To the bright seats in Odin's hall.

GAUKA THORER.

The King said, "And I have a great inclination to take such; but are ye Christian men?"

Gauka Thorer replies, that he is neither Christian nor heathen. "I and my comrades have no faith but on ourselves, our strength, and the luck of victory; and with this faith we slip through sufficiently well."

The King replies, "A great pity it is that such brave slaughtering fellows did not believe in Christ their Creator."

Thorer replies, "Is there any Christian man, king, in thy following, who stands so high in the air as we two brothers."—*Laing's Translation.*

represented it as discontented with its connection with Denmark, and ready to accept almost any other foreign government. It still produced, he said, many students and scholars, who mostly went to the University of Copenhagen.

I found we had an equal admiration for the old Icelandic literature, though I knew it only by translation. A new German translation of the *Eddas*, by Simrock, which I had with me, he pronounced one of the very best yet made, preserving the alliteration admirably.

He attached very little historic authority to the sagas which Snorro Sturleson collected of times before the 7th and 8th centuries. The saga of the discovery of America by the Northmen, he, as most scholars, considered to be based in fact, especially as it is conjoined with the saga-accounts of Greenland and its occupation, which recent investigations by the Danish government into the remains of the early settlements have fully confirmed. His theory of the settlement of Iceland was peculiar—that colonists from Ireland and the adjacent islands, first occupied the island, and these were succeeded by Norwegian Northmen.*

* One of the old sagas relates that a celebrated Icelandic chieftain had his son taught Irish, "that nothing should be wanting to him, if he should ever come to Ireland!"

CHAPTER III.

POSTING OVER THE DOVRE FIELD.

CHRISTIANIA, to most travellers, is merely a waiting-place. People are always preparing in it, and questioning, and investigating as to the perils and trials of the unknown journey in the interior. My perplexities were somewhat increased, by having now a lady to provide for—my wife having joined me by steamer from Hull—and for a woman's travelling in Norway, there seems not the slightest provision. One thing was clear, that beyond the railway and the Mjösen Lake, there was no public conveyance, except a kind of peasant's dog-cart. But whether to hire a double carriage, or a chaise, or carrioles, or to buy one or any of these, was the problem. A carriage and driver to Trondhjem alone would come to about sixty dollars. Luckily we had an honest reliable landlord, who spoke English, to whom I most cordially recommend all distressed travellers, starting for the unknown journey through Norwegian mountains. Mr. Halvorsen, the landlord of the *Hotel du Nord*, remember! After exploring everything else, I took his advice precisely, and it turned out the very best. In fact, no other vehicle would have done at all. I bought two new light carrioles, for seventy dollars, with the privilege of returning them at the end of the journey, and receiving fifty-five dollars back, if they were uninjured. Of these interesting vehicles, more hereafter. Our equipment was also very carefully provided ; and, as I trust, in a few years, a summer-trip over the mountains of Norway will be as common and popular to Americans, as now is a journey to the Springs, I will give it. Baggage, a small valise each, with thick covers (the best is oil-skin), and straps to fasten them under the post-boy's seat. The gentlemen must have an India-rubber poncha, very light, slouched hat, thick shawl, thick over-coat and shoes, and clothes very strong, with walking-stick and wallet and a leathern-bag for small silver and copper coin. This last indispensable. The lady, a water-proof cloak with hood (an excellent article called *aqua-scutum*, can be obtained in London), blanket-shawls, stout leather boots (India-rubbers for change) ; warm winter clothing, and a wallet for tea, and guide-books, etc., etc. *One* bonnet, I am instructed, with change of trimmings!

The great object being to have everything as compact as possible, and to be prepared for the hardest treatment, that clothes, luggage, vehicle, and externals can possibly sustain, for the dust, heat, mud, rain, snow, and bitter cold. Nothing that is taken in the way of garments, it should be remembered, will ever come back in wearable condition. For stores, if the party be inclined to dyspepsia, take portable soup and biscuit, and in any case, tea. I took no brandy or wine, but those who need them should be reminded that the country inns have nothing of the kind.

June ——.—As usual, too late in starting; nobody in the Christiania Hotel in the least hurry—the landlord quietly observing as we leave the house, while he looks at his watch, that he thinks we cannot possibly reach the train, though he knows we have been waiting already two days beyond our time. Our rosy-faced *commissionaire* who had negotiated for the carrioles, starts them off at the same time with ourselves. The clock in the Station already points the hour; the rooms for the first and second classes are crowded with people—sportsmen in grey shawls, and California hats; travellers in oil-skin sou'-westers; gentlemen of business, soldiers and ladies—all gathering parcels, calling for tickets, and hurrying to and fro.

The commissionaire puts the carrioles aboard the freight cars, and I buy the tickets in agonizing haste; but there is not the slightest occasion for it. Our railroad, like everything else in Norway, takes its time. We seat ourselves in a second-class carriage, dispose the bundles—but finding two pipes already beginning to smoke, in different parts of it, change to a first-class before there is any indication of the train's starting. At length the guard, evidently from his face an Englishman, locks the door and we are off. Our car is entirely English, even more comfortable than many English first-class carriages, and we have the cushioned little compartment entirely to ourselves. The scenery on the route is much like that of a New-England railroad—long, sloping, pine-covered hills, glimpses of rivers and white foam through trees, green rye fields and pastures, and here and there a log-house, or little village of red houses. Time, about eighteen miles an hour ; length, forty-two miles.

This road has been built in great part by the aid of English capital, at the cost of fifty thousand dollars per mile. Part of the directors reside in England. It pays only about three per cent. on the whole stock, but is increasing daily in business. From the connection with the steamer on Lake Mjösen, it is enabled to gather in the products and passengers from a considerable back country, perhaps one hundred and fifty miles in extent. It is the only railroad in Norway. Another is much talked of now, which shall connect Norway and Sweden, by *Kongsvinger* on the Glommen, to the northeast of Christiania.

This road ends at Eidsvold. Here we found a very comfortable, sensible sort of station ; boats were in waiting to take the passengers to the steamer—none of our frail, modern boats, but broad, substantial Norsk vessels—into which carrioles, luggage, and passengers can be dumped without inconvenience. Four carrioles and one low-wheeled carriage for two horses were taken up by crane and rope on the front deck of the steamer. For the two vehicles and ourselves the fare of the ferry was sixteen cents. No one put himself out, and in about two hours everything was aboard, and we were under weigh.

As I already find in Norway, charges are low, and no one seems to wish to take advantage of you. (N. B.—Two persons have returned me change to-day, overpaid.)

A polite Norwegian gentleman, travelling by post to Trondhjem, has taken us in charge, and by his thorough kindness we get on admirably. He says that the carriage on board belongs to one of the Bonders,* or peasant farmers on the Lake—the wealthiest class in Norway.

The scenery of Lake Mjösen is not at all remarkable—pretty and gentle with green hills sloping far to the water, sprinkled over with little brown or black houses. A great deal of cultivation is visible, and constantly small villages of neatly-cut log houses come in sight, where the steamer stops—on the whole, the scene is much like Lake Champlain or Lake George.

Every thing is done in the easiest way possible. Broad boats pull leisurely off, the boatmen raise their hats, the sailors raise their caps, passengers bid polite adieus, and calmly smoking step into the boats. A passenger is putting on his coat, and the man at the wheel leaves the helm to help him get it on. The carriage is swung off into a large scow-boat; a gentlemanly-looking man receives it, and pulls off with sweeps, and does not even take off his coat. When last seen, the current has taken him quite below the landing-place, and the boat seems much too heavy for him, but he labors on undisturbed.

The men one sees are tall, florid, vigorous-looking, but generally spare in the face—blond, with wrinkled face near the eyes, and often, with what I observed in Christiania, a

* I shall adopt this English version of the Norwegian word *Baender*, as better than any translation.

slight obliquity in the eyelids. The nose is regular, and is a little raised in line.

There are not many passengers in the cabin—a few Danish ladies coming to the Lake for a pleasure trip, and to see a Norwegian Sœter or mountain pasture, one or two Norwegians, and two English sportsmen, salmon-fishers. These last are desperately bored, and one—generally in the finest scenery—turns his face to the wall and sleeps. They left England because they were so bored; and they find this almost as bad, though once in the mountains they hope for sport.

The Lake is only sixty-three miles long, but we did not reach the town at the end, *Lillehammer*, before eleven o'clock in the evening. It was still bright daylight; a crowd of boys were on the pier—there was no shouting or excitement—boys raise their caps, we raise ours—the little carrioles are lifted up by the cranes on the dock. In a few moments, small Norwegian ponies are harnessed to them and we drive towards our inn.

It was very important that evening, that I should see a gentleman, to whom I had especial letters—the principal magistrate of the province. It was half past eleven at night, though still only a pleasant twilight, and with some trepidation I drove to his house. He was up with his ladies in the drawing-room, and welcomed me, just as if it was a seasonable hour in the afternoon. He spoke English. I desired only to state my objects, and not further to detain them—but he would not hear of it. The guest must at least break bread with them. Some refreshments were brought, and he was gone for a few moments, while I chatted with the ladies. He had said so little, and used so few ceremonies, and I had made such a strange intrusion, that I should not have been surprised at his getting rid of me on the easiest terms. But on the contrary, he had been showing me the most thorough kindness—a sort of English-like politeness which comes right to the point of your wishes, and serves you without words in the most direct way. In those few minutes, he had prepared a plan of travel and given me directions to various parties through the country, which saved me afterwards weeks of useless labor. They drank a parting health, and bade a warm good-bye, and the hostess handing me a bouquet of roses for the lady traveller, we separated, much to my regret.

Our hotel was a droll little place. The rooms seemed to be arranged *en suite*, so that I had to pass through one with two couples in different beds, and one with a single gentleman, before I reached mine, and in that, the door would neither lock nor shut. When such accidents began in Norway, I always put my purse anxiously under my pillow, but soon gave up all that. You very soon see that you are among the most honest people in the world.

An English gentleman, a year or two ago, in travelling from Trondhjem to Christiania, tied his *porte-monnaie*—which is a large leather bag for carrying the quantity of little silver money necessary—on the back of his carriole, and lost out fourteen or fifteen sovereigns on the road. He wrote on arrival at Christiania, to the country judges, and in a few days had every one of the sovereigns returned to him. They had been picked up by the peasants, and handed to the magistrates, who sent them on to the owner. We are constantly meeting similar little instances of honesty. People take money whenever offered, but they always seem content with a little ; and if they are convinced that they overcharge, they are usually willing to take off a portion.

At half past four in the morning, the servant girl was at my bedside with a cup of good coffee and delicious cream ; and in a little time we were safely fastened into our carrioles.

Your first experience in a carriole is no joke. The sensation over a pebbly road is as if your teeth would be shaken out.

The morning was a glorious one. We wound along the back of a giant-hill, with a deep spacious valley beneath, and a stream rushing through far below in the bottom. The sun-beams fell across in great breadths of light ; the grass and grain-fields were sparkling with dew, and distant perspectives, with blue mountains and ponderous pine-covered hills in the foreground, opened before us. Everything was still, and pure, and grand, but yet it was not satisfactory. The carrioles seemed like to shake our brains to pieces ; heads and necks became almost dislocated. After half an hour's travel, we were as tired as if it had been a day's. We agreed that Norway was grand, but this would never do. At length, the lady gives out, and is handed over to a public carriage which runs up a few miles, while one of the English salmon-fishers agrees to drive her carriole.

This vehicle, the American reader should understand, belongs to the general species of our New York "sulkies" for fast trotting. It is a single cushioned-seat, just fitted for the person, with a little strip of wood reaching in front to a narrow dash-board, and swings on a pair of ashen shafts between the horse's back and the single pair of wheels. A leathern apron closely fastened to the seat covers the front part, in which your feet can be stretched. The dash-board has a bag for your wallet, and a place on which to tie umbrellas. The luggage must be tied on or under a little seat behind, where the post-boy sits. It is the lightest thing imaginable, for a man to ride in, and has the advantage of being easily taken to pieces, when you come to a lake or Fiord, and put into boats.

This beginning with the carrioles was not at all a fair instance. The road was stony, and we were not accustomed to them. We soon became used to the motion, and over the perfect Norwegian roads it became a luxury to travel in them. Indeed, the great temptation was to hurry on too much. The little Norwegian horses whirl one on at such a rate, and it is so pleasant to have the union of grand scenery enjoyed at your leisure, with this excellent driving, that you are for ever getting on. The night, too, almost as bright as the day, is so tempting. You come to have a kind of mania for making the station (usually six or seven miles), in the three-quarters. Every one you meet has the same mania. Our two English salmon-fishers, who had nothing in the world to do, were hurrying this day, as if their life depended on it. We ourselves, with all the unpromising beginning, posted eighty-six miles before midnight.

The scenery to-day in the Gulgdbrandsdal has been impressive, yet hardly equal to my expectation. The aspects have scarcely been bold and grand enough. Perhaps the finest effect was in the sensation just hinted at, the fresh exciting feeling of travelling through constantly new scenes of such lonely beauty, the idea of continuousness of enjoyment in Nature, as if for days to come, she would open successive pictures to you.

Then the silence!

The old Scandinavian Mythology placed among its deities, the god VIDAR, son of Odin, who dwells in Landvidi, or the "Boundless Land." He is called by the poets, the Silent. He represents the imperishability of Nature. Of him, Thorpe says, "Who has ever wandered through such forests, in a length of many miles, in a boundless expanse, without a path, without a goal, amid their monstrous shadows, their sacred gloom, without being filled with deep reverence for the sublime greatness of Nature above all human agency, without feeling the grandeur of the idea which forms the basis of Vidar's essence!"

One feels him still in those grand, silent mountain-valleys of Norway.

JOURNAL.

June ——.—*Station E.*—One o'clock.—"Six miles in fifty-five minutes. Good! *Hestene! Strax!*" (Horses! right away!) These are the two magical words. You unbundle yourself, jump out, and rush into the farm-house for refreshments. Everything is very cheap—a breakfast, with delicious coffee, for sixteen or twenty cents. The cream seems scarcely ever made into butter, but to be used at once for coffee and tea, and in cooking. Butter is usually poor, and often imported—a singular instance of Norwegian want of economy, still a by no means disagreeable fact to a traveller. One favorite dish is *sour cream*, eaten with sugar.

These stations are kept up by the peasants by law, and they are obliged to have horses ready, and to furnish refreshments. Every charge is fixed by legal enactment. We pay at the "fast stations"—*i. e.*, stations where horses must be kept ready—almost thirty-one cents for seven miles, which, with a small gratuity to the post-boy, makes the expense of posting about five cents a mile. Every station has a "Post-book," with the law in regard to the rates of posting, the fines, etc., etc. Each traveller is expected to put his name in the book, and if he has a complaint to lodge against the postman or the fare of the house, he does it in these books. The horses trot wonderfully well. We have passed one stage, of eleven miles and three-fourths, in an hour and five minutes—most of it down hill, however.

A Norwegian gentleman has been travelling with us, and at first, it was almost frightful to see him, when reaching a hill-summit, suddenly disappear, and then, on coming ourselves there, to find him plunging at tremendous speed far down the slopes below.

But we have soon become used to this habit of Norwegian driving, and whirl down the hills at fearful rate. We hardly hold the reins in at all—the little horses managing all, without ever stumbling.

Station M.—We have just visited a singular little Lutheran church, built of logs, and entirely covered with large square pieces of slate, instead of boarding. The nave crosses the transept at right angles in the centre. The inside is furnished with plain wooden seats; the altar is ornamented with old gilt carving, and it has a painting and candles. A little model of a ship, a foot or two long, hangs over the aisle. The churches we have passed are very picturesque—painted red or brown, with pointed white spires, sometimes with several parts, built one upon the other in a pleasing proportion. We have passed one, an octagon in shape.

I had a letter to the Head Sheriff of this district, and have enjoyed a very pleasant conversation with him. As usual, the Norwegian officials seem really the first men in the community. This gentleman, who spoke English well, was a person of singular dignity and intelligence. With reference to the education of the country districts, he states that owing to the scattered dwellings of the population, they cannot have many fixed schools, so that the schoolmaster goes from house to house, and gathers in each, the children of the nearest neighbors. Their pay is only a few dollars a month. The higher classes must have tutors for their children or send them to the towns. The churches are equally scattered—still, the people, he thinks, very faithful in their attendance. The morality of the country he considers much improved since the working of the Temperance Societies in Norway. Wine is still drank at tables, but brandy has been much abandoned, and intemperance is uncommon.

I learn from this gentleman, that there are a certain number of Norwegian families who are confirmed gipsies in habits. They are mostly the descendants of a vagabond population, which was scattered over Europe, after the Thirty Years' War. They wander from one end of the land to the other, stealing and begging, and have scarce any settled home. There is a police-book, with the names of every one. An antiquarian of Christiania, Mr. SUNDT, has written a curious book upon this class, the *Fante*. We have, thus far, hardly seen a beggar.

The cultivation along the road has been good to-day—the crops mostly rye, oats, and barley. In some fields, water had been brought from the hills above, in wooden troughs, and men, in the universally worn red caps, stood with ladles and sprinkled it over the ground. The tops of the hills are covered with forest, while the lower slopes are cultivated, and dotted with brown log-houses. These are nearly always groups, arranged in square, of four or six houses—one as the dwelling, one the kitchen, one for guests, and the rest for "the creatures," as the Norwegians, Yankee-like, call the cattle. We pass no villages, yet, on the whole, the country must be populous. All the houses have flowers in the windows. The roads are very good, of stone, covered with gravel. The fences are of poles, inclining between two cross-bars.

Station F.—We have just met two English sportsmen, in carrioles. We not only did not salute, but there was scarcely a look on their side, even of curiosity—hardly more than if we had met in Regent's Park. The country-people generally lift their hats to us. We meet only a few persons travelling, and they are usually in rough carrioles. We find that the lady-traveller makes a great sensation among the peasants. And, indeed, what with the capote and out-flying travelling-costume, and the comical little vehicle dashing along the roads, under female hands, we cannot help having, ourselves, a good laugh occasionally at the droll aspect.

The people at the inns find a woman from America a great curiosity; they examine her dress, price every article, and ask innumerable questions. Yet they are all exceedingly civil and attentive, though apparently a little perplexed at the wants of modern civilization.

Station L.—Not far from this station where we are passing the night, we rode through the narrow way, where more than two centuries ago, an ill-fated army of Scotchmen was crushed to death by rocks and stones, rolled down from the mountain above by the peasants. They were allies of Gustavus Adolphus in his war with Denmark, and were making a bold cross-march over Norway to Sweden, when they were suddenly destroyed. As we passed, a dark storm was covering the sky, and there was a desolate gloom and wildness over the spot.

It is a sombre, fearful way, even on the new road, which Norwegian enterprise has constructed. A simple monument of stone, with an inscription, marks the spot, where Sinclair and his brave comrades fell.

Our hotel is also in a desolate pass;—not a house in sight, only a turbulent river and an immense bare mountain side, with hardly a tree to hide its barrenness. We sit by the great roaring kitchen-fire. The bed-rooms are large unpainted boarded rooms, approached by a stairway on the outside of the house ; water for the morning is brought in a black wine bottle ! Yet every thing is very clean and neat, and the people are anxious to please.

CHAPTER IV.

A VISIT TO A BONDER.

Tofte —. A bit of the old Saga history belongs here—a glimpse of the Norwegian Kings :

"King Harald (Haarfager), one winter, went about in guest-quarters in Upland, and had ordered a Christmas feast to be prepared for him at the farm Thopte (from Tofte).—On Christmas eve came Swase to the door, just as the king went to table, and sent a message to the king to ask if he would go out with him. The king was angry at such a message, and the man who brought it in took out with him a reply of the king's displeasure. But Swase, notwithstanding, desired that his message should be delivered a second time; adding to it that he was the Laplander whose hut the king had promised to visit, and which stood on the other side of the ridge. Now the king sent out, and promised to follow him, and went over the ridge to his hut, although some of his men dissuaded him. There stood Snaefrid, the daughter of Swase, a most beautiful girl; and she filled a cup of mead for the king—but he took hold both of the cup and of her hand."

The saga goes on to tell, in rather plain language, that he fell passionately in love with her, and finally married her, forgetting, such was his passion, both his crown and dignity.

Tofte is one of the old Royal stations. In the chronicle

of King Eysten, who reigned about 1120, the king is represented as having a great dispute with King Sigurd, in their guest-quarters, as to the good deeds of each. Sigurd relates his crusades, but Eysten, among other improvements which he describes himself as making, says, "The road from Drontheim goes over the Dovrefield, and many people had to sleep out of doors, and make a very severe journey: but I built inns, and supported them with money; and all travellers know that Eysten has been king in Norway."

They were at first only block-houses (called *saelnhûs* in the sagas), and uninhabited. The first inn (*tafernishûs*) was built in 1303, by King Hakon Magnussón.

Tofte was one of the stations thus supported by the kings. Even yet, these Post-Houses have peculiar rights—the owners being freed from taxes, and enjoying other privileges.

I had noticed in the room of the post-house some remarkable articles of furniture of black carved wood, with gilt ornaments, and was told that the Bonder who owned them lived on the hill near by. I felt a great desire to see the farm-buildings of one of this class, but was doubtful whether I should be received without a proper letter of introduction. A Norwegian gentleman in the inn encouraged me, saying no one made ceremonies here, so, engaging a guide, I started off.

The Bonder of Norway is not at all a common peasant. In one sense he is the aristocrat of the country; he owns the land, and is descended from the old leaders, and sometimes the princes, of the nation. His class send the most of the Representatives to the National Assembly. We might say, he is one of the farmers, or yeomanry of Norway ; but, so far as my observation extends, the Bonder are not at all like the "farmers" of America, or the yeomen of England. They are a more distinct class ; a class with less of the gentleman and more of the relics of the former peasantry about them—who, though independent, were still somewhat in the power of the great princes. In this—the middle province of Norway—you see them continually on the boats, at the post-houses, and working in the fields. Their features are usually large and strong, with firm and intelligent expression, and the blonde complexion much reddened by the exposure to the weather. They seem vigorous, well-made men. The common costume is a red cap, like a night-cap ; jacket with metal buttons, and breeches. The farm buildings of one Bonder were shown me, on Lake Mjösen, who was estimated to be worth $100,000.

The *gaard*, or estate, of this proprietor was on a hill, commanding an immense view, and like all the farms we have passed, formed with its buildings, a little square, the interior being protected from the winter winds. There was no indication, among various houses, which was the main dwelling, but finding one hospitable-looking door, I rapped with my knuckles, and a servant girl opened. She understood me, and summoned the master. He came soon, and looking at a sort of general letter I had, at once showed me into another of the little houses in the square.

There was something very notable in his appearance ; he was not exactly a "gentleman," in the usual acceptation, not a man of the world, but he impressed you as a kind of natural prince ; tall, strong, with commanding features and long black hair, and an air of genuine dignity. He wore the red woollen cap and the usual costume of the farmers. At each door, as he opened it, he stepped back and bowed, to let me in. I was shown into a large room with a handsame uncarpeted floor. The furniture was singular. On each side of the apartment were some splendid carved cabinets and tables, black, with gilding—one with white panels, having pictures in them—while in the midst of the room a common deal table stood, with enormous legs, and in the corners were small tables and wooden settees—just such as one would see in an English country ale-house. Near the door was a long, old clock, such as every New Englander is familiar with in his oldest village houses. The host had gone out for a little while, as I was observing all this. He returned, and brought with him an old gentleman with a still more noble and patriarchal air. This one welcomed me in the same dignified manner, and told me in a few words that he was a direct descendant from one of the old Norwegian kings, HARALD HAARFAGER. A decanter was then brought in with a cordial, and a glass poured out for me. I sipped, and we all bowed, and quite seriously drank healths. This custom of the welcoming-drink dates back at least to times of the early Vikings. It appears in all the sagas.*

* It is stated in one of the sagas, that when Gangleri asked about heavenly things—whether water was drunk in Walhalla? his informant replied, that it would be a wonderful thing indeed, if the All-Father should invite kings, and earls, and heroes, to himself, only to set water before them!

After some conversation, I asked if they would have any objections to show a stranger the house. They had not, and getting a bunch of keys, the younger took me over one or two of the houses. There were an immense number of bedrooms; some with plain farmer-like furnishing, others with elegant curtained beds and pieces of splendid furniture. Seeing my interest, my host kindly went farther and took me to the store-rooms and attic. There were the winter coats, the bear skins and furs, and reindeer boots and high water-boots; the blankets and comfortables and dresses; then the little sleds and sleighs for the snow; the piles of round oatmeal cakes, each a foot and a half in diameter, kept for the food of the laborers; heaps of birch bark for tanning, spinning-wheels for weaving, shoe-blocks for shoe-making—for on these farms all trades are carried on. Then to the kitchen—a still separate house again, with a sort of stone range in a corner, over which is a little roof completely overshadowing it, and carrying off the smoke and flames of the cooking. In another part was a great tin tub for baking bread, and large vats or vessels for boiling. One side of the kitchen was occupied with beds for the servants. The next little log-house seemed to be for keeping preserved meats; another was used for some common farm purposes, and had a little cupola and bell, which is often seen in the Norwegian farm-clusters, and has a most picturesque effect. It gives a centrality to each group—as though they made up *one* home. There were, I think, eight of these log-houses in this *gaard.*

This arrangement of many separate houses appears in

all the old sagas. We hear very early of a sleep-house (*sympnhûs*); and of two stalls being kept apart from the dwellings, though even at this day, the Danish peasant has animals and family under one roof. The old Icelandic homesteads had often thirty or forty houses.

My host next took me to the stables, though "the creatures," as he informed me, were in the mountain pastures, or saetters. These are beautiful little green pastures on the heights of the mountain, where the cattle stay in the summers, under the charge of two or three dairy maids and men, who there make their butter and cheese for winter. They are famous in Norwegian poetry and romance.

The barns in central Norway, though often old, have the modern improvements—being built usually on a side-hill—with two or three easy entrances to each story, and with apertures for sliding the hay or grain down to the stalls beneath. The lower story is the cattle stable, each stall being constructed of two large slabs of slate, so that you look up, on entering, a long range of upright stone slabs, which make the separating walls of each stall, the floor is of wood, and the feeding place a trough, with bars above, as in our own barns. The barns as well as other buildings are elevated on little stone supports, to save them from the destructive invasions of the lemming-rats.*

* These little creatures are a species of rat which in Lapland is very small, but in Norway attains sometimes the size of a wharf-rat. They have black and tawny spots on their backs, with white head and

Slate-slabs form a very common article of use in this valley. This gentleman has one table, some eight feet by five, made of one slab.

One part of the under story was slabbed out for sheep and pigs. I was surprised to see an old threshing-machine here —the wheels turned by a horse moving in a circle below—a ponderous, primitive-looking thing, but the owner said, very useful. The common crops raised by him are oats, barley and hay. His fields are irrigated by water, brought down in troughs, as I have before described.

He has about one hundred cows, thirty horses, and hundreds of sheep and swine.

I know not how to express enough my sense of the courtesy and the intelligence of this Bonder landlord. With our limited means of understanding each other, he showed such a quickness and keenness—such an appreciation of the point of every question, that I was surprised how much we communicated in so few words. Then everywhere, he manifested such a true and manly courtesy, that I left him feeling the country was very fortunate that possessed such a class. They are evidently the muscle and bone of Norway, and when greater enlightenment and modern enterprise shall reach them, we shall see what a nation this vigorous old Norse people can yet make.

belly, and grey legs and tail. Once in eight or ten years there is a great immigration of these animals—as there is of squirrels in America, directly over the country, up mountains, and across lakes. Nothing can turn them aside, and they consume everything they can get hold of.

The great historical fact, undoubtedly, which gave the peculiar power to the Norwegian people in their early history, and which renders now their peasantry, one of the best of Europe, is that Feudalism had no existence among them. Some of the French historians have questioned this, but there seems now now no doubt of it. Feudalism is always the fruit of conquest. In Norway, the conquered inhabitants, the Finns, melted away before a race so different, or fled to the Northern and most inaccessible provinces. There was no conquered people to render military service. The land was divided among equals. Democratic assemblies governed the people, from the earliest times. Even the petty kings, who were conquered and driven out by Harald Haarfager, were only chieftains from their bravery and skill, and were obliged to refer everything to the Things, or Popular Assemblies. These bodies often chose their king, and nearly as often murdered him. The country became divided up, as it were among a nation of soldiers. Each Bonder was a freeholder, equal to every one else, and owing for his estate no feudal duty, obligation or tax whatever. The only restriction upon him was the Udal Law. By this law, every descendant of the owner had, in the order of relationship, a right in the property. If the possessor sold or parted with the estate, the one next of kin had the power to redeem it, by re-paying the purchase-money ; and if he refused, the one next to him had again the same right. At his death again, it was divided among his lawful heirs. The time of redemption,* is in modern times limited to five years.

* Laing.

By such a law, there could be no primogeniture, and no opportunity for large estates. The nation, in its early history, was a body of equal and free petty land-owners. It is so still.

CHAPTER V.

POSTING.

Dovre Fjeld.—We are ascending now the great plateau, called the Dovre Fjeld (pronounced Fiell.) The main road over it was first constructed in the beginning of the twelfth century, by King Eysten. The scenery is very desolate: there is no vegetation except stunted birch, and the ground is covered with fragments of rock. At a little distance, are snow-topped hills: snow occasionally drifts down near the road. On one side of the way are poles, at regular distance, to mark the path in winter. Though it is near the end of June, the air is cold and cutting, like November winds.

The height above the sea here is about 3,200 feet. We can catch occasional glimpses of a famous snow-peak in the distance—Sneehœtten—a mountain about 7,700 feet high.

Jerkin.—This is another of the old government post-houses, and is considered the best between Christiania and Trondhjem. It is a little *gaard*, or group of farm-houses right in the midst of this desolate mountain scenery—not a house or tree in sight. We were put into a comfortable upper room, with a roaring fire, and a nice supper of Reindeer-steak and pancakes with coffee, was sent up. The old room, with

A NORWEGIAN FAMILY GOING TO THE SAETTER.

its great feather-beds set in alcoves, and its large chairs and quaint furniture, had a very inviting look after our long ride.

I went out soon to examine the farm. The landlord is one of the old Bonders of the country : and the arrangement is very much like that at the farm near Tofte, only on a smaller scale. All the trades are carried on on the farm—smithery, carpentering, shoemaking, weaving, etc., etc. There are various little houses for these and other purposes. In one we found dried meats ; in another, piles of oaten cakes, for the workmen during the winter. One building has, as usual, the little belfry. The stable has the same arrangement of stalls, slabbed off by pieces of slates. The cows were away in the *saetter*—I think the boy said there were fifty of them. There were stalls also for some forty or fifty horses. In the house, the landlady showed us, with much pride, her furs and handsome dresses, and other articles—reindeer coats, bear and fox-skins, wolves'-skins, and eider-down comfortables. Both she and the landlord had much the same manner that a substantial farmer and farmer's wife would have with us—an independent, kind, half-patronizing way. This post-house is a favorite sporting station for the English : there are two sportsmen now in the little guest-house : and here travellers leave the main road to climb Sneehœtten. The charges are just about what they would be at an American country tavern—about seventy-five cents, or one dollar a day. Generally, the whole bill in a Norwegian inn, is not much more than fifty cents a day for each person, provided he does not call for too many dishes. Travelling was once much cheaper in Norway, but the English are said to have corrupted the people, as they have done the Swiss ; still, even now it is the cheapest country in Europe, except Sweden, for hotel charges. Posting, inn-charges and all, come usually to about three dollars a day.

There is in these stations—as indeed in all interior Norway—a curious mingling of habits. You climb a ladder to your bed-room, and find there the cleanest beds, with, perhaps, some rich antique furniture, but the log-walls scarcely covered by plaster. A very nice dinner may be set before you, with napkins, and you begin to imagine yourselves in the most comfortable civilization, when your landlady suddenly empties your slops out of the window, or you discover some singular omission on the table, which could no where else occur with such beginnings.

A little beyond Jerkin, the summit of the plateau is reached, 4,594 feet above the level of the sea.

The descent from the Dovre Fjeld down the valley of the Driv, is a grand mountain drive—road like a gentleman's avenue, hard, gravelled, graded beautifully, and fenced by blocks of cut stone.

On the left, a deep ravine, with a dashing stream, with waterfalls, eddies, flashing currents, cavernous pits, where the waters bury themselves to come out again foaming and hurrying below ; and beyond, the eye looking far down a succession of such glens—add to this, your little Norwegian pony trotting down the slopes at ten miles an hour, your ride changing each moment the point of view, yet giving you time to enjoy each glimpse, and revealing beds of the most exquisite mountain-flowers, passed so quickly, that they seem like masses of beautiful violet, pink, or yellow coloring on the rocks, rather than flowers, and one can perhaps enjoy with us that morning ride down the mountain. The flowers are wonderful, so delicate and fresh in coloring, growing almost from the chinks of the cliffs. The lady can hardly get on, for sending the post-boy to pick them ; but "the stupid fellow" has such a talent for finding dandelions and butter-cups, and weeds, instead of violets and hare-bells, and such like ! *

Stuen.—We are experiencing now some of the fair compensation for the trouble which the Norwegian law allows a traveller to put upon a peasant. We are passing occasionally common or "slow stations," where horses are not obliged to be kept, and where it often takes three or four hours to get one from the mountain-pasture. To avoid delay, I had sent on an order for horses at such an hour. But we have been everywhere delayed, and in consequence must pay wait-money. There is additional money demanded, too, for sending for the horses. I dis-

* Among the flowers which we found were the following:— The draba (*cruciferæ*) ; viola palustris, viola tricolor ; lychnis githago, silene nivea (*caryophyllaceæ*) ; linum ; geranium palustre ; epilobium angustifolium (*onograceæ*) ; sedum minimum (*crassulaceæ*) ; linnæa borealis ; galium mollugo (*rubiaceæ*) ; achillea multifolium (*compositæ*) ; vitis ideae altera (vaccinium), andromeda cerulea (*ericaceæ*) ; linaria vulgaris (*scrophulariaceæ*) ; echium ; pholx (*polemoniaceæ*).

puted and discussed it at first considerably, but finally found it was the legal charge.

I think the Norwegian always respects you for questioning anything that is an overcharge. We had a government post-book with us, and knew exactly what we should pay for every mile. The peasants can always be convinced, if you will reason with them and show your authority. They are generally poor reckoners, and one must not unfrequently pay them more than they claim to give them their legal right. This settling the fare by law is an immense saving of annoyance and disputes. It is good policy to give drink-money, or gratuities to your post-boys, which is but a trifle—with the Norwegian travellers, three or four cents; with a foreigner, perhaps double. If he gives more he injures other travellers, as it is not the custom of the country.

The scenery of this part of the journey is very fine—wide views over deep valleys, and dark pine-covered hills.

At the station, just after we had crossed the Orkel, on the summit of the hill, we enjoyed one of the grandest views on the whole route. An immense valley opened below, filled with sombre pines, and in the midst flowed a calm, dark river, while beyond, surge upon surge of the gloomy hills crossed the valley. At the west it opened into a green dell, with soft, sloping banks, where the stream wound through, beautifully gleaming. A rich glow of light from a summer sunset poured over the whole, giving a wonderful glory and softness to what would have been otherwise only a grand and gloomy scene.

We were delayed now at each station, and did not reach Garlie (our resting-place for the night), till about one o'clock. But there was no darkness; all through the night, the light was almost as it is with us on a cloudy day.

On the morning of the fifth day from leaving Christiania, we crossed the ridge which gave us the first view of TRONDHJEM. The old city lay below on the banks of the beautiful Fiord, with the Cathedral towers and formal houses plainly to be seen, the shipping and steamers in front, the dark solitary island (Munkholm) with its fort in the harbour, and a long stretch on each side of the arms and islets of the Fiord. The city was still eight or ten miles away by road, and the worst road I had yet seen. After a tedious drive, we reached the old fortifications and entered the ancient city. Our carrioles rattled up the broad, paved streets, lined with low, neat houses, toward the *Hotel de belle Vue,* which had been especially recommended. The city is a quiet, formal town, which is redeemed from common-place by the interesting old cathedral, that meets your view almost everywhere. The shops appear all like private houses, with windows high from the ground, to avoid the deep snow in the winter.

We were soon made comfortable in our hotel, with a neat room and a good dinner, and I sallied out to see the city.

There is little to interest a stranger in it, except its historic associations, as the ancient Capital of Norway, and its cathedral. This last is a most remarkable building, both for its mingling of styles, its union of different ages and schools, and the massive effect of the whole structure.

All the wealth and religious feeling of Norway cannot keep it in repair, and the mystery is, how it was ever built. The two aisles are in the purest Byzantine, and the nave in the Gothic. The most delicate and graceful part of it is its choir, now ornamented with Thorwaldsen's figure of Christ; and the Apostles, by his pupil Bissen. These, I believe, were the gift of Bernadotte. The interior is disfigured by a row of wooden boxes, built up on the sides of the nave, like the boxes of a theatre. A large part of the nave is still in ruins.

The two chapels clinging to the choir, the minaret-like spire and the solid tower, the exquisite flower capitals, and the grotesque faces, leave a strange combination of impressions on the mind—of the Eastern imagination, and the quaint Gothic, sardonic earnestness expressed in the singular structure.

June —th, 1856.—I was amused in accompanying a gentleman to call upon another, to see him put on a sou'wester, as if it was the customary June coat for Trondhjem. The wind felt like December air. Most of the gentlemen to whom I had letters, were in their villas in the country at this season. I visited one house, well known to travellers for its artistic treasures and the cultivated host—that of Consul Knudtzen's. He has several of the most famous bas-reliefs of Thorwaldsen—his brother having been one of the first friends and patrons of the great artist. I saw here also the well-known book of Minutoli on the Trondhjem Cathedral.

Trondhjem has a number of Public Schools, as well as a *Real* School or academy, a Drawing-school for mechanics and artisans, and an Agricultural School in the country near by. I attended an exhibition in the Real School, and a giving of prizes for scholarship during the school-term. The teacher of English was very polite and communicative, and gave me much information on Norwegian Schools.

CHAPTER VI.

TOWARD THE MIDNIGHT SUN.

A trip to the North Cape, even in July, cannot be recommended, unless you are sure of the weather. To-day is the second of July, and the wind, which cuts across the deck, is like a February gale in America.

We left Trondhjem, or Drontheim, yesterday in one of a line of steamers run by the government along the whole coast from Christiania to Hammerfest, for the purpose of carrying the mail and providing a connection between the different parts of Norway. The prices are very moderate, and as a business line it would not pay. There are two little cabins, one for gentlemen and one for ladies, and a small saloon in common. The rate of passage is fixed at twelve skillings per mile (about three cents an English mile)—wives or sisters, in company with a gentleman, being charged half price, as is the universal custom on Norwegian boats.

Our company is made up of two or three young merchants returning to the North from business on the continent, a young Norwegian gentleman travelling with his betrothed, a young lady going home from an English school, one or two other ladies, one German artist, one English 'Squire, and, beside ourselves, an American gentleman, with his wife and servant. On the front deck are great numbers of fishermen's wives and farmers, coming back from selling their products at Trondhjem, and taking their sugar, goods, etc., to the Lofoden Islands, Tromsó, Hammerfest, and various, small stations on the north coast of Norway. Among them are three Cambridge-men from England, pedestrians and sportsmen, who sleep on the deck under their blankets.

The weather is horrible—cold, bleak, with occasional turns of driving mist and rain, almost sleet—and then clearing up, to show the grand and gloomy scenery. We are driving on through narrow Fiords, or arms of the sea, with grey, bare rocks, twisted and broken and crumbled as though under the action first of fire, and then of ages of the ocean storms, reaching down close to the white waves. No houses or grass, or trees are visible on shore, nor sails upon the water. Behind the first ledges the land sinks, and then rises into sharp, jagged mountain peaks, drifted with snow even to their base, and wreathed with mist. Large white gulls flutter over the rocks, and now and then the eider-ducks scud off just on the surface of the water towards the shore. Now as I write, we have come out on a larger bay, with heavy waves rolling in. Rocky islands make the horizon seaward, and on every other side the many mountain-summits rise. We steer in at what seems an unbroken dark ledge of rocks, but as we approach, a channel opens, and beyond, another broad sheet of water appears, sprinkled with islands, and opening into innumerable bays and armlets among the fissures of the mountains. There is no soft, summer light, no gently rounded outline, or dreamy perspective —it is all stern, harsh, and forbidding.

TORGHATTAN.—One of the most remarkable objects we have met, is an island-peak—Torghattan—with an immense cavern distinctly visible through the upper part. Murray says "large enough for a ship to go through," but unfortunately the floor must be a hundred feet or more from the water. Forbes* makes the peak about twelve hundred feet high, and the cavern is estimated here as large as a cathedral.

Some fishing boats have just crossed our bows—broad, unwieldy things, with cod-fish piled half-way up the mast like hay, and with one large square sail, which is reefed by untying and separating from the sail successive folds. They have very high stems and sterns; it seemed to me the old traditional form of the Viking "sea-dragons," as pictures give them. Our captain says they are excellent sailers.

We have just passed a harbor where a famous old Viking, Harick, had his nest. It seems the coast to breed Vikings —the sea-kings and pirate-conquerors of the North. The scenery opens now more grand; the mountains are massive at the base, but above broken, and as if tossed about in the wildest confusion. Peak follows peak in endless succession and form. A green herbage is visible on the lower slopes, probably dwarf birches and pines. As I write, the fog rises,

* Glaciers of Norway.

and the sun, near the edge of the mountains, at eleven o'clock at night, pours a golden light into the cabin.

The great peculiarity of the scenery is the rounded smooth character of the hills below, while the peaks rise in abrupt conical or jagged summits above—the latter being, perhaps, a volcanic effect, while the former shows the abrasion of the immense ice-floods which once swept over Norway.

We have passed the "Seven Sisters"—seven stern, weird-looking peaks,* that seemed to reach out snowy hands to each other, and whose frosty brows lowered on us as though, according to the Finnish traditions, they were the spirits hostile to the proud conquering races who had invaded them.

HESTEMANDOE.

July second.—We have just passed the Arctic circle, at a singular island, rising in the form of a giant horseman from the waters. The back of his mantle is the mountain-side, and the crags and cliffs make the horse's head and ears, and the rider's hand. His head was at first veiled angrily in mist; but as we passed, a whiff carried it away, and a grand, calm face, like the face of the Sphynx, stood out, looking solemnly up to the stormy sky. The effect was mysterious and wonderful. These high peaks are great barometers to the seamen, and one can imagine how many a fisher-boat's crew has watched anxiously and supersti-

* Estimated height, four thousand feet.—*Von Buch.*

tiously the head of the giant rider, and, though Christian, has muttered a prayer against Jumala or the Trolls.

The legend of this island is, that a giant who dwelt on it, shot a great arrow at a maiden in Lekoe (eighty-eight miles distant), who had rejected him. The arrow passed through Torghattan, and made the great cave or fissure, already mentioned, and thus failed of reaching the maiden. Both then changed each other to stone, and must so remain till doomsday.

Thorpe says that every Nordlander still takes off his hat, as he sails by, to the maid of Lekoe.

We are winding now through multitudes of islands with occasional little stations, which consist usually of a large log-house, with a Norwegian flag floating above it, and one or two smaller houses, sometimes boarded and painted red. The roofs are frequently grassed, and it is difficult to distinguish them from the green slopes which form the foot of the mountains.

Sometimes, on a rocky coast, the eye wanders over the cliffs for a long distance, without noticing these little brown cabins planted on them. The channels between the rocks are occasionally so narrow, that the steamer is compelled to anchor, and swing round on its bows, in order to return. Last night, our artist and the ladies were on the constant lookout for the "midnight sun," but the clouds utterly obscured the view.

The thermometer stands at thirty-five degrees (Fahrenheit) in a shelter, and continual storms of cold rain or mist sweep over our course ; such cold and gloom at this season are almost unknown. The farmers on board say it has done great injury to the crops. The artist says, "If he could only have good butter, he should not care for the weather !" Every one is shivering, and abusing the arctic summer. Yet there is something in these sudden wild squalls, and the gloomy mists covering and revealing the wintry snow-peaks, and in the cold grey light, well suited to the character of the coast—the stern, grand, repelling scenery.

THE FONDAL GLACIERS.

July third.—To-night I was called up to see a grand scene. A wintry gale was howling over the ship, and to the southward, the drifting squalls hid every thing in gloomy, driving sleet and rain ; but near us, on our quarter, some peaks arose which seemed gigantic, against the misty background. The first was a black, massive cliff, rent and fissured and with twisted strata marked plainly on its side, jutting with deep wall against the sea ; behind it, and following the line of the coast, were several peaks of pure snow, whose tops in the storm above seemed to reach unknown heights.

The snow was drifting in clouds about their summits, and yet every few moments admitting a perfectly clear view into their vast solitudes, so that what seemed tracks were visible down the sides. As the mountains opened to view, glaciers appeared between them, the blue ice obtruding through the snow. On the seaward side again, the cessation of the storm-gusts showed snow-peaks and black, craggy islands.

It seemed the very desolation of the Icy Ocean; or as if you were a witness of the action of the most gigantic powers of Nature, in the antediluvian solitude and chaos. You shrink away, as if too insignificant amid such tremendous agencies.

We are now in the West Fiord, one of the broadest inlets on the coast, and near the famous whirlpool.

THE MAELSTROM.

I quote from Von Buch's description.

"It is from these rapid changes and agitations that the West Fiord is so dangerous for the coasting navigation. The Fiord presses like a wedge between the main land and the high and very extensive islands and mountainous range of Lofoden. The tide surges on at the same time, and the general current from the south to the northern coasts. The narrow sounds between the islands do not afford a sufficiently quick passage for this great mass of water; the ebb returns like a cataract, and the smallest opposition to this motion, such as south winds, occasions immediately broken and irregular waves. A stronger wind, which drives before it the deep waves of the sea, sets the whole Fiord in furious commotion. In all the sounds between the island of Lofoden, the sea flows in as in the strongest and most rapid rivers, and on that account the outermost bear the name of streams, Grimström, Napström, Sundström; and wherever the fall of the ebb cannot extend through such long channels, there arises an actual cataract; for instance, the well-known Malström at Mosken and Väröe. These streams and this fall change their direction, therefore, four times in the day, as the tide or ebb drives the water on; but the Malström is peculiarly dangerous and terrible to look at, when the northwest wind blows in opposition to the ebbing. We then see waves struggling against waves, towering aloft, or wheeling about in whirlpools. We hear the dashing and roaring of the waves for many miles out at sea. But in summer these violent winds do not prevail; and the stream is then little dreaded, and does not prevent the navigation of the inhabitants of Värdöe and Moskenöe. The desire to see here something extraordinary and great is therefore generally disappointed; for travellers, for the sake of travelling, venture up Norway in summer only, and seldom in winter."

All the descriptions I heard from the Norwegians familiar with the coast confirmed this account. At high and low tide the "Mill-stream" is perfectly safe; only at the ebb is it at all perilous. Its latitude is about 68°.

Our "Fourth" was passed in snow-storms near some of the most imposing scenes of the voyage—the Lofoden Islands.

We celebrated it by a good dinner, and one American treated the whole forward deck to a kind of root and ginger-beer of the country. A Negro—an American—passed it around, and was as enthusiastic—poor fellow!—as any one for the day of American Liberty. This Negro is much looked up to by the deck-passengers, as a sort of mysterious Oriental personage.

The peaks of the Lofodens rise like volcanic summits with the most sharp and jagged outlines. The panorama of snowy needle-like peaks from one point is wonderful. One writer compares them to the teeth of a shark; another to vertebræ. They are red granite cliffs, protruded as if by fearful volcanic power, about four thousand feet in height, and with glaciers and snowy valleys among them. Forbes* says the line of this semi-circle of mountain-summits reaches one hundred and thirty miles, and in one point, they occupy a third of the horizon.

Our steamer went far out of its regular course to visit these islands.

Here is the centre of the great business of the north of Norway—the cod-fishery. It employs now probably from twenty-four thousand to twenty-five thousand men, and has a capital engaged of three or four millions of dollars. The fishing is carried on near these islands, from February to the end of May; then it removes, for a few months, to the northernmost coast, for another variety.

The men engaged are the most bold, hardy sailors existing, and are subject to great privations. We have just entered a harbor, and the captain says that sometimes a storm will sweep these boats right from their anchors into the open Fjord. Last year, twelve were thus carried out and wrecked. The business is not as once, merely an exchange of the fish for provisions—thereby giving the fishermen no chance for saving money—but is a regular cash-trade with the Bergen and Trondhjem merchants. There are two modes of curing the fish—one by cutting it, like our cod, into halves, and hanging it over sticks to dry (this is called stock-fish); the other, by packing in heaps and drying them on the rocks. These little heaps you see all along the coast.

* Glaciers of Norway.

THE LAPPS.

"A Lapp! a Lapp!" We all rushed, helter-skelter, on deck, to see the first specimen we had yet met. "Which is he? Which one?" There is no mistaking. A broad, brown face, with high cheek-bones, and half-frightened expression; the hair long and light, eyes blue, forehead common, and nose mean. His cap rises straight from his forehead, with a bright red band around it; he wears a woollen *blouse*, with red fringes at the wrists, blue trowsers, tied with red bands at the ankles, and great turned-up shoes—in the lower part somewhat a Chinese costume. "The shoes are packed with dried grass, beaten down, to make them soft," says the captain. An old woman is with him, also with high cap, with red band; but her face is much darker, her eyes small and black, with a Mongolian cast.

"There they are, at dinnner!" The old woman has pulled out a large cake, like an immense buckwheat-cake in appearance, which she eats with cheese. Edward, the colored man, of course, gets into a talk with them, as he does with every body, though how he makes himself understood, is an inscrutable mystery. He says the cheese is *not* reindeer cheese, and that the cake is rye-bread.

This person is not a Lapp, probably, but a "Sea-Finn"—one of those who live near the shore, and have settled habitations. The "Mountain-Finn" lives a wandering life, with his reindeer We see the huts of the former now on every

Fiord. The "Quéns," of whom we hear a great deal now, as we go farther north, are the inhabitants of Russian Finland, a larger and handsomer race than the Finns and Lapps.

I have conversations continually with the Norwegians, on their dealings with the Finns. They deny all oppression or wrong on their part, and describe these tribes as hopelessly inferior and ignorant. Still the fact remains, that the Finns, like our Indians, have lost their old habitations; and that the conquering race have done, till lately, very little for their improvement. A singular movement has commenced within a few years among them, of which I cannot as yet speak with confidence. It began with terrible outrages, and fanaticisms; the murder of the sheriff of the district, and an attempt to offer a Protestant clergyman as a bloody sacrifice to God—the poor creatures believing themselves acting under divine inspiration. They were punished; and since that time, under the influence of Swedish missionaries, the religious excitement has taken a more healthy direction.

My friends speak of it as merely a "fanaticism;" but, by their own confession, it has driven out intoxication from among these tribes, which had prevailed before to a fearful extent, and the results seem to be of a sound, rational nature. They are represented as deeply attached to the Bible, but not so much revering Luther; as very correct and pure in their lives, speaking with much feeling of their religious hope, but believing in an inner inspiration in each man's heart. Even the magistrates allow a great change in the general morality of the Finns and Lapps, since the "revival movements."

It will give an idea of the proportion of these tribes to the Norwegians* in Finnmark, to give the statistics of a single parish in this neighborhood, furnished me by a clergyman on board—that of *Lyngen:* Normans or Norwegians, 614 ; Quaens, 721 ; Finns, 1,601. Of these, the mingled races are—from Norwegians and Quéns, 92 ; from Quéns and Finns, 119 ; from Norwegians and Finns, 7—this last giving an excellent instance of the affinities between the two races, as compared with those of either to the Russian Quaens.

The Quaens, or Finns from Finland, are a tall, well-made race, and do not at all resemble the Norwegian Finns or Lapps. They are agricultural, and the Lapps nomadic. Von Buch dates their entrance into Norway, only to the time of Charles XII.

With regard to the relation and ethnology of these tribes, there may be some confusion of ideas, owing to the confusion of terms applied to them among the Norwegians themselves. We hear of Finns, of Lapps, of Quaens or Kvéns,† and Russian Finns. All these really belong to but one great family—the Tsjudes—and divide themselves into two

* Lallerstedt makes the number of Finns in Norwegian Finmark, 6,000 ; of Lapps, 13,000 ; of Norwegians, 25,000.—*La Scandinavie, ses Espérances, &c., p.* 7.

† The English word *queen* is allied—this country of Finland, having formerly been supposed to be the country of the Amazons, or of *women*, and thus called queen-land, or *Kvenaland.*

branches, the Polar people, or the Finns and Laps, and the inhabitants of Russian Finland, or the Quéns, formerly called *Suomi.* * The *Tsjudes* are a great Asiatic race, allied to the Mongolians, who have covered the Northern and Northeastern provinces of Europe. They form the under-stratum in Russia, especially in Archangel and the provinces near St. Petersburg, but are utterly different both from the Sclavic and the Germanic families. They divide themselves, according to Prof. Rask, into three great branches, of which it is only necessary here to mention the Finnish.

One of these branches includes also the Madjars, or Hungarians.

The Finnish branch, beside the two divisions mentioned above, has a third, not important in this connection. The languages of the Polar Finns and the Russian Finns, or Quaens, differ as much as the German and Danish, so that the two peoples do not understand each other. The language of Russian Finland is the only cultivated Finnish tongue, having its own literature. The people also are far superior physically, to their relations of the West.

Prof. Munck † limits the proper Finnish territory as follows :—" It is bordered toward the east by a semi-circle, or a third of a circle, from the Gulf of Livonia to the Western part of the White Sea, and towards the west, by a similar curved line, from Malanger in Finmark to Umala on the Gulf of Bothnia."

* Prof. Munck.

† Norskt Maanedskrift, 1st Hefte.

We have just passed Senjen, a remarkable island. The legend related of it is characteristic :

THE GIANT.

In ancient times, when the holy St. Olaf came to instruct the Norwegians in the faith of "The white Christ," and to plant the cross on the heathen altars, he found his efforts much impeded by the terrible monsters, that still inhabited the mountains and the desolate rocks on the coast. Among these monsters was a giant Senjemanden, who lived in this island of Senjen. This giant threatened often vengeance against the strange God, who was about to drive him from his old dominions ; but he was most of all enraged at the pious chantings of a nun, who lived on the island of Grytö. These devout melodies would sometimes make him howl with rage and pain. Happily for the holy nun, his attention became occupied at this time with quite different subjects. In the interior of Kvedfjord, in a beautiful green valley near the Fjord, lived a *Jutuljente,* or daughter of a giant, who was wonderfully rich. Her bulls and black cows pastured the hills by the hundreds ; her flocks of goats swarmed over the mountains ; her sheep, fat and soft-fleeced, fed in the long grass of the valleys ; she had numbers of hens who layed their eggs continually ; eider-ducks on her rocks, who gave her soft covering ; reindeer on the mainland, who drew her in winter over the snows and ice. In her home she possessed great drinking-horns of gold, and cups of silver ; and every one of her twelve dogs had a collar of silver. She had much riches beside, of which nobody knew ; for it is well known that the *Jutuls*, however much they have, always desire to conceal it, and to have more. The giant Senjemand, though he was old and horribly ugly, was so dazzled by all these riches, that he resolved to win the the daughter of the giant to marriage. He commenced by addressing her in his softest tones, but even then, they sounded like summer thunder, and could be heard much farther than in her island, though that was twenty-four miles away. The Jutul-maiden was not a beauty, and had no inclination to perpetual virginity, but she could not bear the addresses of Senjemand. He was too awkward and heavy, and his education had been too much neglected in his association with mermaids and sea-monsters, and such like creatures, so she answered in good Norse verse—

"Miserable Senjemand—ugly and grey!
Thou win the maid of Kvedfjord!
No—a churl thou art, and shalt ever remain!"

Whereupon the Senjemand gnashed his teeth, and in his rage, fitted a stone arrow to his bow, and shot it at the maiden. The arrow passed right through *Toppen*, and split it from top to bottom. At this very moment, the nun happened to be out of doors, engaged in her morning orisons; she was so frightened at the fearful crashing of the arrow through the cliff, that she was changed to stone, where she still stands. The arrow was turned aside by this obstacle of the cliff, and struck the mountain *Elgen*, on the island Hindö, where it may be still seen. The *Jutul*-maiden, in her fear, was seeking to flee away on her horse, but was changed by the magical arts of the giant to stone, with her horse and saddle. The mountain *Sadlen* (saddle) is still to be seen.

The wicked giant himself also became stone from his own rage, and he is so terrible, that no grass or shrub will grow upon him. He is still shown as a warning in the Senjen Island.

CHAPTER VII.

FINMARK AND ALTEN.

Our boat—the Prinds Gustav—is a very pleasant, though a small one, and we enjoy the trip as we approach the North more and more. The captain is a gentleman, an officer of the navy, speaking English very well. The cooking is admirable and the prices are all low. Our party is just large enough not to inconvenience each other, and still to have a good time. We stop at every small station, and are to remain nearly a day at the towns or important places.

People constantly come on board and leave us again—generally government officers, and tradesmen, and clergymen. My American friend, Mr. L., says "he can always distinguish a Norwegian clergyman now by his weight!" They are evidently the country 'squires and landlords, and not peculiarly ascetic in habits. Their duties seem to range from those of magistrates, office-holders and clergymen to the taking of census and numbering of cattle. One on board says, he must give to the government a complete return of all the population and property—even of every horse, cow or goat in his parish.

Among our passengers we take many ladies, who are going

short distances : all have comical little wooden bandboxes calculated to try the Christian disposition of Norwegian husbands. Some are unique in dress : the most, however, European in costume and rather pleasant in appearance, without being pretty. Our ladies have fastened upon one tall, serious, half depressed looking woman of sweet manner, as the original for the heroine in Afraja—sensible and devout, but without doubt about to be sacrificed by a tyrannical father to some suitor whom she does not love, a thing, we hear, not altogether confined to fiction in Norway. She has just left at a little fishing-station, whence a strong-manned boat pulled out to take her. They watched her depart, sadly.

There is an old Lapp-woman on the forward deck, who might well do for one of the witches in Mügge's story. She has been released from the prison in Trondhjem. Her face looks like the lowest style of Indian faces—with a sly, besotted, murderous expression. She sleeps in all weathers under her blanket by the side of the funnel, and speaks to no one—even Edward can not open communications with her.

In our part of the ship, there is a constant warfare going on between the American ladies and the Norwegian on the subject of the only window of their little cabin. There seems to be a strong constitutional objection on the part of the Norwegians to fresh air ; and however many crowd into the little room, the window must at once be shut. From the intimations of our ladies, we should gather also that the Norwegian female travellers are anything but delicate in their curiosity either in strangers' affairs or property. Still, if there is anything one learns from travelling, it is, not to judge of a people alone from its travelling population.

A great want of attention to women is very marked here. They are bundled into boats, or shoved out of them like packages—and need strong arms and much resolution sometimes to avoid accidents.

The worst travelling habit in Norway, is the disgusting spitting. I thought America had reached the lowest grade of nauseating vulgarity in that respect—but it is worse here. The decks are clammy with it. And now that I am grumbling, I may go on to say, that of all European countries, it is the worst for fleas. Even Italy is not so tormenting. The country people are usually excessively filthy in their habits, and most of the inns are merely their houses, provided with an extra bed-room. In Sweden or in Hungary, where the country inns are dirty and disagreeable, there is so much hospitality that in your pleasant quarters in gentlemen's houses, you forget the filthy character of the hotels and taverns. Here, where the travel is too much to allow of more hospitality than is customary in civilized and crowded countries, you feel the full effects of the quality of the public accommodations. Still all these are trifling, compared with the enjoyments and physical benefits from a Norwegian tour.

We are now in the region of perpetual daylight, though bad weather has prevented a good view of the "midnight sun."

This unceasing day gives a new sensation, worth coming

to Norway to feel. It is difficult to describe. You are at first struck with the *strangeness* of Nature—the silence, and the unnatural light. You feel as if something unusual was about to happen. After a time you become more accustomed to the day, and lose the sense of division of time. The sensation is of perpetuity, of unlimited activity, of a Nature working without rest, or change, or shadow.

It is exciting, stimulating, and cheerful; but probably if enjoyed long, wearisome.

Finmark.—As we enter the Finmark Amt, the aspect of the coast becomes even more volcanic, with the sharp acuminated summits, and the contorted strata.

In one place, the curved or *curling* lines of rock melted by fire, would have struck the most ignorant beholder, even a quarter-mile away. We saw, in several instances, precipices with grey limestone above, and some granitic formation below. Of all countries, this must be the favorite for a geologist. It is evident that two of the greatest agencies of Nature in continent-making—volcanic fire and ice floods—have been in tremendous action over the Norwegian coast.

TROMSÖE.

We came on the deck of our steamer on the morning of the 5th of July, and found ourselves in what seemed a mountain-lake, with the little red-roofed town of Tromsöe on the borders. A brisk snow-storm was blowing, so as almost to hide the giant snow-peaks at one end of the bay, the other was shut in by green slopes, with heavy masses of snow lying close on the grass. The town is on an island and sheltered from the sea by a larger island, Kvalö, though this does not at all appear from the water. It shows a number of substantial wooden ware-houses, and we could see some dwelling-houses of a very respectable size. The green grass roofs of the fishermen's cottages made the outskirts. We were soon on shore, and wandering about the town, picking some old friends among the flowers —butter-cups and violets from a grave-yard in one quarter. Every hut had flowers in the windows. The air was cold and wintry. We took breakfast in a miserable dirty inn. At a later hour, we called on a number of persons to whom we had letters—the Amtmand (magistrate) of the two districts of Finmark, By-Foged (sheriff), and others.

In one house, I had a conversation with a very intelligent young pastor, on the new religious "movement." Like almost every person here, he spoke English. "I speak but imperfectly English," said he, "but I shall be happy to tell you of these peoples. They call themselves *opvakte*, or awakened, and they believe themselves to have alone the truth of the Bible. They are against the ordinances—the *daub*—what is it? child-baptism—for they say, no one should be baptist without his own will, and that they do have now the best baptism of the Holy Ghost. And so of the what call you it? the priest's clothes and ceremony, and the forgiveness of sin, which is spoken out by the clergyman. They be also opposed to amusements, the the musique and dance, and to *brant vein* (brandy). Some of them have burned their piano-fortes, but the most are too poor to have any such. They always bring out texts from the Bible, and say they have the true understanding of it. One must confess they show much *moralsk* (moral) in their lives. They will have nothing to do with the office church—what is it in English?" "State Church." "Yes! they have removed themselves entirely, here in Tromsöe, to the number of forty-six, but I believe they come again. It will pass forby."

"Do they believe as you do, in Christ?"

"Oh, yes; certainly, in nothing so much."

I asked about their leaders. The clergyman thought they scarcely had any. Pastor Lommers of Skien, was a prominent clergyman among them, who had just abandoned his place in the National Church. The most, he said, were led by people of their own sort, who pretended to especial inspiration. "They claim, you know, also, to be sinless."

While conversing, a physician came in, who belonged to the new sect, and we had, after a short time, a conversation in German together on the subject.

He was guarded in his expressions, but in his view the movement was "a struggle for Apostolic Christianity." "We do not find," he said, "in the New Testament, that the clergymen should be chosen by the government authorities, and that he should have so much money, and wear such and such clothes in the church. We believe 'confirmation' is altogether a matter of the heart, and not to be fixed by law. Our efforts, mein Herr, is after a life more impressed with religion; we think each man can have a divine light within him."

I asked about Baptism and the Communion. "Yes," he said, "we believe that only old persons should be baptized; and that the great thing is, the baptism of the Spirit." The Communion, he said, they wished made a thing for the soul only, and not a requisition.

Of amusements, his own feeling was, that a redeemed person would have no taste for them; still, they left that to the conscience of each one. Of their alleged belief in perfection, he denied that they ever supposed themselves to have attained to a sinless state. "The main thing in it all, sir, is what you in America will understand—we want the Church utterly kept apart from the State."

It would be presumptuous in me, as yet, to give a judgment on this remarkable religious movement. But from all evidence thus far, I fully believe it is a natural vigorous protest against the State Church, accompanied, of course, with much fanaticism. It should be remembered, in Norway every clergyman is an officeholder, paid by the government. Confirmation—church-membership—is a condition of citizenship, fixed by law at a certain age and after a certain degree of knowledge. That is, no one can hold a public office or receive a license, or be entitled to the fullest protection of the Norwegian laws, without possessing a certificate that he has been religiously confirmed in a certain church or parish. To enlarge on the fatal effects of such a mingling of the religious and the political, is not necessary to the American public.

The clergymen seem very well paid throughout the country, and generally have the best farms along the road. In this town of Tromsöe, containing perhaps three thousand five hundred inhabitants, with the universal cheapness of every thing, the pastor has a salary of two thousand five hundred dollars, and his house. The salary is made up somewhat singularly. Twenty dollars of it are from the *eider-down*,* furnished by a certain island in the neighborhood. Four hundred dollars come from lands, let out to farmers in the outskirts of the village, which belong to the pastorate: the rest is paid by the parish and the State. Among other fees, the pastor has a fixed one for every baptism and marriage and funeral. In the fishing districts, near the Lofodens, it is the custom for each fisherman to contribute a proportion of his fish, if the catch is lucky, so that in a good season the pastor will have three hundred or four hundred dollars' worth of fish added to his salary.

I went with a friend to visit the church of the village. It is a log building, boarded, and painted red. The interior has the usual division into four equal parts, by one portion of the building crossing the other in the centre at right angles.

The altar is separated by a railing from the church; a picture of Christ was behind it, and candles before. The floor within was strewn with juniper twigs, for the odor.

The seats in the body of the church were ugly wooden seats, and the walls were occupied with three tiers of unpainted little boxes, like opera-boxes, for the better

* The down sells here at two dollars a pound.

classes. The pulpit was on one of the angles of the nave and transept. The house was never warmed, they said. Above the altar, hung two little ships-of-war, complete in all equipments, such as one sees sometimes in a marine insurance-lawyer's office, for models to use in court. I asked the meaning of this singular custom, which is quite common in Norway.

"It betokens the sailing of the soul away to heaven," my friend answered.

Another explanation is, that the first church of the Northmen was an inverted boat; and hence, through all the Teutonic branches, the name for the principal aisle of the church became ship* or nave.

Two Russian vessels are lying in the harbor, with meal. The men were walking about in the town. They were much better-looking persons than the Norwegian sailors, with regular features, and full beard and moustaches. They seemed to me to have a certain peculiar gravity and dignity for people of their class. Probably something of the consciousness of a great nation comes down even to the lowest.

Russia has a considerable trade with this town.

I walked out in the afternoon on the hills behind the city. Here the Tromsöe citizens of wealth have erected villas to escape the heats of the summer, and to enjoy the wide landscape. It was the day after the Fourth, so my New-York friends will remember its temperature. I had

* In German, Schiff; Norwegian and Danish, Skib.

two overcoats on, but could hardly keep warm with walking, and was half blinded by the snow-squalls. One gentleman has a kind of Chinese villa, with pretty gravelled walks about it, laid out among trees, which from the water seem a grove of fruit and shade trees, and with fountains and summer-houses. A green lawn runs down from one side of the house, with flowers in the grass. There was something almost touching in this effort for summer. The only trees that would grow there, were the dwarf birch ; the snow yet lay deep at the foot of the lawn ; and the only flowers were the sweet Arctic *flora,* which winter cannot drive away, the yellow ranunculus ; the wild violet, here almost yellow ; the pink heather blossom ; the white multiberry flower, and our unfailing friends, the butter-cup and dandelion. Otherwise no shrub or fruit or vegetable—even potatoes can hardly endure the climate. The view from the *summer*-houses was the usual grand, desolate, Norwegian scenery of this latitude, mighty snow-peaks of jagged outline running down into dark, broken, twisted rock-bases, with broad reaches of water, gloomily hidden or suddenly revealed in the scurrying snow-squalls sweeping across it.

THE LYNGEN FIORD.

The Lyngen Fiord attracted my attention, as we sailed on from Tromsöe, from its mention in Mügge's charming romance. The scenery of it is truly grand. In the upper portions, owing to the condensation of the air, and the collecting of clouds by the hills, the climate is singularly mild and genial. Here grain sometimes ripens—the highest grain-growing land in the world—though at Tromsöe, only the dwarf-birch flourishes, and at Hammerfest, which is but a little distance, not even potatoes or the birch can live.

We pass now many glaciers, and occasionally cliffs of limestone.

The Jökulsfiörd was indicated as remarkable, for having the only *sea-glacier* in Norway—that is the only glacier emptying into the sea. With all these glaciers, are plainly to be seen the signs so often indicated by Agassiz ; the *moraines*, or masses of rock and stone pushed on by the slowly-descending ice, the semi-circular form of the mouth, and the protruding blue ice—with, as we hear, deep crevasses on the sides of the mountains, down which the ice-floods make their way.

Our bad weather is beginning to disappear, and the sun shone out brightly as we entered the beautiful Alten Fiord, in which are the famous copper-works. The inner branch of the Fiord is called Kaafiord, where is a famous headland, Bosekop. The highest peaks are about 3,000 feet high ; many of the hills rounded by ice-floods are visible. The village with the green slopes, and the pretty houses of the proprietor, Colonel Thomas, looked very pleasantly as we came to anchor. The works are a little without the village. One of the most singular sights from the steamer, is the different lines of the old sea-beach, plainly visible some fifty feet or more above the present water-level. The highest of these ancient sea-beaches is now two hundred and forty feet above the sea, showing that the land has been elevated during the historic period, that distance. It is curious that the elevation is greater here than towards the north, so that there is a *slope* towards Hammerfest.*

The copper found in these mines is the common yellow pyrites. The rocks are clay-slate, limestone, and hypersthene, green stone, with a peculiar kind of sandstone, or granular quartz.

As we lay at anchor, a young gentleman—an Icelander—came on board, from the Catholic Mission recently established in this neighborhood. I had known some of his friends in Copenhagen, and we soon made each other's acquaintance. There seems to me about all the Icelanders I have met, a peculiar raciness and enthusiasm. We had a long conversation together, in which I inquired of the mission and its objects. It was commenced, he stated, by a Russian gentleman, who had lost his estates in Russia, from his conversion to the Catholic faith—the Baron de Djunkowsky, or *Père Etienne*, as he is called now.

The mission consists of seven priests, two French and three German, beside himself. They have a chapel and have prepared a catechism as well as a kind of ascetical work. A seminary and college will be opened later. He is very warm about his friend.

"He is a noble man, Mr. B.," he says; "such a man as the Holy Xavier was." He states that the Baron is the Apostolic Prefect of Iceland, the Färöes, Lapland, Greenland, and Polar America.

*Forbes' Glaciers of Norway, p. 84 and 96.

They are to revive the five bishoprics which flourished here in the early Christian times, and they want hundreds of priests. The great question yet is, whether they are a legal community. They are buying land, and they refuse to pay tithes, so that they hope soon to have the question of their independency of the State Church brought before the courts or the government.*

"It is truly a question of liberty in religion," he says. "But we are obliged to present it as a question of education. At present, we are only an educational establishment—and there is no law in Norway against schools by foreigners."

I had some very free conversation with him as to his reasons for joining the Jesuit mission. "I know," he said, in English, "I leave the faith of my fathers, though not of the ancient Icelandic folk—but to me at this time, the Church Catholique seems the only democratic church. If I was in America, it might be different. Look at us here! We alone ask for toleration—such as you give even to the Mormons—and this Lutheran church does try to crush us. We are seeking to carry the cross among the poor Finns, and these rich pastors say, 'No: you must pay for our salaries! you must bring in the tenths! and you must keep up the State-church!' We will not do this. No: I would rather go to Siberia as my father, the baron, has done once."

We spoke afterwards of Iceland and her literature.

* Later information shows that the Mission has been legalized. A new Catholic Church—the first in Norway—the Church of *St. Olaf*, was consecrated August 24, 1856, in Christiania.

"Ah !" he said, "Mr. B., if you could only read our old sagas in the Icelandic ! They are grand. I do think of them every day—such vigor and fearlessness ! We have nothing like them in these days. Those old chieftains who conquered in all countries of Europe—and who sailed away on the unknown seas as the crows flew, and feared never—and finally even reached your noble country. Ah ! what have we now like them !

"People do never acknowledge what they have gained from the Northmen. Do you think they do ? Your jury-trial—your free speech—and your respect for women—are they not from our ancestors ? Christianity has much effected—but I do not believe it so much implanted respect for women as the old Norse habits and character did. *Pardon !* that I run on so. Will you take snuff ?"

We walked up and down the deck, continuing our animated conversation. I asked if he would care to live in Iceland ? No : he would not. It was dull, and was now only a colony and a depressed colony of Denmark. "When I settle, it shall be in Free Amerique, where all sects can have toleration. Europe has much to learn from you in tolerance and free allowance of every religious opinion. Do you see how these Norwegians avoid me ? I am a wolf, because I am become a Catholique. They say, 'See ! he's a Jesuit. He wants an *auto-da-fé* here ! We shall have nuns and a *parc aux cerfs* again !' *Les bêtes !*"

I asked him about the Finns and Lapps, whom they were trying to convert. He gave a better account of them than I had heard from the Norwegians. "A simple, serious folk," he said, "who could not leave their nomade life, but who might be much improved. Not especially stupid or inferior, and very grateful for kindness." He thought they had been much neglected and sometimes oppressed by the Norwegians. I found he spoke German and French as well as he did English.

The valley of the Alten, "the richest and most important on the coast," according to Mr. Lallerstedt, has been selected by the Swedish writers against Russia, "as the point where her ambitious attempts against Scandinavia will centralize." The gulf has three mouths, and each one leads to an excellent port, well sheltered against ocean storms and capable of being well defended.

"A second Sebastopol," says Mr. Lallerstedt, "could easily be erected here." The valley, rich in forests and metals and inhabitants, can furnish the materials for great enterprises. A direct bridle-road to the East connects the Alten valley with the Muonio and the Torneo, which from the frontier between Sweden and Russia. It would need but few days to march Russian battalions across from Torneo to this point. Russia has also in the White Sea, fifteen thousand tons of merchant-shipping, in which ten thousand men, with artillery and provisions for three months, could without difficulty be embarked. There is nothing on the whole coast, north of Trondhjem, to oppose a united attack, thus made by land and sea. With Alten in her hands, Russia at once has a good port towards the Atlantic, securely defended and open, owing to the influence of the conformation of the land and the Gulf-stream, for most of the year.

So the Swedish alarmists have pictured the danger. They have, perhaps, overdrawn the peculiar beauties and fertilities of the Alten valley.

It is certainly much more genial in climate than Hammerfest, where nothing grows, but it would not present itself as a very splendid prize for an ambitious Northern people, desiring to burst out towards the south and the sea. For nine months in the year, it is a cold, gloomy place, and no large population could ever subsist there.

Still it is, perhaps, well to have called the attention of Europe to the possible danger.

TEMPERATURE.

"For eleven years (1837–48)," says Forbes, "the average temperature (of Alten) at 9 A. M., was 34°.50; at 9 P. M., 32°.83; mean, 33°.66. Von Buch estimated it, solely, from the upper level of the Pine (640 feet above the level of the sea), at nearly 1° Reaumur, or 34°.25 Fahrenheit, a remarkable coincidence. The mean temperature of February, which is decidedly the coldest month, is 15°.4; and of August, which is usually the hottest, 54°.3. This range is, however, small, compared with the actual extremes on particular days, which I find to be the following during three years for which they are specified, but of which those for 1848 only are certainly taken with self-registering instruments:—

	1846.	1847.	1848.
Maximum............	83°.3	84°.7	86°.9
Minimum	14°.8	3°.1	20°.2
Range	98°.1	87°.8	107°.1

Hence it appears that the thermometer rarely, if ever, falls below the zero of Fahrenheit, whilst there is not, perhaps, another part of the earth's surface on this parallel where mercury does not freeze in winter. The fall of rain and snow in these three years was only 18.19, 16.81, and 17.19 inches."

Alten is known as the most northerly grain-growing town in the world—barley being raised here.

"Von Buch has remarked, that in Norway and Lapland the planes of vegetation of the pine and birch run nearly parallel to the plane of perpetual snow, the intervals, as observed by him at Alten, being given by the following table of limiting heights of vegetation above the sea:—

VEGETATION IN LATITUDE 70°.

The Pine (*Pinus sylvestris*) ceases at 287 metres = 780 English feet. The Birch (*Betula alba*) ceases at 482 metres = 1580 English feet. Bilberry (*Vaccinium Myrtillus*) ceases at 2030 English feet. Mountain Willow (*Salix mirsmites*) ceases at 2150 English feet. Dwarf Birch (*Betula nava*) at 2740 English feet. The snow line, 3480 English feet."—*Forbes' Glaciers of Norway.*

CHAPTER VIII.

HAMMERFEST.

This is the most northerly town in Europe, lat. 70° 40′ on the same degree in America is perpetual snow, and scarcely any human life.

We reached it at eleven o'clock, P.M., in broad daylight. There was a question, whether there was any hotel there at all, so that our first steps were in search of one. We were directed to one of the best-looking merchant's houses, were received by a dignified host, and at once shown to neat, quiet rooms, furnished in the usual style, with narrow beds with huge feather beds for coverlids, chairs, a pretty birch table set into the wall (we see much exquisite furniture made of the polished birch) papered walls, and uncarpeted floors. The house has an immense number of apartments, a large billiard-room, a pretty supper-room, and the family parlor below stairs. One of the rooms below is the store and counting-house, where is kept for sale almost every article needed by man, and capable of being brought or sold here, from fish-oil and reindeer skins up to oranges and thermometers.

As soon as possible we were out exploring the little town.

It was nearly twelve, but the hour seemed no nearer bed-time than in the morning. Hammerfest consists of some three streets, a square, and a church—the square having a dangerous-looking well in the centre. It was horribly muddy, and impregnated with the smell of the boiling fish oil.

The wharves were hung with the *stock-fisch* (cod), tied together and hanging over poles. The great object of every traveller to Hammerfest, besides seeing the Arctic town, is to get a view of the midnight sun—so we soon started, ladies and all, to climb the hill behind the town.

There were represented in our party England, Ireland, Germany, Iceland, Norway, and America ; and the latter had the largest deputation. There was something singularly fascinating in thus strolling off at midnight with a good company, and still enjoying broad day-light. The ladies were helped along—in part over the snow, and then over the springing, beautiful moss, till we stood on the summit. The sun was just setting, that is, approaching the mountains at the north ; but contrary to my expectation, the light was not at all the warm light of sunset, but rather that of morning.

Our artist, who has been making a sketch, says that Humboldt assured him that he would never find warm colors in the scenery ; that they were always cold and severe. Hammerfest lay below on its little circular bay, hid from the south by a rocky point, now beautifully green, and marked by the crosses of the grave-yard, laid out among the rocks. No tree or shrub, or garden-bed was anywhere visible, though beneath our feet, on the rugged cliff, bloomed flowers so exquisite, as no gardener's art has produced them. Even the dwarf-birch has ceased here to grow, except in the deepest valleys.

The wind began to blow from the North, and there were fears of the clouds, which already half covered the setting sun.

Our Icelander, who loves to quote the *Sagas*, says the North wind was always to the Scandinavians a good sign. The old heroes are represented as praying to the North; and in one battle of the peasants of Sweden with Gustavus Adolphus, they are said to have been greatly encouraged by a bitter North wind. To us weak modern men, the Norwegian north winds are no joke.

"It's just five minutes of twelve! we shan't see it."

"There it is above! See the line of sunshine come down the mountain! We shall have it soon!" There were a few moments of doubt, when the great orb burst splendidly forth below the cloud. "*The rising sun!* THE MIDNIGHT SUN!" It was a splendid spectacle—the rays sparkling over the beautiful Fiord, lighting up distant snowy mountains, shining back from peak to peak far away, and the whole sphere majestically rising and clearing away what a moment before had been the clouds of evening, but were now the mists of morning. The light, too was a different one, at least to our imagination—purer, clearer, and fresher. We watched the first movement, and it seemed, for a time, not to be upwards, but parallel with the hills, and then to be gradually ascending. At length we slowly descended under the full morning sun-light to the village. It was half-past one, as we walked through the streets, but people seemed just as much up and stirring as in the day. Children were playing in the street, and women sewing at the windows, while many came to the doors to study the costumes of our ladies. "Certainly, nobody sleeps in Norway," we said.

I must speak again of these gloriously long days—they are the greatest pleasure of Nordland (to an American)—you are always ahead in your work ; time never overtakes you. At first, you are hurrying in the evening, as if darkness would come upon you and you should not have time to finish whatever you are engaged at ; or you hasten to get through with an excursion, but you soon come into the habit of the perpetual day. The elastic air stimulates, and you seem to live two lives to the one in other latitudes. It becomes hard to sleep. Our lady friends, indeed, complain ; they miss the evening twilight, and the curtains drawn, and shutters closed. One says, "she would give so much to see a good Paris lamp again !"

I find that I sleep usually from one or two in the morning till nine, and though it is broad-day at either hour, it seems to make no difference.

We found that the artist had made a beautiful sketch in water-colors of the place, faithfully portraying the horizon of iceberg-like peaks, faintly colored by the morning, bounding the Fiord ; the singular reddish rock rising in the middle of the bay ; the little semi-circular town, with its red roofs, and green grass roofs of the peasants, and the picturesque turfed cabins of the Finns on the outskirts. He had been hardly an hour over it, but had wonderfully touched the prominent features with the true feeling of genius. Mr. H., we hear, is the best water-colorist on the continent.

THE TRADE.

This is principally in cod and fish-oil—cod-liver oil is well prepared here. Hammerfest is a considerable centre of exchange in furs and skins ; immense quantities of reindeer skins being brought there.

I purchased two or three large, beautiful skins, to be made up into mats, as gifts, for which the price was only one dollar each. The ermine skins are six cents each ; fox skins from three dollars to fifteen dollars. A singular exchange is carried on here. Otter skins are imported, *via* England and Hamburg, *from America*, sold to the Russians, and carried by them overland to China, where they are employed to wrap the dead who are buried in state. There were several Russian vessels in the harbor from Archangel, with most ugly-looking sailors aboard. These bring rye and provisions and furs ; the stoppage of this trade by the war, was severely felt in Northern Norway.

Every thing is much cheaper than I should expect, so far towards the ends of the earth. A good dwelling will rent from \$60 to \$80 dollars. Beef is 6 cents per pound ; mutton, 6 cents ditto ; milk, about 6 cents a quart. Butter is imported, as, like all the Norwegians, the inhabitants prefer to consume their own cream at once. A cow is worth from

$12 to $20 ; horse, $100 ; reindeer, $3 ; sheep, $2 ; a labor er's wages from 42 cents to 63 cents a day, without food. The population in 1846, was 927 ; it is now 1,125.

The English college-men who have been "roughing it" on the deck, are quartered at this hotel. They, with the artist, are going to the North Cape. The steamer which connects with ours, takes them within a few miles, and thence they proceed by open boat—the steamer itself going on to Vadsoe. Our hotel proves a very good one. To-day we had ptarmigan* and reindeers' tongues at dinner, preserved by the landlord in hermetically sealed cans. The only objection to the house, as to the town, is the intolerable smell of burning fish-oil which pervades every thing. This landlord has himself been three times chosen one of the "Electors," for electing a member of the National Parliament. He says that within a fortnight there will be a new election, but that there is no excitement. Hammerfest and Vadsoe and Tromsöe used to send one member ; now they are to send two. The new religious movement in Tromsöe takes all the public interest.

In the afternoon, we rowed over to Mr. R.'s place, in order to see some reindeer, pasturing on the hills. They were feeding by themselves, without any herdsmen, and scarcely let us come within what would be shooting-distance. They were dun-colored, and, seen through the glass, were very thin and ugly. The Lapps drive them down at

* Called *Ryper* (Tetrao Lagopus Alpinus).

this season to the sea, to escape the attacks of a little worm which annoys them excessively. They are considered almost valueless now, for present use. We found the moss everywhere on which they feed.

On our way back, we visited an interesting monument erected by the Norwegian, Swedish, and Russian governments, to designate the terminus of the arc of the meridian, drawn, on a great scale, from the Danube to the Arctic. The following is the inscription, somewhat abbreviated :

"TERMINUS SEPTENTRIONALIS ARCUS MERIDIANI, 25° 28′, QUEM INDE AB OCEANO ARCTICO AD FLUVIUM DANUBIUM USQUE, PER NORREGIAM, SWECIAM, ET ROSSIAM, JUSSU ET AUSPICII REGIS AUGUSTISSIMI, OSCARI I., IMPERATORUM AUGUSTISSIMORUM, ALEXANDRI I., ATQUE NICOLAI I., (1816) AD (1852,) CONTINUO LABORE EMENSI SUNT, TRIUM GENTIUM GEOMETRÆ."

LAT. 70° 40′ 11″.

The weather to-day has been the most splendid autumn-like weather—the sun shining brilliantly over the Fiord and snowy mountains. Women and children are out walking on the heights, and enjoying their few glimpses of summer.

The North Cape can easily be seen from the high hill behind the town.

Von Buch states that to get the mean temperature of Hammerfest, one must ascend from three hundred to four hundred feet higher than the pass of the St. Gothard, in the Alps. It is an instance of the bonds which the great Ocean river makes between most distant points, that, in 1823, casks of palm-oil drifted ashore here, which were traced to a wreck on Cape Lopez, Africa. This stream of warm water alone must make a vast difference in the climate of Norway. It is well known that drift-ice is never seen, even at Hammerfest, or at nearly 71°, while on the American coast it appears at 41°.

At Trondhjem, the difference of temperature between January and July is 40° Fahr., while at Jakutzk, Siberia, in the same latitude, away from the influence of the sea, it is 114°, and the mercury is sometimes frozen for three months in the year.*

In walking about the town, one of us said to a boy, cutting cod for salting, "What do you do with the back-bones and bones?" "Feed the cattle, sir," was the answer; and it is true. Even the horses here must sometimes eat refuse fish and bones.

July.—One of the "Fjeld Finner," or Finns of the Mountain, was at our hotel to-day. He wore the same dress as the one on the boat, though his blouse was of fine sheep-skin, and his shoes were of reindeer-skin. The bright colors of their high caps give a very picturesque effect to a company of them, seen together.

I induced this man to take off his cap, and felt the shape of his head, much to his astonishment, no doubt. He had an excellently-formed head; forehead strong and full, though not high; the frontal portions of the brain rising finely, perhaps highest on the Phrenologic organ of "firmness; and the backside of the head not too full

* Forbes.

in proportion. His hair was light and very long ; eye grey, and cheek-bones very high, the broadest part of the face being at that point ; mouth large, and chin small, with a scanty moustache and imperial, as is usual. A face, I should say, showing some weakness but good capabilities of improvement. On the whole, bearing out what my Icelandic friend had said.

On going off at night to the steamer, our landlord would not go into any accounts, but said, "call it a dollar a day," which, considering that it included use of boat, preparation of four meals and rooms, was cheap enough.

CHAPTER IX.

AN ARCTIC DINNER AND EXCURSION.

Our voyage South began in beautiful weather, like an Italian summer, making the coast seem another region compared with the view on our upward trip. We expect to be in Trondhjem on the fourteenth day from leaving it, which is the quickest time in which this trip can be made by the government steamers.

On our arrival at Tromsöe, we found a pleasant dinner-party prepared to meet us, at our friend's, Mr. ——. The houses here are usually very comfortable ; this is like a German house, with many tastefully-furnished but uncarpeted rooms. Reindeer-skin mats you see about, and snow-shoes, some six feet long at the outside door. The windows are double, with French casements. Beautiful flowers are at almost every window.

The cooking is much like the cooking of a nice German family, and the dinner had the same general arrangement. The pudding—which the Norwegians make inimitably—coming in between the other courses ; the game dishes being eaten with sour preserves, and the dessert as with us, fruits and nuts. One preserve, which is very popular with all classes, is the multiberry (*moltibeer*), a small berry growing close to the ground.

The crowning dish of Scandinavia, is also in use here, the "*rögröd*,"* eaten with cream and sugar. May America soon be blessed with that delicious mixture for a refreshing summer-dish!

The wines used were mostly from the Moselle and the Rhine. The most characteristic things to be observed were, the hearty, manly bearing of the company, and the repeated toasting. I think one would seldom see a table-company in Germany, where there were so many strong, manly-looking persons, and with such a free, independent manner. The conversation showed them all to be persons of cultivation, as well as of much natural intelligence. There was a great deal of quick wit and fun going on, constantly across the table. The Norwegian women impress one very favorably—as quick, intelligent, and kind in manner, with an equal bearing towards the men, as if accustomed to respect. I have seen, thus far, very few beauties among the upper classes; the climate evidently tells on them.

* We append the recipe:—"Take three and a half pounds of juice of currants and three pints of water and sugar, *ad lib.*, with a flavoring of almonds or cinnamon (an ounce or an ounce and a half.) Boil this mixture, and when it begins to boil add one and a quarter pound of ground rice or a pound of sago. Let it boil a quarter of an hour, and stir it often; afterwards it is to be poured into moulds or tea-cups, which have been wet with cold water, and left to cool. Then it should be turned out, and eaten with cream and sugar. Any other juice of acid fruit will do as well."

Almost immediately after the soup a toast was proposed —"The strangers"—with a neat little speech from the host. We bowed our response.

Soon after came another toast to the *Amtmand*—then to the lady of the *Foged,* who was not present; then from one of the company to the hostess and to the host—each accompanied with a speech or a joke. Towards the close, our host offered one toast very seriously, alluding to the Crampton difficulties—"*Peace between England and America!*" The jovial amtmand, with a very hearty, pleasant bit of an oration, gave us "The Thirty-one Stars of the American Flag!"

I responded with a toast in German, to the "Norwegian Constitution!"

In the course of the dinner, I told the amtmand, about the character of his office, as we get it in "Afraja"—the cruel and tyrannical amtmand of Tromsöe. He had not seen the novel, though they all knew about Mügge. They laughed at his romance of the oppression of the Finns by the Norwegians; and his sketches of Finnish magicians and maidens. The feeling towards the Finns and Lapps, seemed to be very much like the feeling of an intelligent Western company towards the Indians. The poetry of the race is quite obscured in their debased or drunken habits. The Lapps are simply ignorant, dirty men, who live in a barbarous way among reindeers, or who catch the cod and the ducks which the Norwegians want. Still Mügge is right. They present a fair foil to the Norwegians, such as a dramatist would seize upon—weak, poetic, roving and unsettled, while their masters are strong, practical, steady, and perhaps tyrannical. They have lost, too, their old possessions and habitations before the conquering race of Northmen. Without doubt, they have suffered much injustice.

"Well: we shall see," said the Amtmand. "I have ordered a little tribe to meet us this afternoon in the valley—reindeer and all. They are generally, at this time of year, far away on the mountains."

I had some conversation with one gentleman—a teacher—on the Public Schools.

"We have many obstacles, Herr B.," he said in German. "Our profession is not yet sufficiently respected here. We can not open as thorough and cultivated schools as we desire."

I expressed my admiration of their Drawing-schools for working-men. He said, that they found their influence excellent on the craftsmen.

"Do the common people read?" I asked. "*Ja wohl!*—certainly," he answered, "all read the Bible and Psalm-book, and many of them other works."

I inquired about these fishermen on the coast. They were rather wild and ungoverned, he said, "but they all read, and are intelligent."

I was talking with another gentleman, a sea-officer, of the coast and the coast-scenery, and in our conversation, I asked him about that which is the terror of every child's life in geographical description, the *Mälström*. He laughed, and said, in English, "That is a myt (myth)! There is noting in it—noting. I have seen your whirl-streams in

America, they are quite as bad. It only is a rapid stream of tide between two rocks, sometime a leetle dangerous to an unskillful boatsman. Noting more ; noting!"

"Like Hurl-gate, near New York, probably !"

"Yees ; very likely, so as I remember."

"Gentlemen," said our host, rising, "you know it is our custom, before leaving the table, to drink one toast. (To me.) We are from the South, and it is our habit always to remember that at a festival—I propose *our friends at the South!* gentlemen !" This was drank heartily, and we left for the drawing-room. There each shook hands with the hostess, and thanked her, and then cigars and coffee were brought, and the pleasant chat was kept up.

"It is time for the excursion," said the active Amtmand, "and we must prepare for rough walking !" It was now 7 o'clock, and we had five miles for ladies and all to walk through a marsh and wood, before we could reach the Lapp encampment, which our friends would show us. Think of such a walk into the forest in any other latitude at this hour ! The light out-doors was a pleasant full afternoon light yet, and in the Northern summer, no one thinks of dusk or sleep. Nature leaves you untrammelled.

We crossed the piece of water which surrounds Tromsöe in boats, and taking up our companions from the steamer, began the walk up the valley. It was an excursion to remember. The paths wound through a kind of thicket, which in the warm valley, showed a much greater variety of vegetation than we had seen on the hill by the town.

There was the mountain-ash (the Scotch rowan and

Norwegian *rön*) ; and elder berries, and alders, willows, and birch, and a number whose names I did not know.

On the ground, we plucked the yellow violet and white multiberry (*rubus chæmæmorus*), and pink-heath, and yellow ranunculus, and now and then an anemone, with the sweet flower of the blue-berry or the hare-bell.

The weather was as different from what we had experienced here in going up, as summer from winter. A rich warm afternoon-light filled the valley with almost a glory, calling into short existence thousands and thousands of little insects and moths. Above us were the mighty hills, whence, whenever we left our merry party, we heard as in the most solemn stillness, the gentle continuous rustling of the torrents melting from the snow in long silvery streamlets—"the whispering of Nature," as one of our Norwegian friends said.

The walk was a very hard one for the ladies—especially for one of the Norwegian—we had to carry them over torrents, guide them through morasses, and rescue them from occasional snow-drifts which yet remained even in summer-heats. The Norwegian gentlemen were evidently accustomed to such escorting, and did their duty in a most creditable manner. C——, a lively fellow from this Province, who only spoke some half dozen words in any language beside his own, made himself as agreeable as if he had the whole vocabulary of each—trying now German, now French, now English, or even Latin.

At length, we came out on a beautiful green intervale, with a brook dashing through it, lying at the base of great snow-capped hills. We were almost upon them, before we perceived an encampment of little turf and wood huts, with an enclosure for cattle, surrounded by a turf and bush hedge. One or two Laplanders stood quietly among them; the whole a perfect fac-simile of the pictures in children's story-books. A place to rest was made on the green grass for the ladies, and the refreshments were brought out, while the Lapps were hurrying down their reindeer from the mountains. I went out, in the mean time, to examine the huts. They were built closely, of turf, with a hole in the top for the smoke, like an Indian wigwam. The reindeer-cheese was shown to us, buried in the ground, in wooden vessels; the milk was in heavy wooden pails. The spoons were of wood and horn, curiously cut. We bought a few, and then my American friend attempted to buy some of their rare jewelry, which they have kept a long time among their tribes, but which they occasionally sell to travellers. They would not part with it.

Of course, the great interest was in the reindeer. The first glimpse we caught of them, was as of a flock of little black animals on the snow at the top of the mountain. Gradually they drew nearer to us, and we could see that they were driven by some little Lapland-dogs, and two boys with whips. Every straggler from the herd was at once brought in by the dogs, and the whole mass was directed towards us. Finally they came, tramping and snuffing, and with a low grunting noise, into the valley, and passed us, some two hundred of them—the bucks bent down under their grand antlers, the does very thin and scraggy, and the little fawns, dun-colored and graceful—all running into the enclosure. They are, as I before observed, a small deer—much more so than I expected—and, at this season, peculiarly ugly. Their motion is a kind of quick trot—not a bound, like that of our deer—and, it is said, they will keep this up for ninety miles a day. The boy, to show us the milk, threw a lasso some twenty feet over a doe, and pulled her up towards him. He milked her in a little wooden vessel. The milk is very rich in quality, richer than cow's milk—and not disagreeable. We are told there are two species of moss, which the reindeer feed on—one, a lichen (rangiferina), with a broad pale-green leaf, which we observe everywhere on the rocks (such as grows on dead trees in America); and another, the little white Iceland-moss, which the Lapps keep and dry for winter. They also eat the lemming-rat. The deer are greatly troubled by flies and insects, and, either to escape these or to get their favorite moss, they draw their masters down at this season to the hills near the sea.

It is a curious fact, that these natural migrations of the reindeer have been the occasion almost of a war between Norway and the colossal empire at the North. In former times, Finnish fishermen used to follow their business on the fishing-places of the Norwegians, and, in return, the Norwegian Lapps were allowed to cross into Finland during winter, for the moss for their reindeer. The Russian Lapps had the same privilege in summer on these coasts. This exchange was settled, even by a treaty between Norway and Sweden, as far back as 1751.

After a time, when Russia had conquered Finland, her government expressed itself dissatisfied with this state of things, and demanded greater privileges for Russian fishermen, and even stations on the coast. These were refused. It then refused all entrance into Finland for the Lapps and their reindeer, and when the poor animals absolutely forced their way to their usual food, they were killed, and great injury was thus inflicted on the Norwegian Lapps. These latter attributed their suffering to their own government, and were exasperated once or twice even into bloody outbreaks. The Norwegian government sent a commission into Finland, to quiet the Lapps, and demanded explanations of the Russian government. No satisfactory replies were ever received, and thus the matter still rests.

As I had expressed my desire of making some inquiries of the Lapps themselves, especially on their religious faith, my friends called forward one of the young herdsmen, and introduced me, through an interpreter. The man was dressed in a kind of reindeer-skin frock, with a red visorless cap, and blue trowsers, tied at the ankle. He took off his cap, and showed a good, intelligent face, and well-shaped forehead, with the usual features—high cheek-bones, small eyes, and long light hair. His height was perhaps five feet six inches. He was a kind of servant or member of the household, the chief of which possessed these reindeer.

"Can you read?" I asked, through the interpreter.

He answered that he had learned of the schoolmasters (they go from house to house).

"Can you read the Bible?"

"Oh, yes; he read it almost every day. He had been confirmed under Lestadius."

This was the great preacher and missionary among them, and the originator of this remarkable religious movement, of which I have already spoken. He died in 1841.

"Do you believe you will live after you die."

"Everyone will live," he answered, very seriously; "but whether he should attain the blessed life, he was not sure; he was trying very hard, but sometimes he was in doubt?"

"Do you think you will live above or below?"

The answer was remarkable: "God is everywhere, above and below. He will do with me what is good!"

I was desirous of seeing if any of the old superstitions still existed among them.

"When there is a storm among the mountains, do you not believe the wicked spirits are at work?"

"They are always busy in evil, both among men, and in the mountains," he answered.

"Do you believe in the old Jumala (the heathen god)?"

I understood from his answer that he considered Jumala to be Satan.

He professed also his belief in Christ as "part man and part God."

I asked, finally, whether he would like to live in the cities, to go into business, and make money, and have a fine house.

He made a gesture of utter disgust. "He would not hear of it; he was only used to this," and he stretched out his hand to the mountains and clouds. "He could not leave the rocks and the reindeer. He would die!"

There was something in his simple and sententious replies that impressed one much. His manner was very serious, and as it were, half-abstracted, as if of a man living habitually under principles and thoughts, not seen by the eye or easily expressed. He seemed a savage when I first addressed him, but I shook hands with him at parting, as if we belonged to more than the Brotherhood of humanity.

The old chief had returned now from taking care of the reindeer. I was introduced to him, as from America. His countenance lighted up at once, and he said, "There is where the son of Lestadius has gone. Does the gentleman know him?" I said no; though I had often heard the name of the good man.

He seemed pleased; and spoke a few words more of the old missionary with great feeling. We held then another theological conversation. His replies were by no means so original as those of the young man, and were mostly Scripture phrases.

Once he said, in reply to a question about the future life, "Men are on earth, the bad below, and the good above."

Of the wicked? "They go into everlasting punishment." Of Jumala and the heathen superstitions, he expressed an utter disbelief. "Is there any fear of demons or evil spirits now among your people?"

"No; except with the poorest persons. We believe in the Redemption through Christ. We do not care for anything else."

Is there much drinking in your tribe?"

"No, none. We never drink now. The spirit of God has been among us."

I tried to draw out something more about this strange Revival. He would not answer much; but what he said, was spoken with great solemnity.

His opinions on religious facts were very clear. It struck me that he generally felt himself too far advanced for my questions. At the close, he turned suddenly to me with the remarkable question, "Does the gentleman believe in baptism of children?" My friends explained that this subject was greatly agitated just now among the Lapps, and that there were two parties on it.

This chief was a believer in the old creed of the baptism of children.

I felt diffident about explaining my own views, knowing that my Norwegian friends would look on a doubter of that article, as some one quite out of the pale of society, and perhaps a little crazed. I explained that the majority of the Christian Church in America, and my own religious friends, generally believed in it, but that I, historically and morally, preferred it as a sign of voluntary conversion, or union with the religious body.

The most touching and interesting thing to me in the conversations, was the evident feeling towards the old Missionary, Lestadius, and the deep, solemn religious faith which they had gained from him.

There are many splendid monuments scattered over the world for the great and wise, but what of them could be half so beautiful as the unspoken gratitude and daily memory inciting to noble thoughts, in the hearts of such poor creatures as these? One could die happy, to know that one's name was thus breathed with the prayers of the depressed and the ignorant!

About ten o'clock, we started on our walk back, in a beautiful afternoon sun-light. The sky was soft and genial in tone, and the colors like those of an Indian summer, delicate violet and warm purple, with a dreamy haze on the horizon. Our common coats felt too warm. We had left our thermometer behind, but I am assured it frequently rises at this season to 94° Fahrenheit. Think of this in the latitude of Greenland and Baffin's Bay (69° 40′)!

In walking through the thicket, I was in company with an intelligent gentleman of Tromsöe, and we had some conversation on the replies of the young Lapp.

"There was something very peculiar about that Lestadius," said he; "his great talent lay in a kind of sensuous and vivid presenting of Scripture truth, which often was really coarseness. I remember an instance. He had been once speaking of believers partaking of the communion supper, and then going off to commit sin, just as before. 'Ye eat the body of Christ!' said he. 'Does it digest? Do ye take it into your vitals? Does it become your blood and your life? No: ye are hypocrites! Ye go out into secret places and *spit it all out!*'"

Another time he was preaching of the marriage of the Church to Christ. "Do ye call yourselves *brides* of Christ, ye selfish and sensual Christians ! No : ye were never married. Ye are prostitutes and harlots ! Beasts have ye married !"

"Still," said my friend, "he had a way of coming straight to the conscience of these poor creatures in a wonderful manner, and he spent his life among them."

I asked what he considered to be the cause of this religious movement among them.

"It seems to me," said he, "that the preaching of Lestadius was the origin of it ; and then the grand solitary Nature in which these people live, has cultivated the deepest religious feeling. People call it fanatical—and so it is—still I have been the witness that it has called forth even among the Norwegians in Tromsöe, the most serious and solemn desires to live more really for what is not seen—and I know that the influence has been exceedingly deep and powerful on the morals and life of many people.

"Whether it may be God's spirit," he continued, "or some less natural influence, I believe that now all through Europe, there are strong movements for a more deep and real religious life. We hear of it in Switzerland and in Germany, and even in France."

Such words spoken under the shadow of great mountains, with the silent grandeur of Nature solemnly attesting, where no other ear listens, from stranger to stranger, crossing each other's paths a moment on the endless journey, have an effect which in no way appears on paper or when repeated afterwards.

When we reached the boats, our ladies were very much fatigued, so that we left them on the steamer, and we went across to take supper with our friends. It was now half past eleven—the children were up at the house and the sun poured a blaze of light into the rooms. After a pleasant meal, we bade good-bye, and towards one o'clock came on board the steamer, while the rising run was lighting up the whole Fiord. It was impossible to sleep under the beautiful morning, and we walked the decks in the mild summer air, and talked of the interesting day and the pleasant people of Tromsöe, till the morning of more southern latitudes had really come.

COAST VOYAGE.

We stopped again at Alten on our voyage back, and as we lay at anchor, the Baron Djunkowski, or Père Etienne, the head of the Catholic Mission, came aboard. He was a small, dark, quick man, with Russian features, who impressed you at once as a person of marked ability. His tact and readiness in the twenty minutes which he spent on the deck of the steamer, were extraordinary. Each person he addressed in his own language—(I heard him speak five languages in that time), and to each he spoke just what was most likely to be in accordance with his habits of thought. To me he said, after a few words, "We are attempting here, sir, just what you in America have so nobly solved—the question of toleration of all sects, under the law. It is the question of liberty! I do hope, sir, to visit one day your countree. The Church Catholique owes to it much gratitude. I have not the pleasure of knowing many of the Catholique clergy in America, but we hear of Archbishop Hughes. I hope to see America—the land of the future!"

I wished him every success in his struggle for religious toleration, and we parted very cordially.

We stopped but a half-day at Trondhjem, and took leave of our pleasant company and the gentlemanly captain, to take a large Hamburg steamer, for Bergen. Our new captain again speaks English excellently. We meet many of the fishing-boats, or jechts, bound from Bergen for Finmark. They make two voyages, one in the spring for oil, and another for fish. The salt fish is sent to Spain ; the dried, to Italy, and sometimes to South America. Our captain says, there is a great change in the habits both of the boatmen and fishermen within a few years : so much less intoxication. He attributes it in part, to the greater import and use of coffee in place of liquors.

The coast between Trondhjem and Bergen is very rich in historic associations. A Norwegian was on board, who had been employed by government in selecting sites on the coast for lighthouses. Though, apparently, not an educated man, he knew perfectly every scene celebrated in the ancient history and sagas of the country. He pointed me out many famous burial mounds, where already some of the most interesting objects of antiquity had been found. He stated, and I find that to be the general opinion, that the abandonment of agriculture for fishing, had greatly reduced the population of the coast, and that the country produced more in the twelfth century than it does now ; "in 1812, there was such a famine, that people were obliged to eat the bark of trees."

These views are to be received with much allowance.

From the nature of the soil, and the appearance of the coast, it does not seem possible it could ever have supported a very numerous population by agriculture. When men lived principally by hunting and fishing, I can well understand that a country like Norway, with its deep Fiords and inaccessible forests, the refuge of wild animals of every kind, might have been much more resorted to than the more open and fertile lands to the South, and that thus a population might have sprung up, very numerous in proportion to the resources of the country. This, with the confusion of names for different tribes, is the probable cause of the representation by ancient writers, of the immense population of Scandinavia.

Molde.—This is one of the most Swiss-like villages in Norway. It is built on the edge of what seems a lake, though really a Fiord, with green fields and wooded hills rising abruptly behind, till they disappear among mountains The front is sparkling water, with a fore-ground of sharp jutting snow-peaks. We counted eighty-one at one point of view. The air has been, to-day, the most deliciously balmy; the fresh, green, and luxuriant grain, and the foliage, are inexpressibly soothing and pleasant after our Arctic voyage. There is such a softness and beauty over every thing, that we seem to be in one of our American summer scenes rather than in Norway. The yards are fresh with dear old New England flowers, lilacs, laburna, and violets, and roses. I have just passed, in our ramble, a grave-yard, beautifully set with flowers like a garden. Often one sees that affectionate piety in these northern countries, and what a contrast are their church-yards to our desolate, forsaken places for the dead in America.

The beautiful twilight, with its soft skies, and gentle, quiet and uncertain light, has come again after our long day, and the lamp and the closed curtains are most home-like, after twelve or fourteen days of sunlight.

Aalesund.—The towns on this coast are wonderfully picturesque. This is built among bare rocks which are curtained in vines, or green with fresh grass ; and as you walk along the streets, your path seems to terminate in the hill-side, or the cliffs when you find it suddenly works through on another group of houses among the rocks, or leads over to some pretty little island.

The great business is the fishing and export of herring and cod. The latter is sent even to Italy and Spain.

July ——.—On our voyage to-day we passed a remarkable headland, with a sheer precipice of 1,200 feet into the Fiord —Hornelen. The sailors and cragsmen have often attempted to scale it and reach the summit, but in vain. Several lives are said to have been lost in the effort, at different times. The tradition which perhaps impels, is that one of the old gigantic Vikings—Olaf Trygveson, I think, laid a wager that he would climb it in his armor. He started with a brave peasant, and after reaching a certain point in the difficult ascent, the man dared neither go farther nor recede. The powerful Viking took the poor fellow under his arm, reached the summit, waved his sword in the air, and brought the man down safely again.

CHAPTER X.

THE NORTHMEN.

We have just passed an island—*Vigr*—in which one of the most distinguished and heroic of the cruel pirates of the North had his residence—afterwards the founder of the line of Norman dukes in France, and the ancestor of the English kings and of half of the royal families of Europe—Rollo, or Rolf Ganger (Ralph, the Walker), so called because his great size crushed any horse he would mount, and he was obliged in consequence to walk. This coast which we are passing, with its multitudinous friths, or fiords, encouraging a constant trial of the sea—its jutting rocks, where the slender soil only in favorable seasons could support the inhabitants—was a natural home for that daring race of pirates and filibusters, who scourged Europe for so many centuries, and who finally infused their savage vigor into its effeminated and superstitious people. Whatever be the attractions of scenery or of the existing institutions in Norway to the traveller, the great interest to the student of history for evermore, is the thought of its wonderful Past. Though such vague associations, with all their constant charm, are not capable of being expressed, yet they are called unceasingly forth in this country by every familiar object.

The type of the features, the color of the hair, the stature of the men, the form of the houses, and the mould of the fishing-boats ; the scanty soil and the stern cliffs ; the names of persons and of objects ; the titles, the laws, and the institutions—all, in one mode or another, remind of that powerful race to whom England and America owe their fame and their good work in the world.

One continually asks, what it was in the rocks, the air, or the sea, which made such a people of conquerors. One wonders how it was that a country which now has hardly more than a million and a half of men, could a thousand years before have sent such destructive and conquering armaments against the most powerful nations of Europe.* Norway is fortunate in still possessing a people who are not degraded in the comparison of manhood with their unconquerable forefathers. In Denmark, one cannot, in the character of the people, trace the historic descent from the Danish Northmen. Among the Norwegians, one feels that the same stuff is still there, and the same essential elements of nature.

* "King Canute the Great sailed to England with 1,000 great vessels; Knut Sveinson came to Norway with 1,200 ships; Harold Gormson sailed from Denmark with 700 vessels; Eymundi made an expedition against Norway with 600 ships; and the Jombourg Vikings alone had 180."

The common vessels had 30 oars and 200 men each, and could carry sail.—*Weinhold's Alt-Nordisches Leben.*

To many readers, who only vaguely know that Normandy and England were settled and conquered by the Northmen a brief sketch of their expeditions may be welcome.* I must say here, that I use the name Northmen rather than Normans, because the latter has come to have a too chivalric or heroic association.

The Northmen were simply, through some eight hundred years, Northern pirates, of the most cruel and bloody class. They had various names. The principal one by which they were known, *Vikings*, is derived from *Viks*, or *Wicks*, the inlets from which their fleets proceeded. By the English, they were called Danes ; by the French, whom they continually annoyed, pirates and Northmen ; by the Irish, whose island they approached usually from the east, Eastmen ; in the sagas, they have the common title of Norwegians, though they came from both branches of the North-Teutonic race, the Danes and the Norwegians. The Swedes, though of the same blood, do not appear to have been often connected with their sea-expeditions, while, on the land, they gained great conquests.

The earliest invasions of which we hear, by sea, from Jutland and the north of Germany, were against Gaul, in 286 A. D. Nearly at the same time, there were emigrations from a branch of the great German family, the Saxons, to England. By the year 480, Saxons had established colonies in Normandy, at Caen, and at the mouth of the

* The facts in this chapter are principally drawn from Depping's Expeditions des Normands, Thierry, and the Heimskringla.

Loire, and were fast changing and becoming humanized under the influence of a superior civilization.

In the middle of the fifth century, they had also been called into England, to aid against the Celtic tribes at the north, and thus at length gained a firm foothold in that island. The small islands neighboring, as well as Scotland, held out much longer than England against these invaders. The Anglo-Saxons were early converted to Christianity, and, from some peculiarity of temperament, appear to have fallen especially under its superstitions. Their success in England emboldened the Scandinavian Northmen, and these commenced to make their fearful incursions against the small islands north and west of Scotland. In this same century, an alliance was formed between a Danish Northman's family and a Scotch royal family. The first really successful invasion of the terrible Northern pirates into England was made in 793 A. D., when they began their relentless devastations of convents and churches, which they continued for so many centuries. While the Northmen were thus pressing the Christianized Saxons of England, another race—the Francs—were just about breaking the power of the same people in their own provinces, in Northern Germany. Charlemagne had opened his vigorous and cruel campaigns against the heathen Saxons in Northern Germany.

This great leader, though successful against these tribes, could not destroy the power which he saw would soon threaten all civilized Europe—the piratical and fearless sea-rovers of Norway and Denmark. His strong hand was able to protect the coasts of France during his life, but after his death, Northmen ravaged unrestrained almost every coast in Europe. The people seemed everywhere to have become weak and superstitious. Feudalism could do little against the fierce democracy of the Vikings. With the Northern robbers, each private soldier was a landholder, and an independent man. Among the oppressed peoples of Europe, the soldier was a serf. Nor could the Christian faith in amulets and relics, and masses, stand beside the strong Faith of these Pagans in the joys of Valhalla, reserved for the brave, and their trust in their own right arms. They burned, plundered, and ravaged without mercy or hindrance. Convents were sacked, churches robbed, Christians carried off as slaves by the thousands. Astute and supple, they used wiles where they could not employ force. They united a boundless ambition and enterprise with the most firm animal courage, and a reckless contempt of death. Pain, and hardships, and dangers were their delight. They lived in the excitement of these perils and exploits. The hope of booty, the lust of conquest, the ideals of religion and of poetry, all contributed in stimulating them to their incessant and daring expeditions. They became almost irresistible. In one century, the ninth, they attacked London, burnt Rouen, plundered Paris, and took Seville, overrunning something of France, Scotland, England, Spain, and Portugal. The only decided check they received during this time, was from a people, equally with themselves fired by fanaticism, and inured to danger, and who had not yet learned defeat—the Moors of Spain. Hitherto the local causes which had originated the piracies from Norway, had been the uncertainty of the harvests and the superabundance of the population, almost compelling the young men to seek their fortunes abroad.

To these was added now a political cause. Harold Haarfager, the first king, who sought to make a united State of the numerous petty kingdoms of Norway, and who first attempted to put down piracy, had fought in 885, one of the great battles of Norwegian history in the Hardanger Fjord. His opponents, the petty chieftains of Norway, assisted by the King of Sweden, were utterly defeated and scattered abroad, and the Royal Power was henceforth established. The refugees, many of them the bravest warriors and sea-kings of Norway, fled to distant islands, and formed new bands of pirates and freebooters.

Some took refuge in Iceland, and founded a democratic Republic, where literature and law flourished, as they did nowhere else in Northern Europe, in that degenerate age. Among the countries that suffered most from these defeated Vikings, were England, Ireland, and Scotland, and the small islands which lie adjacent.

The power of the Norwegian King, however, reached them here. In the Shetlands and Orkneys he extirpated utterly their bands, and gave the Orkneys as a fief to Rognvald, the father of Rollo and the great line of Norman kings.

Rollo is the first of the Vikings who turned his successes to solid use, and who can, therefore, really claim a position in history. His life, too varied and filled with incidents to be told here, was most characteristic of the times. Banished by his old friend and chief, Harald Haarfager, from Norway, for acts of lawless violence, he spent years in piracy and bloody adventure, until he obtained a foothold in the beginning of the 10th century in Neustria, or as it was afterwards called, Normandy. There, at Rouen, the old freebooter and pirate married a Franc woman, and became nominally Christianized, established a government which became known as the most settled and strong government in France, and whose only traces, transmitted to posterity, are the most severe laws against rapine and crime. While he was founding the line of English kings in Normandy, his brother Rholland went to Iceland, and established a family, who are said to be still known as intelligent and industrious farmers in that little island.

The Northmen now held possession of Neustria or Normandy for several centuries, as a ruling and distinct people, gradually becoming humanized, and feeling the softening influences of Christian civilization.

With the efforts in Norway and Denmark to extinguish piracy, and the success of the Northmen in France, the Viking expeditions were coming to a close.

In the middle of the tenth century, one of the last bands of these pirates was formed—the Jombourg-Vikings ; and in 1015, the last eminent Viking leader, Olaf Haraldson, appeared, and ran through with his bloody course. The expedition in the eleventh century of the Guiscards, the descendants of the Northmen, which conquered Southern Italy, had more the character of a conquest than a piracy. In the

Scotch isles, the Northern pirates still had their haunts till the thirteenth century, and in the Orkneys, Norse was spoken till the sixteenth century.

At the close of the tenth century and near the beginning of the eleventh, were those peaceful expeditions of the Northmen which resulted in the discovery of America, but which produced so little fruit, that both they and the extensive colonizing of Greenland, from which they rose, had become one of the fables and sagas of the people, and till a late century, utterly lost to history.

One of the most surprising things to the student, with regard to the settlement made in France by the Norwegian and Danish Vikings, is the little trace left afterwards of their occupation. Though holding an important French province for several centuries, they left behind them no language, no literature, no mythology or architecture. Beyond almost any other people of Europe, the Northmen had a technical and elaborate system of law. Only one or two traces of this appear in French institutions. So completely amalgamated and mingled with the French population had the Vikings become, that within a few centuries, not even their origin was known by their descendants in Normandy. Even the Runes, which follow their course in other countries, are not found here. A few names of places and towns, a few words in the popular language, and occasional features in the peasantry, are the only direct traces which they have left in Normandy. The only substantial popular benefit which history records, as the fruit of the Northman conquest in France, are the vigorous life inspired into a superstitious peasantry, and the establishment of the French fisheries and marine.

In England, on the other hand, with a race more kindred in blood, they seem to have united more naturally—the two races filling out in some degree each other's deficiencies and wants. The Northmen had already gained foothold in many provinces of England, before the invasion of 1066, under William the Conqueror. The English Saxons, even as the other Christian peoples on the Continent, had felt the depressing and unmanning influence of monkish superstitions. They had become a weak, almost effete race. Industrious on the soil, patient with mechanical labor, they had no taste for sea-faring life, or the dangers and toils of warfare. They fell an easy prey to the vigorous, relentless, hardy Northmen. Henceforth England had stamped on her national character the traits of the Norwegian sea-kings; and the American progeny yet bears them even more distinctly. The boundless spirit of individual enterprise—the love of the perils of the sea (which the Saxons never showed)—the recklessness of life—the shrewdness and skill in technical law—the fondness for wassail and wine—the respect for woman, and above all, the tendency to associated self-government.

In Britain, everywhere have the Danish and Norwegian Northmen left enduring traces—in the most familiar words of the language; in the names of towns and villages, of hills, and bays, and rivers; in customs, and games, and popular superstitions; in laws and institutions.*

History, in recording the vices, and cruelty, and lawlessness

* Even the trial by jury may fairly derive itself from the similar institution in Norway.

of the Northmen, will admit that they were a natural product of the time ; and that only such vigorous and unsparing hands could have cut off the superstitions and corrected the unmanly wickedness into which Europe had fallen. They had that which must be the basis of character in Nations, as in individuals—physical, animal vigor. On that, Christianity and civilization have built up what of good is at this day to be seen in England and America.

CHAPTER XI.

BERGEN.

This is a much more picturesque town than is commonly represented, built on different hill-sides of a bay, with many heights and varied surfaces, and broken in upon in part by an island. We found here some very cultivated and interesting people, and enjoyed our short stay. The inns are wretched, beyond description. Everything was in ferment, in view of the visit of three Princes—the Crown Prince, who is making a summer tour in the beautiful scenery of this Province ; Prince Napoleon, who is *en route* for the North Cape, and some Italian Prince. Whatever we wanted to see—Church, Museum, Library, or boarding-house, was being prepared for the prince ! Posts were being painted, walks cleared, streets cleaned in a manner most unusual for this steady and dirty city. Bergen is the great commercial city of Norway.

It is perhaps, also, the most conspicuous town in Norway for its institutions of charity. With a population of 28,000, it appropriates about $30,000 per annum to the poor and sick, besides the means for public institutions. These are, the Old Sailors' Asylum, 100—120 inmates ; the Widows', with

31; the old Wardens,' with 30; the old Citizens', 60; Leprous Hospitals—500–600; Hospital, 120; Insane Asylum, 50.

The mode of disposing of the vagrant and criminal children is similar to that adopted by private organizations in America—the sending them to individual homes in the country, where responsible parties are bound to support and educate them. There seems to be a very regular and exact visiting of the poor by public Inspectors, who are bound to serve without pay, for four years. These report if children do not attend school, or are vagrant, or falling into criminal habits; they also dispense assistance, and give permits for the different Asylums and Institutions.

Of its Institutions of education, beside the *Real* schools, and the Drawing Schools for workmen, there are sixteen People's Schools in Bergen, with 1,700 scholars, supported at an expense of $6,000. The boys are taught in the morning, and the girls in the afternoon. Each school is only held three hours a day. Salary of upper teacher, $200: of under teacher, $100 per annum.

No stranger should leave this city without visiting the old "German Church." The curious gilt carving; the mingling of pictures of Catholic saints and Lutheran divines; the odd representations of Scripture scenes in German costume, make a most droll and quaint picture for the memory. We spent a long time examining its curious details.

LEPROUS HOSPITALS.

July ——.—My friend Dr. ——, took me to-day to various Institutions of Bergen, and among others, to his Leprous

Hospitals. It was a hideous sight—the first I had ever had of that singular disease, except in the cases we had seen occasionally in the streets of Bergen. We passed by each patient, the Doctor sometimes taking the hand, or looking more minutely at him. Some of them showed faces drawn down and distorted, with broad deep marks, as of a burn; others had huge scaly patches crumbling off from their features; others, red rings and white spots around their eyes, and the eye itself, evidently half-bleared; some were lame, some blind; some bore the white scales on the arms and hands and every part of the face; others were bleeding from the red broken seams of the sores. They seemed generally quiet, as if not suffering intensely, but hideous and disgusting beyond description. One breathed more freely again when in the open air.

Dr. —— says, that the difficulty with the peasants is, that they will not confess their disease until it has gone too far for remedy. It frequently follows the law of Syphilis, and passes over one generation, attacking the third. He attributes it mainly to the excessive eating of salt fish, and to the filthiness of the peasantry. There are two Hospitals in the city—one for incurable cases, containing one hundred and thirty patients; the other, a new building, for the usual cases, having three hundred to four hundred patients. So far as I know, it is the only Hospital for leprosy in Europe, except, possibly, one in Italy.

Bergen sustained its character, as one of the wettest places in the world, while I was there. The days were very much like summer days in Liverpool—sun-shine, clouds, showers or fog, continually succeeding each other. The difference of climate between this place and Christiania, is striking, as showing the effect of a seaboard position, compared with a continental. With Bergen, the flow of the Gulf-stream, the warm return trade-winds from the Atlantic, and the peculiar amphitheatre of hills, at once sheltering and condensing the vapors, produce an average temperature of 46°.48 (Fahr.), while at Christiania it is only 41°.5, and a fall of rain and snow of 73 inches, while at Christiania it is 21.2 inches, and at Upsala, in the same latitude, only about 41.5 inches.*

The winters at Christiania have a mean temperature 13° lower* than at Bergen.

This latter is not considered a healthy or agreeable place in Norway.

A stranger is always impressed with the German character of the town, the old Hanseatic ware-houses, the faces of the common people, and the language.

It is the first Norwegian town I have found where German was more spoken than English. Whether it be in the climate, or the dirty habits, or the food—consisting so much of fish and oil—it is certain that nowhere do you see among peasants and poor people, so many distorted sickly faces and diseased bodies. I watched for an hour on a market-day the current of peasants pour in. It was rare to see a tall, strong, well-made man, unflecked with sickness, and without some kind of deformity. This is not

* Forbes.

at all the common observation in Norway. Here Syphilis and Leprosy, the fearful scourges for the two great sins of the Norwegian peasantry—licentiousness and filth—have left indelible scars.

CHAPTER XII.

POSTING TO CHRISTIANIA.

We are again off in our little carrioles which we had left in Trondhjem during our Arctic excursion, and then brought on to Bergen as freight. (Item. The freight for a carriole is the same as for a lady in Norway, *i. e.*, half the full fare. Also, let travellers be warned not to leave their harnesses behind them, from too much confidence in hotel servants, as we did in the Hotel de belle Vue, Trondhjem !) The scenery on the post road beyond Bergen is very much like the scenery in a New England valley—the Housatonic, for instance—dark hill-sides, reaches of streams in the valleys, woods and sudden perspectives up a long opening in the hills.

Houge.—Small station with stone and grass roofs among the bare hills ; peasants making hay on the intervale ; the rows of drying-frames looking like battalions.

No Norwegian summer scene is true without these little frames for drying hay. The object is to dry rapidly, for fear of rain in the changeable summer-climate. They often seemed like little ranks of soldiers.

Garnoes.—Stop for breakfast—nothing but dry oat-cake in the house : we make our own tea : no bed-room or any other accommodation, if one were detained there.

Our carrioles are taken apart and put into a large eight-oared boat, and we are pulled up a beautiful lake.

It is a six hours' pull for four men. The views at the other end are grand; immense hills rising abruptly for thousands of feet. I never was so impressed at once with the poverty and the industry of the Norwegians. In a number of places we saw men, so high above us that they seemed mere specks, making hay on little ledges of the mountains, which could not be thirty feet broad, and rolling the bundles down to boats at the foot, where the only access was by water and where a false step would have cast them down a thousand feet. Others were gathering in the same perilous way the green brush-wood for the cattle. Every place that could be labored, even a small bit of grass by the shore, showed its hay-frames or laborers.

It is a poor, hard country; that is the strong impression left by a Norwegian journey. One does not wonder that the people leave it, and yet it is such soils that grow *men.* It has begotten the Northmen—and all that has sprung from them.

Dale.—We landed here. No house or hut in sight; but a few skillings set one of the men running to the post-station, a mile or two distant. I settled the boat-account exactly according to our book of prices; gave the gratuity: no objections were made, or questions asked. They put the carrioles nicely together, and after a little waiting, we were driving off again. When one reflects how completely he is in the hands of these boatmen and postmen, in such solitary places, he is ready to give full thanks to Norwegian laws and Norwegian honesty, which make mountain-travel so easy.

The drive to *Dalseidet* was grand—right under mighty precipices. We had the fastest little horses, and I, a post-girl to drive, if I wished. They brought us wonderfully quick to another lake, with the most impressive and grand aspects we have yet seen. Here, as usual, most provoking waiting for the people, before the carrioles could be taken apart and put into boats. At length we were started. Every fresh scene now makes us say, "This is the finest yet!" On the Dovre Fjeld, despite the most agreeable novelty, there was a slight, almost unconscious feeling of disappointment. Here there is none. One is overwhelmed—crowded with the scenes of power and beauty. I never felt Swiss scenery so deeply. Yet, in enjoyment of Nature, how much depends on your mood, on your company, on the weather, and the nameless power of shadow and light!

This was an evening never to be forgotten by those who enjoyed it. The magnificent sun-set; the solemn, massive hills overhanging and the fissures in deep shadow; the still waters; the gloom and the glory which lit it up—all are on the memory, but cannot be put on paper. In several places I saw a beautiful phenomenon. The rocks on this lake, or rather fiord, are strangely stratified and contorted—how, I was not near enough to determine. At a distance, the effect is as of the most gigantic strokes on the mountain-side by a great artist, as if, in deep feeling of beauty, he had drawn curved lines of shadow or different lights over the bare rock. It is only when you are near, that you see that this *tone* is given by the material, and not by coloring or shadow. Would that some artist or photographer could preserve these gigantic rock-studies!

Bolstadören.—Beautifully situated at the end of a lake. This is a favorite spot for English sportsmen. The English have fairly occupied Norway for sporting. Almost any stream of any value for salmon-fishing is hired by them. Some have even bought properties, for the sake of the fishing—a profitable thing for the country-people, as, of course, the sportsmen do not want the fish, and bring in besides many gains to the peasants.

We had here a delicious supper of salmon and coffee. However poor a Norwegian inn is, one may nearly always be sure of fish and eggs, and good coffee.

We had again another water-journey in little boats; and, as the wheels would not come off from one of the carrioles, it was put into the stern bodily, with the wheels over the side in the water, which created great amusement among the peasants, and brought after us the shout of *Dampbaad* (Steamboat!)

It was full night when we reached Evanger, but we were determined to post all night, in order to be at our station fixed upon for sleep. We set off under the moon, in most uncertain and romantic light. Between twelve and one, there began to be a glimmer of day; and at two, when, thoroughly tired and sleepy, we reached Vossewangen, it was almost broad day-light. The people were easily roused up, and accommodations found

Sunday.—Fossewangen is in one of the most retired valleys of Norway. It is built on the edge of a little lake, and steeply-sloping hills, covered with green fields, and rich verdure of trees come right down to it on either side. On the west, the lake opens out in a wide reach of sparkling water. The little brown clusters of houses—which make the *gaarde* or farms—are sprinkled over the beautiful hill-sides. There are some thirty or forty houses in the village, clustering about an old whitewashed church with black spire, of an indescribable shape, but evidently intended once to be a cone. There are no fences about the houses, and everything seems open. It is an exquisitely beautiful summer day, and the whole village and church and scene have left on me such an impression of peace and beauty, as scarcely any ever has done. Early in the day, the Bonders of the neighborhood, the famed men of Voss, and their families, began to pour in for the Sunday's service. I watched them from the hill. Little ponies brought some from the hills, even from near where the snow now lies ; others came in small carts, in the independent little sulkies or carrioles, or on foot. Then again, a party in a boat crossed the lake, picturesque in red, and white, and blue colors. The village was soon filled with sturdy-looking men in blue caps, jackets and breeches, and with women in most singular costume. I went early to the church. Before the preaching service, the communion is partaken of, and I found some hundred women and men gathered about the altar. There was on almost every face a very earnest and devout expression ; and though our costume must have been even more singular to them than theirs to us, scarce any woman turned her head as we entered. The clergyman, dressed in black cassock with a stiff white ruff, such as appears in the portrait of Martin Luther, or any priest of his time, with his back to the audience, was repeating or chanting a passage of Scripture. He then turned, and made a short address, which was very intently listened to; and then, as the communicants kneeled at the altar, he placed his hands on their heads and repeated, as he passed from one to another, "Let thy sins be forgiven thee in the name of God the Father, God the Son, and God the Holy Spirit!" This is the Lutheran absolution.

Of all the quaint things about this village, the church is the quaintest. To describe its interior would be impossible —so broken up by odd unaccountable galleries, and columns and recesses. It is one of the first Christian churches, built sometime in the beginning of 1200. The walls are of stone, and the wood-work usually unpainted, with curious imitation of gilding upon it.

The prominent object in entering is an ugly wooden statue of Christ crucified, placed over the entrance to the chancel, with two little wooden boys holding a real hammer and whip, and other instruments in their hands, intended to represent the Jews and their instruments of torture. The flat, unpainted board-ceiling is decorated with most singular cherubic heads; and in one corner is a picture of some Bible-scene, in which Jerusalem bore a strong resemblance to Bergen. The chancel was filled with old rude paintings.

At half-past eleven, the other service began. The crowd of women who had been sitting on the grass outside, began to enter and take their places—the young girls on little raised forms, in the aisles, of the height of a footstool, and the older women in the high-backed wooden seats. Each, as she entered her seat, kneeled to pray, and then shook hands with all near her, even the strangers. It struck me as a beautiful token of their simple faith, and of this, the festiival of their religion—worshp first, and then social feeling.

The body of the church was speedily crowded with gaily-dressed women, and I certainly never saw a prettier and more healthy collection of women's faces. All ruddy, round, with genuine good expressions, and some with the most finely-cut features. What might be called the Norman type was the prominent—slightly aquiline nose, well-cut nostril, clear blue eye and light hair, the forehead generally not high, but well formed. There were some very common faces, but richly sun-browned and healthy. As I stood by one of the curiously twisted columns of a gallery, and looked through the entrance into the space before the altar, it seemed for a moment like some scene on the stage—the clergyman behind, in his long black gown and stiff ruff, and before him, continually passing, without our seeing where they went or whence they came, a succession of the most picturesque figures—first, an old woman, in a white triangular head-tire, reaching a foot each side, with blue dress; then one in black, with red bodice, and white scarf; then a maiden, with her own hair in two plaits, tied around her head, and a red band over, and in velvet and embroidered bodice, with red back; and so on, in the most singular variety.

The galleries were filled with men, and many could find no place. The audience throughout was exceedingly attentive, and solemnly interested; and the whole gave one a most cheering impression of at least the religious feeling of the country.

The exercises began by the clergyman's intoning a passage of Scripture, and uttering a short exhortation, after which he made the sign of the cross over the audience. Then a hymn was given out, the number of which had been already placed in large metallic letters on the walls; the singing was entirely congregational, and of the most *screechy* order, continuing through some thirty verses. After this, the clergyman ascended the pulpit, and uttered a fervent prayer, apparently extempore, which was devoutly listened to; then a collect, the sermon, prayer and singing, and the people dispersed through the village—some to eat their meals on the grass; others to visit their friends, and the most to join little groups, where they were discussing the public events of the time, or arranging bargains for the week.

By a singular chance, there were two other persons from America in our inn—two Norwegians, who had been some fifteen or sixteen years in our Western country, had made their fortunes, and were returned, partly for a visit, and perhaps partly for a speculation—to bring a profitable immigration to their own "claims," or town-lots. They were said to have left the village poor boys, and now they came back as grandees. Through all Sunday, there was a levee of their friends in their room, smoking, drinking coffee, and occasionally taking a bottle of wine. The contrast between the Americanized Norwegians and their countrymen was instructive. These two were complete Westerners of the middle class—"hail-fellow" with every one, sharp, alert, self-asserting, almost nervous in busy activity, with swarthy faces, blue coats and gorgeous velvet waistcoats, and very expensive dress and outfit—using the worst American drawl, and smoking and chewing incessantly. Their friends and companions from whom they came were stately, moderate people, dressed in national jackets and breeches, or coats trailing to the feet, with blonde faces, and long light hair parted in the middle. The women in red bodices, and with brilliant head-tire. They moved, one after another, with slow, dignified pace to the inn, and in the rooms, they seemed like judges or princes, before these restless poppinjays of men. Their faces had an austere impenetrable cast, as they watched the vulgar activity, or listened to the loud stories about the American Eden. There was a wonderful revelation in the contrasts. Only once the national reserve broke down, and their pride in their successful countrymen burst forth—when they heard the Norwegians talking English with us they laughed in exultation, and crowded near. I found my two countrymen very good fellows. They said their journey was costing them frightfully, as every one imagined an American must have his pockets lined with gold, and they objected to no bills. We had often encountered the same impression about ourselves, and had pretty effectually corrected it for future American travellers.

They found Norway horribly dull—every thing so much

behindhand—farming fifty years behind the age. They were home-sick already. Yet this valley, they thought one of the finest districts in the whole country : wheat ripened here very early, just below the snow, and all the other grains : the orchards were good : farms were worth from $2,000 to $5,000 ; but the people were slow. They *would not* attempt any improvements.

Then they could not stand this dress of the women—waists way up under the arm, and short petticoats ! They had been to Church that morning, for the sake of old times, but this absolution by the priest was too much for them ! "It is behind the age, sir !"

I said I liked the services, and the earnest, devout appearance of the people.

"Oh yes : but that humbug of a minister ! He won't come near us, because he thinks we are carrying off his people to America ! Old Norway don't do beside the West, Sir !—Take a cigar ?—We'd show 'em a thing or too if they'd come oute to Wisconsing ! Git back to Elecksion, sir ?"

"Yes. How do you vote ?"

"For FREMONT—to be *sure* sir !"

We afterwards visited the clergyman to whom we had previously sent our letters. He was just hurrying off by post (on Sunday afternoon), for Bergen, so that we did not even see him. The parsonage was a roomy, comfortable house—and we spent an hour with the family.

Norway has had a great reputation for hospitality, but it

deserves it now no more than France or America, or any country with hotels and steamboats. There is too much travel for people to be able to entertain strangers; and they have become so used to them, that a foreigner is of little more interest to a Norwegian, than to a New Yorker or Londoner. Sweden, in my experience, far surpasses Norway in genuine hospitality.

CHAPTER XIII.

EXCURSION TO VÖRING FOSS.

The most famous water-fall in Norway lies in the neighborhood of this village, and we had determined to visit it. We left our nice inn accordingly in our carrioles, at an early hour, encumbering ourselves with no luggage, for Graven. The way was a by-road, yet here, as in the main routes, I was surprised how well the road-building was done. It is a marked instance of the success of individual effort under governmental oversight. Each landholder's property is designated by little stakes, and that portion of the public way he is obliged to keep. We have no roads in America equal to the Norwegian. The farms which we passed on this route were uncommonly good, the best I have yet seen, especially those around the little lake by Graven.

The scenery was interesting ; in some places, really imposing. Among the reminders which we constantly have that we are among our forefathers, was the use on the farms of the long well-pole, with a weight at the end—a quaint contrivance which, though common in New England, has almost gone out of date in Great Britain. The post-boy, too, spoke in Norwegian of "*baiting* (*bede*)" his horses at the inn, and of "*plying* (*plei*)" between certain points —good old English words. At Graven, instead of rowing across the lake, and then taking a horse over the mountain to a station, where were boats, we were persuaded to boat the whole way to Vik. Our carrioles were left in charge of the station-master. We were pulled up the little lake, passing again large farms with people busy on the hay fields. In one spot we noticed a remarkable *bauta*-stone, or solitary burial-stone of the old Northmen. These monuments, passed occasionally in all parts of Norway, give a peculiar association to the lonely lakes and hills. At the end of the lake, our boatman took our wallets and shawls on his shoulder, and led us on for a full mile to a boat-station—Eide—on the Hardanger Fjord. The day was warm and beautiful, and the sight of the neat little inn, with the rich wooded heights and orchards, was most refreshing after our long Northern experience of barren rocks and Arctic vegetation. Our boatman here gave us almost the only instance of an illegal charge (as we discovered afterwards), which we met with in Norway, still it was only a few shillings' difference, and the charge seemed cheap enough.

We took our breakfast, procured two very athletic-looking boatmen, and a good boat; these filled the bottom with branches and piled our cloaks and shawls on, and we were soon having the most delicious gondola-like voyage through grand mountain scenery I ever imagined.

The weather was splendid ; the Fjord sparkled under cheery sun-shine, and the wooded hills were sprinkled with those rich dark shadows which one sees in our American summer-scenery.

Such journeys are the very acme of luxurious pleasant travelling. You have the wildness of savage Nature with something of the conveniences of civilization, and the satisfaction of seeing new and characteristic features of a country, while you are getting an invigorating and healthful exercise. It might seem rather trying for our American women to venture on such a trip as this has thus far been, but it is wonderful how the body recovers tone from this clear mountain air, and continued movement.

The Hardanger is certainly the most beautiful Fjord I have yet seen. The perspectives at some points were exquisite. At one opening, the Folgefond glaciers appeared shining coldly among the green hills. The general character of the scenery is like that on our Maine lakes, only the mountains here are far bolder ; wooded points, leafy islets, narrow openings between green hills, long reaches up sparkling bays with snowy mountains for back-ground, are the features of the pictures.

We reached *Vik* in the afternoon. Here is one of those desperately poor inns, of which all travellers should be forewarned—dirty, with no food, not even milk for coffee, and a pack of the most rowdy and drunken fellows hanging about. It was the first instance I had had of the Norwegian intemperance, of which so much is related.

The landlady and her family were in singular contrast with their surroundings, and seemed very decent, respectable people. Some of her children were in America.

We met here two agreeable German travellers, who were walking, or posting by chance vehicles over the mountains.

The book at the inn was filled with bitter complaints in all European languages, at the fare and lodgings.

This point is one of the favorite resorts of the English yachts, which explore the Norwegian coast. We saw a number of titled names on the post-book.

From this station we *walked* a half-mile to a little mountain-lake, and there took boat for Soebö, the nearest station to the water-fall. It was dusk when we reached the little inn. The people had evidently never had strange travellers, especially ladies there before, and were a good deal confused. There was no sitting-room, but we were lighted to a little separate log-cabin, where was an attic-room, reserved for the furs, linen, etc., of the family. This produced a rather droll consternation with the lady; but as we had made up our minds to "rough it," for the sake of the trip next day, there was no grumbling, except when an unfortunate beam crushed out the only bonnet. They did all they could for us, but the appointments were unique. The man brought up water in a little milk-bowl, and a piece of linen for a towel, while the woman got out her best damask table-cloths for sheets, and the curious colored and worked cloths which one sees in all the cottages, for coverlids. Dried oat-cake and milk were set out for supper. They told us that generally the strangers stopped at Vik for the night, and therefore they were not prepared. But we wanted to begin fresh on the next morning for the mountain-climb, and had thus done in one day what the guide-books give at least two days for. As a last attention, the peasant brought us a whisky-bottle, and a little lump of rock-candy, locking the door of the house as he went out.

Next morning, coffee and flat-bread (dry rye-cakes), and goat's-cheese were brought us, but no milk or cream, as the cows were all away on the saetter.

A nice little Norwegian pony had been already engaged for my wife, and myself being on foot, with a guide, we started. The pony's equipment was original—a saddle-cloth surmounted by a side-frame of wood, and a wooden stirrup for both feet. The morning was very fresh and beautiful; and our path for a long distance wound in an easy way along a dashing torrent, crossing it, at length, on a dangerous-looking bridge. After this point, the road was by no means so easy, frequently creeping just on the edge of a fearful chasm, or clambering over smooth, steep rocks, where a stumble of the little animal would have had disagreeable consequences. Here the guide led, and the pony never failed. At length the path crossed a little mountain-farm, and passed over a well-constructed bridge, recently refitted for the visit of the crown-prince, who had just been here.

The hills rose abruptly to a great height on every side of us, and the only escape seemed the chasm through which the torrent broke. We were at a loss to see how the Great Fall was to be reached. Suddenly the path turned, and we saw that it wound by zig-zags directly up the steep hill in front.

The girths were tightened, the guide took the bridle, and we set ourselves to the steepest climb I ever saw a horse make. It was slow, hard work ; and when at length, on a sudden bend, the girth broke and the lady disappeared down the slope, we concluded it was time to try the feet. Luckily, a little grass plat among the rocks saved her any bad consequences, and the pony proved perfectly immovable. The guide too, for our comfort, pointed us out a rock, which he called the " leg-breaking rock," where an unfortunate traveller had fallen from his horse and broken both his legs. At length, after a long pull, we reached the summit—2,500 *feet in height*—giving us a grand view down the great chasm, as it now appeared. The path now led along a plateau of wet, springy ground, for a mile or more, until we began to see a little cloud of ascending spray, which showed the neighborhood of the cataract. After passing a little beyond it, we stopped at a solitary cottage, with out-houses and cattle—generally white cows—around it—the *sæter-cabin* or cottage for the mountain pasture. Taking a few moments' rest and a taste of the delicious milk, we started for the waterfall. We were almost upon it before seeing anything of it, except the hurrying torrent above, though the distant roar was long audible. The guide brought us suddenly to a projecting point : we lay down and looked below into the tremendous chasm. The water comes silent, swift, with hardly a foam, to the ledge, and then makes its quick leap of 850 feet into the abyss below—but though a stream of fifty feet in breadth when it starts, it seems never to reach the bottom ; first it is foam, then spray, then beautiful descending wreaths of silvery mist, whose intertwining and changing shapes, quick appearing and vanishing in a thousand fantastic figures, one can watch by the hour, and fancy all manner of witching Norse *Nöke*, and water-sprites. The grandeur is more given by the great depth and the worn walls of mighty rock below than by the Fall itself. Yet even the depth you do not appreciate till you throw a stone into the chasm, and count by your watch its time of descent. The guide was in great terror of our falling in, but at length we got rid of him, and placed ourselves in good positions to silently enjoy awhile. The impression—as at Niagara—is first of fear—but soon becomes one more of absorption in the beauty of the scene. One of the most wonderful features in it were the colorings of the rock-walls—caused by the very quality of the stone—varying from the most delicate peach to the darkest brown. As I lay on a little ledge of rock, a ray of the morning sun found entrance into the cavity, lighting up beautifully the dark, seething caldron below, and throwing an exquisite little rainbow over the angry boiling of waters. The effect was wonderful. One can understand, in such places, the Norsk superstitions of the Nöke—the water-sprites, who fascinate and tempt in the beholder. The continuous rush of the waters, the roar below, the dancing, fantastic mist-wreaths put you into a dream, so that you can hardly force yourself to rise. You get a sense of the continuousness of Nature, and you understand that strange influence which so many idolatries have recognized, of absorption in the great displays of natural power, as if one would gladly be swallowed up in and become part of such grandeur and loveliness.

With the Vöring Foss, the effect is very much improved

by seeing the fall from above. A few persons have been at its base ; there the scene must be one of the grandest in the world. Its height is variously reckoned from eight hundred and fifty to one thousand feet.

At the cottage, we found a book with the names of visitors. I had thought that our party would have the first ladies' names—but I found that an English nobleman's family, ladies and all, had made the climb during this season.

No American's name was in the book. After some refreshment, which we had brought with us, we started for the descent under a hot summer's sun, and blessed our prudence in having made the ascent at so early an hour. The little station was reached, and finally Vik ; a dinner of salmon was ready for us, and at five o'clock we were off again for a twenty miles' row in the night with the same vigorous boatmen who had brought us. The wind was high and against us, so that it was two o'clock in the morning before we reached the neat little station at Eide.

The next morning we continued the return-journey, but from ordering horses at too late an hour at Graven, we were compelled to wait two hours, and did not reach Vossewangen till three o'clock of the third day of our excursion. In general, the trip would take four or five days from this village.

The Falls are considered a great curiosity by travellers, and therefore I have described our route somewhat minutely ; still it is doubtful whether, with all the time and labor required, the excursion will repay most parties. The rows on the Lakes and Fjords were the best part of it. For the most impressive scenery, I do not believe the traveller in Norway need leave much the beaten path. The best scenes in Nature are always those which you do not expect, and which come on you incidentally, while you are doing something else than hunt for them.

CHAPTER XIV.

TOWARDS GUDVANGEN AND THE FILE FIELD.

We wished to reach Gudvangen that night, if possible, and we posted on at the fastest speed we could command. The little ponies trotted like racers ; the country was a succession of green, peaceful landscapes, with pretty lakes and rolling hills while a soft evening sunlight filled the valleys. As a sensation, I have had few pleasures like these from our Norwegian drives. As we had not ordered horses, we were everywhere delayed at the stations, though paying the most liberal drink-moneys. One enjoyment in waiting was picking the delicious wild strawberries. The people seemed greatly interested in us, as Americans, and asked every sort of questions. There has been a large emigration from all these valleys to our West.

At first in our journeys, we were much interested by the fact, that all our postmen and the small farmers whom we met, were "going to America next Spring," but we at length discovered, that "going to America" in Norway, was like "going to be good," or any other good resolution in other countries—always belonging to the next year.

It was nine o'clock before we reached the last station, Stalheim, about seven miles from our stopping-place. We waited till half-past ten for the horses, walking on a little way and letting the post-boys overtake us. It was twilight still, and the view before us was one of the most extraordinary I ever beheld. We were on a mountain-plateau, in a desolate, barren country; a little distance beyond the road seemed to plunge down a precipice. There was nothing visible but a dark, yawning chasm, of unknown depth; no gradual descent, or any objects at the bottom were visible. The shades of night added to the fearfulness of the view.

Our carrioles overtook us, and we trotted briskly towards the brink. There we could look down into a deep, black mountain-valley, and distinguished faintly a few objects far below at the bottom. The road which was to take us down could be plainly seen even in the darkness, in white zigzags of the sharpest angles, so steep that we seemed right over the lowest turn, as it led off into the valley. The scene was frightful—and I felt, at the time, the grandest we had yet seen; still, with all that, and though I drove myself, almost hanging over the horse's neck, with this awful chasm below, where a mis-step would have plunged me down thousands of feet,—I could not keep awake! It was most pitiable. I seemed to myself like an unfortunate gentleman under a sleepy sermon. I struggled, cried to to the horse, looked behind, pictured the danger, impressed myself with the grandeur, but it was all useless—my head fell forward, and I was waked from a dream at every new angle.

Luckily the sure Norwegian horse saved me any bad effects. The road in the valley below lay through a pass of perpendicular cliffs, nearly six thousand feet high. We reached Gudvangen about midnight—found almost every room occupied with travellers, but at length secured a dirty sitting-room and doubtful little bed-room.

The next morning a hard rain was pouring, still we both concluded it was better to take it in the boat, than in these miserable quarters; so we had our carrioles and baggage put aboard a large eight-oared boat, and set off, on a branch of the Sogne Fiord, for Leirdals-ören, a distance of thirty-one miles. There were only four oarsmen, and we prepared ourselves for a long day.

Our equipment was thoroughly tested on this day's journey. We sat for eleven mortal hours under almost incessant rain, and did not get wet or suffer any inconvenience from the dampness. My wife's *aquascutum*, and my india-rubber *poncha*, with coats and umbrellas, fully protected us. But to say that the sight, at length, of a large modern hotel, in Leirdals-ören, with comfortable beds and a good warm supper, was refreshing, is, as the reporters say, "a feeble expression."

This Fiord which we have just passed in such a wretched manner, has many interesting relations connected with it. On one part, the scene of Frithiof's Saga is laid—a tale so beautifully rendered by Tegner. The upper portions contain some of the most inaccessible valleys of Norway. It is related of one village on it, that the people are so shut in by continuous winter, that the dead are preserved *frozen* till spring, and are then taken to the distant church for burial!

From Leirdals-ören the road continually ascends towards another of the great plateaux of Norway—the Fille Field. Along the stream which flows through the valley, we saw numerous salmon-fishers. Some were English gentlemen, with their guides. The most interesting object on the route, was one of the ancient Norwegian churches at Borgund. A similar one near Leirdals-ören, was bought by the King of Prussia, and carried to Silesia, for a curiosity.

This church at Borgund is one of the few surviving buildings in Norway, and indeed in Europe, of an original architecture—the architecture in wood by the early Northmen. It bears marks of Byzantine influence, as do some of the oldest cottages in the country—an influence caught from the early expeditions of the Vikings to Constantinople, but it is still a style affected by Northern climate and by the material used. It is almost impossible to describe, and I must trust mainly to the accompanying sketch, to give an impression of it. The first sensation, on coming in view of it, in the solitary mountain-valley, is as if suddenly seeing a huge, mailed animal, with many necks and heads, resting on the earth—of something fantastic and living. You cannot in the least understand its structure or shape as a church; on approaching, you discover that it is primarily a little building of Norwegian pine, with cloisters or galleries built out on it in double rows, the first making part of the interior, and the second being really open galleries or arcades in

THE CHURCH AT BORGUND.

Byzantine style. The whole is covered with small pointed shingles, fitting closely, and smeared with pitch, giving an appearance of scales, or of a coat of mail. The spire has an Oriental aspect, and the gables and summits are surmounted by all sorts of quaint, tasteless heads and angular ornaments—these last probably being the first fruits of the Renaissance transplanted here. The doorway has some curious carving in wood of the ancient mythological subjects—the Midgaard serpent, perhaps, swallowing the works of man before the final destruction.

The nave is only thirty-nine feet long and the circular apse fifteen by fifty-four. I mounted a ladder into its singular little galleries, and saw, over the organ, a full-sized stuffed figure of a reindeer.

The church was built probably within a hundred years after the introduction of Christianity, in the eleventh century. It owes its remarkable preservation to the dry cold climate, and to the preserving effects of the pitch on the well-seasoned wood.

In driving over the highest part of the plateau at night, we passed a solitary saetter-cottage. I stopped, waded through the mud, and rapped at the door. There were two pretty young girls in it, without light except from the fire. They said they spent three months there, making butter and cheese, and scarce ever saw a human being. In the autumn, they drove the cows down the mountain again. They had eighty cows in this pasture, beside goats and horses. Despite the lonely life, they looked very merry and blooming—

"Wer'n't they afraid?" "Oh no: there were no bears there except in winter."

Our post-boy says, that these mountain-pastures are excellent, and that if they did not use them in this way, they should not be able to get the hay down.

We stopped at a very good station, in a lonely place, 3,170 feet above the sea—Nystuen—with only the poorest vegetation surrounding it, and high poles, like telegraph-poles, on all the roads, to mark the path in the deep snow. The triangular wooden snow-plow, seen at every little distance, on the side of the road, shows the wintry situation.

A PARSONAGE.

I had a card of introduction to Pastor S——, at X——, but from my experience thus far of Norwegian pastors was doubtful whether to stop, even to make inquiries. I concluded at length, however to do so, for a few moments. A stout, hearty gentleman, with a pipe, came to the door. He glanced over the card—"Velkommen! welcome!" he said, with a most cordial shake. A lady of sweet countenance was introduced as his wife, and they went out to take my wife from her vehicle and bring her to the house. They almost insisted we should spend some days with them, but we alleged our haste, and said we would merely pass an afternoon, and a pleasant afternoon it was. We chatted with the pastor, enjoyed a social family dinner, and walked over the grounds of the parsonage.

I was asking of the number of people in the parish. "It is

about 2,900," the pastor said, "and we have five churches. Ach! Herr B.," he continued, in German, "this is easy work to what I have had in my life. Once I used to have to journey five miles (thirty-five English miles,) on every holy Sabbath-day—two (fourteen English) on the water, and two over mountains, where snow was two or three feet deep, and then I would find three hundred poor people waiting to receive the sacraments. Here it is pleasant, if our parish were only out of debt."

I told him of our interest in the old Church at Borgund. "Ach yes!—and to think," he said, "that we should have lost that other beautiful one. You know that Frederick William bought it for fifty-five species (dollars). I fear this will go too some day, we are so poor!"

His schools seemed flourishing. There was one established school, and four circulating schools, passing from house to house, with three hundred children in all attending them.

His salary was $500, with the parsonage—(a very neat building of two stories.) I asked of the *morale* of the parish. He said there used to be from fifty to one hundred illegitimate children every year, but now, since he had come, there were not more than five or six.

He showed me his stables; the cattle were at the *saetter's*. He had twenty-five cows, and seven or eight horses.

"Do you see that stone, Herr B., under the stalls? That is a *bauta steen*, with runes. I will read them." He translated a burial inscription, as usual, of little importance. I asked whether many old Norse relics were found still. He said that the most had been gathered and sent to the museums, but still, occasionally they were discovered, and the peasants had much reverence for them.

"Do you find, Herr Pastor, many superstitions among the peasants?"

"Not as many as formerly," he replied, "but still a few now and then. You see that mountain over the valley there—with snow some way towards the foot. There is a cavern in it, from which sometimes the air escapes with a loud noise. The peasants still believe that it is the demons, or mountain-spirits bursting out!

"I knew a cross in a certain burying-ground once, where the peasants used to go to be healed from rheumatism, and certain other disorders. It was a great trouble to break up the superstition."

We had then a very interesting conversation together, about the Norwegian superstitions. That multitude of little sprites, fairies, elves, red-capped dwarfs, giants, Nisser, Thusser, and Vaetter, who haunted their forefathers, still pursue, for good or evil, the Norwegian peasants. They are supposed usually to be the fallen angels, who had not sinned so deeply as to deserve Hell, but who were scattered over the earth in the mountains and waters.

One very common belief is in the *Huldra*. She looks like a beautiful woman, but has, concealed, a cow's udder and tail. Sometimes when she appears among the dancers at a peasant's wedding, this tail betrays her, and if it be noticed, she is terribly offended. She is pictured as a sad being, though wonderfully lovely, and her song has a melancholy tone when heard among the hills. This belief is very ancient, and has a deep moral meaning. The inseparable union of the animal nature with the higher, being viewed as the fitting punishment for sin.

THE WILD RIDERS.

One of the most fearful phantoms to the peasant, is the *Aasgaardsreia*—" the Wild Hunt." These are the spirits of drunkards, and ale-house fighters and perjurers, who have not been condemned to hell. They are compelled to ride over the world till doomsday. They are mounted on coal-black steeds, with eyes of fire, and governed with red hot iron bridles and bits ; and their clanking and rush as they sweep over mountain and lake are heard for miles.

They ride most at Christmas time, and especially love the place of drunken fightings and carousals, or where murder is breeding. Where they drop a saddle on the roof, there will be death. Whoever meets them, should throw himself flat on his face, till the clanking, cursing crew have passed.

This is probably one of the oldest beliefs in Norway—dating before Christianity.

One hears frequently in Norway of the " Gertrud's Bird." The story as the peasants believe it, is thus told by Thorpe

GERTRUD'S BIRD.

" In Norway, the red-crested, black woodpecker is known under the name of Gertrud's Bird. Its origin is as follows: "When our Lord, accompanied by St. Peter, was wandering on earth, they came to a woman who was occupied in baking; her name was Gertrud, and on her head she wore a red hood. Weary and hungry from their long journeying, our Lord begged for a cake. She took a little dough and set it on to bake, and it grew so large that it filled the whole pan. Thinking it too much for alms, she took a smaller quantity of dough, and again began to bake, but this cake also swelled up to the same size as the first; she then took still less dough, and when the cake had become as large as the preceding ones, Gertrud said: 'You must go without alms, for all my bakings are too large for you!' Then was our Lord wroth, and said: 'Because thou gavest me nothing, thou shalt for punishment become a little bird, shalt seek thy dry food between the wood and the bark, and drink only when it rains.' Hardly were these words spoken when the woman was transformed to the Gertrud bird, and flew away through the kitchen chimney; and at this day she is seen with a red hood and black body, because she was blackened by the soot of the chimney. She constantly pecks the bark of trees for sustenance, and whistles against rain; for she always thirsts and hopes to drink."

Throughout my journey, I have been surprised at the extent of these superstitions among the peasantry. If a child is sick, two eggs must be deposited in an ant-hill; if an older person, the witch-doctors will advise the peasant to seek for the fat of a white worm, found at the meeting of two cross-roads.

Decoctions are still made with magical formulæ in the lonely cabins. For rheumatism, I heard in one place of binding the limbs with nine withes of the branches of certain trees. When the cattle are diseased, a snake will be buried near the threshold. One gentleman told me that he saw a soldier shoot with a silver bullet over a paralytic woman to cure her. Steel is a great remedy, and a constant amulet against the evil spirits—a key put in the cradle will keep off the black dwarfs from the infant.

The workman will frequently, while at his labor, hear the derisive laugh of the little elves behind, and sometimes he is called up in the night to find a whole stable disturbed by the invisible intruders. The peasant is so far influenced by modern habits of thought, that he is ashamed to confess these superstitions, except to those whom he knows well, but if he is watched, he will be seen frequently to raise his hat or bow his head, where these spirits and elves are supposed most often to be present.

After a long agreeable talk at the pastor's, we rode away, very much pleased with the conversation, and the simple, hearty people.

Our ride was at first through very grand and impressive scenery; in some places, the road winding just on the edge of frightful precipices, so that our postman insisted on our walking. As we drew on into the valley of the Little Mjösen Lake, it became a most sweet, pastoral country, with rich farms, orchards, luxuriant grain-fields and gently rounded hills. There had been a rain, and everything was fresh and sparkling under the sun of a spring-like afternoon. It was a delicious drive. We noticed that every farm-house had its own little grist-mill, turned by a running stream. The number of streams and water-falls is one characteristic of this country. I do not believe I spent two nights in Norway (out of the cities), where I was not lulled to sleep by the murmur of water-falls.

We stopped for a day in this valley at an excellent inn. Our two large rooms looked out over a wide reach of vale and wood, far away to snowy mountains. The landlady was very neat in her housekeeping and obliging, and we had acquaintances in the neighborhood, so that the rest and intercourse were very pleasant. One gentleman, to whom we had letters, was a wealthy pastor, living in a large handsome house of two stories. His family seemed educated and refined persons—not peculiarly different from people of this class in every country. The father, I think, besides being a clergyman, is also a member of Parliament.

CHAPTER XV.

A COUNTRY PASTOR.

Among the others in this neighborhood to whom I had letters, was a clergyman, living at a little distance off the main routes. I started to visit him. The road to his house lay right over the mountain on one side of the valley of the *Little Mjösen.* It was a tremendously steep ascent, sometimes a grass-track through stones and rocks, and finally descending into a beautiful retired valley on the other side. Nothing but a sure-footed Norwegian horse, with a carriole, is fitted for the road. The little animal walked rapidly up, and then plunged down the mountain, without a check or hold from the driver—never making a false step or a stumble—doing the six miles, up mountain and down, within the hour. The parsonage was a neat, cream-colored, wood house, long, with French casements and of two stories, looking like the houses in a small German or French town.

As is usual, there was no village, but little groups of brown log-houses (*gaarde* or farms), were scattered about on the hill-sides. A pleasant green bank, with roses, was in front of the house, and the foreground was made by a quiet lake, which stretched away as far as the eye could reach among the mountains. A most sweet, peaceful scene.

I was shown into a moderately large room, without carpets, but with pretty furniture, mostly of birch-wood, and the unfailing ornament of Norwegian houses of all classes—flowers. There were also some good paintings and sketches of Norwegian scenery on the walls.

The pastor was not at home, but the lady soon came in—speaking German or French as I preferred, and a little English. She said they had a very quiet life there—seldom seeing an educated person, and they welcomed a stranger gladly. I was equally glad to meet intelligent people, who understood the country—so we were soon in conversation.

I asked about her husband's duties. She said they were lighter than is usual ; the parish was small, only having 2,000 souls, with three churches. He preached in one every Sunday, once a day, going some three or four miles ; he sometimes wrote his sermons, but often spoke merely from an abstract.

Did he also have charge of the schools ? I asked. "Yes," she answered ; "he catechises all the children, and at the end of a term examines them in their other lessons. There are five 'circulating schools' and one established school in the parish. Mr. Z. has always taken a great interest in educational matters, and he is trying now to do away with the 'circulating schools'—those you know which go from house to house—and have them all 'established.' He is obliged beside to make a return of the attendance, and the character of the scholars."

I said that the country clergymen in Norway seemed the general fathers and directors of the peasants.

Yes, she said, it was so. They came to Mr. Z. for all possible aid and advice—and as the only magistrate or lawyer was fourteen miles off, he had often to settle their legal squabbles. Besides, the government made him take the census of the parish—and he must return the number of cows, the produce, the population, and all that. Still, she said, the labor was not burdensome, if one could only see more of the moral fruits sometimes.

I inquired as to the general morality of the *bonders* of the province. She thought that there had been a great improvement. Intoxication was certainly very much diminished. When they first came to the parish, seven years ago, every bonder brought his brandy-bottle and knife with him to the church, and perhaps to the communion altar; then, after service, they would take their meals on the grass by the church, drink, quarrel, and sometimes have very disagreeable scenes. Mr. Z. had finally put a stop to that, and government had made it so difficult to get brandy, that, altogether, there was a great progress. In respect to licentiousness, though there was much improvement, there were still considerable numbers of illegitimate children every year in the parish. Marriages were scarcely ever known to be broken. She could only think of one, even disagreement, for many years, between married couples—but this evil prevailed everywhere in Norway. She thought the great cause was an old custom, which is still followed throughout the country—of lovers being allowed to visit the servant maids or peasant girls Saturday night.

It is a strange thing to an American car—but everywhere in Norway this crime is attributed to this old custom, which began innocently, and is still, in some districts, innocently observed, but which is now mostly clear licentiousness. The estimate of those who have investigated, is, that *every tenth* child in Norway is illegitimate.*

In this lady's judgment—and she had a clear, sharp sense—a great deal of the religion of the farmers and peasants was merely *religiosity*—a strong feeling of reverence, and a susceptibility to ceremonials. It seemed to her that their consciences had something of the toughness and hardness of their bodies. They were able to endure anything physically, and sufferings or trials or thoughts of death, did not affect them as they do others. They came in crowds to church and communion, but she could not say that religion, in her observation, had a strong hold over their practical life—still there were exceptions, very beautiful ones, and the evil might be no greater there than it is everywhere.

We spoke next of some of the Lutheran doctrines, and I asked for the passage in the Lutheran service, where the clergyman says, "*I forgive you your sins,* in the name of the Father, the Son, and Holy Ghost." After some little search, the church-book was found in which the service was contained (a book used only by the clergymen), and the context was even stronger than I suspected. It read "by authority of God and my office"—and as Christ has given us full power to remit sins, etc., "*I forgive,*" etc.

She admitted it was hard to defend, and said that many objections were now raised against it, and that Pastor Lom-

* See Appendix.

mers had taken the position that there could be no Absolution without full Confession.

While we were talking, the pastor came in—a thoughtful, earnest-looking man. His views of the low state of morality and religion among the farmers were stronger even than his wife's. They were still suffering, he said, from the long period under the Danish rule, when everything had been put under the will of absolute power. "There was one king, sir, who considered himself to own all our churches, and who *sold* a large number to obtain money! The farmers have never recovered from the evil effects of that time."

He agreed to my explanation that the Reformation had not taken so deep a hold of the Norwegian and Swedish peoples as of other nations; and had been more forced by the rulers on the people for pecuniary objects. "The worst is," said he, "the State-Church! We can do nothing—we are fettered."

His wife suggested that the government was very liberal. "Yes," he said, "but in a Lutheran direction. The moment we leave that, we are exposed to censure. There is no genuine liberty in our arrangements. I believe in liberty as the best atmosphere for a church. Here, now, in our parish, the people have not the least share in calling the pastor, or in managing the church. I have studied your American system—especially among the Independents—and I much prefer it."

Like most thoughtful persons, he is expecting, before a long time, a disturbance in the church of Norway. "Ideas," he says, "work slowly among his countrymen, but with great power."

He informs me that Pastor Lommers has entirely seceded from the State-Church, but that the government has acted with very good sense, and offers to pay him a pension, so that there may be no disturbance. So far as I can understand, the position of Lommers is rather technical than founded on any deep principle. He objects to Absolution, for instance, not because no man has the right to forgive sin, but from some quibble that forgiveness cannot be declared without statement of the particular guilt.

The *Hougianer*, a kind of Methodist sect, still exist, though Houge, their founder, died in 1824. Pastor Z. says that their views do not materially differ from those we meet with at the North—being founded especially on a belief in the inner inspiration of each man, and in the doctrine of regeneration alone by grace.

"We have not yet had the dissent, Herr B.," said the Pastor, "which has shown itself in other lands, but it must come."

"We have spoken hardly of our people," said the lady, "but you must remember these are the Valders-people—the *Jews* of Norway! Have you not experienced how very avaricious they are in their charges?"

I replied that I had not: on the contrary, I had found them very honest, and I related an instance which had just occurred in our inn. My wife had left a valuable ring in her valise, and in drying this in the kitchen, it had rolled out, and was found by a servant, and returned, as a matter of course.

"Good! that is not common," she said; "the fact is, the

mode in which they were converted to Christianity seems to have affected them always. You have surely read it in Snorro Sturleson's Sagas?"*

* We subjoin the account in Laing's translation: "The King proceeded to Valders, where the people were still heathen. He hastened up to the lake in Valders, came unexpectedly on the Bonders, seized their vessels, and went on board of them with all his men. He sent out message-tokens, and appointed a Thing so near the lake, that he could use the vessels if he found he required them. The Bonders resorted to the Thing in a great and well-armed host; and when he commanded them to accept Christianity, the Bonders shouted against him; told him to be silent, and made a great uproar and clashing of weapons. But when the king saw that they would not listen to what he would teach them, and also, that they had too great a force to contend with, he turned his discourse, and asked if there were people at the Thing who had disputes with each other, that they wished him to settle. It was soon found by the conversation of the Bonders that they had many quarrels among themselves, although they had all joined in speaking against Christianity. When the Bonders began to set forth their own cases, each endeavored to get some upon his side to support him; and this lasted the whole day long until evening, when the Thing was concluded. When the Bonders had heard that the king had travelled to Valders, and was come into their neighborhood, they had sent out message-tokens summoning the free and the unfree to meet in arms, and with this force they advanced against the king, so that the neighborhood all around was left without people. When the Thing was concluded the Bonders still remained assembled; and when the king observed this he went on board his ships, rowed in the night right across the water, landed in the country there, and began to plunder and burn. The day after the king's men rowed from one point of land to another, and over all the king ordered the habitations to be set on fire.

A very social meal was now enjoyed, well-served, and after coffee, the lady played and sang for us some national music on the piano. This music is not, in my judgment, equal to the Scotch or Hungarian national music, but it contains some very pleasing airs, both lively and plaintive—some named from, and perhaps springing from the popular superstitions, and others associated with the peculiar peasant life.

After this pleasant amusement, the pastor produced some cigars, and we went out for a walk. Beside other places, he took me to a Bonder's farm, near by. I found here the usual division of houses for each separate department—one for a carpenter's shop, one for a grist-mill, store-house, machine-house, smithery, etc., etc.—every trade being carried on upon the farm. They were building one new house, and on inquiring, I learned that it was for the father. He was about, as is customary, to give up the farm to his son, and

"Now when the Bonders, who were assembled, saw what the king was doing, namely, plundering and burning, and saw the smoke and flame of their houses, they dispersed, and each hastened to his own home to see if he could find those he had left. As soon as there came a dispersion among the crowd, the one slipped away from the other, until the whole multitude was dissolved. Then the king rowed across the lake again, burning also on that side of the country. Now came the Bonders to him begging for mercy, and offering to submit to him. He gave every man who came to him peace if he desired it, and restored to him his goods; and nobody refused to adopt Christianity. The king then had the people christened, and took hostages from the Bonders. He ordered Churches to be built and consecrated, and placed teachers in them."

be supported henceforth by him, though still himself in full strength. I talked with the old man about his farm. He said they would be very glad of some of the new American machines : he had heard of the horse-rake. The reaper would not do well here, owing to their hilly and stony ground. He had one machine, which he had invented himself for sifting, which he showed me. They had the usual thresh-machine, turned by cattle or horses.

He said that they had sent twenty-five men from his *gaard* alone, to America, who were doing well.

"Would you go ?" said my friend.

"Not to be king," said he, "if they had one."

We went into his house, a log-cabin of two stories. It was kept with perfect neatness. There were no carpets, but bare boards throughout, yet it had some articles of furniture quite rich and handsome. The sprinkling of the juniper-twigs on the floor instead of sand, struck me at once. It is an old Norse custom, appearing in the earliest sagas. The peasant woman showed us the bed-rooms, and her own bridal gifts of dresses, with much pride. In one room was a complete fit-out for a soldier. This gaard is obliged to send at least one soldier to the National forces. The gun, I observed, was a species of Minié-rifle, loading at the breech.

The manner of the peasant through our visit was extremely dignified and self-possessed. The only contrast to American habits was in his bearing towards the clergyman, and the clergyman's to him, indicating a much greater difference or separation of classes, than we know in similar circumstances. I inquired about wages. They are much higher than they were formerly ; at present 16 cents a day usually, except in harvesting, when they might be 63 cents. A servant maid had $16 a year, double the wages of a few years ago.

CHAPTER XVI.

RETURN JOURNEY TO CHRISTIANIA.

The scenery through our whole route, till we approached the Mjösen Lake again, was very interesting; in some places bold and mountainous, but generally more peaceful and luxuriant than we had previously seen.

In the village of M——, we stopped to visit the *Sorenskriver*, or Justice of the Peace. A family of intelligent ladies were in the house, who made us welcome, and though we had only an hour or two to spend, it was a very agreeable visit. Delicious mountain strawberries, with the national dish of solidified sour-cream were brought in, and afterwards excellent coffee. The ladies plucked some beautiful flowers for my wife. They had a tutor in the house, and all spoke English or German.

In the course of the conversation, I asked the Judge about the effect on the peasants of this system of posting—whether it did not tend to make them idle, and to injure their regular business?

He said it did not: that it was certainly hard now and then, to take a peasant's horses just in the midst of harvesting, but the wages paid were so high, that generally they liked the duty, and made money by it.

We spoke of this class of *Fante* or gipsies. "An abominable set," said he, "we can't get rid of them. We are losing all sorts of good capable Bonders, who are emigrating to your country; but these never go! We shut them up, and it does no good!"

I asked about his duties and appointment.

He is placed, it appears by government, and cannot be removed, except by impeachment, and is required to have taken a degree in law in the University. He has a court in every parish under his control, and holds a session there at least once in the three months.

His duties seem to correspond to those of a Justice of the Peace with us, except that property is registered in his court, and all cases affecting titles are brought before him. The peculiar Norwegian characteristic of this officer is, that in company with the Sheriff and the Governor (amtmand), he must appoint a standing jury of eight tax-payers, to act with him for the year. He judges alone, in trifling cases, but in all important cases, the Justice and the jury make one body, each person with only one voice, and frequently thus the jurymen outvote the Judge, and decide against him. There is an appeal from his Court to the Provincial Court, and all his decisions are to be revised there, and if on criminal causes, they cannot be executed, till there sanctioned.

There are sixty-four of these courts in Norway. As of all the officials in Norway, my impression of this Justice was most favorable. In some way, the Norwegians have hit much better than either we or the English on the essential requisite of government—putting the right man in the right place.

The fact that the great mass of the people are property-holders, with a permanent interest in the country, and without the great wealth which would lead to indifference of public affairs, is probably the explanation of this intelligent, and practical administration in this country.

COMPROMISE COURTS.

One of the most characteristic institutions of Norway, is the Court of Compromise. It is of Danish origin.

The arbiter or judge, who may be of any profession but the law, is elected in every parish by the resident property-owners, once in three years. In the larger parishes, he is allowed assistants. He serves for a merely nominal salary. Every case whatsoever must be brought before him, but always by the parties personally. No lawyer's aid is allowed. The statement of each of the litigants is entered on the minutes of the Court, and the arbiter decides between them. If they accept his opinion as final, it is brought to the Justice's Court, and, if approved, entered, and becomes a legal decision. If one or the other objects to his arbitration, the party objecting appeals to the Justice Court, but he will be obliged to pay the whole expenses of both litigants, if the proposal of arbitration is found just and reasonable. In this Court, and henceforth in all the courts to which the case may go, the parties can employ counsel, but through them all, the only evidence or statement of facts received are the minutes of the first Compromise Court.

In another point of legal institution, Norway stands almost alone—in the *Responsibility of Judges.* I quote from Christian V.'s code, as given by Laing:

> "Should any judge deliver a wrong decision, and that happen either because he has not rightly instructed himself in the case, or that the case has been wrongly represented to him, or that he has done it from want of judgment, he shall make good to the party whom he has wronged by such decision, his proven loss, expense, and damage sustained; and can it be proved that the judge has been influenced by favor, friendship, or gifts, or if the case be so clear, that it cannot be imputed to want of judgment, or to wrong instruction upon it, then he shall be displaced, and declared incapable of ever sitting as a judge again, and shall forfeit to the injured party what he has suffered, should it be to the extent of fortune, life, or honor."

It is also provided, says Laing, that if a judge die during the course of an appeal from his decision, his heirs are responsible for the damages. The inferior justices, where there are no damages to pay, are fined for wrong decisions; and if these are reversed three times, they are displaced. The law provides, too, against long delay on the part of the judges, before giving their decisions.

There is much difference of opinion on both these peculiarities of Norwegian law—the establishment of the Compromise Courts, and the rendering the Judges responsible. The Norwegian lawyers do not seem to hold them in high estimation, though travellers and foreigners have generally found them worthy of much commendation. To me, they both seem reasonable, calculated to lessen litigation, and further the ends of justice.

R. L——d.—We stopped here at a large parsonage. The yard was filled with children, who were present for instruction, previous to Confirmation. This teaching is not only in religious matters, but in all common-school branches, and must be a very heavy burden to the clergymen. The ladies within were sitting in different parts of the large saloon, sewing and embroidering, and the pastor, with pipe and smoking-cap, had been studying. He informed me that his parish contained 10,000 people, with five churches and two pastors; there were in it 11 circulating schools, and one established school, with 14 teachers in all, and about 1,200 scholars.

With respect to the moral habits of the peasantry, he gives for his parish the usual average of illegitimacy—one in eleven.

S——.—An excellent hotel, with large, neat rooms, and modern conveniences. The charge for service, beds, and breakfasts, was thirty cents for both!

We turned off from the main road, in order to catch the steamboat on the Mjösen Lake at *Hun.* The last station is at *Mustaed,* where I had a letter to the inn-keeper, who is one of the best farmers on the Mjösen. He took us all over his farm. There was nothing in it materially different from what I had already seen, except that everything seemed under very careful management. His stables were on the best modern principles for drainage and light; the granaries were very large and neat; we saw in one part great piles of the *fladbröd*—dried pea-cakes, a foot and a half in diameter—kept for the winter's food. He had the usual clumsy thrashing-machine, but ploughs of modern construction—I think American. Most of the products seemed to be consumed on the farm.

The most interesting thing about this estate is its history. The landlord showed me a new barn, built where, a few years before, was one of the most interesting relics in Norway, visited, he said, by people from every country. This is the story, well authenticated, though I did not get the dates accurately.

Some hundred years ago, a hunter was following his game through the woods near Lake Mjösen. Suddenly, in the midst of a dense thicket, he came upon some walls overgrown with weeds and bushes; surprised at this, he worked his way among them, and, at length, found himself at a moss-covered door of an ancient house. From its firmly supported roof, a young grove had sprung up, with all the flowers and rank weeds of the wilderness. Everything outside was dank and gloomy; the casements had fallen in, and glossy vines had crept out from within. He touched the door, and the worm-eaten wood fell away from the hinges; he entered, awe-struck, the damp lonely rooms, and rats and mice ran over the floors, and night-birds flew out of the windows. The remains of furniture were about, and, as his eyes became accustomed to the gloom, he plainly distinguished, in one corner, on the ruins of a bed, the bare skeleton of a man. Shocked, he left the room and entered another—there again was a skeleton, and another! Some were sitting, others lying on the floor; there was no noise, except the rattling of the rats through the empty rooms. The ghastly company lay scattered about, as if they had been stricken with fearful disease, and had died helpless and deserted. Overcome with the fearful sight, the hunter rushed from the house of death, and stumbled among the ruins of other houses, and fled to the nearest village. He told his terrible tale there, and finally the oldest men remembered that there were traditions that before the devastation of Norway by the "Black Death," there had been a settlement near the lake—though exactly where it was, no one had known. The ruined houses were now investigated, and it was found that this was probably the place. The dead were decently buried, and the hunter took possession of the property, calling the place *Mustaed.* The forest was cleared, new houses were built, and, till within a few years, the old ruined house was still to be seen.

Such stories are not uncommon about different parts of Norway. In Valders, where I lately had so pleasant a visit, I was told of a church still called the "Bear-Church," from the following incident:

A hunter had wounded a bear, and it took refuge in the midst of a dense thicket. The man forced his way in, and discovered the ruins of a church, inside of which he at length shot the bear.

The discovery was made known, and people flocked to see the ruin, and it was at length remembered that there had been a thriving Parish here before the Plague had desolated it. The most intelligent persons in Norway believe that this part of the country was once much more thickly peopled, than it is now ; and that one of the causes of the diminution of the population was this attack of the Plague.*

As we drove away from Mustaed, a man, who looked like a workman, asked me in very good English, if he could ride behind me. On inquiry, I found he was a laboring man who had been in America, and had returned to see his friends for a short time. We drove on together towards the lake, holding a great deal of talk about the comparative condition of a laborer in the two countries.

"I cannot bear it here, sir," said he, "in no way. I had a kind o' expected to have stayed till fall—but it's too lonesome. There isn't nothing going on."

"I suppose you are very well off now in America?" said I.

"Oh yes ; I have one of these farms of mine own in Wisconsin, and I let it out for the summer. When I was here, I used to have a terribly hard time. I tell you, sir, I've worked from 4 o'clock till 8, month in and month out, and only got seven cents a day and found! They say now it's about sixteen cents."

I asked about machines.

"They don't know nothing about machine-work. Look at 'em—there they'd keep six men for a week to mow twelves acres, and I'd just take one of our mowing-machines

* One of these occurred in 1372, A. D.

and dew it all in one day. They never seed a Reaper—nor even a horse-rake, nor any of 'em!"

I asked about food. He replied, that they had pretty good fare in Norway, though not so much meat as in America. At four o'clock, he said, coffee and "flat bread" used to be sent out; then they would rest at seven o'clock and have breakfast, consisting of bread and butter, cheese, smoked salmon, and a glass of whisky. Then they rested again at half past ten, and took a nap till twelve o'clock, when they ate dinner, usually of herrings, potatoes, and barley-soup. They stopped once more at three, and then worked till eight; having four meals in the day, and resting four and a half hours.

His reports of the change in drinking-habits corresponded with all I had heard. They used formerly to have a little still for whisky on every *gaard*—but now the duties were so heavy on distilling, that it was manufactured only in a few places, and was difficult to procure. Among the farmers, he found coffee to be much drank in place of alcoholic liquors.

We had a great deal of this sort of chat, till we reached Hun, with its pretty little inn.

I had made a wrong calculation, and found myself just out of Norwegian money, with nothing but some English pound notes, which could not be exchanged, of course, in such a place.

I told this man my situation, and there was something truly "Western" in the way in which he pulled out a bag of specie-dollars, handing me twenty or thirty—refusing to take any receipt or note, and telling me I could pay it back in Christiania, or New York, as I chose.

The next morning, we were moving in a steamboat slowly down Lake Miösen, and by evening we were in our old rooms in the Hotel du Nord, Christiania, and soon among the cheerful, social people who make that city so pleasant in memory.

Christiania, July ——.—A friend took me to-day to see the hall where the Storthing, or National Assembly is held. It is a simple room, with seats radiating from the desk of the presiding officer, capable of holding one hundred and fifty or two hundred people comfortably.

When we hear of Norway as under a monarchical government, we are liable to form an erroneous idea of her constitution. The truth is, that in all essential repects, she is as thoroughly self-governed as the United States. Her Congress, or National Assembly, is chosen through "electors" by the people—the only restriction being that every voter must be a land-owner, paying taxes, or a citizen of a town, or a possessor of real-estate in such town, to the value of $150. The Assembly has almost sole authority, and over the same class of subjects with our Congress. Even the power of veto, which rests with the king, is null, if a bill passes three successive sessions of this body.

This was illustrated in the passage of the act in 1815, which abolished hereditary nobility in Norway. It passed the house in 1815, and was vetoed by the king ; it passed again in 1818, and was again vetoed ; but in 1821, though the Court used every means of intimidation and corruption, it became a law. By a wise provison, also, no change affecting the constitution proposed in one session can be passed till another, three years later—thus preventing important measures, as is so often the case in our Congress, being passed through before the people have understood them, or before they have elected representatives with reference to them. The Assembly of Norway does not even allow, as does the English Parliament, a member of the Government to propose measures (except by writing), or to vote on any question. It receives the oaths of the king on coming of age, and in case of the royal line becoming extinct, it could, in conjunction with Sweden, elect a new sovereign. It meets by its own right every three years, and does not require the summons from the throne. In its internal structure, it divides itself into two houses ; the whole Assembly choosing one fourth of its members to form the Senate, or *Lagthing*, which has judicial rights like our Senate. The remainder form the House of Representatives, or *Odelsthing*.

Every part of the government administration comes under the control of this body, and its authority in the country is quite as great as that of our Congress. It can impeach and try before its Senate, even the ministers of the crown, and the supreme Judges of the country.

Its number of members can not be over one hundred, representing both towns and country, in definite proportions.

This Constitution, framed by Representatives of the people, in 1814, has been a wonderful blessing to the nation, and with a free able press, has made Norway one of the most free and well-governed countries in the world. The people hold to it against the attacks of the Swedish government, with a peculiar jealousy ; and even dread all improvements proposed, for fear that a change once made, may draw after changes more vital.

THE SCHOOLS OF NORWAY.*

Norway, with respect to education, labors exceedingly under the difficulty of a scattered population.

Out of her 1,400,000 inhabitants, only about 180,000 dwell in towns, the remaining 1,220,000 being sprinkled here and there over an area of 5,750 square miles. As a consequence, stationary village-schools are hardly possible in any great number. The law, from which the present school system of Norway dates its origin, which was passed in 1739, did not require, very wisely, an education in any particular place ; it simply demanded that the parents or guardians should instruct every child, or cause it to be instructed, in the branches usually taught in the district schools—the test of such instruction being the catechetical examinations by the clergyman, and the examination, previous to the con-

* The facts in this article are principally derived from the conversations and reports of one of the great leaders of educational improvement in Norway, Councillor Nisson, of Christiania.

firmation, which last, the American reader must remember, is a necessary condition for all civil rights in Norway and Sweden.

Circulating Schools.—To meet the difficulty of the separation of the population, the law also required Circulating Schools in every parish, as well as stationary. The parish is divided into a certain number of districts, and the teacher travels from one district to another—the children of each forming for the time his school. As an average, the term of each school is only eight weeks during the year. The lessons are given in the farm-houses, in the rooms where the peasants have been sleeping and eating—often uncomfortable and ill-ventilated apartments. The branches required to be taught by law are religion, reading, writing, singing, and arithmetic ; in point of fact they limit themselves to reading and "religion" (*i. e.*, very dry theology), with a little of writing and arithmetic. The teacher's salary is from $12 to $40 for thirty weeks' teaching, with his board. The whole number of these itinerating teachers is about 2,000, and of the schools about 7,000.

Stationary Schools.—These stand somewhat higher than the class of schools first mentioned in the quality of their instruction. The teachers also are better paid, the salary being about $90 per annum, with board and a piece of land for free use. They number about 380, with 24,000 pupils in attendance, and their terms are from 16 to 40 weeks in the year. The whole number of children attending both the circulating and stationary schools is estimated at about 213,000.

Upper District Schools—These are a small class of pay-schools, corresponding somewhat to our High Schools in America. The branches taught are those already mentioned as taught in the other schools, together with history, mensuration, natural history, and a foreign language—generally English.

These schools require a slight payment from the pupils, but are supported by the parishes and by occasional grants from the Storthing or National Assembly.

All the schools established by law are managed by the Town or Parish Council and the clergyman. No tax can be laid for their support except by a grant of the council. The head management in each province is in the hands of the High Sheriff and the Bishop of the diocese, who report again to the "Governmental Department of Church and Education."

The total expenses of all these Schools in the towns and country, together with that of five Normal Schools for teachers, and including the expenses of boarding teachers, are estimated by Councillor Nisson at about $195,000 per annum.

Citizens' School.—These are a higher class of Schools, both public and private, belonging to the towns. The pupils are taught in common branches, in drawing, natural history, and German, French and English. The number of these is more than twenty ; the pupils about 3,000 ; expenses, about $30,000 per annum.

A still higher rank of these schools is called *Real Schools.* These have been established by the Government in eleven towns, and are associated with the "Latin Schools." The latter prepare for the University with a five years' course; the other, after their pupils are fourteen or fifteen years of age, send them out to practical life, or to the technical and military schools.

In the Latin Schools, Greek and Hebrew are taught; in the Real Schools, beside the usual instruction of the best schools, bookkeeping, commercial correspondence, the properties of goods, etc., are sometimes among the branches.

There are also three Latin Schools, not connected with Real Schools, at Christiania, Trondhjem and Bergen, where the usual order is reversed, and Latin is studied before any foreign language. These three schools are supported by their own funds. Number of pupils in the eleven united schools, 700; in the three Latin schools, 300; total, 1,000. Annual expenses of both, $64,000.

No one can be a rector in these schools unless he has passed two public examinations. The conditions for the under teachers are equally strict.

Beside these, there are Charity Schools in many towns for the children of poor laboring people, where the children remain the whole day, while the parents are at work. These are supported by both public and private contributions. Amount expended, about $6,000.

There are four asylums in Norway for the instruction of the deaf and dumb. Another class of schools whose introduction would be highly advantageous to America, are the *Agricultural* and *Drawing Schools* for workingmen and mechanics. There are fourteen Agricultural Schools where young men from eighteen to twenty are taught thoroughly in practical and scientific farming, in the application of manures, the construction of farming machines, the management of dairies, and the like.

Throughout Norway there are eight Drawing Schools. To these of an evening the mechanics and laborers come together and receive instruction in modelling, drawing, mathematics, and natural philosophy. By the law, any person who would be a tinman, gun-maker, copper-worker, turner, brazier, goldsmith, wheelwright, instrument-maker, jeweller, painter, sadler, smith, stone-cutter, chair-maker or clock-maker, must produce a testimonial from the managers of this school. The effect of the instruction is found to be excellent on the taste of this class in their various trades. The Drawing School at Christiania is the most distinguished, and costs nearly $3,000 per annum. The other seven are supported together at about the same rate.

From what has been said of the condition of schools in the Norwegian towns, it is apparent that education is in a favourable state of progress, even compared with America. The working classes have better opportunities than they enjoy here.

Of the country schools one can draw by no means so favorable a conclusion. Schools circulating from cabin to cabin, with teachers receiving $12 per annum as salary, and instructing each circle of scholars only eight weeks in the year, could not be of much value to the mental improvement of the nation.

Still the country people of this kingdom are by no mean

inferior in natural intelligence or in information. The same causes which in that latitude, on a wintry Island, gave birth to a literature whose vigor and originality and high imagination have not been surpassed in the early literature of any modern race, still work upon the descendants of the Northmen.

Now, even as ten centuries ago in Iceland, the people enjoy a kind of democratic kingdom, where one man nominally is chief or king, but where the real power is in the hands of the Bonders or peasant-farmers. They have the free communal life—the right to govern themselves in small matters as well as great. They are continually trained in oratory, the arts of an Assembly and the management of public affairs. This, of all schools, is the best, and can overbalance the advantages from books and teachers.

The climate and the vast solitudes drive men within their own homes during the long winter evenings, and give occasion still, as of old, for a Saga literature—a literature of tales and history, and almost stern poetry, which is transmitted year by year around the roaring fire, from one generation to another. Such people, though not drilled in mathematics and physics, cannot be called ignorant. They have unwritten histories and poems not in books ; and thoughts, nurtured by their grand solitary scenery, which are not given by religious writers, and yet which touch on the greatest mysteries of existence and immortality.

The strong, weather-beaten features of the Norwegian peasant give you no impression of ignorance. The expression is shrewd, reserved, and often sad or solemn—as of men much with great thoughts, which they could not or would not express. The questions you are asked show everywhere quick, active minds.

When, at length, the defective system of "Circulating Schools" is improved, we may believe that Norway, in an intelligent and educated population, will stand equal with any country in the world.

II.

Sweden.

CHAPTER XVII.

GOTTENBURG.

After a most agreeable rest in Christiania of a week, I took the steamer over to Gottenburg, my wife returning to England by the Hull steamer. We had a passage of some twelve hours, and, on arriving at the quay, the luggage was examined as strictly as if it were a strange country—a circumstance which called forth many sarcasms on the Swedish *Union* with Norway.

The hotel at which I was lodged I found intolerable—the *Götha Källare*—dirty, bad-smelling, with no conveniences for eating, or hardly for sleeping. Price, about twenty-five cents a day for a room. I had no cause, however, to complain, for a very agreeable and intelligent gentleman to whom I had letters, took compassion on me, and carried me out of town, to his villa, a little gem of a home, where I have been staying since. In his neighborhood are a variety of very handsome places—houses with large gardens and groves—where people live in considerable style. They are principally the villas of the wealthy merchants, doing business in the city. All speak English, and their manners are exceedingly cordial and agreeable, with a certain sincerity and half-seriousness of tone, which inspire confidence. They seem usually intelligent and even cultured men.

I had the opportunity, on my first Sunday, of hearing Bishop Thomander preach—the leading pulpit-orator of Sweden. The church was crowded to the doors. The order of exercises was the same as I have already described in Norway—the usual Lutheran liturgy and form. The Bishop was attired in a black surplice, with a brilliant embroidered cross on his back. Like most great orators, he was a man of large, heavy *physique*. His manner was very easy and voice rich and powerful, as of a man accustomed to address large audiences. So far as I could see, he read his sermon, with occasional bursts of extemporaneous oratory. From my want of familiarity with the language, and the distance where I stood, I could make out but little of the address. He has the reputation of a man more fervid than profound.

Aug. ——.—I have been visiting with my friend, the various charitable institutions of Gottenburg—among these, the *Willinska* School for the poor. In this institution, carpentry and smithery are learnt by the boys, beside the regular school-lessons—and by the girls, knitting and spinning. Some of the mechanical work was excellently done by the lads. The monitorial system is adopted in the classes, and little semi-circular iron rods are fastened before the walls, around which the class stands, the monitor being within.

Without being able to speak from much examination, the teaching left an impression on my mind of not being of the best quality. Still, the first thing with a class of this kind, is to elevate the morals and affections—not to sharpen the intellect.

The managers had employed the plan so successfully carried out in New-York, of sending the children away, to be placed in reliable and religious families, rather than keep them in an asylum. They had not, however, connected with it the method of constant communication with these children thus sent out, as has been done at home, with such excellent results.

The *Poor-House* seemed a better managed institution than such are usually with us. The buildings were of the best quality, and the arrangements for ventilation and warmth very practical. The principal work was *mangling*, which the inmates do for the public.

The *Chalmerska Skolan* is a higher class of school, being a kind of polytechnique school for laborers and mechanics. Here drawing and modelling are taught, and various natural sciences. There are laboratories, and well-furnished rooms of philosophical instruments, connected with it, together with a reading-room. The whole is free *for working men!* An institution so enlightened, neither New-York nor Boston yet have.

I visited another school, principally for teaching drawing and designing, intended for the same class. The public schools are usually of a high class. There is here, also, a Normal School, for the instruction of teachers.

THE CITY.

GOTTENBURG leaves a pleasant impression on one. There are many handsome, busy streets in it, and the country surrounding is picturesque. The river, the Göta, is thronged on its banks and on the water with trade, and the town has stretched far beyond its old limits.

The story of its foundation is, that the king, Gustavus II. Adolphus (in 1618), on a visit to the neighborhood to determine the situation of the new city, stood on the top of the mountain, Otterhällan, surrounded by his counsellors and generals, when a small bird, chased by an eagle, flew to the feet of the king, and there sought refuge. This seemed to the king a sign from Heaven, and he at once resolved that the new town should be laid out at the foot of the mountain. In the words of a friend, "Future has proved that the king was in the right, and trade has often, in the safe and always open harbor of GÖTHEBORG, found a refuge against its enemies and oppressors."

The first inhabitants were mostly Dutch merchants, called into the country by the king. The city still retains the memory of them, in the appearance of the town—especially in the canal-intersected streets, once shaded by trees.

Gottenburg rose very slowly to its present rank. The first great impulse to its growth was given in the latter part of the last century, by an enormous herring-fishery, which was carried on, on the west coast of Sweden, for about forty years. Great riches were accumulated by it;

but suddenly, in 1812, the fish left the coast from unknown causes, and have never returned.

During the years from 1810 to 1815, the wars of Napoleon and the Continental System brought in a rich harvest to Gottenburg. All the trade of Northern Europe then passed through this city, as it was the only open port, through which the manufactured goods of England could be imported into Russia and North Germany. The harbor could not receive all the ships that entered, the goods were stored in the open street; and wealth increased immensely.

With the fall of Napoleon, the city again retook its former position. The only lasting advantage which remained from these prosperous days, was the handsome style in which the town was rebuilt, and the splendid houses erected by the merchants for their residence. Property fell so much, that many of these buildings could not sell again for half their value.

In 1832, a work was concluded which has steadily raised Gottenburg to its present position—the opening of the Götha Canal, "that splendid and immortal work of a poor Nation," as a Swedish friend calls it. By this canal, through which vessels can pass Sweden from the North Sea to the Baltic without paying the heavy Danish Sound-dues, Gottenburg became the new centre of the imports to Sweden, and at the same time, the great commercial entrepôt for the exports of the rich central provinces of Sweden. The town now commands the largest inland navigation of any town in the country, and it is believed, that when the railway, now being opened between Stockholm and Gottenburg, is finished, the advantages to its trade will be scarcely less than from the canal.

For the last ten years, the business of the city has been continually increasing; and the Swedes claim that next to Marseilles, Dantzic, and Constantinople, Gottenburg has made the greatest progress in that time of any of the trading cities of Europe.

Within the same time, the city has been lighted by gas, the streets paved with cut-stones, sidewalks laid with sandstone, all the quays rebuilt with hewn stones, a large hospital has been erected, and an extensive Work-house for the poor; and last year a plan for a harbor was drawn up and immediately adopted, at the estimated cost of seven hundred and fifty thousand dollars, embracing in its features the furnishing the banks of the river, for nearly two miles, with granite quays

The last three years have been equally fortunate for Gottenburg, with the rest of Sweden. The war of the neighboring powers, the improved agriculture, and the more enlightened commercial policy of Sweden, have all contributed to swell immensely the business of the country. Ten years ago, the export of grain was almost unknown, from Sweden. In 1855, Sweden exported nearly two millions of barrels of grain, amounting in value to more than the whole of the iron exports. Gottenburg and its immediate connections on the western coast, partook in this to the amount of five hundred and sixty-nine thousand two hundred and forty-four barrels; of these, three hundred and eighty-seven thousand, nine hundred and thirty-two barrels were of oats, which went almost all to England—making nearly *one third* of the whole exports of oats into England from all countries for that year. The greatest part of the rye exported goes to Holland.*

The whole impression left on my mind by these facts, and my own observations of Gottenburg, was that it contained a very enlightened and public-spirited population, much superior, as I afterwards discovered, to the mercantile people of any other city of Sweden.

* For these statistics, and much of the information about Gottenburg, I am indebted to a very intelligent gentleman, well known in the mercantile world, Mr. OLOF WYK.

CHAPTER XVIII.

COTTON SPINNERS IN SWEDEN.

The gentleman whom I was visiting, kindly offered me the use of his pleasant travelling carriage, to post out to a very retired and unknown district some fifty miles distant, where we could see something of the *home manufacturing* of Sweden. He said, beside, we should meet a class of people which were quite peculiar to Sweden—the ancient peasantry or Bonders, changing into rich manufacturers. I was, of course, very glad of the opportunity. The kindness and courtesy of the offer corresponded to what met me from the beginning to the end of my journey in Sweden.

We started out on a fresh August morning, over a rocky country, with occasional pine or beech woods, and cleared fields, where oats, or barley, or potatoes were growing, being much such a district as one would pass over in New England—many streams and lakes near the roadside, and woods covering the hills in the distance. Now and then a white church tower, with its black conical top, crowning some summit in the distance. The country seemed poor, and not much populated: sometimes we passed long stretches without seeing a house. As in Norway, there were no villages, but large farms, where a number of people lived together. The houses had not the peculiar Norwegian character of brown, neatly laid logs, but were red or yellow frame-buildings, not different from our American farm-houses. The post-stations seemed the important places on the road, and had evidently the best fields and buildings about them.

Posting in Sweden is not at all so easy a matter as in Norway, unless *Förbud* (orders for horses) are sent on before. The people now have great need for their horses in the farm-work. At the second station we waited two hours, while they sent to the peasant whose turn it was to furnish horses. Probably he was obliged to take them from haying in the middle of the work, to have them beaten and worked for the next course (six miles), as only post-horses are worked. For all this, he gets from the traveller, for both horses, one dollar banco—or forty cents. It is a burdensome and stupid system, which ought long ago to have been changed in a country where horse and man are of any value. Near this station we came on the first evidence of the manufactures we were approaching: a long train of little one-horse carts, each with his bale, or bale and a half of cotton, driving laboriously on to the spinners and factories. This alone would show the difficulty of manufacture in such an out-of-the-way spot. The freight from the sea is several dollars on each bale.

As we had no introductions to any one, and but few knew much of the district, we were obliged to inquire from station to station. They all said the same—that these new cotton lords, though peasants, were very rich and would welcome strangers gladly.

At length we came to one of the best-looking farming establishments on the road, with the side to the highway open. Everything was extremely clean and comfortable in appearance ; no dirt or carts or pigs about the court-yard ; but large barns and stables, as if all was stored and housed properly. The best of the dwelling-houses was shaded with cool, green beeches and lindens. We went at once to the door, and a bluff ruddy man, dressed like a farmer, met us. My friend introduced me as an American, and said that we desired to see something of his manufacturing. He replied very cordially, and invited us in. Sherry and port, with cigars, were brought in at his order, by a maid. He asked some questions about America—then rose, poured out the glasses, and we rose, sipped and bowed to each other. He said that unluckily he himself could only show us his stock, for the work was done by families in the neighborhood and by his factory at some little distance.

I inquired about the mode and amount of his manufacturing.

He said he supplied the spinners in the families with the cotton, and the weavers with the yarn, which they made up for him, getting so much a piece. He also had a share in a cotton-spinning factory. He kept employed about 1,500 spindles in fifteen different counties, and some 1,200 looms in families.

The cotton he imported amounted to nearly 2,000 bales a year; the wages paid out by him were some $3,000 a month.

The weavers (women) could earn about thirty-six cents a day, which was about the same as the wages of a farm laborer.

We went out to look at his stock. The "shop" was one of the dwelling-houses of the square, and here the country people came to purchase of him. The different packages of calicoes were in piles in the bed-rooms of the house—mostly patterns of bright colors for peasants' dresses or 'kerchiefs ; some very neatly colored, and nearly all stamped with the hand. A few he had stamped and colored in a neighboring factory. He always sold, he said, at twelve months' credit. The handkerchiefs were six cents to eight cents an ell (two-thirds of a yard) ; common calicoes, five cents ; cloths, twelve cents. For the weaving of these, he paid two cents an ell.

After spending some time here, we went, at my request, to his farm buildings. The barns have not the Norwegian improvement of an entry on the second story, but are like the old-fashioned barns with us. The stables were very neatly kept. He had eight or ten horses, some of good blood evidently, valued, he said, at from seventy-five dollars to two hundred and fifty dollars. The grain in his granaries was mostly rye and barley. He has a separate brew-house and bake-house. The farm implements were more like our own than I have found in Norwegian husbandry. The only machinery I saw, was a large threshing-machine turned by horses. All that he raises is consumed by his own family.

At about nine, we were called in to supper. At first, we

all eat, standing, *smörbordet* or a little bread and cheese and anchovies—the others taking a small glass of corn-whisky along with this. Then each with folded hands stands a moment for a silent grace, which is closed with a kind of obeisance—and we sit down.

The first course was perch, handed by a neatly dressed maid to each; then pieces of stewed hare, served in the same way; then a very delicious cake, eaten with sauce (*munkar*). No tea was on the table, but beer and port and sherry. The only thing characteristic of our host's position, was his working dress, and the fact that his wife did not come to table. At the close, we rose and shook hands with our host, thanking him for the meal.

At a good hour, we were shown into a handsome bedroom; the maid took our boots and clothes to brush, and we laid ourselves each in little feather-beds, soon to be dreaming of places far away.

August ——. — Coffee was brought to the adjoining room at a comfortably late hour the next morning. This apartment is the *salon*—the ball-room of the house, with some very handsome pieces of furniture, white secretaries, painted and gilded, and a clock about seven feet high, white, with gilded edging. There are some pretty little tables, but no curtains, and the floor is of plain boards. At nine o'clock we met in the room below stairs, for breakfast. This room, again, had some very rich articles of furniture of polished birch and another huge clock; handsome silver plate was on the table. The floor was uncarpeted, with little spittoons here and there filled with pine twigs, for the Scandinavian habit; and in each corner of the room was a plain wooden bench, like those in ale-houses.

Our host is a jovial fellow, and gives us a hearty greeting. We again take of the bread and butter and salt meat, as a prelude, declining the usual glass of port; the same silent grace again, and we fall to work. The *Patron* (as they call him) asks questions of America; says he gets his cotton direct from Mobile and New Orleans, through agents in Gottenburg, but has to pay heavily for freight from the port to this place. He thinks the Americans a most clever people; but he says—the old theme—"How can such a nation as you are endure Slavery? I am sure you will finally abolish it." We ask whether the tendency of Sweden to Free Trade will injure his business. He thinks not; says the English cannot make coarse goods cheaper than the Swedes, and they never will have goods of enough different colors to suit the people here; "they cannot, except by hand-work. In fine muslins," he says, "they are far ahead of us, and will be."

As one of the landed proprietors, or squires of the country, we ask him about the schools. He does not know a great deal about the matter, but thinks the people used to be well enough before the new School Law, and he considers the one "established school" for the parish as not practicable. He prefers instead some "circulating schools," which shall go from house to house. They were taxed very heavily already, he said, and they did not like the burden of the school. I tried to give him an impulse in relating what we were willing to be taxed in America for education; but it made no especial impression on him. He thought the pastor ought to attend to it! It appeared that the pastor was an old man with a good farm, and two or three assistants (Comministrar), and did not trouble himself much about such modern matters.

In giving the sketch of our conversation, it is difficult to convey the tone of indifference and lack of interest this man—one of the great peasant aristocrats—had in the whole subject, and yet he himself was a "self-made" man; by his own cleverness and perseverance he had erected a very considerable manufacturing business and won himself wealth. A vigorous, shrewd man—one of that class who will yet raise Sweden to modern enterprise and activity.

I should not forget our breakfast, which was most hospitably and properly served, with napkins, wines, fish, and various dishes in course; with no tea or coffee. The wife, evidently a peasant, but impressing us as a very dignified and intelligent woman, did not come to table. The *patron* was much like a central New York or Pennsylvania farmer of little school education, and great education in the world. We asked him once about politics. He shrugged his shoulders, and said he had nothing to do with them. One peasant manufacturer in R——, was always sent as member to the Parliament, and no one ever opposed him. The crown and clergy, I understood him, had it all their own way in the representation of the yeomanry. He had the right to vote as a member of this class for *his* House of Parliament. We bid adieu to him finally, truly grateful for his hospitality, and very much interested in our visit.

HAND-WEAVERS.

He directed us to some of his manufacturing hands, who lived at a little distance. The houses were pretty little log-cottages, among flower-beds and potato-patches, each having, perhaps, two rooms. In the first, there was an arched room with several windows—everything clean and whitewashed within, even the fire-place. Four women, with ruddy, cheerful faces, were at work at hand-looms; one was quite young. They were weaving common handkerchiefs and shawls of bright colors. Everything looked comfortable and happy in the place. There were curtains at the windows perfectly white, and flowers. The women all wore silver brooches. They were paid by the master by the piece, earning from twenty cents to twenty-seven cents a day; the youngest, a mere girl, only twelve cents —not poor wages in a country where a carpenter frequently only gets thirty cents a day. One thing characteristic of Swedish peasant life, was the several beds for both sexes in the room—here, as usual, in wooden bunks built into the wall, and in one instance, covered with curtains.

The girls talked to us very pleasantly and modestly. As we went out, we marked the pretty pointed, almost Gothic, doorway, of unpainted wood, built on the house. The impression, as we re-called it, was very agreeable of peasant home manufacturing. We compared their cheerful, healthy faces, with the worn faces of English "factories," and the aspect of a certain position and dignity in them with the usual expression of depressed toil in working women, with much commendation of "home labor."

In the next cottage, they were weaving plain white cotton cloths, all the arrangements being similar, and the girls with the same robust, pleasant looks. One very old man was spinning the yarn on little reels. We talked with them; they expressed no discontent, but seemed very happy in their work. My friend says they can all read and write, as indeed every one must who would be confirmed in the Lutheran church. On the Sundays, he says, you will see them splendidly attired, sometimes with very valuable silver ornaments, handed down from their forefathers.

We rode on for some distance through pretty cross-roads, among hills and woods, to visit the factories beyond. I have been told this is a very populous part of Sweden. If so, we are away from the inhabited districts. We seldom pass a house, and never a village. The farms, too, are poor, and the soil thin. Many streams flow across the road, and like our New England, it is evidently a country best adapted for manufacture—and what capacities the soil had for agriculture have been neglected for this newer labor. The crops are oats, barley, rye, potatoes, and grass. We saw no orchards.

CHAPTER XIX.

SWEDISH HOME-MANUFACTURES.

THE first factory to which we were directed, after visiting the weavers, was built, I think, in 1853. The building is of stone, but the surrounding boarding-houses of wood. The clerk introduced us into his sitting-room, and wine and cigars were of course produced. We begged off, finally, and drank his health in pure water. Fortunately he spoke English, and, I found, had several English foremen and workmen. The factory is for spinning yarn. There are 200 hands employed, and 16,000 spindles. The capital was originally about $150,000 ; some $170,000 has been laid out on it, thus far, with very good return. One of the Englishmen accompanied us over the works. Most of the hands were women, though many children were at the spindles, seemingly working very skillfully—some must have been as young as seven or eight years. Generally, their faces looked pale and not healthy.

The foreman pointed out to us child after child who had been beggars on the highway, and were now industrious workers in the establishment. Each one has to attend school a certain number of hours every day, he said ; and, according to Swedish law, every factory employing children must sustain a school. I asked him about the capacity of the Swedes for machinery. "They have a great capability, sir, for the spindles; they are such a patient set, you know. But the women, sir, there's the rub! They were never accustomed to such close work. Always at 'ome, they've been in the 'abit of talkin' and chattin,' you know, as they work, and I find it very 'ard to keep 'em hattentive and considerate some. And they *are* so tricky. Why, two Swedish women can't possibly meet without a little dance, just together, which won't do you know here, sir. But they'll learn. It's a young nation, sir; very young. Everything is young here—even the craggy rocks; they are all *primary*, you know! It will take time—time, sir, before they do as the English and Americans."

I inquired as to the morality generally of the factory.

"It is good, sir—good! And there's been a great progressive movement in the last two years. Of course, it isn't like England. You know how it is with the women—they don't look hon some things as we do. I believe they really think it a credit to be found in a family-way, nobody knows how. Then they all sleep so, men and women in one room, and they don't seem to think anything of it. They don't care for some things which an English woman never could put hup with. But I believe we don't 'ave more than one or two illegitimates every year—which is very good, you know, here."

"How is it with the drinking?" I inquired.

"It is not so bad now. There's been a great reform in that, too. When I first came here, a gallon of finkel used to be about nine pence, and now it costs three or four shillings. Government has laid such a duty on the stilling of it, and it's so hard to get it. Of course, some days they will 'ave a ' burst,' but it isn't often."

The women, he says, earn by piece-work about $1,50 to $1,75 a week; men, from $1,50 to $3,50 ; and the children from 10 cents to 24 cents a day.

The freight from Gottenburg, or from Warberg, by the peasant's carts, is alone five or six dollars, ($1,35 to $1,62) for every bale. When the railroad to Borăs is done, they will be quite near the great means of communication. The machinery is all Manchester work.

We visited the school. There were fifty-three scholars in it, with a rather stupid-looking old man as teacher. All the children were bawling out their catechism together, evidently with no more idea what the sacred words meant than if they had been Indian incantations. And this is what the Swedes everywhere call " teaching religion."

As we went out, the Englishman said: " You see it haint here just as it is in our countries. They don't know much about all that ; but they have to be confirmed, helse they couldn't be citizens or anything else, and they goes into the sacrament as a sort of business, you know. Perhaps some of 'em really feels it, poor creatures !—but I don't think the most of 'em cares or knows much about it. They leaves it to the parsons."

We again drove on through a rather picturesque country, with no especial cultivation, as yet, and sparsely peopled, to some new factories. The first one at W———, was a great stone building, in the style of our best factories at Lowell or Lawrence. It was not quite finished, though the machinery (all from England) was already there. It was to have six hundred workmen, with about one thousand looms—mostly, I believe, for colored cottons, worked, as are all by water-power. This mill, with those we visited afterwards, are owned by one peasant—SVEN ERICKSON—who has raised himself by his skill to be one of the richest manufacturers. His next mill, a few miles farther on, for weaving and dying cottons, sheeting, wool, cloths, etc., was at Rydboholm. The number of hands employed is 450 ; looms, 282. Produce, annual, $800,000.

This factory had a number of buildings for dyeing, drying, etc., as well as for the homes of the workmen. The office was a *bonâ fide* store for goods, not a dwelling-house. Mr. E.'s house was near by, looking very neat and comfortable. He has built, we understand, a church, and sustains a school for his operatives. The wages of women here are about twenty-four cents a day ; men, $1 00. A number of Englishmen are employed about the works.

As we stood waiting, several carrioles drove up, which were supplied with horses, and then, after the gentlemen had conferred a little with the people within, drove on. These are the buyers, we hear, who are very handsomely entertained and forwarded from one factory to another, free of expense.

After leaving this factory, we entered on a much more

cultivated and rich-looking country—a broad valley, with very nice and roomy farm-houses on the hill-sides, one farm having sometimes six or eight houses, and fields showing a far better culture. The houses were usually of wood, two or three stories, painted some pleasant modest color, with French windows. Many have large stables, and handsome travelling-carriages in the yards. This is the especial district of the rich peasant manufacturers—men as proud and independent as any in the land, but not yet having lost all the peculiarities of their class. They form a kind of turning-point between the ancient and the modern world.

I was interested to see near some of the houses on the edge of the river, bathing-houses, in modern style.

We drove to one of the handsomest houses, entered and said to the gentleman, we would like to look at his goods. Here, again, as in the other houses, they were piled in bed-rooms and sitting-rooms—colored shawls, handkerchiefs, cottons for dresses, etc., etc. The people worked for their master in their own cottages, and brought it to him ; here he sold, also, to the peasants, always at twelve months credit, charging two per cent. a month. The prices were very low.

The manufacturer himself, in this case, was much more peasant-like than any we had seen, having a low, animal face.

From this we drove to the parsonage, a comfortable three-story house on a hill, amid gardens and trees, and introduced ourselves. The parson insisted we should take supper with him, and then was equally urgent for us to spend the night. We resisted long, but the refusal seemed so to injure his hospitable feelings, that at length we gave way, and carriage, servant and all, spent the night there.

THE PARSONAGE AND SQUIRE.

Our host was not the chief clergyman, but a vicar or assistant (*comminister*). His house looked very neat and comfortable, with marks of sufficient means about it. He himself impressed one as a mild, amiable gentleman. I told him soon that one of my especial objects was to investigate the schools of Sweden, and inquired about those in his parish. I had touched evidently on a sore topic. He uttered sadly his grievances. Since the new regulation of the ministry, establishing a school in every parish, the former circulating schools had been given up, and now the peasants live so far from this school—some four or five miles—that the children did not attend regularly. Besides, breaking up the old system separated the children from the parents very much. Before, the teacher of the circulating school would be aided often by the parents, and they felt a personal responsibility in the improvement of the children. Now, it is all in the hands of the teacher, and he is not fully competent. He has been a year at the Normal School at Gottenburg, but that was not enough to improve him; and in matters of religion, especially, he could not teach the children properly.

I suggested whether it would not be a better arrangement

to take the whole matter of religion out of the hands of the teacher, and leave it in his (the pastor's) hands. "Yes," he answered, "it would be ; but if they can have a foundation laid of the knowledge of the first principles, it would assist me very much in afterward instructing them for the confirmation." My friend suggested that two schools, one circulating and one established, might meet the difficulty regarding the distance, etc. Mr. L. admitted that they would, but doubted if the people would be willing to pay the tax. There was much opposition already to paying so heavily for schools.

We mentioned then Count Rudensköld's plan—which has already been tried—of having little *infant schools* taught in the houses by some old woman or intelligent girl at a small price, and making these the preparation for the "established school," so that the parents might have some share in the education, and the difficulties of expense and distance be avoided. He thought such a plan might succeed. We asked whether this teaching of Religion, as a school study, did not make children think it was merely a lesson and not a matter of life. He allowed it often did ; but still they ought to know the facts, he said, and they require it for Confirmation.

Of the morality of the people—the factory workmen, and the weavers—he gave very nearly such an account as we had heard before, along the journey—that the people, though needing much improvement, were better than the mass of the same classes elsewhere in Sweden.

Certainly, statistics begin to show that not manufacture

but agriculture draws after it the lowest state of morals; that is, where manufacture really is a means of living, and not a means of crushing the poor and weak.

The Temperance Societies, he thought, had mostly failed. The people only signed to break, but the consumption of brandy had immensely diminished, especially owing to the restrictions placed upon it by government. His parish, he informed us, numbered between four and five thousand, and had four clergymen and five schools.

We sat down, at 9 o'clock, to a very simple, good supper, with milk instead of the almost universal accompaniment, wine; and after the silent grace at the close, and shaking hands, we were showed to comfortable beds in an upper room.

From this point our ride was through a much better country, with well-kept fields of wheat and rye and oats. The farm-houses were of two or three stories, well painted, and with nice windows, and had all spacious guest-houses, and bakeries, and stables. Here dwell the rich, aristocratic peasant manufacturers of Sweden—a class not yet raised out of its ancient position, but, with wealth and enterprise, certain soon to be thoroughly modernized. The clergyman accompanied us to one of the oldest of these manufacturers and squires, now retired from active business. His parents, we understood, had been so opposed in the beginning to the manufacturing in Sweden, that they had made it a boast never "to have worn in their lives a *thread of cotton!*"

The farm was the usual square of houses, painted red,

and we entered the principal dwelling from the court-yard within. The peasant-proprietor met us at the doorway. He is a tall, dignified man, with small finely-cut features, hair parted in the middle, and an expression of much intelligence and character on his face. His coat was of the national costume, black, reaching to the ankles; he wore breeches, a close-buttoning black waistcoat and black neckerchief without collar. His wife, a very hearty, lively woman, had the usual colored bodice. We were shown into a large saloon, unoccupied, with plain benches in the corner, and the usual large white gilt clock; from this into another smaller room, not differing from any modern parlor, with handsome sofa, centre-table, and French lamps.

The talk at first was on the weather and persons of the neighborhood. The only thing characteristic was a remark of the wife that "Fru X. had gone to Dr. D.'s for her bilious attack, to try the *Gymnastik.*" I asked what the cure was. She explained that it was the taking small doses, instead of large ones. My friend said, "Oh! you mean Homœopathy." "Yes," she answered, "I knew it was one of those new cures; I have been recommended the *Gymnastik.*" It appears, this practice of medical gymnastics is as regular and profitable a one in Sweden as Homœopathy is with us. It consists of a scientifically arranged series of muscular movements and exercises, which is said to be of immense benefit to women, especially in nervous disorders.

Of course, wine was ordered to welcome us, but we declined, and some fruit and milk were brought out to an arbor in the garden. There the peasant read to us a petition that he and others were preparing to lay before the king on the subject of schools. As the pastor had told us, the present arrangement did not answer well. These rich peasants wanted several circulating schools to be started in the parish, and supported from public tax.

The clergyman, as I understood it, was somewhat against this, still he did not wish to displease his wealthy parishioners, considering the plan too expensive. On a recent meeting of the Common Council (*socken stämma*) of the village, it happened that those in favor of the additional schools were not present; and though it had been previously voted that there should be more schools at the public cost, the present meeting re-considered the question and carried the other motion, and sent the resolution to the government. This petition was to state the facts, and request an interference of the Ministry in favor of the more liberal measure. My friend said it was a very well-written document.

After much conversation the peasant took us to see his stock of goods. They were in one of the houses of the square, and stored in very handsome rooms—in quality mostly like those we had before seen. He had not a very large stock, as he was nearly out of the business, and occupied himself with his farm. The peasants who made them, brought them to him, and he bought on twelve months' credit—making a discount of fifteen or twenty per cent. if he paid cash.

Before we took leave, he insisted on a drinking of healths, and the servant brought in hock, claret, and champagne.

Through the whole, there was a singular mingling of the modern customs of the rich, and the old habits of the peasant.

He impressed me, in the whole visit, as a wise, dignified man, who was a gentleman by nature in whatever peasant's clothes. Such men will eventually raise their class—wealth and wealthy habits will bring with them the intelligent wants of riches. Their children must have education. (The son of the house, in this instance, was at the Gottenburg Commercial Institute.) They will be superior—at least in culture—to their fathers; and in a generation or two, will make a class not essentially different from our New-England countrymen—the Yankees of Sweden.

This county (Elfsborg), with a population of 246,000, *sold* the following home-made stuffs in the following years:

		In 1846.	In 1849.
Cotton Stuffs	Eng. yds.,	4,458,300	5,828,259
Linen	"	317,800	299,990
Woollen	"	392,080	419,998
Shawls and Blankets	Pieces,	1,502,956	1,393,212

In Gefleborg, amount *sold* in 1849	1,458,666	Yards.
Westernorrland	200,600	"
Halland	257,650	"

CHAPTER XX.

THE GÖTHA CANAL AND STOCKHOLM.

This grand work of mechanical science and business-enterprise is well known through innumerable descriptions. Making use of the natural communications of lakes and rivers, and cutting through the solid rock in its way, it has thrown open a great inland route of navigation, through the richest parts of Sweden.

The beauty of scenery in its course, it seems to me, has been much exaggerated. It is a pleasant pastoral landscape usually, and at Trollhättan, truly picturesque ; but to one coming from Norway, nothing more. As a voyage of pleasure, it is detestable. I have, in earlier travels, been thoroughly inured to rough conveyances, and all sorts of fare; but I never experienced anything so thoroughly disagreeable as the accommodations of Götha canal-boats. I had applied a week beforehand for a state-room, but was told they had all been engaged for months, and so was obliged to take a place in the general cabin. We were packed there as they might have been in the Black Hole ; on tables, under tables, on chairs, on seats, in hammocks, on shelves—in every assignable square inch of space that the little room could furnish—one *woman* waiting on the whole company, and managing to steer around among the sleepers.

I saw an English nobleman packed on a settee, and his servant sleeping by his side. In this imprisonment we spent three days and two nights ; here we ate our meals, and shivered away the days, when the cold storm blew over the deck. Of course, feeble old gentlemen were determined that the windows should not be opened, and the state of air in our cell may be feebly imagined.

What a relief it was, when a bright Sunday morning we got our first glimpse of the beautiful "Venice of the North" (as the guide-books call it), STOCKHOLM, scattered about on its islands, with picturesque church-towers and massive buildings, and innumerable boats plying to and fro, to supply its pleasures and wants.

I had been warned of the hotels in Stockholm, and I went at once to a handsome lodging-house in Drottning's gatan well-recommended. I obtained two nice rooms for about two dollars and fifty cents a week ; and in half an hour felt myself comfortably settled.

* * * * *

Stockholm is a delightful city. The variety of aspect, the gay water, and the busy cheerful streets ; the bridges, and gardens and quays, the monuments and grand buildings make a wonderfully pleasant impression.

You move about much in boats, and, if on the outskirts, amid most picturesque bits of scenery. The finest Park—in advantages of Nature—of all Europe is here. A great reach of woods, and hills, and rocks, with almost natural rambling paths, the sea skirting both sides—old, moss-grown, still, and secluded ; such a place for pleasant strolling walks as is not, except in our own forests.

Then on another side of the city are beautiful groves and rambles, towards the ancient Church of Solna.

OF THE ORIGINALE AND SITUATION OF THIS KINGLY CITY.

(*From Olaus Magnus.*)

"This chief city of the Swedes and kingly place, Stockholm, was built from the foundation by a most illustrious and famous man, who was the king's tutor, whose name was Birger Jarl, and he fortified it with walls and other buildings in so fit, necessary, and invincible a place, that it is supposed that he could never have done anything more commodiously; for it is a place that is on all sides fortified with Torrents (and was formerly only for fishermen's use), and is so placed, between fresh and salt water, that it may be called the port of all Sweden. For formerly the Estones, Muscovites, Russians, Tavesthi, did constantly pass through the mouth thereof, and plundered the Swedes privately, who suspected no hostility, and destroying great multitudes of men, they freely and unpunished, loaded with great booties, returned to their own countries. In which incursion they slew John, the second Archbishop of Upsal in his own mansion-house, Alme-Steck, and some other noblemen. But when this Stockholm was built, all and every man enjoyed a long peace, and the enemies were in continual fear, who finding such a strong garrison raised for the time to come against all enemies, forbore to plunder Sweden any farther. If any man shall presume to beleaguer this Stockholm, and think to take it, he can never win it; though he should continue resolute in the siege thereof every way. For it is situate in the most deep waters and most swift rivers, having only two gates on the south and north parts, with long bridges between them, which gates and bridges cost the king of Denmark more money in a siege that came to nothing, than ten of the greatest cities of his kingdom. Nor can it be besieged but by three most potent armies, divided into islands that are parted by firm land and water, yet those armies can never be secure from bowmen that will put them into fear. Let him try that will, and he shall find it worse."

Though the hotels are so poor, the *restaurantes* of Stockholm are agreeable. One celebrated establishment of this kind, is in the Great Park or Deer Garden, Djvrgärden. The manners of people, in families and in shops, strike one as very polite and agreeable. The city is not at all in its season—the most of the people of rank, as well as the Court, being in the country. They can hardly flee the city for its heat, as these August days have the sharpness of our November, and one needs constantly an overcoat.

I spent most of my time while here in seeing sights, with which one is always bored and which one dare never omit. I made—what was much more to be valued—the acquaintance of some agreeable and intellectual men, not to be forgotten. Among them Mr. SILJESTRÖM, of whom I shall speak again ; Professor RETZIUS, the distinguished Professor of Anatomy—a man whom our Western orators would certainly call "a perfect steam-engine"—such vivacity and fire he has ; and Rector SVEDBOM, Editor of the *Aftenbladet*, the principal Stockholm paper, a liberal daily.

It will certainly not be out of place to express here my obligations to our Minister Resident at the Swedish Court, Hon. FRANCIS SCHRŒDER—a gentleman who has made our country respected through Sweden, and who has used the facilities which his diplomatic character gave him, to furnish our own country with a vast quantity of useful scientific information relative to Sweden. The truth is, our *diplomates* at every Court, ought to have it understood, that one of the principal objects of their foreign residence, is to transmit to the Department useful matters of information with reference to other countries. Thus, and thus only, would diplomacy be an endurable evil.

Stockholm is a very gay place in the winter, but it does not seem especially expensive for housekeepers. Two or three hundred dollars would be a high rent, as almost every one lives in the flats of large houses. A good income for a lawyer or physician would be $1,500 or $2,000. Teachers and Professors seldom get over $1,000.

THE MUSEUMS.

The most interesting museums to me were the Kraniological collection of Professor Retzius, and the "Collection of Antiquities." This last is vastly inferior to that at Copenhagen—still very interesting. The best divisions of these remains are the Danish—the separating them according to their periods—thus making four ages: (1) the Age of Bone, (2) of Stone, (3) of Bronze, (4) of Iron. In the first, the weapons and implements being the rudest possible, of the bones of animals ; in the second a little higher, though probably used by the same people, of flint-stones, or stones sharpened by rubbing. The arrow and spear-heads in this Age, are almost precisely the same with the flint arrowheads used by the North American Indians. In the third of Bronze, gold appears also in beautiful workmanship, and in connection also with the Age of Iron—sometimes in great abundance. It is remarkable, that the bronze swords—probably belonging to the Keltic race—and those of iron, the weapons of the Teuton, all have smaller handles and are of lighter weight than similar weapons now. These and other indications have led antiquaries to believe that some of the former races inhabiting Sweden were of inferior physical power to the present. Of the ethnological conclusions to be derived from these remains, I shall have occasion to speak hereafter.

August ——.—I met to-day a young gentleman from Finland. He had come over to make enquiries of Mr. Siljeström, in regard to the improvements he had brought back from America in the School-system.

He said, that the young Russian Emperor was beginning to be in favor of Popular Schools ; and some of those interested were trying now to find what had been done elsewhere. At present, they have nothing in Finland of value in Institutions of popular education. A progress, however, was beginning. It is well known, though this gentleman did not state it, that it is the policy of the Russian Government now to encourage the Finnish national spirit, in order to counterbalance any attachment towards their old masters or countrymen, the Swedes. For this object, the revival of the old Finnish literature, of such poems as the Kalewala and the Kantelitar, has met with great favor from the Russian authority. The great Finnish University, as is well known, has been removed from Àbo to Helsingfors, where it can be more directly under Russian influence, and at present no Swedish is allowed in the language of instruction. This process of *Russianizing* goes very skillfully on, year by year. The nobles are enticed by honors to Russia ; the offices in Finland are filled by Russians, and the peasants made to forget as much as possible their old connection with Sweden. From all accounts, these efforts are succeeding. The peasantry is becoming attached to the government. Russia has never kept, of course, her promises in regard to States Assemblies with local powers in Finland ; but she is now forced by the spirit of the age, to do something for popular education.

This gentleman, like all the Finlanders I have met, was very guarded ; yet you could not help remarking a certain depressed or sad expression, both in his appearance and in the few words he said of political matters.

My friends say this depressed feeling is generally true of the Finlanders. You instinctively know it is the shadow of despotism.

I asked this gentleman about the feelings of the people during the late war. He states that the cruelties and barbarities of the English upon the poor fishermen and lumbermen on the coast, quite changed the first favorable disposition towards the allies, and very much exasperated the peasantry.

He had known the lieutenant who was engaged in the barbarous affair at Hango. He was young, he says, and was supposed to have acted thus, because he was confused and not really knowing what he was about. Though the

Government did not punish him, he lost caste every where, and was disgraced.

I found he had the usual impression, derived from the tone of a few of our papers, that we sympathized in America with the Russians. I was glad to correct and explain it.

Many of the Swedes think the king made a great mistake, in not at once throwing the fortunes of the country, into the late war, with the Allies. They believe Finland, in the beginning might have been easily re-won, the old disgrace of Sweaborg wiped out, and a flank-march directed on St. Petersburg, which would have effectually weakened and humbled Russia for years to come.

At first, the peasantry were entirely favorable ; the Russian force in the country was a mere trifle (much less than was known by the allies), and with the assistance of the fleets, and an allied reinforcement, they might have carried everything before them, and removed the great thorn in their side—the Russian Finland. Others, on the contrary, and I think more wisely, believe such an attack would have involved Sweden in a long war, which she could not afford ; that even if she had re-conquered Finland, it would always, henceforth, have been a bone of contention between the two powers, and that the great hope for Sweden is in the development of her industrial and agricultural powers, and not in conquest. Generally in Sweden, there is a great contempt for Russia. A common phrase one hears, is that "one Swede is equal to three Russians at any time ;" and except for the great commercial profits of peace, nothing would have been so popular as a decided part taken in the late war, by the government.

All feel that the great danger eventually to the country, will be from the over-grasping power of the Northern Empire.

CHAPTER XXI.

A SUNDAY IN STOCKHOLM.

THE Sunday seems more quietly spent than in Germany. The churches are well attended. I have been to-day to the Lutheran "High Mass." The forms are somewhat complicated. The officiating clergyman first, with his face to the people, repeats the "Holy! Holy! art Thou," etc.—then kneels and utters a prayer. The congregation do not kneel nor respond. He then rises, singing the "God have mercy upon us!" and the congregation respond. The Prayer book, or "Hand book," requires responses when prayers are sung, but not when read. After this, he turns to the altar and sings the "*Gloria in excelsis!*" this is followed by a long hymn* from the worshippers, from ten to twenty verses. The clergyman then turns to the congregation and says the "Lord be with you!" they responding; next, facing the altar, he reads the extract for the day (he sings it on feast-days.) Here he makes another prayer, which is succeeded by the reading of the Epistle, and the reading or singing of the

* The composers of these hymns, so much beloved in Sweden, are Spegel, Swedberg, and Arrhenius, of more ancient times; and Wallin, Franzén, Geyer, Hedborn and others of modern.

Creed. During the first part he faces the audience, during the latter, the altar. At the name of Jesus, all bow the head. Another hymn is sung, and the sermon follows, which was short. After this, prayer again, and, on feast-days, they tell me, the Litany ; and then the royal proclamations, notices of marriage and of death, and the like. The last exercise is a prayer by the second clergyman at the altar, and then, after a few words, the beautiful blessing of Moses. The principal priest is dressed in a white "mass-shirt," trimmed with lace, over which is a rich red velvet Cope, with a gold cross embroidered on it.

The communion service is characteristic. At the altar, the following prayer is made :—"Lord Jesus Christ, who in thy holy communion dost give us bread and wine, thy dear body and blood, grant unto those who intend to have part in it, thy holy Spirit, that they may worthily receive it, to strengthen their assurance of forgiveness of sins.

"Grant grace, that they, with right-minded hearts may be reminded of thy bitter suffering and death, that they renew the promise which they have made in baptism, and with faithful determination to hereafter live, with thy help, in true faith, godliness, love, firm hope and Christian patience, and thus not to violate the vows made before thy holy face *at the shrift*, (*skrift*) that they with all the believers may be partakers of the great supper in Heaven. Amen."

The priest puts the bread or wafer into the mouth of each communicant kneeling at the altar, saying to each, "Jesus Christ, whose body thou receivest, preserve thee unto everlasting life! Amen."

The last prayer is, "We thank thee, Father Almighty, who through thy Son, Jesus Christ, hast instituted this holy Supper for our peace and salvation, and we pray Thee grant us grace so to celebrate the remembrance of Jesus on earth, that we also may have share in the great Supper in Heaven. Amen."

A custom still prevails in the Swedish Church, of restoring a criminal, or backslider, after public penance. The subject, usually some man or woman from the prison, with worn, depressed expression, stands on a bench near the door, a guard by his side, and before the great congregation is addressed by a stout comfortable-looking man in full canonicals, who has had from his cradle, perhaps, the whole current of life on his side and so has never openly sinned, on the enormity of his guilt, and after a brief confession to his fellow-mortal, receives his blessing and is restored; or, if he refuses to confess, he is sent back to a more severe punishment.

The Commandments have what we are wont to consider a Romanistic arrangement. The First is, "Thou shalt have no other gods before me," with no allusion to the graven images. The Second is on Profanity. The Third, simply, "Remember to keep the rest-day holy!" with no reasons, except those given in the Catechism :—"We should fear and love God, so that we do not despise preaching and God's Word, but consider it holy, hear it gladly, and learn." Which certainly, if the Festival of the Resurrection be borne in mind, seems a much more *Christian* basis for the observance of the day. The Fourth is on the "Love of Parents." The Tenth is divided into two, the Ninth and Tenth, as if distinguishing the two kinds of coveting.

There still survive on the Swedish Church Book, the rules for Secret Confession to the Pastor. It is still resorted to for the worst class of sins; and the clergyman is forbidden under the strongest penalties to disclose what is confessed. Only in cases of treason, or where assassination or murder is threatened, can the clergyman warn the objects, yet still without disclosing the names of the guilty parties. In former times, the pastor has been known to forbid the Sacrament after such confessions.

RELIGIOUS SOCIETIES.

The Tract and Bible Society of Sweden appear both to be active. In 1852, the Foreign and the Native Bible Societies report as already distributed by them, more than a million copies of the Old and New Testaments.

The Tract Society (founded in 1809), have scattered in thirty years nearly three millions of tracts. The "Swedish Mission Society" was establish in 1835, especially for Christianizing the Lapps, among whom they have opened schools and churches. Their annual income is about thirty-seven thousand dollars. Many other societies have also been formed in the last few years—for Orphan Asylums, for

Sunday Schools, Charity Schools, and the like. There is one Association of Deaconesses at Stockholm.

The "Inner Mission," which has done so much in Germany, has met with no success here. Among the religious papers, are the "Mission Journal of Lund," with six thousand subscribers; the "Bible Friend" (Bibelvännen), with nine thousand; and the "People's School" (Folk-skolan), with two thousand.

STATISTICAL FACTS OF STOCKHOLM.

BIRTHS AND DEATHS.

In 1849,	births to population, as	....	1 to 29
"	deaths, " "	....	1 to 25
Sweden "	births, " "	....	1 to 30
" "	deaths, " "	....	1 to 50

DEATHS EXCEEDING BIRTHS IN STOCKHOLM.

Year 1849	by 377
" 1839	" 738
" 1829	" 1941
" 1819	" 1146

SUICIDES.

In 1847	227
' 1848	244
" 1849	225

ILLEGITIMATE BIRTHS.

	1848.	1849.
Stockholm,	1 to 2.20	1 to 2.27
Other towns,	1 to 5.07	1 to 4.95
Provinces,	1 to 15.31	1 to 13.08
Kingdom,	1 to 11.74	1 to 10.96

ILLEGITIMATE BIRTHS.—*Continued.*

In Sweden, from 1780–85.	1800–05.	1820–25.	1840–48.
1 to 29.5	1 to 17.1	1 to 14.3	1 to 11.9

In France, 1820.	1840.	In Denmark, 1811–15.	1835–39.
1 to 14	1 to 13.3	1 to 93	1 to 87

Prisoners in Stockholm in 1850,	3,394	or 1 to 28
" Sweden, "		1 to 261

In New York State,	1 to 1608
" Massachusetts,	1 to 2232
" New Hampshire	1 to 4376

POPULATION OF STOCKHOLM—(RUDBECK'S *Svea Rike.*)

Year 1760,	69,108
" 1780,	75,107
" 1790,	68,986
" 1800,	75,517
" 1810,	65,474
" 1815,	72,652
" 1823,	73,210
" 1845,	88,242
" 1850,	91,544
" 1855,	95,950

From these statistics,* some interesting conclusions may be drawn. In the capital, it appears, that various causes consume life faster than it is produced, so that if left without immigration from the country, Stockholm, before many years, would be depopulated. The ratio of suicides is immense; in 1849, one out of every four hundred persons, or probably one out of every two hundred adult men and women.

* Mostly collected by Hon. Mr. Schrœder.

Out of every hundred children born into the world in the city, nearly *fifty* are illegitimate. In the whole kingdom, one out of nearly eleven. The consumption of human life in the Swedish capital, and the prevalence of vice, are facts not to be dissociated. The whole kingdom appears to have been steadily retrograding since 1780, in this regard ; in 1840 there being fifty per cent. more illegitimate births to legitimate than in the above year, and a worse ratio than in France. However, there are extenuating circumstances in regard to Stockholm, which do not appear in figures, and it is very possible that Stockholm is not materially worse than New York, or Paris.

There are scarcely any houses of ill-fame, it should be remembered, in the city. There is not such a desperate, abandoned, God-forsaken class of women as in our large cities. The *grisettes* of Stockholm preserve some decency and have a chance at least of a better life. They are occupied as seamstresses, or servants, or shop-women, and frequently after many years of unlawful companionship, are married. The cause of these numerous *liaisons* is probably here as with us, the difficulty of woman's earning an honorable support. The laws, too, of former times, which forbade the clergy from investigating the illegitimate births, must have furnished an additional safeguard to the guilty parties. It should be borne in mind also, that the parents of an illegitimate child in Sweden, are frequently married, subsequently to the entry of the name on the Church books, so that an exact judgment of the present state of morals of the people cannot be formed from these certainly rather alarming statistics.

It is significant, in this connection, that the Swedish Prayer-book, alone, perhaps, of all the Church-books of the world, has a prayer for "Mothers, who have been deceived by promise of marriage;" * and the Swedish law recognizes that the promise, if it can be proved by reliable witnesses, secures, even before the marriage, to the children the right of legitimate children, and to the woman all the rights of a wife.

* Prof. A. C. Knös—Swedische Kirchen Verfassung, p. 145.

CHAPTER XXII.

DALECARLIA—UPSALA.

Ever since reading, as a boy, of the faithful peasants of Dalecarlia, who sheltered and fought for the brave Gustavus Vasa, I have had an interest in the people. I fancied beside, in Stockholm, that the Dalecarlian boat-women, with their honest nut-brown faces and stalwart arms, were the best specimens of peasantry I had seen, and I resolved to visit their Province—the kernel of Sweden. But it is a difficult matter to travel comfortably here. At length, after some trouble, having provided myself with a travelling companion and a carriage in Stockholm, I started by steamer for Upsala.

The views on the trip are not interesting with the exception of a glimpse gained of one object—the ruins of the ancient Sigtuna, the oldest town in Scandinavia, and one of the centres of the worship of Odin.

Upsala itself is in a wide plain, and would be a commonplace town, but for the old Cathedral—which is one of the most remarkable structures in the country, of pure Gothic, and dating to the thirteenth century—and its ancient University. This was founded in 1477, by Sten Sture the elder;

it received its greatest endowments from Gustavus Adolphus, and has continued to be the leading university of Sweden. It numbers many great names among its professors—Linnæus, Geijer, Bergmann, Svanneberg, Wallin, and others.

In passing through the streets, I noticed an ample, well-built house, evidently for public objects. "For the Stockholm *Nation*," my friend said. Each province is called a Nation, and has its own quarter and house. The students of the Nation have many things in common, and usually a place of amusement, with library and reading-room, like this building. The same division is used in classifying the students.

There are 14 Nations in the University. The number of students is 1,350 ; professors, 26—four each in Philosophy, Law, Medicine, and Theology. Adjuncts, 18, and docents, 29 ; beside a number engaged in the library, and in teaching modern languages. Annual revenues from property, about $30,000. Of the rare literary treasures of this university, especially of the famed *Codex Argenteus*, the envy of scholars, it is not necessary I should speak. Guide-books and hand-books give full information.

THE SCHOOLS

are, the Cathedral School, with 300 pupils ; the Lyceum and Real Gymnasium, with 50 pupils each ; the People's Schools—as the Duke of Uppland's, with 300 scholars, the Princess Eugenia's, for infants, with 90 ; the "School of Exercise," and a School for Vagrants.

There is also a good Poor-House, and but little beggary is seen in the streets.

A telegraph connects Upsala and Stockholm. The population of the city is 7,288.

I had the pleasure here of making the acquaintance of an accomplished jurist, well known in America, Prof. B—— with whom I spent a whole day talking over the Swedish Constitution.

This university sends two members to the Parliament, who take their seats with the "House of Clergy." Yet not one of these gentlemen, professors or teachers, can be elected by their fellow-citizens to Parliament, or vote for any candidate out of the university. Nor have they the slightest share in the city elections in Upsala, where they have spent all their lives, and where their interests are. They are not strictly members of either of the "Four Classes"—Peasants, Citizens, Clergy, or Nobles. By one of the innumerable anomalies of Sweden, they can be *voted for* to a town-office, though they cannot vote. The professors are appointed for life. Prof. B. says, "Even the King himself cannot unseat me." "But if an incompetent person holds a chair, how do you get rid of him?"

"It is very difficult. He must be tried, and proved to have committed something worthy of punishment, and then he can be unseated."

The legal Professors act the part also of "consulting lawyers," gratuitously. Sweden is yet in that state of primeval innocence, that it is destitute of lawyers. When I first fairly understood this, I could scarcely believe it.

"What do your people do," I asked, "when they fall into a difficult law-dispute ?"

"*They go to the Judges,*" said Prof. B., "and get their opinion, or they come to us, and we are expected to advise."

"But it would take up all the time of the Judges, I should think, and besides, sometimes the thing must need a long investigation."

"No," said the Professor; "you see those two octavo volumes there. They are our law. Your lawyers must consult between six and seven hundred such volumes. The fact is, we have no "common law"—only statute law—and a peasant, if he has a case, can work it out from these books and plead it himself. Sometimes an ignorant man will get the sheriff to state his case, and there are a few cunning men who are employed by the peasants to plead for them, but they have no professional character. In Stockholm now, there begins to be a class of government officials, who are more like your lawyers, still they have nominally other business."

I was often afterwards struck with this peculiarity of the Swedish polity—people pleading their own cases, or stating them to the judge, and leaving them to his decision, without argument. It is still inexplicable to me, especially where anything like complicated commercial law is concerned.

One hears now through Sweden many complaints against Upsala and her conservatism; many wish the university transplanted to Stockholm, so as to give it a more cosmopolitan character. Most unwisely, it seems to me. A large city absorbs an intellectual institution.

"GAMLE UPSALA."

About two miles from Upsala is *Gamle Upsala* (Old Upsala), which is now merely an old Church, and a few cottages. The central part of this church, at this time under process of enlargement, is called the oldest architectural ruin in Sweden. It is built of rough stone, and has no especial architectural character, except the round arch.

It was undoubtedly the great National Temple of Odin, and is described even in the eleventh century, as a building of great magnificence.* Near it are numerous instances of the tumuli, found so plentifully over Scandinavia. One author says, there are six hundred and sixty-nine here.

Laing supposes,—it seems to me correctly—that these

* Olaus Magnus says of the Temple, that it was built so magnificently, that there was nothing to be seen on the walls, roof, or pillars, but shined with gold; also, the whole upper part was made with glittering gold, from which a golden chain hung down, and is recorded to have gone round about the Temple to the walls and tops of the house. Hence it was, that the Temple, situate on a large plain, by the admirable lustre of it, begat in those that came near to it, a venerable fire of religion. There grew before the doors of it a huge tree, of an unknown kind, that spread with large boughs, and was green both in Summer and Winter. * * * *

Let this suffice for other nations to understand some of the vain customs of the Goths.—(*History of Goths and Swedes, translated in* 1658—London.)

were natural formations, but used as burial-places, and as places for addressing the people. One of them, a lofty mound, is still called the *Ting's* mound, or place where the great National Assembly of the Bonders was held in early times. It has been excavated, and the entrance to the interior is carefully guarded by a gate—my companion said that many small ornaments of value had been found here for the museums.

The "*Ting*" was a purely Democratic Assembly, like the Norwegian *Ting*, composed of all the free-holders: was the governing power of Sweden in the days of the Vikings. It made kings and unmade them; voted supplies, passed laws, called out levies, and, though sometimes overawed by the kings, was on the whole, a most powerful and independent Assembly. The Bonders had certain men among them, who, from their talents or character, came to lead and represent them at these *Tings*, called *Lagmän*—the Swedish Tribunes.

There is a very characteristic scene given in the Saga of "Olof the Saint," (Laing's translation) of a national Ting, held at this very place, in the spring of 1018. The question before the Assembly was, whether King Olof, of Sweden, should give his daughter to King Olof of Norway, in order to put a stop to the war waging between the two countries. A certain Earl present had, in a set speech, strongly urged the king to this measure—but the king had as strongly refused, in a speech very bitter, both against the Earl and the King of Norway. A lagman (named Thorgny), who is represented as having a white beard reaching to his knees, when he sat, prepared himself to reply, or in the words of the Saga—

"Then Thorgny stood up; and when he arose, all the Bonders stood up who had before been sitting, and rushed together from all parts to listen to what language Thorgny would say. At first, there was a great din of people and weapons; but when the noise was settled into silent listening, Thorgny made his speech. 'The disposition of Swedish kings is different now from what it has been formerly. My grandfather, Thorgny, could well remember the Upsal king, Eric Emundson, and used to say of him, that when he was in his best years he went out every summer on expeditions to different countries, and conquered for himself Finland, Liflland, Curland, Esthland, and the eastern countries all around; and at the present day, the earth bulwarks, ramparts, and other great works which he had made are to be seen. And, moreover, he was not so proud that he would not listen to people who had anything to say to him. My father, again, was a long time with King Björn, and was well acquainted with his ways and manners. In Björn's lifetime, his kingdom stood in great power, and no kind of want was felt, and he was gay and sociable, with his friends. I also remember King Eric, the victorious, and was with him on many a war expedition. He enlarged the Swedish dominion, and defended it manfully; and it was also agreeable to communicate our opinions to him. But the King we have now got allows no man to presume to talk with him, unless it be what he desires to hear. On this alone he applies all his power, while he allows his scattlands in other countries to go from him through laziness and weakness. He wants to have the Norway kingdom laid under him, which no Swedish king before him ever desired, and therewith brings war and distress on many a man. Now it is our will, we Bonders, that thou, king Olaf, make peace with the Norway king, Olaf the Thick, and marry thy daughter Ingegerd to him. Wilt thou, however, reconquer the kingdoms in the east countries which thy relations and forefathers had there, we will all for that purpose follow thee to the war. But if thou wilt not do as we desire, we will now attack thee, and put thee to death; for we will no longer suffer law and peace to be disturbed. So our forefathers went to work when they drowned five kings in a well at the Mula-Ting, and they were filled with the same insupportable pride thou hast shown towards us. Now tell us, in all haste, what resolution thou wilt take.' Then the whole public approved, with clash of arms and shouts, the Lagman's speech."—*Heimskringla*, vol. ii. p. 93.

The King, of course, yielded. It is such a spirit among the old Norse Folk which has finally given birth to *Magna Charta* and the American Republic.

Old Upsala was, without doubt, the centre of the religious worship and the capital of the monarchy of the ancient Swedes, as distinguished from the Goths in middle Sweden. The conversion of this part of Sweden to Christianity was characteristic, and perhaps has not been without its influence on the later aspect of its religion.

Hear the Heimskringla.

CONVERSION OF UPLAND KINGS.

"When King Olof had dispatched Björn and his followers to Gothland, he sent other people also to the Uplands, with the errand that they should have guest-quarters prepared for him, as he intended that winter to live as guest in the Uplands; for it had been the custom of former kings to make a progress in guest-quarters every third year in the Uplands. In autumn, he began his progress from Sparsborg, and went first to Vingulmark. He ordered his progress so that he came first to lodge in the neighborhood of the forest habitations, and summoned to him all the men of the habitations who dwelt at the greatest distance from the head-habitations of the district; and he inquired particularly how it stood with their Christianity, and where improvement was needful, he taught them the right customs. If any there were who would not renounce heathen ways, he took the matter so zealously that he drove some out of the country, mutilated others of hands or feet, or stung their eyes out, hung up some, cut down some with the sword; but let some go unpunished who would not serve God. He went thus through the whole district, sparing neither great nor small. He gave them teachers, and placed these as thickly in the country as he saw needful. In this manner, he went about in that district, and had three hundred deadly men at-arms with him, and then proceeded to Baumarige. He soon perceived that Christianity was thriving less the farther he proceeded into the interior of the country. He sent forward everywhere in the same way, converting all the people to the right Faith, and severely punishing all who would not listen to his word."

POSTING.

From Upsala we commenced our land-journey towards Dalecarlia, taking Dannemora on the way, and intending to pass over a little of Södermanland.

It is wonderful how long the Swedes have submitted to the inconveniences of travel in their country. To travel in a province, a hundred miles from their capital, or even twenty miles, one must take his own carriage, convey it to and fro by boat, hire at every station his two horses, for ever annoyed with waiting for horses or hurrying them, with paying *wait-money* if he is behind the time he has set by post, with feeing *hällkarlar* (ostlers) and post-boys, never accomplishing more than seven miles an hour, and paying about the price of our American stage-coaches, or double that of the railroads—five and six cents a mile,—this, where, in some seasons, the travel is incessant over the roads.

Yet it has also its pleasures. This traversing a country in your own comfortable carriage, giving you time for visiting and talking with people, and the excitement of accomplishing the stage in full time, are not disagreeable experiences to a traveller. On one of our first stages, I had an experience of a different people from the Norwegian we had just left—the little rogue of a post-boy cribbaging some small articles which we could not well spare.

DANNEMORA.

These iron mines are well known to the whole world. The sight was one of the grandest I ever had, as the crane swung us off at a giddy height into the black chasm: the little insects of men pecking away at the rock far below, the mighty columns and arches disclosing gloomy vistas, as in some subterranean rock-temple, and the grand craggy walls of the mine—a mountain-side. We wandered about a little in the chilly vaults, and collected some specimens. There are over three hundred workmen employed; each has a house, a plot of ground and certain privileges, as well as the day's wages paid by the job—about twenty-five cents a day. When old or disabled, he and his family are allowed a pension. A great many children are at work above, on the outside of the mine—as usual with the miners' children, a sad, miserable-looking set. The whole population connected with the mine is about thirteen hundred. The water is pumped out by steam, and conveyed a considerable distance. The iron owes its adaptability to the fabrication of steel, to the quantity of magnesia contained in it, and its excellent quality, to the small quantity of sulphur and phosphorus. The ore yields from forty to fifty per cent. There are seventy-nine different mines, some but little worked. The first working of them, say the books, dates back at least to the 15th century. The annual expense of the works is one hundred and seventy-one thousand rix dollars. The produce is roughly estimated at about ten thousand tons. The Superintendent of the mine is a government official, though paid by the proprietors. A physician and nine other officers are engaged in the service of the company.

Beyond the mines one of our first stations was Alfta. We stopped to change horses and called for tea. The landlady did not know anything about the article. We took out our own, and, to the great admiration of the children, began the preparation. The woman then remembered that some travellers had once left a little there; but she had never used it, supposing it to be a medicine.

GEFLE.—This is a thriving town with considerable commerce. The houses are white, and mostly of two stories; and the streets paved with cobble stones, without side-walks. A railroad is soon to connect this with Fahlun. As usual, the hotel was wretched, but charges are very moderate. Seventy-five cents a day will cover the expenses in most country hotels.

MO-MYSIE is the best station in all the North; with large, neat bedrooms, and good, substantial fare. At a station near this, while waiting for horses, we walked over to the parsonage, to make a call on the clergyman. We found it the best house and farm in the village—the building new, and painted white, of two stories. The maid, who accidentally found us in the hall—for there is never a bell, or knocker, or any means of communication, in most Swedish houses, showed us up into a large attic, and there left us. It was occupied by a miscellany of objects, deer-skins, spinning-wheels, books, clothes and odd chairs. At length we spied a door, which might conduct us to the parlor. It was opened to the rap, and a stout, important-looking gentleman looked up from his writing. He had the unfailing pipe in one hand, a smoking-cap on his head, and in the corner near him was a *chevaux de frise* of pipes. When we had stated our objects, he welcomed us, and then begged us to excuse him a moment, while he attended to the baptism of a child, who was just then brought by a peasant for the purpose. This, as in all Lutheran countries, is a legal requisition, and for which the clergyman is always paid a fee.

On his return, we had a long conversation. Education, he thought much progressing among his people. The parish numbered 6,000, with two preachers; there were six "circulating schools" and one established, with some 500 scholars. The pay of a common teacher was about 21 cents a day; of a higher teacher, $100 per annum. The great difficulty was with the teachers—to get good men on such a miserable pay. After discussing the merits of the new

Swedish school-system, we were about to go to the inn, when he insisted on our staying for dinner.

We were shown out to the large dance saloon, in the middle of which, the little round table with its pure white Swedish linen, was set. Flowers were here, as everywhere, at the windows and on the tables. The walls were painted in fresco, by a village artist. The dinner was simple and good; home-made beer was served to each, and coffee was brought in immediately after the silent thanks at the end. Then an offering of cigars and pipes, and a courteous farewell, as our post-carriage comes to the door.

A———.—We had a letter to the clergyman of this village, and drove into the great court-yard of the parsonage. The pastor at once, on reading the letter, ordered our horses to be taken out and detained us for the night, to which we were not averse. After a little chat over the cigars, we all set forth to see the Church and the villagé.

This last has some very comfortable houses, the property of rich peasants. The church is only a little distance from the parsonage. Before entering, the pastor deposited his cigar on a tombstone, and reverentially uncovering, we stepped within. The building was large, of the simple cross form, but with no columns or arches to interrupt the view; the usual audience is about two thousand. The pastor took us to the sacristy to show his dresses—the splendid crimson cassocks with the gold cross, the common white and black, and others with various embroidery and ornaments. Pastor F. states that his parish contains four thousand four hundred souls, and extends some eleven Swedish square miles. He has frequently to ride thirty-five miles to preach, and he must catechise at forty-five different places through the year, sometimes in the coldest weather. He is much discouraged by the licentiousness of the peasants—the proportion of illegitimate children being very large. In drinking habits, he sees a vast improvement, especially since the new laws, which make brandy so expensive.

There are, in the parish, five circulating schools and one established, having together about four hundred children in attendance. Here again is the complaint of poor teachers and poor pay; some receiving only six dollars per annum, with board! Dissent, he informs me, is beginning to make havoc among his flock. The excitements of *Läsarne* (a kind of methodism) have already produced sad results, physically. It was a commentary on his remarks that we met, in our short walk, three persons, crazy from the overtension of their religious feelings. The Baptists and *Läsarne* have not dared, as yet, he says, to come out and build chapels, for fear of legal measures, but he thinks they soon will. The parish, he informs me, is a royal parish—that is, the King appoints the clergyman, though usually the Consistorium presents three candidates, to select from. The salary is a certain pro rata sum fixed by the parish-meeting (*Socken stämma*) and collected in driblets of produce or money from each peasant; every man being obliged by law to give a certain amount.

This village is in Helsingeland, and the peasants have a peculiar character. They are by no means so intelligent as the Dalecarlians, but there is more wealth with individuals, and greater extremes of condition. We visited a number of peasants' properties. According to the universal Scandinavian arrangement, for rich or poor, there is a little square of houses, one being for guests, and for the family, and another for the servants and for store-room. The doorways to the principal houses were highly decorated, and had almost an Oriental aspect. Within, each room was perfectly neat and clean, with large beds and good plain furniture. The floors were sprinkled with twigs of pines. In some, we saw a singular article of furniture, consisting of a bedstead, painted white and gilt, with a secretary for the foot-board, and a *clock* for head-board. Others had large bed-rooms, used as store-rooms; some were quite prettily painted within. The most notable thing was the neatness. I saw no book except the Bible and Psalm-book. The women who showed us their rooms were usually healthy, cheery looking working women, dressed somewhat in colored costume. The pastor says that generally they are well instructed, but that there are some superstitions remaining among them, which he cannot break down. When they are sick, they always send first to the old witches, before they apply to the regular physician. A Helsinglander, who buys a horse, is careful to take him out the first time *backwards* from the stable, to avoid the evil spirits—the *Tomt!*—and with the most, the mountains and desolate places are still beset with the legions of spirits who haunted their heathen forefathers.

When we returned to the house, at about 8 o'clock, a

good supper was served up for us, and we sat long, talking of America and Sweden; for this family, like so many in Sweden, has its members in the New World. A Swedish military officer was present. In the glow of the conversation, he could not refrain from an enthusiastic outburst for his country, such as I have often heard since—"After all, as we look over the nations of the world, there is no country so blessed as old Sweden. Here every one can speak or write as he pleases; there is no slavery here, and we have a *good* King. Yes, we are the happy people!" The others smiled, but evidently considered him quite right.

I ventured to object, partly for argument's sake, and asked how a country could be called blessed where there were such multitudes of ignorant people, and spoke of the licentiousness and drunkenness. "The proportion of illegitimate births in Stockholm are fifty per cent." He replied, that as to the ignorance of the people, he would not compare them with the American. "But look at the English peasantry and the German! How many cannot read or write! Here it is very seldom that you will find a peasant who cannot read. And for brandy-drinking, it was, indeed, bad some years since; but the people improve every day in that. And, for my part, I do not believe them worse than other nations in the matter of licentiousness. You cannot judge from Stockholm, sir. It is true there are very many illegitimate children there, but *there are no prostitutes.* We hear of fifty thousand women in London who are damned for this world utterly. There is hardly one in Sweden. Even if a woman has an unlawful connection, she can still raise herself up again, and she lives at least in a human relation with her companion."

"But the children! What becomes of them?" I asked.

"The State takes care of them," he answered. "It is bad, I know. But which is worse—that, or your infernal prostitution?"

Iron Works.—On our ride, the next day, we stopped at a wretched village adjoining the iron works of D., which we wished to visit. Why is it in Europe that manufactures always draw after them such a trail of poverty? This was the most miserable, ragged population I had seen. We entered the "Works" through a gentleman's house, and very tasteful grounds laid out on the stream that gave the water-power. The proprietors were two young bachelor noblemen, who at once welcomed us to brandy, fruit, and cigars. We declined the former, and sat down to a little chat over some delicious hot-house fruit. They are manufacturing bar-iron—employ three hundred laborers—wages usually one rix dollar (twenty-five cents) per diem. I inquired how it was that they, as noblemen, were manufacturing.

"It is very common now, sir, in Sweden," Captain D. answered. "We younger branches must do that, or belong to the bureaucracy, or try to get a commission. The fact is, sir, we are the most unhappy class of the community. You know, by our admirable Constitution, we cannot vote because we are not of the elder branch. We get very little of the large estates, for they are all '*fidei commiss*' (settled on the eldest son), and so we are all dependent on the elder brothers, or we must work, to which we have not been trained."

"Can you never take a seat in Parliament?" I asked.

"Yes—if the *caput familiæ*, as we call him, will resign his seat to us. Sometimes we can buy a seat from a poor noble."

The forges which we examined afterwards contained nothing remarkable. The great hammers were raised by a very rude contrivance—the outside spokes of a wheel carried by water, striking the head of the hammer, once in a given time—it falling again by its own weight. The furnaces were heated with charcoal. I observed in one part of our walk, a pretty school-house of stone, which these gentlemen were erecting for the children of their workmen.

We stopped for the night at a kind of chateau, belonging to another iron-manufacturer—a most simple, gentlemanly person. He is manufacturing chains and iron cables and the like:—two hundred and fifty workmen—produce 100,000 rix dollars per annum—wages from twenty-five cents to thirty-seven and a half cents per diem—number of hours of labor, eight. The cables are tried by a hydrostatic machine to such a tension that a quarter-ounce difference in the weight will break or preserve them. When the new railroad is finished from Söderhamn to Bolnaes, all these iron works will be greatly benefited. This gentleman informed me that his establishment has a vote for a member of Parliament, as now the iron interest is represented by five members in the House of Burgers. This concession was made a few years ago by the Parliament in order to quiet some of the grumblings against the unwieldly Constitution. Like the other great factories, his establishment is obliged to have a school for the children of the workmen, and for others in the parish.

We were very hospitably entertained here. The house was prettily furnished, and had a great number of French engravings, especially of the heroes of the French Revolution. In the better class of Swedish houses, one often sees these indications of the former well-known French bias of the nation. I bid adieu the next morning to this gentleman and his courteous hospitality with regret.

Orsa.—The beginning of our ride towards this village was through very desolate pine barrens. The characteristic Swedish scenery are woods of pines, with glimpses of lakes under the sombre branches, and occasional sun-lit glades, varied by groves of that exquisitely beautiful tree, the Northern drooping birch. The glory of Scandinavia is the birch groves. We have nothing like them in America. The glimmering, trembling leaves, the graceful droop of the branches, the light and shade—the *tone* which nature herself, in truest feeling, has impressed on the bark of their gigantic trunks, so that without sun-light, there is a perpetual variety of light through their checkered arches—make unforgetable pictures in the traveller's memory.

A pleasant cheerful tree, which we met near the villages, is the mountain ash, with clusters of the most brilliant red berries. This tree, so familiar to the student of Scandinavian mythology, is still cherished by the superstitious of the peasants. Its name sounds almost precisely the same as the Scotch "rowan-tree"—*Rön.*

As we entered Dalecarlia, the costumes began to change. Hitherto in Helsingeland, we have seen black caps with red tassels, dark jackets and breeches ; now the peasants have white cap and jacket, sometimes with curious tassels at their knees. The faces are generally swarthy, with high cheek bones, eyes dark, but hair light and long. We have passed one village of log-houses—Skattungeby—utterly deserted, the people being all in the fields. Each farm has precisely the same arrangements—the gate opening through the barn into a little square, each side of which is a log-cabin. The servants and animals sleep in the same building. There is not a framed glass window in the village, or a frame house. The church only is a handsome, modern-painted building. In the middle of the town is a high "mid-summer pole," with garlands still upon it, and bristling with wooden swords and arrows of ancient shapes, perhaps all in the form established by the worshippers of Odin and Thor.

A Postman.—(Postman, overwhelmed in astonishment,) "From America ! *Gud bevars !* (God forbid.) Did the Herr come by land so far ?"

"Water ; and 3,000 miles in eleven days."

"*Ha !* I suppose every one makes money there ? S. B—— has just come back here to live, with pockets full. He was in—in—"——

"Louisville," said my companion, who knew the case.

"What are wages in America, sir ?"

"Four riks, and meat every day."

"What a country ! We cannot make twenty-four skillings (twelve cents) a day here. And I have never eaten meat for seven months, and my wife and we all ate *bark bread* * last winter."

We asked whether he drank liquor. He shook his head lugubriously. "We have no money, Herr, for brandy, it costs too much." My companion led him on to the subject of the Dissenters—the Baptists.

"Oh, yes, Herr, I knew some. One poor devil in T——, says he will never have his boy baptized by the church. They have a little chapel not far away. But God will destroy the infidels! People say that they are going to stop all dances, yet every one knows that they sleep together, men and women, every night, and then go about screaming and praying to frighten honest people. They will all go to hell, certainly!" There was much gusto in the tone with which he disposed of the unfortunate Baptists.

Gradually, in our route, we began to descend towards the valley of Lake Siljan, the historic part of Dalecarlia, and the seat of the bravest and best population of Sweden. Here Gustavus Vasa concealed himself from the victorious Danes, until at length his eloquence roused the peasantry to the first resistance, which finally freed the country. Geijer says, that in these speeches of Gustavus to the peasants, the old men reckoned it as a good sign that the north wind always blew, "which was an old token to them that God would grant them good success."

We were well pleased to enter a cultivated country again,

* This is the bark and resin of the pine, mingled with a little bran.

with homesteads and marks of prosperity, after so long an experience of the pine woods. The Swedes are very enthusiastic over the *Siljan* scenery. It is gentle and pleasing—that is all one can say, and to a traveller fresh from Norway, it seems tame and commonplace.

The sturdy Dalecarlians were at work in the fields, men and women, in very picturesque white, black, and red costumes. As we rattled by into Orsa, the post-boy put them all into excitement by his cries, "An American! an American!"

We are now among the genuine Dalecarlians, or "Dalesmen"—the dales being made primarily by the two branches of the Dal River, which unite below, near Fahlun. There are many glens and cross-valleys, beside the two principal valleys. The whole number of persons inhabiting these, may be 150,000.

Mora.—We did not stop in Orsa, but hurried on to Mora, as one of the most characteristic points of the provinces. The village is built on the northern extremity of Lake Siljan, near the mouth of the Oster Dal River. Our hotel was unusually good, still poor enough—the walls decorated with prints from Frithiof's Saga. The pastor, to whom we were especially recommended, lived but a little distance; a man of large proportions in heart and body, with a sort of fatherly-arbitrary relation to every one, which was very agreeable. After the first introduction, we sat in front of the house under the old trees, the party smoking and drinking the home-made beer.

"We have seldom had the pleasure of a visit from an

American," said the old man. "Wälkommen!" clapping me heartily on the shoulder, "but we have one or two peasants who speak English."

I asked how that was? "You must know," he answered, "that our Dalecarlians are the most migratory people in Sweden. They wander all over Europe to sell their little wares—hair-chains, bracelets, and watches. There are about two thousand now absent from my parish. They go to Russia and Italy, and even England. But they always come back. They love nothing so much as this poor country. They are the proudest people! The Fru Prostinna will tell you what trouble we have with servants. We must send to Helsingeland, and other provinces; no Dalecarlian will be a house servant!

"They are a brave people," he added, seeing my interest, "the most honest people of the world, I think. If you will pass through these villages at any hour, you will see linens and furs and various things of value left out, and no one ever loses a *styfver* (stiver). And there is something so strong and inexpressive in them! I remember when the first little steamboat plied on this lake. I happened to be out and saw it first, and turned and told a Bonder who was ploughing, 'There's the steamboat! Have you seen it?' He turned and looked at it, and I have no doubt was overwhelmed with astonishment. It was the first he had ever seen, but he only answered, quietly, 'I see it,' and went on ploughing! They never will betray their feelings. Lately a proposition was made to my church to have a picture of Gustavus Vasa placed in the building, in commemoration of the great services of their ancestors. 'No,' they said, 'what our fathers did does not need any pictures or writing. Every man knows it'—and they refused."

They are exceedingly ingenious with machinery, the pastor says. He has known a peasant after a single examination of this little steamboat, go home and construct a miniature steam-engine. The telegraph runs now along all the great roads in Sweden. One of these men told the pastor, on seeing it, that if he could only once examine the marking machine, he would engage to construct a telegraph from his house to the parsonage!

Our host's account of the morals of his parish corresponds with all we have heard of Dalecarlia. There are 9,000 souls in it, and he never has heard of more than two or three illegitimate children in the year. Yet, with this remarkably favorable condition of morals, there exists here as everywhere in Dalecarlia, the singular custom of the *Fria.**

When a *Bonder* would woo a maiden, he is allowed by the parents to sleep with her, both being in their full clothing. When there are several lovers, three or four will frequently pass the night together. For this purpose beds of immense width are in use among the peasants. Sometimes for more unreserved communication, they will sleep in the cattle-stalls, as otherwise they are in the same room with their parents. Saturday and Sunday nights are the universal

* Got *frijon*; Sansc. prinami; Gr. *φιλημι*, *πριαπος*.—*Säve.*

nights through Norrland for the "wooing." The custom has furnished much subject for the poets of the country, and probably will be one of the last which the *Bonders* will abandon, under the influences of advancing civilization. It exists only occasionally in Sweden out of Dalecarlia; but, as we have seen, in many parts of Norway, in Finland, and, it is said, in Switzerland. Here, it seems entirely pure and innocent. A friend tells me he has known a Bonder thus woo his maiden for nine years! One great preservative in Dalecarlia against vice is undoubtedly the early age at which marriages are made—the groom often not being more than eighteen.

The father, in the marriages of the peasants, has great authority—frequently giving away a daughter with very little regard to her feelings. There is a secret contract and ceremony before the marriage in the church, about which little is known. The Bonder is as aristocratic in his connections as the Noble in his. A Burger would be much more likely to marry the daughter of a peasant, than a *Bonder* (a free-holder) the daughter of a *Torpare* (a farm-servant paying his rent by labor). One of the evils of Dalecarlia is the division of land. It is customary for the father to divide his land equally among his children; and the consequence is, that the estates at last come down into the smallest parcels, and a man will own a lot not larger than a small bed-room in one spot, and another of equal size, perhaps half a mile away, so that you see everywhere the fields cut up by innumerable lines of fences. One great object of marriage accordingly is to unite neighboring lots, and all else that concern the two parties is often sacrificed to contiguity. These little properties are frequently pawned to the larger proprietors near, and still paying taxes, they are eaten up at last by the burdens.

The custom of the *Fria* has a corresponding custom in New England, which undoubtedly existed in all parts of it in our early history, perhaps derived from the Norwegians of Northumberland—the Sunday evening "bundling."

CHAPTER XXIII.

DALECARLIA.

While we were sitting by the parsonage chatting, a young peasant came up, in leather apron, white wool cloak, breeches, and thick cumbrous shoes. He wore a black felt hat with cockade. As the parson clapped him on the shoulder, his manner was modest and submissive, but when he took off his hat, he revealed a very intelligent face, and a well-shaped head, with an expression of much native dignity. "Our Representative to the House of Bonders, and Secretary of the Sockenstämma," said our host. "He is just chosen for the first time."

This was a lucky fortune to me. From the beginning of my journey in Sweden, this class had, more than any, interested me, and more than any was difficult to comprehend. They were evidently not gentlemen, or exactly our "farmers," or the English yeomanry, or the German *Bauer*. Their whole position, and privileges, and character seemed original.

I asked about this Sockenstämma. "It is," said the pastor or *Prost*, "a kind of parish meeting, which manages all the affairs of the parish. The freeholders alone have the right to vote. It takes care of the church matters, the roads, the poor, and the schools. We usually now have a separate committee for each of these. You see, now, they are repairing my parsonage, unfortunately for my guests. They have the right to choose the clergyman, where the parish is not a royal one ; that is—the Consistory presents three, who preach on trial, and the meeting chooses from them. "Who presides over them?" I asked. "I do, in my parish—*ex officio*. This young man here is the Secretary, and has a small salary. He has shown himself a thorough business-man there, and that has made him elected for this. Talk with him ; you will find he is no boor. Will you take snuff, sir?"

"No, thank you. What is he paid?"

"The peasants determine that—probably five dollars riks yäld ($1,25) a day."

"Will he wear that dress in Stockholm!"

"Certainly—that is—his best national costume. If he did not, he would never be returned again. The last member was a little ashamed of it, and it ruined him here. He cannot be elected again."

We started out on a walk towards the church. I tried to get the delegate into a conversation, and asked him what position he intended to take on the question of reform in the Representation. "I go to Stockholm to school," he answered sententiously. I asked if the peasants were much in favor of railroads. He said those in his Province were beginning to see how necessary they were, and he had already bought two shares himself in the Bolnaes road. "Why should the peasants object to any man's voting in their class, if he owned land?" I asked. "Is it right to exclude very useful men thus from the State?" "It seemed unreasonable," he answered, "but he had not fully considered the question."

The pastor pointed out on our walk, some large meadow lands, which were public property formerly, and had occasioned them much trouble in the different claims of individuals to a share in them. Now, he said, the Secretary had just framed a plan of dividing the lands among the freeholders of the parish, in proportion to the taxes they paid ; and after a hot discussion, it had been passed.

As in every circle I have visited in Sweden, the conversation fell soon, between the pastor and me, on American politics. The clergyman explained to the delegate, that "America, the freest land in the world, has the stain of slavery upon it;" and that this election turns on the extension of it. The peasant knew it, and inquired about the chances of Fremont! "No Swede in America," added he proudly, "will ever vote to have a slave." They were much interested in the Know Nothing party, as in opposition to Romanism. "Oh, *the sects!* the sects!—that is the disgrace of America!" said the clergyman; and the peasant nodded a sad assent. "What can Christ's church be worth, when it is broken up into so many little parties, all quarrelling with each other?" I replied, warmly. But as these discussions occurred with almost every new acquaintance (and I shall have occasion soon to mention one), it is not necessary to repeat it here. The first conception of religious freedom has scarcely entered the Swedish mind.

We entered the church—an immense cruciform white building, with the inner architecture somewhat in a crypt form, the ponderous arches meeting and uniting in massive columns—an exceedingly roomy and impressive arrangement. The interior was white. There are frequently five thousand people comfortably seated at the Sunday service. The building dates back to the thirteenth century. All the galleries are decorated with quaint paintings of Scripture scenes—sometimes an allegorical series, in which the tortures of the damned were a prominent feature.

The *Prost* thinks there is a profound religious feeling among the people shown in these solemn and crowded Sunday services; and he finds the same well tested in the practical life, in sorrow and misfortune. The hard-drinking habits have much decreased. He has been making great efforts for education. The new ordinance of the ministry left a little choice to the clergy in respect to the established school in his parish; the distances were too great for the children to attend any one school; accordingly he had opened home schools (after Count Rudensköld's plan) in certain of the private houses, where the youngest children are taught by women, whom he paid from the moneys voted for education. An informal but effective system, he thinks. There are about one thousand children in the home schools of his parish. They need, very much, thoroughly trained teachers for the older scholars.

When we returned to the house, we found some of the peasants there who had been in England, and we had a long conversation together.

One of them said to me: "They used to tell us in Scotland—'You are very far behind in Sweden—no iron roads, no improvements, and so on.' But I always said—'No such crowds of poors, and not so much whisky in our country.' I saw so bad things in Glasgow!"

"What books do you read at home, here!" I asked.

"We read only the Bible, and sometimes the Psalm-book. Then a few peóple takes the *Wäktaren* (a newspaper) from Stóckholm."

I tried, next, to draw out from him the belief of the people about witchcraft and such matters; but he was too cautious to give much information—"Some believes in good spirits, and some in bads."

"Do your peasants care much for politics?"

"No, sir—if they be let alone."

"Do you vote?"

"No, sir; I have no hemman (freehold)."

The pastor asked him if he had an English Testament. He said he had, and then read very well from one which was brought to him. As we were about to go to the village, our host ordered out some ginger-beer, and it was given to all who were gathered about the door—among others, to the member of Parliament, who took off his hat respectfully on receiving it. On bidding good-bye to the peasants, I attempted to give a small gratuity to the one with whom I had been talking, but he would not take it, and it was only with considerable difficulty that I induced him to do so.

It was a lovely sunset, as we walked by the quiet, peaceful lake, towards the hamlet—a broad beam of golden light falling over the rich harvest-fields near the mouth of the *Dal,* and the gentle rounded hills on the horizon, and gleaming from the coppered spire of the church; the pastor leading the way, pipe in hand, talking most earnestly. The *Adjunct* (vicar), in demure black cap, on one side, and the delegate with his picturesque costume, behind; the rest of us keeping up with the rapid pace, and talking as eagerly.

The pastor pointed to the hills and said: "Those are the mountains—Oestberg, and the next—where the peasants believe the *Troll,* and the fairies, and witches still have their revels. They are poor, ignorant creatures, some of them!" I expressed my interest in these old superstitions. "You will not meet with many, Herr B., here," he answered. "The Dalecarlians are too enlightened; but in other parts of Sweden, there are very singular beliefs. Indeed, lately here, I found that there was a certain spring, out of which the peasants would not drink, without first *spitting* into it, in order to avert the influence of the evil spirits!

"But these are not the only hills, Herr B. See you there! that rounded small hill near the river. There the great Gustavus first harangued the peasantry of Mora, before they took up arms for the country!"

I asked if the people really cherished these recollections. He replied that they did; but now without much speaking of them.

"Over there again, on the other side of the lake, is the *cellar of Utmedland,* where the King concealed himself."

They spoke of the Baptists, who had just opened a

chapel near by. "They are liable to the law—every one of them," said the clergyman. "The last Parliament made it a criminal offence for any layman to administer the ordinances. They could be fined and banished."

"Why do you not enter proceedings against them? they are disturbing the whole country," said the vicar.

"Because I am doubtful of the expediency of it," he replied. "It is a long affair, besides. They must be warned by me a certain number of times first, and then the case may be carried from court to court."

"Was not this whole thing brought before the courts a few years ago?" I asked.

"It was: but by the old law, those who administered the ordinances with motives of mockery, were alone liable; and though the first court condemned them, the higher court of appeal reversed the sentence—rightly, in my opinion, for certainly these poor deluded people had no intention of mockery. But now, under the new law, they cannot escape."

I spoke of the folly of persecution—that a good cause never gains by it, and the bad, when persecuted, takes on a better appearance to all men of humane feelings. The pastor admitted it philosophically—"but the time has not come here, yet, for conscience-freedom. When we are ready for a Republic, we will be ready for that!"

"And for a man not to baptize his own child! Atheistic!" added his vicar.

"Besides, look at America! We have seen there what religious freedom is. Every preacher is seeking to advance his own sect—not the evangelical spirit of religion. You have Methodists and Baptists, and Episcopalians, and Mormons—and there is sometimes hostility among them, as you just admitted. I have here a parishioner who was in your country; he gives melancholy relations of the want of evangelical piety and interest in the churchly ordinances."

"Where was he, Herr Prost?"

"In Süd Carolina, I think."

I explained then, that we would not admit a Slave State to be a fair representative of the religious character of our Union, and then gave them more fully, than in the previous discussion, our American position with respect to religious freedom. The aspects which individuals take of truth *must* be different—it is a necessity. Why should not then religious bodies represent some of these endless differences? These various sects were all united in the grand principles—Love to God and Love to men—but consented to differ on these other points. My own experience was, that the preachers were not especially given to urging on the interests of their sect, as opposed to other sects; that the most popular clergymen were those who were least sectarian. In private life, certainly, sectarian differences had very little influence, and we never troubled ourselves about the theological position of our associates. I believed our people as thoroughly imbued with a deep religious feeling and principle as any other, though the great Sin of a part of our nation had certainly poisoned all in contact with it.

Our great principle in America—as we believe, the principle of Protestantism—is that the conscience must be free; that liberty is the true atmosphere of the soul, and without it, religious life withers and dies. We conceive that this has nothing to do with republicanism, or with forms of government—that it is universal and eternal—true in all times, through all societies and in all countries.

They listened respectfully, and as I had spoken in German, the *Prost* translated to the delegate, who made no reply.

"Here we are at Andersen's gård (farm)!"

This again had the same arrangement of houses in a little square, though the farm was in the midst of the village. A woman sat in the doorway to the kitchen, eating—some little girls frolicking behind her—such sweet children, brown cheeks with a color richer than the freshest peach-bloom, loose flaxen curls, dancing blue eyes, and forms so plump and healthy! This is our general observation in Dalecarlia; the children are wonderfully pretty, but the women, though very healthy-looking, show the effect of hard work—their faces are thin and forms stumpy. This woman was dressed in the usual red bodice and white skirt, with a white cap on her head. A number of men stood around, tall, powerful figures, in white garments like the *blouses*. Their faces were usually florid, with long light hair, blue eyes and high cheek-bones; an expression in the countenances of subdued force and of seriousness.

The *Prost* introduced me to the woman, and after a few words, asked for a bit of her bread to give me. I took a small piece, hardly larger than a dollar, and tasted it; it was coarse oat-cake: then, not liking to hand it back to the woman, I inadvertently dropped it on the grass at my side. Her face changed in an instant, the eyes flashed, but before she could speak, the pastor had picked it up and placed it on her lap, and I, seeing my mistake, complimented it, and she seemed mollified.

"That was nearly a bad affair," whispered the *Prost* immediately after. "Every Dalecarlian looks on it as one of the worst sins *to throw bread on the ground.* They have a perfect superstition about it. The whole village would have known it immediately. All the glories of America could not redeem your reputation, if the people thought the Americans ever threw bread on the ground."

We went into a kitchen soon after, where they were baking on iron griddles, great round rye-cakes, a foot and a half in diameter. These are kept and thoroughly dried for the winter. The house-mistress had a hearty, laughing face, and seemed much pleased at our interest in her operations. She took us into the upper rooms, to see her wardrobe. Two large attic-chambers were hung around with dresses—colored prints, snow-white wool aprons with brilliant red borders, silks, linens, embroidered bodices, wool-jackets, deer-skin coats, snow-shoes and winter-boots. Taking up one little spencer of soft lamb's-wool, she said, "*Litet Lamm!*"—one instance among many of the resemblances of our languages. We met here the man who had returned from America—a pale, cadaverous-looking fellow. He had had the yellow-fever in Charleston, and nearly died; "thought his own country much better." As he bid me good-bye, the peasants all laughed with delight, to hear him speak a foreign language.

Late in the evening we returned to the parsonage. Again a hospitable supper was served, with the silent, reverential grace, preceding and following, as if every meal were a new indication of the universal Providence. A pleasant talk around the table followed. It was noticeable that this gentleman had no wine or spirits on his table—a moderation rarely seen in Sweden. Hearty shakes of the hand were given—"Adieu!" "*Farwäl!*" and we had parted from the warm-hearted family.

CHAPTER XXIV.

TOUR IN DALECARLIA.

Rätwik.—The Rätwik parsonage is another of the great hospitable parsonages—one house being for guests and summer enjoyment, another for the winter, another as a study for the clergyman, and still another for the servants. In the large dance saloon, called the King's Hall, in memory of a royal visit, where we meet, the outside doors are wide open, and the bountiful dinner is brought in by courses, and is placed on a little table in the centre, for every one to help himself as he wishes. Before commencing, the usual prelude is gone through of a glass of whisky and bread and cheese—the gentlemen helping themselves first, and then the ladies. We eat standing. It is a generous room, with pine planks twenty or twenty-five feet long, making the flooring.

"I suppose you have great times here, with the dances on Christmas eve and the holidays?" I said.

"*Bevars!* Not alone then—every Sunday night!" said a spirited young lady. * * *

"What is the history of that picture," I asked, pointing to a painting on the wall. "A wonderful painting!"

"Ack that! the Herr Pastor received it at a lottery (of an Art Union). It is very good—by Malmström, the '*Norna Gest.*' The tale is this. One of the old skalds, in the time of the Vikinger, was visited at his birth by three wise Norna-women. The mother had lighted two candles at the cradle, as was commanded, and the old witches began to prophesy. They told her he should be wise and great and rich, and surpass all of his day—when suddenly the youngest *Norna Greytur* burst in, offended at not being treated with ceremony, and she said: 'Boy! thou shalt not live longer than the candle that burns beside thee.' The mother was in terror, but the oldest witch took the candle and put it out, and gave it to his mother and bade her keep it. She did so, and when the boy grew and became a famous bard, she gave it to him. He lived for three hundred years and played divinely at many courts, and celebrated the great battles. But finally he sighed for Valhalla, and became tired of so long a life, and he took the candle from the interior of his harp, and lit it, and watching it, he died."

"Is it not a good saga—and has not the artist hit it?"

It was an old man in antique barbaric costume, of florid Northern face, with long white hair and an expression, though pained and exhausted, still noble. He leans on a quaintly ornamented harp, holding the dying candle between finger and thumb, watching with deep haggard look each hair's-breadth lessening of the taper. His gaze was penetrated beyond the fatal omen into the dark futurity. The weakness of death is falling over him, with the flickering light; his other arm, unmuscular as becomes his vocation, with the blue veins of age on it, and decorated with golden armlets—Odin's golden serpents—the prizes of many chantings of sagas and war songs, drops relaxed by his side ; his breast seems to rise feebler and feebler, and the fatal hour foretold by the Nornas will soon be at hand. Behind is a mysterious Runic column, dimly seen. The ornaments of his harp and of his dress have a wild, intelligent character. The colors are fresh as life, still soft and mild in tone. It is a picture which you cannot escape from. Whatever you are doing in the room, the eyes wander back to that mysterious Rune ; you are away in dreams in the dim early ages of the Scandinavian peoples, among those wild poets of courts and battles, whose wonderful mythology and Delphic poetry make a never to be forgotten literature. You gaze exhausted at the dying candle, and look out with the old saga-bard into the dim unseen, where wild forms of evil and of good pass and repass—the Nornas, the mighty Thor, the evil Loke, the giants of the frozen North, the awful Midgaard serpent which is to swallow all, but where, at length, after the final destruction, " a new heavens and new earth shall come forth and Baldur, the god of love, forever rule."

The church adjoining the parsonage is one of the historic places of Sweden. Here Gustavus Vasa called the people together for insurrection.

"He bade the old consider well, and the young to inform themselves, what manner of tyranny foreigners had set up in Sweden, and how much they themselves had suffered and ventured for the freedom of the realm. Sweden was now trampled under foot by the Danes, and its noblest blood had been shed; his own father had chosen rather with his associates, the honor-loving nobles, in God's name to die, than to be spared and survive them. Might they now show themselves men, who wished to guard their native land from slavery, then would he become by God's help their chief, and risk life and welfare for their freedom, and the deliverance of the realm."—(*Geijer.*)

The building dates back to the twelfth or thirteenth century. Again, we have the interior of heavy round arches, meeting at points like the arches of a crypt. On the fronts of the galleries were the names of the different clergymen of the parish in gilt letters, going back to the Reformation. In one corner I saw a number of portraits of the Swedish Kings, Charles XII., Charles XIII. and Gustavus Vasa, apparently laid aside as rubbish.

Near the church, the pastor had built his school—a neat dwelling-house, with rooms for the teacher and for one of the vicars. There are four clergymen in this parish, which numbers 8,800 inhabitants. The chief vicar is called *Comminister*, and the others *Adjuncti*. Among the pastors, *Prost* is a higher title than *Pastor*, and *Dom Prost* the highest under the Bishop. These clergymen in Dalecarlia are among the richest and most powerful in Sweden. Their incomes from the regular tithes, and the gifts of their parishioners, who are much attached to them, amount to 12,000 or 15,000 riks dollars ($3,000 to $3,750) per annum, which is very large for the interior of Sweden. They all keep several carriages, and their hospitality is unbounded. They are the principal school managers, the leaders of education, the chief members of Parliament and legal advisers, as well as spiritual directors of the peasants. The influences which the clergy in other provinces of Sweden, from their lazy habits and worldly spirit, have lost, these still retain. They are usually men of the best culture, and of truly democratic feelings—their relation to their flock being very familiar.

A Dalecarlian always says "thou" to his pastor, which is like calling a man by his first name with us. A friend relates that one of the clergymen in these provinces, who was a very distinguished preacher, was too much given to strong drink. One Sunday, after a most impressive and eloquent discourse, when he had come below in his robes to return home, an old peasant, much respected, came up to him, and clapping him on the shoulder, said—if we can give the equivalent in English—"Harry, thou preachest like a whole-souled man, but thou tipplest like any tavern-keeper." This public rebuke is said to have had an excellent effect.

When once a parish has an unsuitable clergyman, it is very difficult to unseat him; and nothing but drunkenness or some glaring offence can give sufficient cause to the Consistory to expel him. The choice, in the first place, except in the Royal Parishes, is directly from the people, but limited to the three candidates presented by the Bishop and Consistory.

This clergyman had done unusually much for education. He had twenty-six circulating schools, and two established; though the time spent in school by the children is by far too short, being only two days a week for fourteen weeks. Their studies are the Bible and catechism, reading, writing, and reckoning, and a little history. The preacher examines them all once or twice a year; and though the children are not obliged by law to attend school, they are obliged to pass this examination before the pastor will "confirm" them; and without confirmation, there is no civil right in Sweden. The teachers, again, receive miserable pay—some only twelve riks dollars ($3) a year and board.

As we sat in the roomy "King's Hall" afterwards, over our coffee, the pastor, with long pipe, gently puffing light clouds out into the summer air, I spoke of the very different position of a country pastor in America—how much more simple and spiritual his duties are. "Would it not be possible here to simplify the Constitution," I said, "dividing the Parliament into two houses, and giving, if you desire, to the clergy a share in the Upper House; or, what we would consider far better, confining them entirely to spiritual and moral duties? Does not this taking part in political life injure the spiritual tone of the clergy?"

"It often does, God knows!" he answered. "The parish would not be so frequently neglected, and the vineyard desolate, if our pastors were kept from *Riksdag*. Still, the great interests of the kingdom require a watchfulness from the priesthood. The working classes might press us into unhallowed courses, if we had no lot in the affairs of the state. They are already seeking to take the schools from us, and to banish that which is next to the Word of God—the catechism."

"But was not your house of clergy erected in an age when the clergyman alone was the educated man of the community, and when the relics of Romanism still survived in the public influence of the priesthood? Is it so necessary now?"

He allowed that it was not, and that he would gladly see a change which would not too much remove the shepherds from their flocks. Still, the clergy must not lose all share in the state. They have a right there.

"Yet it is often a grievous burden for us of the other clergy," he added. "I pay twenty-four riks dollars ($6) a month as my proportion of the salary of our member, though he receives no more than the pay of a Bonder by the day—four and a half riks ($1,12)—which is little enough in Stockholm. But your coffee is cooling!"

As we sat talking, the young ladies brought in some flowers, and I heard them in a discussion. "It is—it is the *spirea*." "No, it is a *ranunculus*." "Father, is it not the *spirea ulmaria*?" And the father decided. Some other plant was mentioned—perhaps the well-known *salix daphnoides* on the lake—and a careless young medical student at once gave the correct name and description. It struck me then, as it often did, that botany was much more an habitual branch of knowledge with them than with us.

It may be interesting to know the names of the old magical plants of Scandinavia. Those which drove away death in the old sagas, were plants that now are not remarkable for healing power. The books give them as *enpetrum ingrum, fragaria vesca, gnaphalium alpinum, leontodon taraxacum, ranunculus hederaceus, stellaria viviflora,* and *vaccinium occycoccos.*

LEKSAND.

August ——.—Of all the homes we have visited, this parsonage is the most glowing with hospitality and good feeling—such great rooms, such loaded tables, and, above all, such a stout-bodied, great-hearted host, the Domprosten H——, who wrings one's hand like a vice, and claps one on the shoulder with a blow which shakes you to your boots! "Hah! *Amerikanarè!* An American *here!* Ha! ha!" He talks to me in French, German, English or Latin, and sometimes in a mixture of all, and is said to speak Greek as well as any. He is well known and much beloved through the whole country, and was a successful member of Parliament. His parish, as he tells me, contains twelve thousand people, and has *forty-six* schools.

The sight yesterday morning (Sunday) at his church was one of the most impressive I ever saw. I rose at half-past six, in a cool brilliant summer morning, and the people were even then beginning to straggle into the great church-yard—the women arranging their *toilettes* in the angles of the church-walls. At seven, a fleet of boats from various parts of the Lake (Siljan) were flashing and ploughing through the water, all directed towards one point, and pulling with regular strong beat, as in a boat-race. At one time, I counted thirty-one large boats, with thirty or forty people in each. They were all in costume, and the boats glistened with white and red, as if it were some festal procession. As each struck the land, it emptied itself of the brilliantly-dressed party—the women in broad white head-dresses, or in red, and with red bodices ; the men wearing long black coats reaching to the feet, and black "Kossuth hats," sometimes with embroidery on their shoulders. As they came up the hill, with their various colors fresh in the morning sun, it made a most picturesque train. Each carried the psalm-book wrapped in neat cloths ; and those in the rear bore the baskets of biscuits and onions for the meal after service.

The men were much the finer looking, though the women had most hearty, pleasant, sun-browned faces, with the whitest teeth; while there were some young girls of exquisite and regular features. The head-dresses have their peculiar meaning, and are almost a police in themselves. The maidens wear simple colored bands, the hair braided in a kind of coronal ; the wives, white caps ; those in mourning, or about to join in the Communion, pointed white flat triangular head-tires ; and those who have children, unmarried, still another kind of white decoration, which betrays them to the whole community, and is one of the strong safeguards against licentiousness. Yet few, out of the peasantry, know of the exact appearance of this head-dress.

By eight o'clock, the streets of the little village were crowded with a great multitude of peasants ; and it was notable how large a part of the place was made up of rows of little buildings, used alone as stables or carriage-houses on the Sunday. From land and from water, they came pouring into the church-yard. Soon a denser crowd gathered around a particular spot—a sad procession, with hearse and mourners, entered—the young *Comminister* read the service over the grave, and the whole multitude in the open air joined in a grand solemn hymn.

At the same time, another large company were receiving the Communion in one part of the church. At half-past ten, when I entered, an imposing spectacle met the eye. The spacious church, with the two tiers of galleries, its long seats and aisles, was crowded to the full; the chandeliers and little pronged supports black with hats, and every available standing-place filled—all by the peasants alone. I saw but one European bonnet and gentleman's coat in the house. It was a vast array of stalwart working-men, and ruddy, sun-burnt women, in their parti-colored, picturesque costume. All were there—the nursing child and the hobbling old man—no one was left at home. I saw many women suckling their children. The men took the seats first; those who stood up in the aisles were women. Some of the mothers were feeding their infants with onions. As each person entered, he stopped a moment, covered his face, and made the silent prayer. After a little time, a hymn was commenced by the congregation—a monotonous, melancholy kind of chant. The organ was a powerful one, but it was almost drowned in the surges of sound which rolled up from the vast assembly. This was continued a long time—through some thirty or forty verses; while in it all, mingled the cries of children, of whom there were so many in the church. At length, the clergyman, in black robes, ascended the pulpit; a short, apparently extempore prayer was uttered, and the sermon was read. There was profound attention through the whole audience. After it, a quartette was sung with beautiful effect; and with another long chant and some reading of Scriptures, the assembly dispersed—many standing without to admire the new crown just placed on the Byzantine-like tower; others gathering in knots, to discuss business and village affairs.

My friends computed that there were *seven thousand* persons present in the church, and this on no unusual occasion.

The people have evidently a reverential and devotional disposition, and the degree of self-government granted to each church, strengthens the interest of the members in it. I was impressed in seeing the audience, with the wonderful opportunities granted to the Swedish clergy for influence over the peasants. In such remote provinces, they are almost the sole guides and directors; there are no nobles, or judges, or governors here, and every Sunday, they have these vast audiences, upon which to impress humane and liberal, or religious sentiments. The Swedes are plainly susceptible to oratory; and there never was such a field for a great Reformer as Sweden is now. But who is there who will come forward to work it?

We are occupying the lower rooms of the Parsonage—large, pleasant rooms in one of the houses; above us are the saloons for company. On the other side of the square, is the kitchen and servants' house, and on still another side, the house for the pastor's family. The doors are all open, and in the kitchen department, I observed a number of the poor peasants taking food ; in the pastor's saloon a little table is bounteously filled, from which we are to take and eat, wherever we can find a seat. A glass of whisky, and bread and anchovies, are offered to each first, as usual. A number of persons come in and join us in the meal. The servants bring in course after course, in most liberal measure. After the dinner, we start for a long walk by the pleasant lake, while the Prost goes to the parish-meeting.

Sunday evening, at the pastor's, is the *fête*-evening always, but more especially now, as they wish to celebrate the crowning of the Church tower.

The large guest-saloons are thrown open, as well as the state bed-chambers, and by six o'clock the guests begin to come. The gentlemen are in one room, and the ladies in another, and as each gentleman enters, he shakes hands with the pastor, and then with every other gentleman ; and then goes through the ladies' rooms, bowing to each, very low and formally, seldom shaking hands. The ladies have a similar ordeal—each one bowing and courtesying all through our saloon, to every gentleman whom she knows. It must be no joke to come late to a Swedish *levée.*

I am standing near a lively young gentleman, who entertains me with descriptions of each new arrival. "There! you see that handsome man with white gloves—that's our great singer, from Stockholm! He led the quartette this morning. But there's something for you Democrats!—you observe a very tall man in long peasant's clothes—a Bonder—with hair parted in the middle?"

"Yes. Do peasants associate with the upper classes so?"

"Certainly. He is a delegate to the *Riksdag* (Parliament). A good-natured fellow—rather weak though—the nobles lead him by the nose. He lost his election once on account of it, and another was chosen, who was so much worse, that they were glad to keep this man."

"But who are those two men in peasant's clothes, near the door?" I said.

"Oh they!—they are the *héros du jour*. Don't you see how every one shakes hands with them? How awkward the poor devils look! They are the workmen who put the crown on the spire at last. *Dom Prosten* (our host) is almost ready to hug them—how he claps them! He is a democrat for you!—But there!—you see!—Captain S——, the gentleman with the moustache, he doesn't shake hands with them. He is a noble, you know. Herr V. and N., and all the burgers do at once.

"It's a singular thing," he added, "those poor fools are hardly intelligible to a Stockholmer. I suppose you could make nothing of their dialect. I know their jargon now, I have been so much among them. The Prost does say though, that it's more like the old Norse than any other language now used. They have a diabolical drawl. But you snuff, do you not? No?" He sneezed, and several "*God bless yous, and wälbekommet*" at once were earnestly uttered, to which he bowed.

"Did the pastor have the crown put up?" I inquired. "Ack!—no. It was all the peasants, it is their Church, you know. But there is a beauty for you! Have you such women in America?" A light graceful figure—blonde golden hair wound over the head—blue eyes—features very regular—the expression so animated and sweet, and the manner singularly kind and genial. Her dress, a white full dress, as for a dance. "It is Fröken C——." I told my companion I found the Swedish ladies of the middle classes, as if somewhat depressed or kept in the background, and the men not especially attentive to them. "You have right," said he, "it is so too much, but this charming creature is of a higher family. There again!—there's another of these *Bönder*, you have such an interest for—a fine manly fellow. He is the *Nämndeman*."

The *Nämndeman* is a sort of a juryman. In every village, the Courts of Justice are composed of a Judge and twelve jurymen, who sit at each session of the court, for many years.* The Judge always determines the sentence, unless the jurymen are unanimous against him; in that case, they can reverse the decision of the court. The jurymen are not paid: it is a public duty for every peasant. No other class has anything to do with it. The Courts are called *Ting*—the old name for popular assemblies, one meets so often in the sagas, and the Scandinavian history.

I was sitting by the pastor afterwards and asked him

* The original idea of this Jury seems to have been that it should represent the natural equity of a case as opposed to technical law. "Because," says an ancient judge, quoted by Geijer, "all cases which may arise, cannot be set down in a law-book, but where no written law is to be found, men must borrow their decisions from that natural

if he had ever known an instance of the jurymen reversing the sentence of the judge. "Oh, yes;" he answered, "there was a *Ting* in T—— village lately; a criminal case came before them. The judge felt himself obliged by the evidence to decide against the accused, though it was plain he felt that he was innocent; the Nämndeman at once reversed the decision. Still, they are very often a stupid set. I remember hearing of a Nämndeman in P——, who went home and threw himself down with groans on his bed, "Well, we have done a business to-day!" "What is it?" his wife asked, anxiously. "We have sentenced so and so to be hung!" "*Ack* God! and what for?" "That's what I should like to know!" he answered, groaning terribly.

Generally, the judge does everything, and they only listen; but here's the Delegate! Here!—come! An American—let me introduce you!"

The Delegate being at a loss for conversation, took the opportunity to inquire for a Herr L., who had fled to America with some stolen property. "You have very many men there whom we are glad to be free of!" I told him, we could not prevent, of course, the vagabonds of Europe from taking refuge there; and then passed into conversation with some others standing near. The man was a boor by nature, evidently—and all the Riksdagar could not change him.

law which God hath implanted in our hearts and brains, therefore the law-book saith in many places touching doubtful questions, let the jury of the hundred (or næmdemen) examine this!"—(*Geijer*, p. 85.)

I was next presented to the Nämndeman—a very sensible man. The pastor said, "You take an interest in Swedish politics. We have still another thing, as good as the *Ting*, you may not have heard of it—our *By-ordning*. It is a sort of assembly, chosen by the peasants, which takes charge of the moral matters of the village—a sort of half-juridical affair. They try and punish for petty offences against morality and law. I am afraid, we shall lose it, though; it is being attempted now to merge it into the Courts. Indeed, it has no legal existence—but there's Lieutenant S——. I must meet him!"

A friend has since given me an instance of the operation of this *By-ordning*, somewhat characteristic. A Dalecarlian maiden returned in the autumn from the usual summer's labor in the Capital, and was observed to have a gold ring on her finger. A circumstance so remarkable attracted the attention of the other peasants; she was questioned, and replied that it had been given her by a gentleman with whom she was working. The people doubted, and finally she was brought before the Town Council, which, after an examination, decided that she should be kept confined by her father, and whipped every day until she should confess. The father carried out the sentence, and at length she confessed that she had stolen it from this gentleman. The ring was at once sent back to the owner, with the message, that the girl would be prosecuted if he desired, but for the good fame of Dalecarlia, they hoped he would drop it, which of course he did.

Punch in small glasses had now been brought in, and

the pastor, with the little cup in his hand, stepped out among the company, called for silence, and said, "My friends! I am happy to offer a toast. It is the health of the two brave peasants who have given us the opportunity of holding this feast; we all saw their daring on Saturday. To the Bönder V—— and T——, who put the crown finally on the tower! *Skăl!*"

Every one went forward and clinked his glass with those of the peasants, saying, *Skăl!*

"*Prosten* likes the peasants," said a gentleman near me, "and they like him! Hear him; he speaks of you!" and I heard him telling, in his hearty tones, the different groups, "Ha! the Amerikanare called the meeting *storartaat* (grand) this morning. Ha! ha! It is only a spectacle to him—and a grand one!"

Another toast. "My friends, I have another health for us to drink. By Providential chance, a gentleman is present with us this evening from a distant country—*America.* Sweden and the New World are widely separated by oceans, and they have different forms of society, but they are united in religion and in political liberty. We have shown that science, and arts, and freedom, and prosperity can grow under a Monarchy, and they have proved it equally under a Republic! I propose the health of our American friend. May he have from God a prosperous journey! *Skăl!*"

Next the healths of the Delegate and Nämndeman were drunk, then of the ladies and of various gentlemen, and now began the dance. The great saloon shook with the tread of the dancers. The waltz was the favorite, danced with great spirit and life. The Comminister who spoke at the grave, and led the communion in the morning, was now moving cheerily among the waltzers, though I think not dancing himself.

After the dance, some songs were sung—mostly from the people's melodies. They were singularly plaintive and wild. The "*Necken*" is one of the most popular. The religious quartette was also given again. At ten, we all went over informally to the house on the other side of the square, and found a large table prepared in one saloon. The ladies helped themselves first, and then the gentlemen—afterwards separating into different rooms.

It was one of the hearty old Scandinavian feasts. Dish after dish was brought in—meats, puddings, game, pancakes, milk-soup, salad, *gröt* (or rye mush) and milk, fish, cakes and creams; and everybody fell to with vigor. Nothing was drunk at the meal, except the unfailing prelude of a glass of whisky, until late, when the servants brought in a great silver flagon, with curious ornamenting, foaming with beer. This was a gift from a former parish to our pastor. It was passed around, each drinking by turn. At twelve, the company began to disperse, the hearty old *Prost* giving his vigorous clasp to each hand, with "*God Natt!*" "Guds frid vare med eder! God bless thee!" Warm-hearted old man! May his great ruddy face still be gleaming friendlily on the poor and rich in Dahlarna!

FAHLUN AND SOUTHERN DALECARLIA.

Our journey continued the next day towards the south. The driver was the owner of the horses, and a very respectable-looking squire. The country along the road, even to the Wester Dal, was a pleasant, fertile district, and he pointed us out many good fields, which belonged to himself. The crops, as usual, were rye, oats, potatoes, and grass. We made slow progress, owing to horses not being ready at the post-stations, and did not reach FAHLUN till five o'clock. The approach was through a desolate country filled with slag, and breathing out sulphurous smoke, showing the neighborhood of the copper-mines, which stretch for miles under ground. The first streets were long rows of little houses for the miners' families, very dirty and impudent little children playing in front—justifying the popular reputation of Fahlun for a wretched population.

The town was filled with sulphurous odors, and vegetation seemed much dwarfed or killed through the whole neighborhood by the works in the mines.

THE MINES.

We first went to the edge of the immense excavation, where a great slide had been, throwing open, as the books say, some thousand feet of the mine. No work was going on in this. Our guide brought us dresses and old hats, to protect from the drippings of the mine, and we commenced the descent, he holding a lighted torch, made of small pine links bound together by a copper ring.

The first passage was simply a dark stairway, with a banister. After fifty or sixty fathoms of this, we began deep descents by ladders, down through one dark pit after another, then into galleries, glittering with ore under the torch and dripping with moisture. Our guide stopped us occasionally, to take us to the edge of some black chasm, and throw off fragments of the burning torch. We could see the pieces flash and glimmer, and hear their fall, at great depths below. There were various historical chambers, too, to be shown: "Carl Johan's," where the King and Queen had a brilliant dinner, and where his autograph is still preserved on the wall, and "Prince Oscar's," and others of older date, hollowed out of the solid rock.

We descended hundreds of fathoms, and followed the gloomy galleries for miles, only occasionally seeing torches and meeting the solitary inhabitants of these dark caverns—yet we did not traverse a twentieth part of the mine. This mine dates far back in its history, even to the eleventh century. Its produce, which has much fallen off in modern times, in 1853, was 4,277 *skeppund*, or about 1,710,000 pounds.

There is a mining-school here, where engineering and chemistry, and other natural sciences, are taught.

It is thought that the railroad now being constructed between Gefle and Fahlun, will be of great advantage to the latter place, in affording a more convenient transit for the metal to the coast. For this road, the company borrowed of the State, $400,000.

The population of Fahlun in 1854 was 4,522.

As we were in a hurry, and had a good comfortable travelling-carriage, we pushed on the same night towards Sala, reaching it in the next afternoon. This district is famous for its silver mines, of which we visited one, about a mile southwest of the city. This mine dates back historically to 1187, A.D. Its produce in 1850, was 3,835 marks. The mining population seems a superior one to that of Fahlun. The whole number of inhabitants in Sala, is 3,208. Between this point and Westeräs, is a rich farming country, with very substantial farm-houses. Westeräs is a well-built town, with some interesting public buildings, and a valuable Library. Population in 1853, 4,027.

The impressions left on my mind by this tour through Dalecarlia, are, that in no country of Europe can a peasantry so independent, honest, and virtuous be found.

This cumbrous Constitution, though blocking now every useful reform, has at least preserved the peasant in his ancient rights. Having his own House of Representatives, his own peculiar privileges, his costume, his church, and above all, his local self-government, he has not been crushed by the superior privileges of the nobility, or humiliated by mingling with classes more cultured and refined than his own. He is proud that he is a *Bonde*. Each man has an independent bearing. There has evidently been no serfdom or feudalism here. Yet this very isolation and pride of class has kept the Dalecarlians ignorant and superstitious. The country needs, what all Sweden needs, railroads and schools. Its mineral products and lumber should have an easier market, and the ingenious talents of the people be employed on more profitable manufactures than they are now. The first interest for this province is Education. Give such an intelligent population as the Dalecarlians, good common schools, and they will be able to accomplish anything. There is excellent stuff in the character of the people. The country is the New England of Sweden. As in all Sweden, much of the progress of the people will depend on the clergymen. This body has, as I have already stated, an astonishing power in this remote province. If they were true to their duties, and had ideas at all corresponding to the progress of the age, the Swedish peasantry would speedily be in a very different condition. We believe, however, that more is being done for genuine improvement in Dalecarlia, than in any other rural district of Sweden.

CHAPTER XXV.

VINGÄKER.

In the central part of Sweden, near Lake Hjelmaren, is one of the characteristic counties—Vingäker: a land of lakes and groves and rich fields, showing some of the best agriculture in North Europe. My objects here led me more among the gentry and the large proprietors. The peasantry yet preserve the national costume in the centre of the country, but they are by no means so independent or well-informed as the Dalecarlians: the explanation for which lies, no doubt, in their tenure of land, and their relation to their landlords, as we shall hereafter see. I attended one large Church at K——, where the Bonders were all dressed like a respectable farmers' audience at home, in black coats with gloves, though the women had white head-tire instead of bonnets.

S——Y.

This estate lies in the midst of a pine forest, approached by the roughest roads, which wind around among pretty lakes and ponds. The first indication of its neighborhood was given by some cleared ground, and a neater class of peasants' houses. Then came a Church, sheltered in a beech grove, and a school, and then an avenue under old trees. The house of the proprietor was a long, two-story stone house, painted a grave color, with smaller houses on each side of the usual square, and a pretty flower-plot in the middle. On the other side was a handsome garden, with very rich dahlias and brilliant flowers, laid out in terraces somewhat formally ; beyond, meadows and corn-fields stretched out to the edge of the forest. Again, on the wings, were the conservatories for fruit, and the stables hidden by shrubbery; and still farther on could be seen the rich masses of the park trees. A liveried servant came to the carriage, and took in my letter and a card. I was shown into a saloon hung with old portraits. Almost immediately a lady entered, who welcomed me in French, most sweetly, expressing her regret for the absence of her husband. Nothing could exceed the grace and simple-heartiness of her manner. She led me to the drawing-rooms, and entered at once into lively conversation.

The family is one of the old historic families of Sweden. Sir C. has the reputation of being among the most cultured public men of the day, and has filled many offices with honor.

Everything in the house and surrounding, showed a much higher class of tastes than I had yet seen in Sweden. The furniture was not costly, but the walls were covered with paintings, which any royal gallery of Europe might covet.

In the drawing-room where I sat were original Correggios, Wouvermans, Guidos, Claudes, and Salvator Rosas. In the next drawing-room were celebrated modern works; and in the billiard-room, some animal pieces from Rubens. Exquisite bits of statuary from Bissen and modern sculptors, were set about here and there; and in one saloon was the unfailing ornament of rich Swedish houses, the cabinets with curious old china. The library was a gem, such as in our democratic societies an individual can seldom possess—old valued Bibles, travels and works of art issued by governments, of great value; books of costly and rare engravings, and works on philosophy and science and history in all modern tongues, were in the collection, the owner speaking with fluency nearly all the European languages. I was glad to see that the best of American literature was there.

I asked Lady C. if the ladies read much of our authors. "No," she answered, "not much—only your *novelistes.* I am so glad," she added, "that those detestable French *romans* are no more the mode. We get now, in the English and American writings, all the amusement we sought in the French, with a healthy moral tone. I remember when I was young, nothing was read but French, but now I dread to put a French author of light literature in my daughter's hands. The German is not much read, except by the scholars. We find their romances very *ennuyantes.*"

I inquired, what American authors were most read. "Madame Stowe, of course, first; then much now that authoress of stories—I forget her name—Wide World and Queechy. You know we have now Danish translations of all these, and of M. Emerson and Hawthorne. Ah! what a sombre *génie* is that man—do you know him? Your poet, too, who has translated Tegnèr—Longfellow."

I told her that we had other translations now of Tegnèr—of his Frithiof's Saga, which was greatly admired. She seemed much interested, but said "I have not seen the translation: still it is not possible to translate that. You must lose the fine quality."

According to the universal Swedish custom in the upper classes, fruit is brought into the drawing-room about six o'clock—grapes, peaches, and apricots from the conservatories—and then a cup of tea. The party was a most interesting one, as we sat in the twilight—Lady X., whose face still shows, under traces of many sorrows, the noble beauty for which she is distinguished; several spirited young ladies, and some fresh, active-looking young gentlemen, who have had, evidently, a thorough manly education.

Something in Lady X.'s feeling gave a sober tone to the conversation. The ladies spoke of the position of the Swedish woman in society, and how little she exerts the influence which belongs to her. "We learn from Mam'lle Bremer what your ladies, Monsieur B., do in America. But here very few feel the responsibility. We are content to enjoy ourselves, and to be admired. Yet, mon Dieu! what multitudes of poor people are around us! Frederika Bremer has truly labored to give occupation to our ladies, and I hope she may succeed!"

I asked if they had all read her Travels in America. "Oh, yes," the young ladies answered in English; "but tell us, be there so many wonderful people in America? Every one seems a hero to her to be!"

"It's horribly dull," muttered one of the young men. "I never could read it!"

* * * "Have you remarked the *similarités* between our languages?" said one of the ladies, "especially in the Scotch!"

"He must call for the cork-screw in the next hotel," said one of the young men, alluding to the phrase, "Give me the cork-screw" ("*Gif mig kork skrufven*"), a well-known common phrase to Swedish and English. We then recalled the common words: "Bra' hus" (*bra hus*), "reek" (*rök*), "timber" (*timmer*); "Come, let us go!" (*Kom lät oss gä*), "potatoes" (*potatis*), "speer (ask)" (*spira*), "room" (*rum*), and numbers of others.

I asked about the Danish and Norwegian—whether they understood or spoke these.

"No," said they; "we speak them not often, because the Danes and Norrmans (Norwegians) comprehend us and we comprehend them, when we converse."

The conversation turned on the Danish literature, and the celebrated Reformer, Kirkengaard. "That is a spirit noble and pure," said Lady X. "Perhaps he went too far in condemning all the church, because his branch was lifeless, but he had the true fire within him. I think he has done us much good in Sweden."

"Still, mother, was he not too extreme?"

"Yes, he was; but the sins of his church drove him to it. But, Monsieur B., shall we not have a little music?"

Some beautiful national songs were sung, and exquisite pieces played from the German classical music. During the playing, the physician of the family estate came in, and the Superintendent of the Forests, both residing on the property.

We conversed together of the mode adopted by Baron X. in cultivating his estate. It appears that he has put the cultivation, as much as possible, in the hands of his tenants, not attempting himself much of the labor of agriculture. "You must know," said one of the young gentlemen, speaking in German, "the Baron has given up for ever his *jus patronatum*—that is, the peasants can choose their own clergyman now. Before, he was the patron, and had the sole power. You saw the church and school, as you entered the avenue. He built both; but he thinks it better for the peasants to have this right of election, and thus far we have had no trouble. *Leider!* (alas!) it is not always so!"

I asked about the transmission of the estate. "S——y is a *fidei commiss*," he replied; "but that you may not understand. You have a word—*ja das ist-es—primogeniture*—the oldest son must have it all, and so keep the property together." I asked, if he was obliged to support the other brothers and sisters. They answered that he was not; but still the usual custom required that he should give assistance to the poorer members of the family, and beside, the father commonly bequeathed his personal property to the other children. The law gives a peculiar authority and privilege to the eldest son; and it struck me often that the son assumes something of a paternal or authoritative relation to his brothers and sisters. These gentlemen talking with me were all noblemen, but their views on the Constitution I found more liberal than those of the peasants. They were in favor of widening the suffrage, and of lessening the privileges of the elder branches of the noble families. "We find it absurd, Herr B.," said even the young heir himself of this estate, "that the *caput familiæ* (the eldest son) should alone have the right of sitting in the Riks ständ. He may be a stupid dolt, or he may not have the leisure, and tnen he must give or sell his seat.

"Many of us are in favor of doing away with the whole cursed system of the Four Houses, and having a simple Parliament of Two Houses. It takes an age for any liberal bill to get through. The parsons like one thing, and the Bonders another, and the citizens and nobles are against them both perhaps. The conservatives with us are the peasants and the clergy. Those parsons lead the Bonders by the nose. We might have had good railroads and schools years ago, if it had not been for the *verfluchte* (cursed) stupidity of those Bauer! *Sacra-ment!* it makes one groan!"

I mentioned the instance of Capt. B., who owned a fine estate, and yet had no vote.

"*Ja wohl!*—there it is! Such a wretched arrangement! The men of property and intelligence shut out, and the clod-breakers voting! There ought to be a law admitting all to suffrage, in some one class, who own land. It is just as stupid in the cities. There is Doctor S. and Prof. N., you know them—they cannot vote, because they are not Bürgers (citizens or members of a guild). *Bien!*—it is a slow world here!"

"Pardon, Messieurs! *Souper!*" said Lady X., taking my arm, as the servant opened the doors. The customs here were much the same as in other classes, except that the meal was simpler. Bread and butter, glasses of milk and pan-cakes, were the whole, we helping ourselves generally, without aid from the servants. Every body was in high spirits, and much fun was going on.

The most remarkable thing to an American was, the evident contrast between the ladies of the party and the ladies one meets generally in the middle classes. A certain expectation or graceful habit of receiving little attentions, as if their position to the other sex were long secured; and a style of information and conversation, even if not indicating talent, yet showing an habituation to world-subjects—these were the distinguishing qualities, and which at once brought me back to our intelligent American society. This contrast in Swedish society, is by no means so apparent between the men; indeed, the gentlemen of the middle classes are superior to any in the kingdom in thorough education, and quite equal in refined habits. I was impressed here with the influence of *quiet*. This gem of a home, placed in the midst of forests and mountains, containing in itself the influences which educate and ennoble, had shed a certain light of peace and repose on its inmates. There was no vulgar strain after effect, or restlessness, or hankering for the excitements of cities, but that species of calmness which arises from long habituation to nature and to a residence in the same home. It may have been fancy, but these seemed to me the excelling traits over our American homes. Afterwards, in a walk in the park with one of the ladies, I spoke of this, and asked what they did in the winter ; whether they ever found it dull. " No never," she said. " We ride in släda—what call you it ?—sleighs, and we have little dance amid the neighbors—you know there are *some* neighbors, and we read and talk much, and sew, and have musique every evening. Then we do go sometime to Stockholm, but I am fatigued of it. There we dance every night, and go to Court, and to suppers and balls, and I am glad when it is over. We go not again soon."

"Yes : you have reason. There is nothing like the old home. I know every old tree here, and the lake there, and the walks, ever since I can remember I was here ; and there are the same peoples, the servants and gardeners, and my dog and my pony are almost so old as I. Yes—I do hope I will never leave it !"

The hours for retiring seem very early in Sweden, at least in country-houses ; we have supper usually at eight, and bid good night at nine. Then with breakfast at half-past eight or nine, there is a long night for all. These sufficient rests in their chambers must add much to this effect of repose on the character. My fancy impressed this all abundantly on me, and the long calm line of historic faces which looked on me in the neighboring chamber, as I entered mine, did not lessen it. They seemed to say, "No vulgar activities, no modern restlessnesses here ! They do not enter. Be calm ! You are in the shadow of the Past !"

And in the stillness of the night, sunk in the comfortable

bed, the musical voice of the night-watchman, who patrols the estate, seemed to strengthen the security.

"Gud bevare värt
Hus och land
Frän eld och brand!
Klockan elfva slagen!"

"God keep
Both house and land
From ill and brand!
Eleven o'clock
Is striking!"

CHAPTER XXVI.

THE MANORS OF SWEDEN.

There is something impressive in all the northern nations, in their respectful salutations morning and evening; the "Good night!" "May you sleep well!" or "Good morning!" and the almost anxious inquiries, "Have you slept well?"—forms which every one makes a religious duty to observe. The "God bless you!" when you sneeze, is a part of the same. This is a healthy race and it makes much of the body: these formalities come from times when there was truly a terror by night, and to see the morning safely was something for gratitude. Then, as Emerson says, each one comes to the others every morning, as a "new stranger from a distant clime:" that is, without straining the impulse, there is an element of genuine Courtesy in these trivialities—a coming out of one's personality to recognize the personality of another. And it is just such petty habits that tend to cultivate one part of politeness; they aim to guard and to respect personality. The higher part—of self-sacrifice,—these are merely a path towards.

Our breakfast again was a cheerful, pleasant meal—very much like an English breakfast, with tea, coffee and cold meats; our hostess showing us the same peculiarly kind courtesy as before. Liveried servants were in waiting.

Afterwards we walked out in the park, which was a picturesque grove of old trees, with a lake, but not well kept. The whole estate consists of about 20,000 Tunland (about 15,000 acres) much of it in forest.

V———o.

My hostess kindly forwarded me in her own travelling carriage to her neighbor, Herr T., to whom I had letters. His position, again, is peculiar to such a country as Sweden. A large proprietor, on an estate which he and his fathers have occupied for generations—a gentleman, much travelled, speaking many languages, yet an alien still in political rights. The property was a beautiful one, much more so than those of the nobility; placed on the banks of a large lake, with groves on each side, and terraces of beautiful flowers and shrubbery running down to the water's edge. It is wonderful how the dahlias grow here—such pure rich colors I never saw on them in America.

The approach to the house was through a fine avenue of beeches and oaks. The house was in the usual style—of two stories, with a great number of rooms, opening into each other on the ground floor. The furniture, very rich, with a few paintings—no carpets, and the flooring, parquette. The windows had a beautiful outlook over the lake.

Herr T. showed me over the property. In one part was a school which he had founded, as the other proprietors have done. The peasants' houses seemed very comfortable—better than those in Dalecarlia. T. says that the people are now in process of transition from *Bauer* to gentlemen, and they feel very self-important.

In the garden, I noticed an old scraggy oak, much decayed, and said something of it.

"Ach!" said he in German, "there is a story about that. It is a *habitation-tree.** I can't get it cut down!"

"*So!* How do you mean?"

"There has been a long time a superstition about that tree among the Bauer, that whoever should cut it down or injure it, should certainly suffer harm—I suppose from the *Troll* or fairies. When I came into the property, after my father's death, I ordered the tree to be cut down, as it is in the way of my garden, and looks, as you see, rather unsightly. But no one would do it. I tried one and another, and at last a young Bauer attempted it. He worked awhile one day, and the next day fell sick. I induced another, and after a little, he became ill and finally died. The rumor was spread through the whole country, and I was much blamed by the *Bonders*—so that finally I gave it up—and there you see the tree! The Bauer find the fairy-rings† now on the grass often!"

* The habitation-tree (boträd), in the heathen times of Scandinavia, was thought to be inhabited by a certain elf, who would protect it and reward those who took care of it.

† Luxuriant grass made by the dancing of the elves—the *cynosurus cœruleus*. Hear Olaus Magnus on this:

"OF THE NIGHT DANCES OF THE FAIRIES AND GHOSTS.

"Also travellers in the night, and such as watch their flocks and

I told him I wished we had such tree-fairies in America. They would find most humble worshippers there.

* * * * I made some inquiries and remarks about his political position. "Yes, that is true," he said. "In that sense, I am not a citizen. The *Bauer*, whose cabins you saw, can vote, but I cannot. You know why. I am not of noble birth—at least Swedish, and I am not a Bauer. It makes little difference to me, though. I have my own affairs, and do not care for politics."

"Why not be a Bauer?" I said.

"*Gott bewahr!* No; it would be disagreeable to them and to me." I wondered the country had not demanded a change. "*Ja! wir sind langsam!* We are slow—slow, here! It must be changed, though, before many years."

In the evening, I was presented to the ladies. The cur-

herds are wont to be compassed about with many strange apparitions As King Hotherus (so Saxo reports) following three nymphs to their caves, obtained a girdle of victory from them: yet sometimes they make so great and deep impression into the earth, that the place they are used to, being only burnt round with extream heat, no grass will grow up there. The inhabitants call this night-sport of these monsters, the dance of fayries; of which they hold this opinion, that the souls of those men that give themselves to corporeal pleasures and make themselves, as it were, slaves unto them, and obey the force of their lusts, violating the laws of God and men, when they are out of their bodies, and wander about the earth. In the number whereof they think those men to be, who even in these our days, are wont to come to help them, to labour in the night, and to dress horses and cattle; as I shall show hereafter in this very book, concerning the ministry of the devils."

rent language was French—as is usual, a French *gouvernante* residing in the family, though there were no children. In inquiring about the pastors, and their relation to the people, I found the same feeling which seems almost universal through the middle and upper classes—of utter distrust and dissatisfaction towards their religious teachers. They spoke highly of a gentleman (Captain H.), who had been building a little Chapel for his workmen, and laboring among the *Läsarne.* "He may be a fanatic, but he is sincere, Monsieur! But these men—they have no belief! It is an affair of the pocket. Look at Doctor S., at N. He is known for an Infidel, and says openly, the Bible is a myth, but still preaches and gets his tithes. Our pastor here, is nothing but a very genial gentleman. He has his 12,000 riks ($3,000) a year, and that is all he cares about. He knows no more of the spiritual matters of his people, than if he were a thousand miles away. There is a droll story between him and the peasants lately—they bear him little love, you understand. He demanded of the *Socken-stämma* double windows for winter, in his parsonage. They refused to supply them. He argued and threatened, and at last had to get them himself—at the same time saying, that when he went away, he should take them with him. They replied, that there would be no need; for when he went, he would go where there would be no necessity for double windows!—implying they should never get rid of him till he went to a rather warm place!"

* * * * I was installed at night in a very comfortable guest-house, and the next morning was driven over

by the gentleman himself, with a handsome pair of horses, to Count B. of S. Castle. We stopped on our way to see a clergyman, to whom I had a letter—Dr. X. He speaks English perfectly—a most jovial, sociable gentleman. He is said to be very old, but springs about like a young man—attributes it all to his "never having had any regular habits!"—called his vicar "the old man," though he is ten years younger than himself. He took us to his Church, one of the famous churches of Vingäker, having an assembly often of three thousand people. There was a catechisation going on of school-children, in the vestry-room—the same dull, mechanical teaching of so-called "Religion," which one finds everywhere in Sweden. Dr. X. is something of a scholar, and is still engaged in literary works; he gave me a new derivation of "Viking."

* * * * * *

Castle S. is famous through Sweden, and I only intended visiting it, as one of the public sights, as I had no letter to the Count and I thought my friend would not be on such terms with him, as to introduce me familiarly. But to my surprise instead of delivering us up to a servant, the Countess herself, with the most simple and sweet courtesy, showed us slowly through the apartments where the pictures were. A most choice collection, gems of art and historic association. Rembrandt, Claude, Lely, Domenichino, Guido, Correggio, Salvator Rosa, with fresh modern works from Swedish artists. The common drawing-rooms and saloons for the family were set with these beautiful adornments—works whose feeling and beauty must grow in impression on one, as do glimpses at home of exquisite aspects of nature, seen day by day. Each room had a little catalogue of the paintings. We visited beside the conservatories and orangery, and finally the great library. The Countess courteously invited and even pressed us to dinner, which we declined. The library must be one of the richest private collections in North Europe. It seems in bad order just now, though the Count has a scientific librarian constantly employed. After much searching we found one of the books I was in quest of—the first Bible (probably) printed in Sweden, bearing date "Upsala, 1541." There were some splendid collections of engravings and travels—the "Voyage to Iceland and Scandinavia," in which M. Marmier took part, issued by the French Government. I think the large editions of Humboldt's Travels were there, and other works of the kind, which usually only National Libraries can possess. If any connoisseur in sketches should visit Sweden, he should certainly inquire for the "*Teckningar om Asarna*, by Wahlbom" (1834.) They show great power.

I found a fair representation of American Literature—among others, Hildreth's History. I made out, at the Count's request, a brief list of our best late works in history and politics, for the new additions to his shelves. So much time was spent over this rare collection, that we accepted per force the cordial invitation to dine.

I was shown to one of the state bedrooms to dress. Each room is numbered on the door. The style of furniture is almost palatial. The dinner was more like our city dinners of style, than any I have yet seen. It is the only table in Sweden where I have observed more than two kinds of wine. The table was beautifully decorated with flowers and fruit. Here, as elsewhere, the old Scandinavian custom of the whisky and bread and butter and cheese first—the ladies being helped before the gentlemen. Even the children had their slices: though very few took the whisky. There was no other company present—a family party, with the teachers, governesses and physician only. Three servants were in waiting. The lady helped the soup, and the servants carved the meat, and then a platter with slices, after the German style, was handed to each person. This is certainly the true mode for a dinner-party. It is remarkable how much better all the Europeans understand this art of eating and dining, than we do. One is often at home so bored with questions of, "Is your meat right?" "Will you have it well done?" "Will you have celery?" etc., etc., that all conversation is blocked. You want good eating, but you want it as it were unconsciously—as a side-dish—an *entremet* to the conversation. The intercourse is the first thing; all else is subservient to it. Whatever turns away from free, easy conversation, is a defect in your dinner, and of course bad cookery or unsavory viands do that. They distract you, disagree with you and annoy your hostess. First, good nourishing dishes, well cooked—which means always simply cooked; then easy attendance, like this Swedish mode, which does not interfere with your talk; and—assuming, of course, that you have an intelligent company—you have the components of a dinner-party.

There seems to be no toasting in the Swedish parties, such as I saw in Norway. Indeed, I never saw wine-tables where so little is drank. The most seem only to sip. Sometimes the host asks to drink with a guest, but the latter is not obliged, as he was ten years ago, to empty his glass. At the close, the host fills his glass, looks around, and the others who choose, fill theirs, and with a bow to him drink or touch their lips, and rise. The company stand a moment with folded hands, and then each takes his lady back to the drawing-room. There the guests bow and shake hands with the hostess, thanking her for her hospitality. Coffee is always served after dinner.

In our conversations, we spoke of the clergy, and I found the same serious dissatisfaction with them here as everywhere. The Count thought that the support of the clergyman should come from the State, and then he would not be falling into these eternal bickerings with his people for every dollar of his stipend. It appears, he is entitled to certain *pro ratâ* portions of the produce of his parishioners, and also expects gifts to a large amount; so that, from this man he claims his one-tenth of corn, from that his one-sixteenth of barley, from another his two chickens or leg of mutton, or eggs, or flax. Where there is love to the pastor, these all come in gladly and easily; but where there is not, he must be continually on the lookout, lest he lose something. When a poor creature comes, inquiring what he shall do to be saved, his first thought may be, "You owe me seven bushels of rye!" or, "Have you paid in your proportion of mutton yet?" and he *must* follow up each of these little perquisites, or he will lose the major part of his salary. "Monsieur B.," said the Count, in French, very gravely, "*il y a un soif dans les cœurs du peuple*—there is a thirst in the hearts of the people for true Religion, and they cannot satisfy it with such teachers. The holy office becomes a means of support only; and the preachers are rendered covetous and greedy. We need a different mode of collecting their salary, and a different relation between the people and the pastor." The lady, too, with fewer words, expressed even deeper discontent at the state of the Church. I did not agree with their remedy, but did not discuss it. They spoke with much appreciation of the gentleman whom I was hoping soon to visit—Captain H. "He may be a Methodist (Läsare)," said the Count, "but he is a true Christian."

The estates of this family contain their tens of thousands of tenants. Countess B. had the sense which a true noblewoman should have, of her responsibility for the poor and ignorant under her control. I described to her the plan of our Industrial Schools in New York, and I think she saw that some such thing was necessary among the poorest peasantry here.

The parting with us was peculiarly graceful and kind. We drove to the estate of a gentleman to whom I had a letter, a man who has taken a prominent part in the modern history of Sweden.

COL. A——'S ESTATE.

It is a quaint old place, on a property which indefatigable agriculture, under-draining, clearing woods and careful sowing of crops have redeemed from the pine forest and swamp. The barns, with high peaked gables, were even more conspicuous than the house. This was long and low, and near it were some fine old trees. We entered an octagonal room hung full with pictures.

The Colonel was a dignified old gentleman, who received us with great hospitality—like many of the public men in this country, a man of various accomplishments. I have already visited a number of gentlemen, prominent in political life, who sketch and draw with talent—some of whose works are engraved, and command a good price. At Baron V.'s, I found the whole early history of Sweden, illustrated by his own hand, and already lithographed; the Sagas, too, had been represented by him, with great boldness and talent.

Such accomplishments, when one considers what those men have *done*, show a higher style of public men than one usually finds in America, or even in England.

Col. A. had a prominent part in the Revolution which overthrew the king, Gustavus IV. Adolphus

The Colonel again had some beautiful works of art—of great value. It is a wonder how these collections have been made in Sweden. Except in Vienna or Italy, there can be few collections more valuable in Europe.

My host showed me over his property ; the barns were large and well kept, but with nothing peculiar in the arrangements, except the great furnace under one for drying the grain. His crops are mainly wheat, rye, oats and grass, with large fields of turnips for cattle. In his stables, were some very fine Normandy horses, pure white, of large heavy frames. The prices, I think, were not very high for these ; If I understood aright, not more than two hundred and fifty dollars for a gelding of first quality. There were some other horses of English blood. Each horse had a separate little enclosure with a lock.

We found again a school and church, built by the landlord, for his tenantry.

I regretted extremely that my limited time kept me from making the nearer acquaintance of this gentleman. He impressed me as a true, modest, noble-spirited man, with whom only to meet, is something to be gratefully remembered.

CHAPTER XXVII.

THE COUNTRY GENTRY.

L——.—At this estate was a school, which I had greatly desired to visit, and as the proprietor was a remarkably intelligent gentleman, I spent a part of a day there very agreeably. Capt. H., again, is one of the non-voting proprietors, though very rich, and having a thousand tenants on his estate. The property is a beautiful one, far better kept, and with more natural advantages than the estates of the nobles, near by. The avenue was through rocks and old oaks. The houses, built in the usual form, low, and very neatly painted and begirt with flowers, were on the banks of a pretty lake; a rich, terraced flower-garden was in front. The saloons and the furniture seemed very costly and rich, though but few paintings were on the walls. As I saw in this case but little of my host's interior arrangements, I may take the liberty to speak here of the astonishing backwardness of the Swedes in practical conveniences.

There is hardly a house, palace, or cottage in all Sweden, with a bed-room bell, or a bath-room, or an outside bell, or speaking-tubes, or dumb-waiters, or any of the little modern labor-saving contrivances in American houses. If you go to a friend's house, you pull about the handle of the door, stumble in the hall, as hall-lights are equally discarded—rap your knuckles sore, and often at last go away, utterly baffled at arousing any one. In your own bed-room, you must often shout out of your window, to call any servant. If there is a bell in the hall, it communicates usually with the court-yard, and awakes the whole family and all the dogs of the neighborhood, if you ring it rashly. It excited great surprise when I said, that our city-houses in America, and the best in the country, had now as a necessity, their one or two bath-rooms, and hot and cold water in every bed-chamber. There are, at the present time, in Sweden, only four, or possibly *five* cities which burn gas—Gottenburg, Stockholm, Örebro, Norrköping, and I think Lund. Hardly one has good side-walks, and a day spent on foot in the streets is really torturing. The principal conveniences, as compared with those in American houses, are in the warming apparatus, which consists universally of a large brick stove, prettily covered with white porcelain. This, with little fuel, gives out a mild, equable heat when closed for the whole day, or open makes a cheerful fire, like the old-fashioned fire-side ; and however used, produces an infinitely better atmosphere than our furnaces, with their blasts of fiery air, destructive to brain and lungs.

There is also in the Swedish kitchens, a kind of roof over the range or stove, such as I have described in Norway, which carries off the odors and fume, so that one is not at once, on entering a friend's house, saluted with the exact components of the dinner, as in some of our houses at home.

Our host, Capt. U., walked about with me over his estate.

He has an extensive farm, with the usual crops. The barns were very large, with some fine cattle in the stables. Hearing me express an interest in the different costumes of the peasants, he said to one of his workmen, who was in the cattle-yard—" Hey ! Gustav, bring up three or four Bonders in wedding-dresses, to-morrow morning to the Hall, at seven o'clock. An American gentleman wants to see them !" The man looked puzzled, but took off his hat and said he would. We walked on to the park ; on the way, a peasant was about to drive from a cross-road over our path. It would just have been quite as convenient for us to wait for him, but my companion shouted sternly, " Thou !—hey ! Stop there !"—and the man stopped submissively, though sulkily. We were evidently not in Dalecarlia. " You have no idea, Herr B., of the *Dummheit* (stupidity) of these boors" said the Captain, in German. " I have tried to do something for their education, and I think I succeed, but it is slow work."

" Are there many free-holders among them, Captain ?" I asked. " No," said he, " the most belong to the land, and pay their rent in labor or in produce."

" You do not mean that they are serfs," said I.

" *Ach nein!*" he answered, " there are no *Leibeigene* (serfs) in Sweden—but these men, or rather their fathers, have, as it were, bought their lands on a perpetual rent. They are owners, as long as they pay their yearly *Abgabe* (tax), but if they fail to do that, the land falls back to me. I have some *Frälse* (regular tenants) beside, who have hired their land of me, and pay annual rents."

BONDERS.

It will be in place here, to mention distinctly the different classes of peasants or Bonders. It should be remembered that, as in Norway, there was strictly no feudal system in Sweden. At the end of the tenth century, Sweden appeared like a union of various confederations of freehold peasants under a nominal king at Upsala. The first confederation being of a hundred families or haerads; then of several haerads, making up lands or provinces; and finally of the provinces or nations to form a kingdom. The first Bonders were all owners of the soil, with certain obligations to the king: but gradually some of the weaker began to come under the power of the stronger, and free-holders became tenants. Then the large estates of the leaders and nobles were let out on a long lease to their followers; or the property of the crown was farmed by peasants who had been faithful to the king; so that at length, three very distinct classes of Bonders began to show themselves, along with smaller subdivisions.

First, The *Skatte* or free-holders, owners of their lands.

Second, The *Frälse Skatte*, or Bonders who have bought their properties of the owners, but who pay for them in an annual tax—holding them under a kind of perpetual lease.

Third, *Frälse*, or mere tenants, who pay for their farms annual rent of labor, produce, or money.

There are, besides, *Torpare*, or Bonders, who rent small pieces of land from other Bonders, and pay by labor; and there were formerly *Höferii*-Bonders, who were bound by law to give so much labor to the estate, and who were exposed to much cruelty.

I asked the captain, in our conversation, if it was not generally true that the tenant-Bonders were much inferior to those who owned their properties. He thought that they were. "The tendency among the Bonders everywhere now, is to own their farms. In many cases, large properties of the nobility have been bought up by the peasants. And as no new *fidei commiss'* (entailed properties) can be formed since the law of 1810, the large estates dwindle away. We do not find the small properties owned by the cultivators so good for the great improvements in agriculture," he added, "but they certainly make a better class of people—such as those you saw in Dalecarlia."

I asked how the nobility bore these encroachments of the peasants.

"It is something disagreeable," he answered, "but they can not help it. There is Baron P,—a gentleman I know, whose whole property of some thousands of acres is being bought up by the Bonders—and what is more, they get *Frälse Hemman* by this (*i. e.*, estates freed from the old military taxes). You know, since 1809, any one, noble or not, can own such tax-free properties, if he can buy them. So you see, we are equalizing ; but I am sorry to say, these Bonders become cursed aristocrats, and without the *Bildung* (culture) of the nobles. But here we are in the park !"

Our walk had brought us to a stately grove, of considerable extent, laid out on the banks of the lake, with walks, and arbors and boat-houses.

We spoke of his school for the peasants. "The truth is Herr B.," he said, "I was driven into that school by the stupidity of the clergy. We had too much catechism in the schools!"

I told him, my own observations confirmed what he said. Everywhere I found a mechanical drilling in the words of theology and certain dry facts of Biblical or Jewish history —and this was dignified with the name of "teaching religion," though it evidently had no more connection with religion than with topography. Religion was never taught in such memorizing, technical lessons—and indeed, I believed even the immortal freshness of those divine narratives might be dulled and begrimed to a child's mind, who was forever conning and repeating them, as laborious parts of a school exercise.

"I have opened a school," he said, "where some practical lessons shall take the place of a part of this learning and repeating the Catechism. I felt that for the Bonder's child, one of the first things is to have some good means of support for the future. I have introduced, accordingly, trades; cabinet-making, carpentry, and such things, and have them regularly taught. You shall seesome of the specimens, presently. The children do them wonderfully well."

"Do you not meet with much opposition from the clergy?" I asked.

He replied that he did; some cried "Infidel!" still he was determined to carry the thing through. If the people were ever to be enlightened, the schools must be a little more in harmony with the times. The priests seemed to think nothing was for a moment to be compared in importance with their catechisations.

I told him, that we in America believed the main religious instruction must be given in the family, or in Sunday Schools, and not in day-schools. We spoke then of books. I said that I thought one of the worst indications of the intelligence of the Bonders, and the greatest obstacle to their improvement, was the want of books among them. I had been in many Bonders' cottages, and had scarcely ever seen any book but the Bible, or occasionally a volume of sermons, and the people seemed to have very little taste for reading. I had thought of one plan, to publish a weekly edition, for instance, of the *Aftonblädet* of Stockholm, which should have well-arranged information, and should be sold cheap, and try to scatter it among the great masses of the peasantry.

"You have touched precisely on what I have been so long laboring at!" he answered. "*Ach!* it is hard to cause these people to read! I have bought the 'people's books' which we publish in this country, but they cannot read them! They are too high above them! Then I tried histories, and I found that some, especially about Swedish battles, they would read, but not many. Then I got this 'Reading Magazine for the People,' which you will see in my office. That they sometimes can understand."

"Will they not read Miss Bremer?"

"No. She is not easy enough. Your English books

are much better suited for us, if they were only translated. Something strong or imaginative, but very simple, would be the thing."

"Are there not authors who write for the people?"

"*Jo!* (yes,) but they fly too high. You know that gentlemen instructed in Education are trying in Stockholm to get up such books, and they have a plan to collect libraries there, which they will distribute in the various parishes needing them. Gott sei Dank! that something is being attempted. And the *armen Kerle* (poor fellows) are truly eager to read good books. I have opened a library here, and all the simple practical books, travels and such like are continually taken out. Your plan is a good one about the weekly paper, if it could be once well-started; still it must have pictures. But here we are at the house! I will send for the models our boys have made."

After a short time, the servants brought up some baskets, with wooden models of ploughs and harrows, etc., and with little horse-shoes and basket-work, which they had manufactured. This industrial feature in the common school, he said, was quite new in Sweden.

In the house, afterwards, we met a very lively party—the family—tutor, and some ladies, with a few gentlemen from the neighborhood.

There was some talk about driving me over the next day to a nobleman's residence, to whom I had letters of introduction. My host was engaged, and the question was whether some of the others would go. They were unwilling, and it was finally arranged that I should go by myself.

"Frankly we must tell you," said one of the gentlemen to me, "we have nothing to do with Count W. We are independent men, and we will never associate where we are looked upon as inferior. He is a great Lord, and we are nothing; but we have our own place and we are content with it, and we will not invade his, nor he ours." * * *

It is an incredibly agreeable thing to an American in Europe, that he can utterly ignore the distinctions of society. If he has education and the refinement of gentlemen, there is nothing to prevent his associating on an equality with princes; and at the same time, he may have social chats at peasants' firesides and count any worthy man of any class his friend. He has no fixed position; no title to herald him (if he be not by wonderful chance Colonel or Major-General); no weight of aristocracy above him, or immeasurable distance below him. If he be a gentleman and make no claims, passing himself simply for what he is, he will be so received by all classes and his position in European society will be the most sensible and agreeable than can be imagined in this conventional age.

* * * * * * *

I was curious to know whether these gentlemen felt the anomaly of their Constitution, which prevented them from voting. They spoke of its absurdity and injustice, but I think they cared very little for the loss.

I found them much interested in our tremendous struggle in America. They could not doubt of the victory of the Free Party. "Your country marches on, sir," said one, "it must finally free itself from this disgrace and clog. But it is a fearful question. We are watching you." Much more was said, showing the intense sympathy and anxiety with which the Europeans regard our struggles.

Our conversation lasted till a late hour, when I was shown to the guest-house, where a bright fire was lit in my room, though it was only the beginning of September. In the morning, the servant who brought my coffee, announced that the "Bonders had come." I hastened out to the other house, and there, in one of the drawing-rooms, the four peasants in wedding costume were standing sheepishly to be looked at. The costume was highly-colored and picturesque, with many peculiarities borrowed from the modern Greeks, our host said. The women had red and white head-dresses, reddish bodices with white skirts and half-mantles ; the men, white coats with embroidery and gilt upon them, belts about their waists, and, I think, leather trowsers, ornamented.

What struck me more than the dress, was the evident position or relation of these people. They were Bonders, but a very different class from the Bonders of the North. No reward could have made a *Dalkarl* exhibit himself and his wife thus at the word of command. But this gentleman had "*bestält en Bondquinna*" (ordered a peasant) at a certain hour, as we would a horse. The difference lies mainly in the different effects of freehold property and tenant property on a poor class.

CHAPTER XXVIII.

ÖREBRO, AND A MODEL FARM.

I SPENT but a short time at Örebro; the inn being the worst I had found in Sweden. My room was a kind of ante-room to another chamber, where slept two travellers, and was also peculiarly frequented by fleas.

The new parts of the town have a pleasant appearance, and have been built since a fire a few years ago, which destroyed about one third of the place. The Parliament loaned the corporation 275,000 riks dollars to assist in rebuilding the city. It is a town of some manufacturing importance, containing twenty factories. A telegraph connects it with Stockholm, and a small railroad is being built between it and Hult. Population in 1850, 5,177.

From this point, I set out to reach the place of Captain H., of whom I had heard so frequently, both for his skillful agriculture and his enthusiastic labors among the peasantry.

To reach his estate, I had a slight experience of Swedish means of communication. In Örebro, no travelling vehicle was to be hired or borrowed, though it is a town of some five thousand inhabitants, so I was seated in a little springless cart—like the rag and bone carts of New York—and with a little post-boy by my side, began the journey. The road was a much travelled highway, but no public vehicles ever cross it—indeed I believe there are but two or three lines of stage coaches in Sweden—and with delays for horses, we were six hours accomplishing the eighteen miles

The entrance to the property was through a pine wood, little improved by art, but forming for nearly a mile a very picturesque approach. The house was on a little knoll, hidden by trees, and we wound through a handsome avenue of beeches, passing a grass-grown ruined gable (the remains of a monastery) before we reached it. It was a plain, sensible building, of two stories neatly painted, with a flower plot between it and "the guest-house" on the other side of the usual square. The barns and out-houses were concealed (contrary to the usual custom) from the buildings, by shrubbery. The view from one side of the square, was of an English landscape—a lawn, another avenue of trees, a building among the trees, and below without separation by fence or hedge, beautifully-rolling grain-fields as far as the eye reached.

This farm had, like those in Norway, the picturesque little bell-tower on one of the buildings; a thing which should be imitated by our American farmers of taste.

The host met me with great cordiality, on learning my objects. I found him a cultivated gentleman, speaking several languages. After some conversation on his peculiar efforts for the peasantry, he took me over the farm. It is a truly model farm, such as is hardly to be seen elsewhere in

Sweden. It covers about 2,300 acres—much of it, when the present owner took it, marsh-land and uncultivated. Now he has it thorough-drained, by tile and stone-drains. One hundred and ninety acres are in wheat, thick, full grain, of a quality which last year gave Captain H. a first prize in the Paris exhibition. The yield, if our reckonings of Swedish and English measures were correct, was about thirty-two bushels per acre, weighing sixty-four and a half pounds per bushel. There were other immense fields of turnips of the best quality, and of oats, clover and grass. All were bounded by ditches,—hedges, as he explained, collecting the snow and killing the neighboring plants in the spring. For a similar reason he had adopted the English division of "lands"—now I believe beginning to be abandoned in the Scotch farming—in order to drain the snow-water from the surface. He took me to see his new English drilling machine (Garrett's), worked with a pair of horses by three men. In another part of the field, Scotch harrows of a new construction were at work, and in still another, the best Scotch plows. A number of women were also employed in breaking clods. In the barns was a large threshing machine, driven by four pairs of oxen, with connecting pulleys for even draught; Scotch winnowing machines and horse-rakes were also employed. Reaping machines he greatly needs, but the difficulty thus far has been that the wheat is often so much *laid* and tangled under the rains that no machines he has seen are fully adapted for it. There is no country where quick reaping is so important as in Sweden, for the weather is very uncertain, and the summer short. (We have frosts now every night, though August has a week yet to run.) In his barns, he pointed out as an experiment, which was quite strange in Sweden—the use of shingles instead of thatch or slates on the roof!

The stables were built on the latest approved plan, with drains for urine, stone troughs for water, and apertures from the hay-loft above, and a little contrivance of his own, to keep the cattle from drawing their food under their feet. There were stalls for 100 cows. These were feeding between two fields of oats, with nothing to keep them from the crops but a cowherd with a little white, snarly dog. Capt. H. assured me, that this dog could drive the hundred cows in a lane not ten feet broad, right through grain fields, without their doing the least injury. It was certainly the most beautiful herd of cattle I ever saw—all Ayrshire cows of the first quality, not very large, but so tight-skinned, small-headed, with straight back, muscular fore-quarters and full dew-laps. Many were mottled with white.

Twenty are owned by the government; which intrusts them to this gentleman for the sake of improving the breed in Sweden. All he is obliged to pay as rent is the price of one bull-calf a year. Two-year old heifers he sells for about $111; bulls for $200. The butter and cheese he sells in Stockholm.

In the horse-stables we saw some noble white Normandy horses, the same breed which the old knights favored, and which Wouvermann so often paints—a ponderous, strong breed, and with them a few Norwegian horses.

The wages of his laborers he thinks now high, in proportion to the cost of living ; yet he pays only an average of 16 cents a day, and food. It was formerly 12 cents. His cowherd—a very valuable man—gets $25 a year and board. The whole number of men employed is between 80 and 90. Several of his workmen are soldiers—(he himself was an officer,) and he related to me many interesting facts of these men, which I will mention afterwards, in connection with his more important works. The grooms in his stables were also some of them old cavalry soldiers.

He considers his experiment in "high farming" thoroughly successful. The peasants laughed at it at first, but they are glad now to imitate it where they can. His property, which he bought for about $25,000, he holds now worth at $100,000. I have no doubt, he has given an impetus to the agricultural improvement of all Sweden. Such men are public blessings of such a country as this. This gentleman, again, with all his interests in the country, has no vote and no share in the political affairs! He does not belong to any one of the four classes!

His efforts in another direction beside agriculture are equally remarkable. He is a gentleman of education and of fortune, but has had the courage to leave his old associations and to violate public propriety under the impulse of his conscience. He is a Läsare,* or "Reader," which, to most Swedish ears, has a sound as horrible as "Socinian," or "Shaker," to most American.

* As a sect, the *Läsare* may be said to date back to the middle of the last century.

In the beginning of our walk over his fine property, I had observed a very plain wooden building among the old trees: so exceedingly bare and simple that I remarked it, and wondered that he did not break the outline at least, by some cupola or bell-tower. "That is my chapel," he remarked, "and I am obliged to make it as unlike the churches as possible, in order to avoid any trouble from the clergy." Here, every Sunday afternoon, when the church service was not held, he assembled the country people, simply to hear the Bible *read* and explained. One old woman walked thirty-one miles, the men fifty and even sixty miles to attend this service, where the only exercises besides were singing and a prayer. He had commenced first with daily prayers among his house-people and workmen, who numbered about sixty, then went on to Sunday services, and now every Sabbath afternoon for two or three hours, nearly a thousand of the poor peasants were present, listening most eagerly. As I went around among his fields, he pointed me out one and another, whom he thought greatly changed in life since this began. "You see that tall man there, driving the machine—he is a soldier—I knew him when I was in the army—a violent, cursing fellow. He is so different now—I really believe the truth has taken root in his heart.

"There's another—the man hoeing. He was greatly given to brandy and other vices. He came of his own accord to the 'reading,' and one day I took occasion to speak of the sin of taking the communion-supper in the church, merely because of the law, when the heart was full of evil. The Spirit seemed to bring it home to this man, and he was deeply affected, and now he is known as an outwardly good man. I believe he has the true Life in him."

I asked Capt. H. how he was induced to begin this. It is not proper to state all the causes which led him to these works, but the principal were those which, in every country, cause the human heart to feel the deep things of life—private sorrows. He was besides staggered and discouraged, as a master of a household, by the general licentiousness of his servants and of the country peasantry. The usual moral motives and influences seemed mere straws against the currents of passion and habit. The *Church* did nothing. His pastor was a very kind, jovial country gentleman. But with ten thousand riks dollars a year, a good farm, and placed for life, how was it to be expected he should make himself uncomfortable, with such questions from poor lust-beset peasants, as, "What shall I do to be saved?" or, "Who will deliver me from the body of this death?"

Probably, kind man! he gave the fellow a glass of beer, and told him to come and repeat the catechism at the next church-examination.

The Captain's earnestness, and an impression with the peasants that he really believes what he says, has probably taken the place of much theological training. However that be, they come, and from great distances, to the unpretending service, and he thinks they show good practical effects.

The whole thing has made a great sensation in the coun

try. The clergy oppose it bitterly. It is opening the flood-gates to dissent. Substantial squires laugh at a *gentleman's* turning Methodist!—and building his own chapel. The bishop has visited him and investigated the matter; he fears that it may be illegal, and that Captain H. may expose himself to prosecutions. The Captain replies respectfully that he is simply instructing his own workmen in religious truths, at hours when they were usually carousing, and that if others choose to come, he cannot conscientiously prevent them. He does not propose to break off from the State Church, but only to fill out its instructions in this plain way. "Then," says the Bishop, "you should be ordained as a clergyman." But the Captain does not at all feel himself adapted or educated for that; so at length the Bishop retires, very courteously discomfited. Captain H. has also had a conversation with the Ministry of Public Worship at Stockholm. These gentlemen are obliged to allow that, as yet, he is not going beyond the pale of the laws—so for the present, Läsarne will not be broken up. In addition to the chapel, Mr. H. has a school on his estate, as is the custom with the large landed proprietors.

My visit at this hospitable home was delightful. One takes away from such places a purer and better atmosphere. A few words with any man who really holds himself in the presence of the Unseen, and lives for it, is the best sermon. To my own mind, there is something unnatural in this specifying and cataloguing the events of the soul's life, even as in the outward life, as my friend did in his conversation. It is dangerous besides—yet here, where for a time the soul was more a reality than the body, and people were aroused by mighty truths before hidden, one could pardon and appreciate it.

Captain H.'s enterprise, humble as it is, is another of those grand evidences which meet one continually in Europe, of the irrepressible *demand* of the human soul for religion. Rich priestly garments do not satisfy; catechisings, liturgies, communion-suppers are not enough; jovial clergymen, hospitable parsonages, a recognition of the Church in every act of civil life, do not meet the soul's hunger. Moral essays and the "Ten Commandments" learnt to a satiety, and catechisms oft-repeated, are not sufficient to restrain the surging lusts and passions of the heart. But at length, a man without surplice or cassock, with no help of organ or paintings or architecture, opens the old unworn story of the Redeemer and under the light of great truths, talks quietly and earnestly. It is all real to him. He has proved it in the storms and when the floods of great waters were on him, and the people believe; they flock to him; old habits are changed: Love beams where Selfishness was; the great truth that man is to look out of himself, and so cease to count his petty virtues, and to love and depend on the higher One—the REDEEMER, works on the soul as it has done in every age, and of itself spreads the very air of purity and morality in the foul heart, where before every effort at self-redemption had been in vain. This is the despised Läseri at present in Sweden.

CHAPTER XXIX.

AN OLD CASTLE.

The next morning I was forwarded to Count X.'s estate, in my friend's carriage, the horses being supplied at the post-stations. The entrance of the property was through an old stiff avenue of beeches, perfectly straight, leading to the front of the castle. It is remarkable how poorly placed and ill-kept are many of the estates of the highest nobility in Sweden. The rich middle-classes seem usually to possess more tasteful properties. Here, we came first upon the barns, brick buildings with high pointed gables, not at all screened ; then to a mill, built upon what was the old moat probably, now a rather unseemly weed-grown stream. There was nothing of that nicety of care, one sees in such places in England ; but the broad, carefully ploughed fields on each side, and the herds of Ayrshire and Durham cattle on the meadows, showed the owner an agriculturist, perhaps more occupied in that direction at present than in beautifying.

September ——.—I am in a comfortable old bed-chamber on the ground-floor, looking out on the court, which is enclosed by two brick wings with little Gothic turrets. An ancient clock is in the centre, and the date says 1642—probably the date of the restoration of the building. My room opens into a huge dining-room, not now used apparently, and lined with old portraits. There is a heap of new books in their paper wrappers, unopened, on one of the side-boards, just as they have been sent from the agents and publishers. A servant in livery in the hall, has especial charge of me and my wants. It is two o'clock, and we are having the hour to ourselves to dress for dinner.

I have already made the friendly acquaintance of a very enlightened and generous-minded lady, Countess S., visiting the castle. She has resided long in Germany, and we have many subjects in common. High rank with her has not had the common effect, of contracting the mind and sympathies. Her album has the most interesting collection of historic names and personal memoranda from great men, I have ever seen. One from Bernadotte struck me :

"Celui qui sert l'humanité et qui la défend mérite le titre de citoyen du monde."

Bernadotte was an orator always, and something of the *elation* of the French Revolution seems to run through all his sentiments. She says his conversation was one of the most interesting she ever enjoyed, and when, after dinner, the ladies were in one circle around the Queen, taking coffee, they were often really listening to the King, talking to his circle of gentlemen. She has in her book, bars of music from distinguished composers, sketches from artists, and even poetry and music from the present princes. One gentle song she treasures, from the young Prince not long deceased, whom all Sweden yet mourns, the favorite of the whole line—Prince GUSTAF, second son of the present king.

I have been kindly shown over the castle by Countess S. Three large saloons—those most used by the family—were filled with costly paintings. Here as so often in the rich houses of Sweden, I have been surprised at the rare collections of art. Even the English castles, especially in the medieval art, are not superior ; and only some Austrian and Italian private collections can be judged finer. Guido, Rubens, Caracci, Rembrandt, Wouvermann, Poussin, and numerous others—each of which is a gem. There were also pretty collections of China. Plate is not shown, as it is in England, or perhaps not so richly possessed. The rooms were usually uncarpeted, with parquet floors : furniture solid and tasteful, with now and then some antique oak or walnut piece, quaintly carved. The bedrooms have very heavy hangings over the beds and at the windows—the pillows and all being covered with red-drapery. The charm of the whole was in the antique grandeur of the apartments, and the historic air from the portraits. Each room had its paintings, and its ancient faces, connecting the Present with the far-away Past : sweet womanly looks, cheeks fresh as if copied yesterday, stern and manly countenances, and one or two crowned heads—for the family numbers these among its ancestors.

In one wing was a very pretty library and study for the Count. The collection of books was by no means equal to those in the other castles and halls I had visited.

The antiquity and the association with the past seemed gradually to affect one's mind, and as we passed out of an old saloon with portraits, into a sombre bed-room, hung with ancient paintings and engravings, I listened almost unsurprised to a story of the lady's about this very room.

She was sleeping there, she said, one night, as she had often done (though never since, thank God!), her maid slept in a little tower adjoining, when suddenly, in the middle of the night, she was awakened by three distinct raps on the panelling of the chamber. She raised her head, thinking it was the maid, when she heard them again on the opposite side, towards the saloon. She looked there, and the door was open, and against the light of the windows within this room she saw a *white mist* drifting in, which seemed, as it approached her, to assume a gigantic human form. She tried to shriek, but her throat could not utter a sound; she gasped, and at length had strength enough to drop her head on the pillow, when she felt a cold sensation pass over her neck and shoulder, as if an icy hand had touched her. She nearly fainted—but at length in her exhaustion, slept. The next morning, she questioned her maid, but the woman had heard nothing; when she went down to breakfast, she told her experience to the old Countess A., whose son is the lord of the estate. This lady turned very pale, but made no reply, and the subject was never alluded to again between them. The next day, she happened to journey away, and when she returned, she took care never to sleep in that chamber again!

I asked her if she had ever spoken about it to others, or had ever heard any legends, which might account for the spectre.

She said, she once asked Colonel F., a friend of the family, if anything had happened to him at P. Castle? He shrugged his shoulders mysteriously, and said he should never sleep at P. Castle again!

It appears in olden times, a very wicked woman lived here, who was thought by the peasants to have sold herself to the Evil One; and when she died, a puff of white smoke was seen to issue from one of the castle windows. This bed-room was perhaps her room.

I heard another instance lately of these interesting experiences among intelligent people.

A lady who is descended from the famous family of Oxenstiërn, told me that while in her castle at W., she observed one day the workmen making some repairs in the walls of one saloon, at the command of her father, and that they had placed a valuable painting on the floor. She was fearful some injury might happen to it, and she said to the workmen that they could hang it on an unoccupied nail in her chamber. The picture was a portrait of the old Chancellor Oxenstiërn. On the other side of her chamber, though she did not then observe it, hung a portrait of Queen Christina. Now, as is well known, there was between these two during life a most bitter feud, which was never reconciled. This did not occur to her, however, and she undressed and retired to her bed as usual. In the night, she was aroused suddenly by a curious rustling; she listened, and it evidently came from the wall where the picture hung. She raised her head, and gazed at the old portrait by the light of the night-lamp, when she heard distinctly proceeding from it, a deep, hollow groan—then another—and then a third. She was fearfully alarmed, but really had not strength to shriek, and her room was at a distance on one wing of the castle, where she could only arouse people by an alarm-bell. She thought of arising and fleeing to her maid, when suddenly again came the sepulchral groans. She could not stir; her voice failed, and at length she fell back exhausted—to sleep. The next morning, nothing seemed moved or different in the picture, "but I assure you, Monsieur B.," said she, "I removed the portrait at once to another room, and I have never been troubled with anything of the kind since! But, it *was* horrible!"

A servant announced dinner as we were sitting in the drawing-room, and another opened the doors from the great hall into the dining-saloon. All stand a moment by the table, with hands folded; then, with the usual obeisance, we take our seats. Two or three servants are in waiting. There is very little formality and no display—a pleasant family-table—the ladies not in full dress. Some beautiful dahlias make the principal ornament of the table. A preparation of sour milk and a soup is handed first to each to choose from, then fish, a kind of sturgeon, then quails, and pancakes, and another dish of meat already carved. Only one kind of wine is passed. The children sit at the table with their governess; our hostess the Countess, is a most affectionate, careful mother. The conversation at table is almost entirely in French or German—the company, as usual, using the language of the guest, even for their own intercourse.

The German lady, who has so kindly been my *chaperon* thus far, talks to me in under-tone of the society of Sweden.

"The ladies are shut within their cliques too much," she says. "They do not see enough of the world, and one does not find the spirit of humanity enough among them. To me, *the air is close* among them. They speak languages, and they read, but they have not many thoughts, and it is hard to interest them in anything—still they are sufficiently amiable."

We spoke of the morality of the higher classes. She thought there had been a great improvement since the accession of Carl Johan (Bernadotte). The old French indifference and sensuality had much passed away, under the citizen-king and his family. "Yet there is a great deal of *Leichtsinn* (laxity) among the young men. I have seen such fortunes wasted among them!"

At the close, according to the usual custom, we stand a moment for silent thanks, and then go carelessly to the drawing-room, where each shakes hands with the hostess, and thanks her.

Coffee is served up, and we chat and listen to music, until a walk is proposed. The grounds are singularly poor and formal for such a property, the main attention evidently being given to the crops. As is universal with the gentry there are hot-houses and orangeries and wall-fruits. The peach and apricot will sometimes ripen here against a wall, but more generally they are kept under glass. The principal superintendent met us—called "Inspector"—who has the charge of the place, apparently a very sensible, well-informed man, and treated very politely, by the ladies. The tenantry on the estates of Count X., number about ten thousand.

On returning to the drawing-room at six o'clock, fruit is served—grapes, peaches and melons.

We are called to supper at eight o'clock. The Countess makes tea, and we each eat a little bread and butter and cheese, standing; then sit down, and one or two light dishes are handed by a servant—pan-cakes and a dish of milk. No one takes more than one cup of tea.

It should be noted, now that I am cataloguing small customs, that this is almost the only table in Sweden, where I have seen salt-spoons or at dinner, finger-glasses. While we are eating, the children come around and bid us each good night, and are taken off by a servant—their little rosy faces quite melancholy at the cruel word "bed-time."

We sit a little while in the drawing-room after supper, by the French lamp, and although the castle is miles from any post-office or town, the Stockholm papers and letters, and some telegraph-dispatches are brought in. They read to me with much interest the American news, and the slavery question, and Fremont's chances are eagerly discussed.

Among the despatches, the Countess read one indifferently, that the young Princes from the Court were to pay them a visit on the following Saturday. My partings were most courteous and kindly from the ladies, and it was arranged that I was to be forwarded to the next post-station in one of the Count's vehicles, and thence by post-carriage to N——.

CHAPTER XXX.

NORRKÖPING.

As I was waiting for my carriage at the first post-station, a young gentleman, wrapped up in a pelisse, and just about to enter his own carriage, which was at the door, said suddenly in English, "You ride till Norchœpping, sir ?"

I answered, Yes : after a few pleasant words, he proposed an exchange—that I should come in with him, and his maid should go on in the other vehicle and meet us in the city. I accepted without ceremony, and we were soon rolling easily off in a most elegant little turn-out, with a mustachoed coachman in top-boots on the box. My companion was a young nobleman, travelling across the country some two hundred miles, with his own horses. He was a fair type, I suppose, of the majority of his class—intensely patriotic, a little bigoted both in politics and religion, not remarkably cultured, of serious turn, and with a very generous spirit of courtesy and hospitality.

We spoke of the Russian and English war. "Ah ! such a blunder as was that !" said he. "We had only to throw ourselves in and Finland could have been certainly re-taken. Such a chance to drive those cursed Russians for ever out !

But we waited, and we negoced, and it was in fine too late. It will never come again—such an opportunity. We all would have enlisted, to a man. To be sure, we have not so large an army as the Russians, but every one knows one Swede is worth of three Russians. Look at Pultowa !" And he hummed fiercely—

"Ur vägen Moscoviter !
Friskt mod j gossar blä !"

"Out of the way ! out of the way ! ye Muscovites !"
Up and at them ! up and at them ! boys of blue !"

This gentleman again was of the younger branch of a noble family, and shut out from many of the privileges of nobility ; but he informed me that, through the favor of a relative who did not want to take his seat in the Parliament, he expected to sit. "Ah, yes," he said, "our Constitution needs much rebuilding. It is the priests who are in the way. The King is in favor of all rational reforms—he *is* a good king—such a king no country ever had ; but these clergy—they are always in fear for the Church." "Know you," he added, "that in many province, the *paysans* are already buying the property of the nobles, and unless something be done to give all our gentry a share in government, we shall have nothing but *prètes* and boors to rule us !"

I found that he had the same feelings about the formalism of the clergy and Church, which prevail every where.

"We want the Reformation," he said, "as much as they did in Luther's time. You know Dr. B., of Stockholm—such men never preach the Gospel. It is not the doctrine of grace and faith, but only works, works! How they hunt Capt. H., where you were, merely because he is a truer Protestant! May the Devil confound them all!" * * *

We spoke of America, of which he knew very little. I think he inquired if we had not recently abolished slavery!

Learning my objects of studying the condition of the people, he was very anxious to take me with him to his father's, Baron H., in Småland, whom he was going to visit. He said that the Baron, like Capt. H., had erected a church for the people and had called in a schoolmaster from the peasants, to preach to them. Crowds came from a great distance to hear him, and yet it was nothing but a simple, earnest exposition of Scripture. His invitations were the most cordial, but I finally concluded that the excursion would take me too much out of my route. We reached Norrköping in good time.

This town is one of the leading manufacturing places of Sweden, for woollens and cotton. I never saw a more cheerful and picturesque manufacturing city. The streets are broad and clean, and through the midst, a beautiful stream, with broad reaches and flashing water-falls, runs merrily, giving the great water-power. Some of the views on the bridges of this river—the Motala—are exquisite. I met here also some very agreeable and cultivated men of business.

SWEDISH MANUFACTURES.

The value of all the manufactures at Registered Factories in Sweden was—

In 1839	$5,439,123
1846	7,084,947
1848	8,368,348
1850	9,891,072
1852	9,859,524
1853	10,151,724

COTTON.

Raw Cotton—Import in 1853, 9,883,572 pounds—exceeding that of previous year by 1,247,041 pounds, and of 1850 by 5,200,000 pounds.

Twist—1853, manufactured in Sweden, 7,715,961 pounds, mostly of numbers under 26, and valued at $1,655,336. In 1852, 6,653,790 pounds, and value, $1,467,950.

Cotton and Linen manufactured in 1853, valued at $346,886—exceeding 1851 by $82,000.

TOBACCO.

Import of unmanufactured tobacco, in 1853, 4,831,638 pounds, excess of 1852, 413,722 pounds.

Import of manufactured tobacco, 66,588 pounds—more than one half from United States. In 1853, from United States, 3,107,193 lbs.

COMMERCE OF SWEDEN.

Imports from United States—Tobacco, rice, cotton, oil, sugar, coffee, cocoa, spices, dye-woods, resin.

Value.

1840.	1846.	1847.	1848.	1849.
$450,156	346,000	450,000	760,000	1,070,800

EXPORTS.

Iron and Tar to United States—

1840.	1846.	1847.	1848.	1849.
$1,029,796	388,000	886,400	1,002,400	730,800

BRANDY CONSUMED.

In 1851, 30,000,000 galls. per annum—9.1 for every human being! The consumption is much less now.

DUTIES.

Cotton (raw), free. Cloth less than 76 threads to an inch, and width less than 6 quarters, fordidden.

White cloth, per pound, 1 riks banc (40 cents); printed, per pound, 1.04 (41 cents).

Yarn, undyed, per pound, .04 (1 cent); Turkey red, .8 (2 cents); Woollens, .2 (one-half cent).

The iron-trade has increased immensely this year (1856). The value of exports and imports is equal to $50,000,000, or nearly double that of 1853, and one third greater than that of 1854. The customs' revenue alone from this article is about $3,500,000, which is beyond any previous years by $1,600,000. The annual export of bar-iron is about 80,000 tons; to the United States, (about) 13,333 tons. By the Decree of December, 1855, the export-duty on bar-iron was abolished, which would make a loss of some $40,000 in the annual revenue. Pig and ballast iron, export and import, pay a duty of 40 cents on a *skeppund*.*

Seven eighths of the iron-export business to the United States is done by Messrs. Naylor & Co., New York.

* About 266 pounds.

CHAPTER XXXI.

THE SWEDISH SCHOOLS.

From Norrköping I returned to Stockholm, where I spent my time especially in investigations in the Swedish Schools. The American friends of Education will be glad to hear of a vigorous progress in the modern school-system of Sweden.

The first organized popular school in Sweden may be considered to date back as far as 1646, when the Bishop Rudbeckius, at Westerås, commenced his labors in this direction. The first practical instruction for the teachers was arranged in 1690. About this time, a general law was passed, forbidding any one to take out a license to marry, who could not read the catechism. The laws which followed, relative to the examination of the children, who were about to be confirmed, and the custom which requires every one to be able to read, before he can receive the confirmation, and thus be a citizen, have caused for some centuries a very general knowledge of reading and writing among the Swedish people.

The last ordinance passed by the Parliament in June, 1842, establishing schools in every parish, has been productive of much good. Before this, there were small "circulating schools" in each district, passing from house to house, but the teachers were poor and poorly paid, and the accommodations miserable. Now, each parish must have at least one established school, with a Normal School for teachers, with proper rooms and conveniences. The pastor exercises a careful supervision over it, and himself examines the pupils twice a year. The difficulties in the way of the country-schools have been in the lack of interest among the people, the poor state of the Teachers' Seminaries or Normal Schools, and the scattered condition of the population. In a parish reaching twenty miles, with 10,000 people in it, it became almost impossible for all to attend a school at one point, so that the Government has been obliged to allow the pastors to open circulating schools. It will be remembered, in Dalecarlia, in the parish of Leksand, I found thirty circulating schools, with one established.

Great efforts are now being made to advance this whole subject. At the head of the movement is one of the most enlightened men in Sweden—a gentleman favorably known in this country—Mr. SILJESTRÖM, of Stockholm. His work on the "Schools of America" has been invaluable for Sweden. He is now getting out a book with the plans, etc., of our latest improvements in school buildings. It was often said to me that Mr. Siljeström was doing more for education in Sweden than all the Committees on Education of the Riksdag for the last quarter of a century. His great efforts now are to awaken interest in the public mind on the subject, and at the same time to improve the education of teachers. He is also seeking to form parish libraries all over the kingdom, through some central agency in Stockholm, as at present the mass of the peasants read nothing but the catechism and an occasional newspaper.

The school buildings which he took me into in Stockholm seemed equal to the best of our city schools, with large airy rooms, good light, and means of ventilation, and improved seats, though I think I saw none of the single iron seats.*

Those in the country were generally dwelling-houses, where the teachers resided, but were provided also with suitable accommodations. The great defect is the poor pay of the teachers—some in the country not earning twenty-five dollars a year beyond their board. This is collected by taxes on the parish, laid by the town meeting of peasants. With new interest and enlightenment, the scale of reward for such services will rise.

Charity Schools.—Of these there are not many. I visited two in Stockholm, two in Gottenburg, and one near Lund, and a few private schools on gentlemen's estates.

The defects in them, as in the public schools, lie as I have so often indicated, in the too great value attached to technical religious instruction—the catechism taking the place both of usual school studies and of genuine religious inspiring; so that the effect on the minds of the pupils seems to be a stagnation of the intellect, and a substitution of words for the feeling of religion—the catechism becoming

* I am informed by Mr. Polman of New York, that he has received orders from his friend, Mr. S., to send out to Sweden this spring various iron seats and tables.

a kind of Protestant bead-telling, like that, of use in reminding, but inspiring no life.

Normal Schools.—Both Gottenburg and Stockholm have schools for the training of teachers ; still the system of teaching is poor, and the quality of teachers sent out is generally very inferior. There are also such schools in some of the smaller towns.

Gymnastics.—There are two respects in which the Swedish school-system is far superior to ours.

One is in the universal teaching of *gymnastic exercises.* Every school-building has its large, high room, with earthern or matted floor, and all sorts of implements for developing the muscles—ladders, poles, wooden horses, cross-bars up to the roof, jumping-places, ropes for swinging, knotted ropes for climbing, etc. The scholars are not allowed to exercise on what they wish, but there is a regular, scientifically-arranged system. They are trained in squads, and move and march, sometimes to music, at the word of command.

At a large public school in Stockholm I saw the lads in their noon lessons at gymnastics. The teacher gave the word, and a dozen sprang out towards a tall pole with cross-bars, and clambering up it, each hung with his legs, then at the word all together dropped their heads backward and hung by the feet and ankles, then again recovered themselves and let themselves down. Another party, one after the other, squirmed up a naked mast ; another pulled themselves up hand over hand on a knotted rope ; others, in succession, played leap-frog over a wooden horse ; then they marched to the beat of the drum. The smaller or weaker boys begin with the lowest grade of exercise, and follow up, according to a scientific system, arranged for health. They all seemed to go into it with the greatest relish, and showed well-trained muscular power. I could not but conclude that the superior *physique* of the Swedish men is not entirely due to climate. When will America learn that health and strength have their unescapable laws?

This gymnastic system is a regular medical system in Sweden. Prof. Ling has an elaborate treatise on it. I found the treatment in much use for nervous, bilious, and dyspeptic disorders, both among men and women, the most intelligent people having great confidence in it.

Our public schools in America ought to be up with this step in education. Every Ward School, High School, or school of any importance, should have its *gymnasium*. Of all nations in the world, ours, with its intense and constant stimulus to the nervous system, needs the balance of healthy exercise for the muscular. Children are growing up puny, and nervous and delicate, most of all, perhaps, for the want of such training during the time when their brains are in most constant activity. Mr. Barnard, of Hartford, Ct., one of the great reformers of our common school education, is deeply interested in the subject, and has models and plans of the Swedish implements and machinery for this purpose. The introduction of a good method of physical training might change the whole bodily and sanitary condition of our growing population.

Scientific Schools for Workmen.—The other superiority

of the Swedish system, lies in the advantages it offers to mechanics and laborers. In a small Swedish town, not larger than Bridgeport, for instance, you find an evening school, where mechanics can learn drawing, modelling, or the practical application of the natural sciences, without any expense. I visited one in Stockholm in which Mr Siljeström is much interested, which was truly a "School of Art." There were in it beautiful plaster models of Greek sculpture, and bas-reliefs of Italian statuary, and of the best of Danish bas-relief—than which modern art has nothing more pure and classical—beside plaster casts of heads, fragments of limbs, mathematical blocks and architectural ornaments, from which to draw and to model. An original device struck me here, of natural forest-leaves arranged to draw or mould from. All this with lessons and teachers in the arts, lectures on chemistry and the sciences, is open every evening for laboring men and women. The consequence is, as in France, you have a class in Sweden, which America has not, of *artisans of taste*—artistic mechanics, men and women, who show ingenuity and a tasteful originality in the manufacture of furniture, the decoration, painting and frescoing of rooms, the making of common ware and implements. Whatever you are obliged to buy for a house in the shops, without ordering, has not that hard, awkward, angular look, which such articles have with us. Then these schools provide the women with a new and beautiful means of livelihood—the arts of designing, painting, drawing, and the applying of science to manufacture. Such schools for laborers exist all through Sweden.

It is truly a disgrace that in them America should be so far behind. Except the excellent Schools of Design for women in Boston and New York, I know of nothing of the kind in the United States.

Our city evening schools are good in their way, but they are suspended at certain seasons of the year, and they do not teach the higher mechanical and artistic branches. The New York Free Academy has a good modelling and drawing department, but is open only in the day, and designed for the lads of the school.

Perhaps the great "Cooper Institute" will eventually supply the deficiency.

America—the country of all where Labor is honored—ought to hold out advantages to the laboring classes, equal at least to those in the old and aristocratic Kingdom of Sweden

CHAPTER XXXII.

THE ISLAND OF GOTTLAND.

A STEAMER runs twice a week between Stockholm and Kalmar, touching at Wisby the principal city of Gottland.

The trip to this Island, is a favorite pleasure excursion in the summer, from the capital ; and with good reason. There is not in North Europe so picturesque a town as this old commercial city of Gottland. The first view from the water is of broken towers, battlements, gables, ruined churches and half-demolished spires, with small houses closely crowded among them. You land on a wharf quietly, and go up narrow paved streets, between low, quaint houses, and now and then pass an old tall, gabled warehouse, reminding of the days when Wisby was a leading Hanseatic city. You come soon on the ancient wall encircling the whole city, which has some forty-five towers yet remaining, though much defaced and broken.

This wall is built on the limestone rock, and follows each change of surface. The towers are some of them still used as granaries or prisons. As you wander carelessly about, you come upon a ruined church—some quiet scene with a green grass-plot, and the stone walls and arches rising distinct againt the beautiful blue sky of this latitude. You enter, and find yourself under columns and arches, still simple and chaste as in the best Gothic periods ; amid ruins belonging to the earliest times of Scandinavia, built before William the Conqueror had touched the soil of England.

If you observe, you find your architectural principles shocked by a mingling of periods, once most severely separated—the sturdy round arch of the Saxon, side by side with the graceful, aspiring, pointed arch of the early Gothic, proving in art as in ethnology, that the Saxon has had vastly more than his deserts from the world.

The "Church of the Holy Spirit," an octagonal tower, with one crypt-like room opening into another above of similar form, by a hewn aperture in its stone ceiling, is one of the most remarkable architectural structures in the world, and thus far, I think, unexplained. Nearly all these buildings show a great completeness and fineness of work. The town only contains some 5,000 inhabitants, yet there are now the ruins in it of from twelve to twenty large churches, most of them dating back to the tenth and twelfth centuries.

Such a collection of mediæval remains, it seems to me, does not exist in Europe, and it is surprising that we have nowhere a good pictorial description of them.* The con-

* An American artist of talent, Mr. W. U. C. Burton, of Waterbury, Ct., has made a beautiful series of sketches of these wonderful ruins, the most complete series existing.

trast of these chaste, finished structures, requiring such advanced taste and such great wealth, with the poor miserable town, though a common one elsewhere, is here very impressive, because the story of the rise of this splendor and its passing away is so hid in the mists of history.

The Scandinavian Vikings, from the early centuries, as has already been shown, did not alone bring back the plunder of their piracies. Some of the fruits of their adventurous expeditions were the introduction of foreign arts and commerce, and the ministry of the new Christian Faith. They traded with Constantinople, Italy, Russia, the East, and the islands and coasts of the Northern Ocean. The centre of one of these connections of trade—long before the existence of the Hanseatic League—became this city of Gottland.

The productions which the East brought to Northern Europe were conveyed in caravans to the Russian city of Novgorod, itself founded by Swedes, and from there sent to Wisby to be exchanged for the iron, copper, fish and furs of Scandinavia. Immense numbers of Asiatic coins have been found in Gottland, and in various parts of Sweden. In Stockholm alone, there are said to be preserved near twenty thousand coins issued under the Caliphs. Coins have been found, also, indicating a considerable commerce between England and Wisby, from 959 to 1066. In the twelfth century, Wisby was in high prosperity. Foreigners from various countries were settled there, having their own separate churches, built with much splendor. Great warehouses lined the streets, and her wealth was famed through the commercial world. One church is yet shown which, tradition says, had an oriel window set with such rich pearls, that they shone far out at sea to the approaching sailor.

In the thirteenth century, German merchants were settled here and the city was intimately associated with Lübec; and in the fourteenth she became the head city, and some claim the founder of the Hanseatic League. The high-gabled warehouses show still the evidence of the German occupation and wealth.

The code of Mercantile Laws,* first applied by the Germans and Northmen of Wisby, has become the foundation for the European code of Maritime and International Law since.

The decline of the city dates from its beleaguerment and sack by Waldemar, King of Denmark, in 1361. After this, its rival Lübec and its enemies, the Danes, sought incessantly to injure it; trade found new channels, and the city sunk to be only a relic of what it had been.

A curious relic, both of the barbarism and the unconquerable spirit of that race, which laid the foundation of its wealth and the liberty of modern days—the Northmen—is shown on this Island—a *suicide cliff*, where the Norse chief-

* Pardessus and other French writers on maritime law, following him, do not hold that the maritime code of Wisby originated there. Their theory is, that this code was a compilation of all the local commercial laws among the mercantile cities of the Low Countries, and of North Europe—Wisby among the number, and that it was only brought forth in that city.

The oldest copies are in Gothic and Low German, dating near 1320. Good editions can be seen in the Astor Library, New York.

tains, who were in danger after a life of battles, of the dis grace of dying in bed, came to throw themselves off. The Sagas relate that it was often thus used. Many of the most interesting relics of the Scandinavian museums have been found on this island.

There is great need of a thorough description of Gottland —of its early history and the quaint superstitions and customs of its people ; its antiquities and unequalled architecture. There is nothing of value so far as I know, in any language on it. A very learned gentleman in Wisby, with great taste for such investigations—Mr. Säve—has been collecting, for many years, the material for such a work. The only difficulty, probably, will be, that he has too much material, and can hardly make a salable book for general readers.

During my visit there, I was very hospitably entertained by a Swedish gentleman, well known in England, Consul ENQUIST. He had a fine place without the city—the house almost like a château. He is much engaged in a large enterprise for draining a tract of some 14,000 acres within the island ; 4,000 have already been made cultivable, and the rest is yet being drained. It is one of the largest operations for agricultural improvement in Sweden. Gottland is a ledge of encrinitic lime-stone, rising up unaccountably near the primitive rocks which make the coast of the peninsula, and naturally has an excellent soil for wheat. The climate is much milder than that of the coast near by ; and the grape, chestnut, and mulberry ripen here in favorable situations, though the island is in the latitude of the north of

Labrador—57° 30′. The weather, while I was there (in September), was like our most beautiful June weather in America, a soft mild air, with dreamy blue skies and a really summer heat under the sun at noon-day.

Among the institutions of Wisby, which I visited, were some popular schools in large buildings, well supplied with libraries and other means of education. I saw on Sunday, a school of young working-men, which was taught gratuitously, first in religious matters and then in the usual secular instruction. The teachers with whom I became acquainted were all men of culture. There is one large bath-house for the people on the principle of the English bathing establishments for the poor. In leaving the place on the steamboat, I was introduced to several Scotch farmers, of whom some were returning to Scotland, and others had already settled on the island. The great inducements to them were the cheapness of the land—$4 to $6 an acre for a good wheat-raising farm being a common price, and the low wages—$20 to $30 per annum, with board ; yet they did not seem very well satisfied. They felt the difficulty which always meets such experiments—the impediments from the *spirit* of an old backward society, such as cannot beforehand be reckoned in figures and yet which hampers every new undertaking.

My last view of the picturesque old city was in the light of a rich sunset. The broken cornices were gilded anew ; the harsh outlines of dismantled walls softened ; the ruined towers filled out in the shaded light, and the upspringing lonely arches crowned with a wonderful glory.

Gradually, the distinctive objects became confused, the buildings were masked in dark shadows, until at length the low island itself was lost in the splendor of the waters under the evening glow.

From Gottland, we steamed down the coast towards Kalmar. It is a most interesting reflection, as one passes this Swedish coast, that at this day, one of those grand mysterious internal movements of the earth, which raise continents and open the bed of oceans, is quietly and continually going on here.

As early as the beginning of 1700, Celsius observed that the waters, both of the Baltic and the Northern ocean, were constantly sinking. He estimated the fall to be 40 Swedish inches in a century.

More careful and comprehensive observations showed the fact to be that the land was rising. In 1807, Von Buch, after his celebrated tour over Norway, expressed his conclusion that the whole country was rising—Sweden more than Norway, and the northern part more than the southern part.* In 1834, Sir Charles Lyell, one of the most careful and candid of the observers of natural phenomena, compared the marks made by the Swedish officials at various periods in this century, on the coast north of Stockholm, and concluded that the land had risen 4 or 5 inches in that time, and that the rise diminishes from the north of the Gulf of Bothnia towards the south. He states, what every travel-

* Von Buch—and Lyell's Principles of Geology, vol. ii., p. 402.

ler must confirm as true, that the character of the coast—consisting, as it were, of two lines of coast, one, the shore, and the other, a series of broken reefs and islets—makes it peculiarly easy to determine whether the rocks and landmarks and channels have changed. The rocks, beside, are of gneiss, mica-schist and quartz, and of course, less likely to lose the peculiar aspect which make them familiar to the sailors and fishermen. It is well known all along this coast, that many islands have sprung up and become wooded, and that old channels are become filled and impassable.

This movement of elevation, Lyell supposes to go on over a territory some thousand miles in length, from Gottenburg to Torneä, and thence to the North Cape, and extending several hundred miles in breadth, far into the interior of Sweden and Finland. The evidences of it are numerous, in the change of the height of waters, in the disappearance of old landmarks, and especially in the discovery of many deposits of sea-shell, hundreds of feet above the water, and even as far inland as 70 miles from the present shore—shells of the same genera with living species in the Baltic.

The appearance, in many districts, is of subsidence and re-elevation. While all the centre and north of Sweden seems thus being forced gradually by tremendous agencies from beneath, whether of heat or gases or galvanic action, above the surface of the water, the southern part—Scania and the country we are passing—is gradually sinking, to such a degree, that the streets of several of the old cities nearest the water, are now submerged ; and ancient streets are discovered, many feet below low-water mark.

CHAPTER XXXIII.

KALMAR AND SMÄLAND.

KALMAR is famed in Swedish history as the city, where for a short time was made real the idea of Scandinavian Unity. Four centuries and a half ago (1397), the three kingdoms of Denmark, Norway, and Sweden were here brought under one Queen. Eighty-six years later, the Union was again renewed in this place; and through it the aristocracy reached the highest power which they have ever gained in Sweden, while the Danes were left in reality the masters of the country. The nation was finally freed from the tyranny of foreigners, by the heroic exertions of Gustavus Vasa.

The present town is a quiet, quaint Provincial place, containing about 7,000 inhabitants, with the old historic castle still standing, where these great events occurred. Among the modern changes, a German has opened a hotel in the principal square, which is a great improvement on the Swedish houses of the sort. I met here again some intelligent agreeable men, who showed me much kindness. In general, Kalmar has a poor reputation for cultivated society. The people are very much absorbed in business; and there is a great want of the usual Swedish family life. Gentlemen live at their club-rooms or billiard-rooms, and the wives suffer for it at home. It struck me that Miss Bremer, in her pictures in Hertha, of woman's inferior position and influence in Sweden, must have had in mind just such towns as this. And yet the fault is very much with the women. They have not the wit or the accomplishments to make home more attractive than any thing outside.

I was desirous to see some of the characteristic Smäland peasantry, and was recommended to Dr. V., as one of the most intelligent Pastors of the country, who could put me in the way of seeing them. His reception into the old parsonage was most cordial, and he himself, with his pale, intellectual, spiritual face, must remain to me, as to every one who has enjoyed his acquaintance, a most pleasing memory. We sat under the old beeches, in the front of the house, all the day and talked ; and then, in company with his *Adjunct*, visited some of the peasants. During the day, many of the people came up to consult with the pastor—among others, a stalwart young peasant, who went away at length looking very much cast down. The Doctor explained—Some years since, the mother of the young man bought him a fine little farm. As he was still a minor, she could not register it, as the law requires ; afterwards when he was of age, she neglected it. Now, after having labored on it for years, and improved it, under the increased value of all such property, the original owners, who had discovered the mistake, demand back the property, on the ground that the law has not been fulfilled. The young man came to the Pastor as his legal adviser in the matter. The Pastor was obliged to say to him, that nothing legal could be done, except to attempt to recover the value of his improvements. He himself offered to try the effect of a moral appeal with the other parties, though with little hopes of success

The laws on woman's holding property in Sweden, are even more strict than this. The Doctor says, that an unmarried woman, if she be seventy years old, can not hold property in her own name ; but if she were a widow at seventeen, she has all legal rights during the rest of her life.*

In the course of the day, another peasant, with a downcast, sneaking look, entered the yard, and was taken up to the Pastor's study. We inquired of the case. "Ack !' said Dr. V., speaking German, "it is the oath-taking !"—We looked surprised. "You should know," he added, "that sometimes people here are only *half*-condemned, or half-acquitted. For instance, if there be but one witness, or the testimony be doubtful in character, or for some other reason the Judge is not satisfied, he half-acquits him. That is, before the final sentence he sends him to his clergyman, and after being instructed in the nature of an oath, he takes a most solemn oath that he is not guilty. If he refuses to receive the oath from his pastor, it is strong presumptive evidence in the mind of the Judge that he is guilty. If he takes it, and

* In the Royal Speech during this last winter (1856–57), one of the many liberal recommendations was, that the laws in regard to the minority of women should be changed. Miss Bremer's especial object in *Hertha*, was to cause a reform in this oppressive legislation.

is afterwards proved guilty, he is liable to greater punishment. I have such persons sent to me constantly. This Bonder took the oath in a quibbling way, which I shall report to the Judge."

"But how do you account for such a custom?" I asked. "What has the clergyman to do with the law?"

"It is entirely consistent," he answered. "You are to remember that with us the State and the Church are one. The judge and the pastor are both officials in the same organization. The sanctions of Religion are to be applied to the courts of justice, as much as to the more immediate institutions of Religion."

Seeing that he was philosophizing on a favorite topic, which interested me, I drew him out.

"Do you regard Confirmation, as a condition of civil rights, in the same manner?" I asked.

"Certainly," he replied. "I have indeed had my doubts, and I have thought much on the subject, but let me explain. The State commences as a Christian State. It demands that all its members shall be Christians. For this purpose, it enacts that all who wish to be citizens shall pass through the outward rites of our sacred religion. Every one must be baptized. Then, for the same reason, it requires that every one shall be instructed and approved by the pastor, and *confirmed* in Christian doctrine. If he cannot show the evidence of this instruction, in his *Schein* (confirmation-papers), he is presumed not to be worthy of the privileges of citizenship. You see our stand-point?"

"But do you not see," said I, "that you gain no real

Christianity by this? You get outward ceremonies, and conforming—that is all. And more, you are far more liable to cultivate hypocrisy than true faith. I should expect a Church, under such a system, to be lifeless."

"*Ach!* Sie haben recht! You are right. Our beloved Zion is almost *todt* (dead) now. But that is the result of other causes. In this system which you deplore, we at least gain that every man and woman and child shall be instructed in the principles of our holy Religion."

"I would not discuss here the subject of public education in Religion," I answered, "but in our view, the partaking of the Lord's-Supper is a testimony of certain states of the heart, with which Law can have nothing to do. To enforce it under civil penalties, is to *command* the faith of the heart which cannot in its own nature be a subject of Law."

"Es ist ganz recht! It is quite true!" burst in one of our party, Herr T., a very generous, impulsive young man. "The Herr Americaner has hit it. I confess to the Herr Doctor, I suffer from this every year. The Herr Doctor will remember that I was confirmed before I could really understand these doctrinal problems. Now, it is the law that I must attend public Communion once at least a year. But I cannot. I do not care for it. I do not believe all the words which are said to me there. And yet I must. If I should stay away, that verfluche—*pardon!*—that infamous N—— would inform against me, and I might lose my business and be fined heavily! Is that right, Herr Doctor? I am a hypocrite!"

The Doctor was a little perplexed, for no man was ever

more open to truth than his pure soul ; but for the time, he took refuge in the easy assertion that the Herr T. should try to make the blessed Abendsmal (Communion-Supper) a reality and nourishment to himself, and then the yoke would be easy and the burden light !

Our host was anxious to know what had been the effects of the separation of Church and State in America. He had the same general views, common here, of the sad disturbances of sects, the unworthy rivalry of preachers and the growth of all possible heresies in America, which I have before described.

I gave him our theory of the office of sects.

"Yes," he said, candidly, "theoretically that is true. We are many limbs in one body, which is Christ. That system may be useful for the young, free America. It will not be so here—though, alas ! our beloved church sometimes here seems crumbling in its walls. It is true, that the pure Faith is now not often to be found among us."

Here our young friend broke in.

"I have told Herr B. that in my view, not for centuries are we ready for *Gewissens-freiheit*—Freedom of Conscience. I believe in a Republic, but I do not think Sweden fit for it. So with Freedom of Conscience. When we have a Republic, then will we have all sects among us !"

I told him that I could not see that the two went at all necessarily together. The liberty to worship and to think on religious subjects, and to express and organize one's thoughts, was universal and eternal.

"But look, Herr B. ! See these *Läsare* now ! I detest

them! See what vulgar, hypocritical fanatics they are! We used to be quiet here in Småland, and now they have turned everything upside down. The next thing will be your Mormons, and forty wives to each man, and all sorts of disturbances. No; I am for keeping down these cursed fanatics with a strong hand. Let them go to the dev—, ahem—*pardon!* Doctor!—America, I mean!"

I will not follow out the discussion. Enough is given to show the spirit. Our friend, Mr. T., is one of the "young Sweden" party—a Reformer and Liberalist. On every other matter his views are expanded and humane. Though not precisely true of him, yet in general one may say, that the spirit of bigotry has its peculiar residence in Sweden. There is not in any other country of Europe, so far as I know, so narrow and persecuting a spirit—not more in Naples or Austria.

"Shall we visit the Bonders?" said the amiable, little adjunct.

We were ready, and in a comical bit of a wagon, rode out in the woods. The groves in this part of Sweden are far finer than in the North—the elm, the oak, and the beech, are the principal trees. We came first to a small cottage, just at the outskirts. There was but one large room in it, neatly kept, but with an air of destitution. A laboring man and his wife with a few children were in it. He took the visit in good part, and we had considerable conversation on crops and weather, and the like. Hearing that I was from America, he took out a well-worn card of

Natural History, with pictures of serpents and various wild animals of the tropics, to know if any of them came from my country. He had no books except the Bible and one religious novel, which the pastor had just loaned him. The man had more the aspect of one of the German *Bauer*—the peasants of the Continent, than any I had seen—as of one who had had no fit opportunities of development.

I inquired about his position, and heard that he was the tenant of a "*Stamhemman*."

The various kinds of *Hemman*, to a stranger in Sweden, are utterly confounding. This was interpreted, as a cottage belonging to the pastorate; in this case, taken from the monks, by Gustavus II., as I understood.

Beside this, there is the *Krono-Hemman*, a property belonging to the Crown, but farmed by a peasant. Then the *Krono Skatte Hemman*, an estate formerly belonging to the Crown, now bought free from the rent to the State, by the capitalization of its rents and by the paying of high taxes. Still further, the *Frälse Hemman*, that is, a freehold liberated from the customary taxes for supporting the military. Formerly, this kind of privileged freehold could only be possessed by the nobility, as a reward for great services. Since 1809, all classes have been allowed to hold them, and the peasants have bought up a large number from the decayed gentry.

Finally, is the *Säteri Hemman*, a property liberated from still other taxes—in some cases, as an encouragement for making improvements thereon. According to the old laws, the taxes of a province were divided among the *Hemman*.

A district must provide, for instance, six oxen, or a hundred hens for the soldiery, so that finally on the tax lists a Hemman would be found charged with the thousandth part of an ox, or seven-eighths of a hen, or nine-tenths of a lamb. These taxes still remain in form, to the great enjoyment of humorous antiquaries.

We visited some other cottages of the wealthier peasants —houses much superior to any of this class in the North. They were usually freehold properties. The crops were the same as hitherto mentioned, with the exception of more wheat and occasional fields of flax.

We chanced, in the evening, to speak of the habits of the people with respect to drinking, and I heard the same report here as in other provinces, of the wonderful improvement in the last five or ten years.

A gentleman was present who had led the temperance movement in Southern Sweden—Magister STRÖM—and who, against much obloquy, had at length in Kalmar carried out preventive measures against the evil which has so cursed Sweden. His account of his efforts to awake public attention—the statistics—the numeration of calamities he was obliged to set forth—the cry of fanatic and ultraist aroused against him—the insult and almost imminent danger of losing his business, for his reformatory measures—was very interesting. He was not a total-abstinence man or for the Maine Law. His object was simply to limit the use and sale of the common cheap drinks which so inevitably degrade the great masses of the people addicted to them. The method, as adopted in Kalmar, has been entirely successful, and deserves consideration by our reformers in America.

The main feature is the making the drink too expensive for the common peasants. This is done by allowing no one to sell liquors, except the licensed dealers. These are heavily taxed by the city—so much a *Kanna* (about two quarts) ; and it is assumed that no seller has less than eight hundred Kannar. Then no one is allowed to sell a less quantity than a Kanna. If he does, for the first and second offence, he is exposed to very heavy fines ; and, if I understood rightly, to imprisonment for the third. The consequence is that brandy which used to be twelve skillings (four cents) for two quarts, is now several dollars (Swedish).

The topers with small means cannot get their usual draughts. The poor peasants must club together to obtain their Kanna of brandy ; and any disorderly conduct on the premises, or even the selling the liquor to women and children, is considered cause sufficient to remove their license. A volunteer society watches these liquor-shops and reports to the police, and carries on the suits.

The measure has not been so extreme as to defeat itself. Even the lower classes—especially the women—begin to like it. It is observed that the potatoes which used to go to whisky are now eaten ; that the neighboring districts of Skania, which once imported wheat—so much was their own employed in distilling—now have enough to export. Crimes and distressed cases of poverty are of much less frequent occurrence. The lower classes of the city have a different aspect.

For my own part, I should consider such measures in our American cities vastly more practical and probable to succeed, than any entirely preventive laws. The great difficulty with us would probably be, that what a man wants in America, he can generally afford to get. We could not make brandy so expensive that topers would not buy it. Still we could control somewhat the poorest, and the indifferent, to whom the price would be an object; and we could prevent public disorder on such premises.

CHAPTER XXXIV.

A COUNTRY HOME.

From Dr. V.'s we posted on to the house of a gentleman of distinction, to whom I had been kindly recommended, whom I will call Mr. X.

Of all the Swedish homes which I was permitted to visit, and whose hospitality I enjoyed, this made the most agreeable impression on me. A seat of repose, of refinement and culture, where the people seemed mated to the surroundings. Here, rank and high position had not lessened the spirit of genial humanity, or cramped the activity of the intellect. A high-bred Swedish lady is, to my mind, the perfection of that kind. She has the settled air of one accustomed to deference, which sits so well on many of my countrywomen, and something of their best culture ; she has the grace of the Frenchwoman, yet with a certain kind and sweet courtesy, and a repose, if not seriousness, of nature, which belong to neither the Americans nor French. Our ladies—and it is more true of the English—are not usually *kind* enough in their courtesies ; a certain coldness, or reserve, or indifference, restraining them too much. The great peculiarity, it seems to me, in the manner of the Swedish lady of the higher classes, is this graceful and sweet kindness. I do not think the Swedish women are remarkable for beauty. The severe climate tells on the wealthy classes, and those of the lower are too much worked for preserving any delicacy of *traits*. The ladies have often the slight, fragile appearance of our American women, but nearly always a grace and ease of carriage, which quite make one forget the want in this regard.

As I have remarked before, there is in manner and general bearing a distinct line between the women of the middle and the aristocratic classes.

A common phrase about the Swedes, repeated in all descriptions of them, is that they are the "French of the North." It does not seem to me true, and must have taken its origin in superficial resemblances, and in another age. There is a tact and politeness with the most aristocratic classes, which is somewhat French. They use the language also much, and in the last century were much imbued with French ideas. But the essential groundwork of the Swedish nature, is anything but French. They are a sober, serious people. The severe skies and dark forests of evergreen, and their Teutonic blood have brought forth a solemn, almost superstitious, temperament.

There is much ardor and force apparent in all classes, the natural accompaniment of their vigorous constitutions and sanguine habit of body. But with this always, a certain seriousness or religiosity, not a poetic sadness, as in the Hungarian temperament, or an overstrained earnestness, as in the American,—but a soberness as from a tendency of the mind to fasten on unseen and spiritual phenomena. This too being a matter more of feeling than of reflection ; for the Nation does not at all impress you, as do the Germans—as a people, skeptical or given to inquiring into spiritual truths. The same thing is true of the Norwegian, though not to so great a degree. The Norwegian is a modern democrat by the side of the Swede, the old aristocrat ; rough, ready, manly, intelligent, equal to any one and accustomed to battle with the most stern powers of nature. The Swede is more refined, courteous and gentle, with more of poetry and superstition clinging to him, but still with the old Norse power in him.

I confess of the two, the Swede is to me the more interesting, though by no means the more valuable to the world. Both nations are essentially inclined to superstition.

My friend's house was on the outskirts of the pine forest. We were walking under the barred lights and shadows in a beautiful September afternoon, and spoke of these things. I mentioned the superstitious experiences which I have already detailed, in the old castles I had visited. "These are nothing new Herr B.," said Mr. X., in German. "I do not think out of every ten people, you could find one who had not encountered such adventures. Before I was in public life, I was a great deal among the peasantry. Many and many a night have I been called up to see or hear the *spökeri* (witchcraft or ghostcraft). The peasants would recount, that in an upper room they had distinctly heard the spirits throwing the tin vessels and the chairs at each other—then a violent struggle between the demons, and then all would be quiet.*

"At other times, regular steps would be heard passing over the floor, or lights be seen ; sometimes the cattle and horses are attacked, and they stamp and neigh in an unaccountable manner. I always went at once, no matter at what hour of the night, to the place which was haunted, to break up the delusion among these people. Sometimes in an attic I would find a cat, sitting quietly in one corner ; sometimes rats would run over the floor—more generally every thing was still, and there were not the slightest signs of any thing being moved. I remember a singular instance of this. Sit you down while I draw out the position of things." He then marked on the sand with his cane, two houses at the ends of a hypothenuse of a triangle. "I was in this house, you see, when late one evening I was called down to see a fearful *spooking*, in the other house there" (pointing to the other end of the line), "which had been long uninhabited, bright lights were plainly visible through the windows, and figures of men and women were seen passing to and fro. The people were greatly frightened. I asked for the key, and against their strong dissuasion, offered to go over to the haunted house, if some one would

* The old historian of Sweden, Olaus Magnus, thus confirms this. "Of the hurts done by the devils. In the Northern parts (where the devil hath his seat really) they mock the people that live there with unspeakable delusions, under various forms, and do them hurt also, throwing down their houses, killing their cattle, spoiling their fields, making a desolation of castles and waters."

accompany me. After some hesitation, one of the young peasants consented, and we walked over the fields to the house. We reached the door, but the lights and figures had all disappeared. The house was empty and dark. I put the key in the door, and it sounded with a hollow reëcho, as in an empty building. We went into both rooms where the light had been, but everything was still and untouched. It was clear, no mortals had been there for a long time. I was at a loss. Of the figures and the lights, I could not have a doubt. They had been there. At length, on going back to the room where the brightest lights had been, I looked out of the window, and there was the explanation! You see this head of the triangle—well, there was a cottage with a bright open fire in a large fire-place, and men and women were passing before it. The reflection first struck full on these windows, while some inequality of the ground prevented its being seen from the other house. Was it not a good instance of our *spökeri*?"

Mr. X. has taken a philosophic interest in these superstitions, and investigated them somewhat closely. There is often a deep poetic truth in them.

THE TOMTE.

Two peasants—so believe the people—start in life with equal blessings; each has his rich grain-fields, his patch of wood, his red-house, his horses and cattle. One thrives continually; his stacks are fuller every day, his crops better, his beasts healthier, his house more protected from storm and winter. With the other it is the reverse. The roof leaks, the cows die, the wheat mildews, the hay rots, the land grows poorer.

What is the reason of the difference? Manifestly, the first has his *Tomte*, or little attendant spirit. The last has offended him. The *Tomte*, as all know, is the spirit of some poor heathen slave, who must work out his salvation before doomsday. He is a repulsive, deformed little fellow, hardly larger than a babe, with an old shrewd face, and wearing a red farmer's-cap and grey jacket and wooden shoes.

One of the peasants had seen him at his usual time, in the noon day, dragging wearily along an oaten straw to the stack, or one ear of wheat to the barns, and scorned him and railed at him, saying he might as well bring nothing as such trifles. Then the Tomte went sadly to the other, and he grew rich, while the first became poor. If the Tomte brings only an acorn to the barn, no one must despise him. The proverb says, "The woodman holds the axe, but the Tomte fells the tree."

THE PUKE.

The Puke is more commonplace. He is a kitchen elf, whose excrements are frequently seen in the milk-kitchen. Certain old women sell themselves to the devil, in order to get possession of these elves, for then they will have milk and cream as much as they desire. If any one wishes to discover these old women, he will burn the excrements where three roads meet, with bits of wood from *nine* different trees, and then they must appear.

The Swedish superstitions have a characteristic tone to them—a more sober and religious element than the superstitions of other European peasantry. This is particularly true in those where Heathendom and Christianity are, as it were, struggling. The mysterious spirits of the streams and mountains are not merely fairies—creations of pleasant fancy. They are the unfortunates who did not enjoy, in their mortal lives, the light of Christianity, and are now awaiting Redemption. They are often almost despairing, and even the passing traveller may bitterly wound them, by proclaiming too severe condemnation on them.

NECKEN.

I have spoken of the plaintive melody of the "Necken." This being appears in different forms—sometimes as a young man with beastly extremities, representing the power of animal passion which has brought him to this; sometimes as an old man, but more often as a youth playing the harp on the water. The best offering that can be made him, is a black lamb, especially if the hope of eternal salvation be at the same time expressed. Two boys once said to Necken, "What good dost thou gain by sitting here and playing? Thou wilt never gain eternal happiness!"* whereat he wept bitterly.

* Svenska Folk Visor—quoted by Thorpe.

In a locality of West Gothland, a *Neck* was heard singing to a pleasant melody these words—"I know—I know—I know that my Redeemer liveth!"

THORPE quotes a beautiful story of the Neck:

"A priest riding one evening over a bridge, heard the most delightful tones of a stringed instrument, and, on looking round, saw a young man, naked to the waist, sitting on the surface of the water, with a red cap and yellow locks. He saw that it was the Neck, and in his zeal addressed him thus: 'Why dost thou so joyously strike thy harp? Sooner shall this dried cane that I hold in my hand grow green and flower, than thou shalt obtain salvation.' Thereupon the unhappy musician cast down his harp, and sat bitterly weeping on the water. The priest then turned his horse, and continued his course. But lo! before he had ridden far, he observed that green shoots and leaves, mingled with most beautiful flowers, had sprung from his old staff. This seemed to him a sign from Heaven, directing him to preach the consoling doctrine of redemption after another fashion. He therefore hastened back to the mournful Neck, showed him the green flowery staff, and said: 'Behold how my old staff is grown green and flowery, like a young branch in a rose-garden; so likewise may hope bloom in the hearts of all created beings, for their Redeemer liveth!' Comforted by these words, the Neck again took his harp, the joyous tones of which resounded along the shore the whole livelong night."

It was characteristic that while talking over these superstitions with Mr. X., our young friend with us, Mr. T., volunteered a confession of no less than two most astonishing supernatural experiences which he had met with—one being the reappearance of the spirit of a lost friend, and the other the apparition of a dog! Both he implicitly believed.

The whole mode of life at my friend's was extremely comfortable and agreeable. Breakfast was at nine, dinner at three, and supper at eight in the evening. The house was a long one, and nearly the whole family lived on the ground floor. There was a pleasant garden, in which we often walked. The service, housekeeping and management was of the most quiet, refined description. I had some comparing with Lady X. of the wages of servants. For her chamber-maids she pays about twelve dollars *a year*, and that is liberal. The footmen and coachmen earn about double this. Two thousand dollars would be reckoned a handsome income for a judge or even a bishop. The common expenses here for food, rent, etc., are wonderfully small, compared with the American.

There were endless inquiries after our modes of life in America. Hearing of the tyranny of conventionalities already beginning with us, a gentleman present related his struggles in one of the Swedish cities. He had small means, and, as he was about to be married, he determined to arrange matters very moderately. He accordingly induced his lady to put the ceremony in the morning, and invited only a few friends, with a simple refreshment. The thing was town-talk for a month; and people could hardly agree that there had been a proper marriage.

When his first child was christened, in place of a grand feast and numerous sponsors, he only asked one or two intimate friends, and had a glass of wine. This too was thought an extraordinary eccentricity.

I had much talk with Lady X. on the position of woman in the higher classes here. She says that even with the wealthy, the household demands much more personal care than in England or other countries. So much is made and produced on the estate always, that greater supervision is necessary. She thinks there has been, within a few years, great progress among the ladies in the ideas of their higher duties—especially those towards the poor. It seems the same problem here as all the world over, for the woman to systematize time, so that duties to herself and to her family and to the world, may not conflict.

* * * * * *

Mr. X., gratifying my hobby of studying the condition of the peasantry, has taken me to some of the Smäland Bonders. The first one whom we proposed to visit, had some office in the parish, and lived in a very comfortable style. His house was a large two-story house, like a well-to-do farmer's at home, approached by a winding road. We knocked and groped about for some time, without effect, until at length the mistress—a common-looking laboring woman—came forth. The husband was away, but we could see the house. The building and furniture were new—the latter mostly of birch, and quite as good as in a Connecticut farm-house. In one room was a writing-desk, with protocols and papers on it, and newspapers hanging filed near by. In another, were the pictures of Luther and of Swedish heroes. There were a number of sitting and bed-rooms, besides one large ball-room.

No books, however, were to be seen. I had visited no peasants' houses, since those near Gottenburg, showing the owner in so comfortable a position. The fact is important, historically, in the condition of this great class.

The next visit was to a Bonder, who was an alderman of the village. He lived in a three-story wood house, with a large farm about it. His reception of us was very friendly. He brought forth a bottle of some sort of cordial and some curious little cakes, which he almost forced upon us. The house was even more comfortably furnished than the other. He owned eighty or ninety cows, eight or ten horses, and six pairs of oxen. There was a large threshing-machine on one of the barns, and an American plough in the yard. He had been draining and under-draining his whole farm. He had heard of the American reaping-machines, and thought they would be just the things for Sweden. After being quietly seated, we had a long conversation.

I asked him whether he thought the "House of Peasants" would be in favor of railroads in the next session. He thought they would, though many took a long time to see the necessity of them. He should advocate the government's making a permanent loan to the companies, receiving a regular interest, as from a bank.

I spoke of a reform in Representation. "For my own share," he answered, "I should have no objection to a change, and I should prefer to bring in the other classes.

There is no reason why Herr X., or any one owning land, should not vote with us and act in our House, as well as we. And I am sure that it would be better for us, as we should gain some good speakers and men of business. Now we often have very poor Houses. Still many of our Bonders will be jealous."

I found him equally liberal and enlightened on the subject of schools. He felt the country to be far behind in that respect, and he hoped that his House would help on the measures for popular education.

We asked him about books—what he had? He seemed scarcely to have any; seldom read any thing but the newspaper and the Bible. He had heard of the tremendous contest in America, and understood the question: was proud that Sweden would not allow a slave on her soil.

His manner in the conversation was not at all so obsequious or diffident as one generally sees in the Bonders towards those of the other classes. He had his own views, and evidently did not fear to utter them.

THE MAGAZINE.

In riding back to the house, we passed a large brick building, near the parish-church. On inquiring, I learnt that it was the Parish Magazine. That is, under a remarkable *socialistic* arrangement, the people are obliged to bring thither certain small proportions each year of their crops. This grain is kept, and when a year of bad crops comes, it is loaned out at a certain interest—paid in grain—to the members of the parish ; or, if any are absolutely suffering from want, it is given ; and thus it becomes a kind of permanent social institution for the help of the parish. Similar storehouses exist through all Sweden.

One difficulty in making public provision for the public poor in Sweden, lies in the internal organization of the country. There are no Provincial Legislatures or Assemblies. The only administrative bodies are the Parish meetings ; so that it sometimes happens, that a petty matter, which belongs exclusively to the district, will go through several instances even to the king. This is the case with matters of pauperism.

Sweden needs two great changes in her internal administration. First, a more permanent, active representation of her parishes (*Socknar*), which shall have the character of, but be more efficient, than the present *Socken-stämma* (Parish-meeting); and second, a representation of counties (*Län*).

We stopped on our way home at the village School. It was held in a very neat-looking dwelling-house, the other part of which was occupied by the teacher's family. The children looked singularly pale and feeble, as much so as the poorest in our Charity Schools at home. They were, I learned, the children of poor laborers, who at this season, did not have much good food. The Teacher was putting them in a dreary way through the unfailing Catechism. (I ought to remark here, that I do not remember ever to have entered a popular School in Sweden, where this species of religious tongue-exercise was not going on.) Each boy droned over the replies, as he would over a definition in chemistry. Truths, which if believed, would rend human society as a rotten web ; Facts which are the echo of the grandest experience that man has yet worked out ; Definitions upon which the most acute minds of all ages have incessantly differed, were sung sleepily over by these children, and thus, as the catalogue says, they were "*taught Religion !*"

CHAPTER XXXV.

THE RIDE TO CARLSCRONA, AND THE FLEET.

WE stopped first at a very handsome place, V——, the property of Capt. M——.

This is the old estate of the Oxenstiern family, famous in Swedish history. It had the only real park I have yet seen on a private property : a grove of magnificent oaks and beeches, broken up with knolls and lawns, and little lakes and arbors, stretching down to the very shores of the sea. It is laid out in the best English style. The owner, a hearty hospitable soldier, took us over it, showing with much pride the grand trees. Some were as fine as any in our American forests. Only a few elms were to be seen ; the trees were principally knotty oaks, with rich foliage, and the compact, clean, muscular beech, with its twinkling little leaves. As is usual, an orangery and conservatory, were in one part of the grounds. The European chestnut begins here to grow in the open air.

The house or Hall is a quiet unpretending building, with large old halls and chambers. We spent some time examining the paintings, of which, the collection though small, is valuable. The choicest were some pieces of the Holland school.

Our reception in the family was kind and hospitable. We dined with them ; the table was served in the usual Swedish style, with much simplicity, for people occupying such a position.

CARLSCRONA

We found here a very good inn, and after a comfortable night's rest, proceeded to see the great attraction, the dry-docks and the shipping. The town itself is a pleasant one, with the air of a fortified or military station.

Two young noblemen, officers, to whom we had letters, accompanied us, and were very polite and attentive. They both spoke English, and had visited America as common sailors. Many of the officers, they say, serve in foreign marines for the sake of the experience, and some even in the merchant service. We found five new frigates in dock, and we went aboard of one line-of-battle ship, the *Carl Johan*, fitted with a screw propeller. Our officers complained much of want of service. They had hoped for a brush with Russia. The service is overrun, they say, with young men from the noble families, who merely come in to find a berth, without really taking an interest in their profession.

SWEDISH FLEET.

The force is 1300 guns, on 10 two-decked line of battle ships, 6 frigates, 4 corvettes, 3 brigs, 100 gunboats (schooners), 125 other boats, 7 mortar-boats, 9 steamers, 21 messenger vessels.

Personnel.—228 officers, 35 marine regiment officers, 280

petty officers, 40 non-commissioned officers, 255 boys, 400 apprentices, 150 gunners, 800 marine soldiers, 5694 seamen (furnished from naval militia), 2427 extra seamen, 25,000 conscripts (liable to service in time of war), 2500 merchant-seamen (similarly liable).

Officers.—1 admiral, 1 vice-admiral, 13 rear-admirals, 5 commodores, 10 commodore captains, 20 commanders, 60 captain-lieutenants, 60 first lieutenants, 60 second lieutenants, 30 supernumerary lieutenants.

MINISTRY OF MARINE.

In Sweden, the Minister of Marine is member of the Council and the Cabinet, and adviser of the king in naval matters. He issues the Royal orders, and has chief command in the navy, and makes all appointments, high or low.

There are two bureaus in this ministry. One for affairs before the Council of State, called "Bureau of Office Affairs," the other for affairs of ordinance, called "Bureau of Command." The chief of the first may be a civil officer, appointed by the king; the chief of the second must be a naval officer.

Under the care of the Ministry of Marine is an institution, called "Administration of Marine Affairs," which is in the form of a College, and consists of a chief (an admiral), two other superior officers of the navy, and one member of the civil service.

This is subdivided thus: 1. Bureau of Construction; 2. Bureau of Pilots; 3. Bureau of Maritime Charts; 4. Bureau of Accounts.

The duties of Naval College are, general inspection of naval affairs, control of pecuniary means, of material and of workmen at all stations, superintendence of naval establishments, purveying of clothing and provisions, hydrographical operations, pilots, lights-houses and signals.

Corps.—Officers of navy, officers of construction, officers of mechanicians, sub-officers of marine, with sailors, workmen, and coast-guard.

Budget (1853).—$571,700 per annum, voted at every Parliament for three years.

Education is obtained at the Military School at Carlsberg. A corvette with fourteen young officers is annually sent out on an expedition for ten months, to train for service.

THE MERCANTILE MARINE.

In 1840, the Parliament made an appropriation of $4,000 per annum for naval schools, which they subsequently increased to $5,500 for the purchase of books and instruments. The Terms are from May to October. At the end of each, examination qualifies for masters and mates of 1st and 2d class.

Masters of 1st class can command in all seas. Masters of 2d class can only sail to European and Mediterranean ports. No mate can sail beyond the Baltic without passing two examinations.

One of the most useful and practical naval institutions in Sweden is

THE SEAMAN'S HOUSE.

Each port must have one, under the government of a committee, a magistrate and a sea captain, called Director. The duties of the director are to register all vessels belonging to the town, to control their certificates, to see that they pay the poor-rates to the community, to provide that every vessel leaving port be duly provisioned and manned, to settle petty differences, register apprentices, give a list of crews, and to see that they are regularly paid off in proper proportion. He is also charged with the promotion of sailors, according to their merits. When a commander wants a crew, he goes to the Seaman's House, and chooses mates and men in presence of the Director. The latter makes a list of the crew, on which every person writes his name. After this, the captain, mates, and men are mustered at the Town Hall, and swear in the presence of the magistrate to obey the navigation laws, etc., etc. The list is signed by the magistrate, and from that moment, the crew belong to the ship for the time and distance agreed.

When a crew is paid off from a ship, the Director of the "House" musters them in presence of the commander, and receives them back from his hands.

Every seaman enrolled in the Seaman's House is freed from conscription, except in war, when he is bound to serve in the royal navy, if called upon, having the usual pay.*

* These statistics and facts have been gathered by the Hon. F. Schroeder, Minister at the Swedish Court, and furnished to the author.

It appears from all this, that in the education of a Swedish seaman, knowledge of a ship's husbandry, the stowage of cargo, exchange, etc., etc., is reckoned a necessary part. The Seaman's House also gives great facilities for ascertaining the character of both crew and commanders on the merchant ships. There is less probability of tyranny, or of mutiny, with such an arrangement. Many of the first class merchant-vessels are commanded by Lieutenants of the Navy, who take the place for the sake of the experience gained. * * * * *

BLEKING.

Sept. ——.—The ride south from Carlscrona is a beautiful one. It is like journeying through a park ; the landscape is a gently undulating country, with scattered groves of oaks and beeches. The crops look finely, and the grass is more rich than any I have yet seen in Sweden. With a rich afternoon sun-light gleaming across through the branches, and the distant aspects of the sea, it makes a ride to be remembered. Posting is now very agreeable. I obtained in Kalmar, an easy old carriage, looking like a cast-off family chariot, which moves on very comfortably, so that in uninteresting districts we can post all night. At every Station, usually once in seven miles, we get a fresh pair of horses. The carriage is to be sent back by steamer from Malmö. A gentleman from Kalmar has kindly offered to accompany as guide and travelling-companion. We sent on orders for horses at certain hours, and as usual, are some two hours or more, too late, so that at every station, we pay *wait-money* ; a thing which slightly exasperates my companion, though I bear it philosophically. We are now in Bleking, the outskirts of the old Danish kingdom of *Scania* or *Skonia*, the provinces which have so often been lost and regained in Swedish history. Here flourished the first Northern civilization and commerce, when Germany and Jutland were covered with dense forests.*

Småland separated this kingdom from its enemy and rival on the North, Gothland.

They tell us that even yet, the feud rages between the Blekingers and the Smålanders. The only traces one can see of the Danish influence, are the high thatched peaked roofs of the cottages, and the smaller number of out-houses —both of which are peculiarities of Holstein at this day, as compared with North Sweden. The accent of the people is decidedly different.

I was never so impressed, as on this whole Swedish journey, with the multitude among men of the workers in the ground. We speak of the scholars and gentlemen and ladies as the important class, and in one view they are. But after all, what mere exceptions are the rich and the cultured, if one considers the great masses of humanity. The millions in all ages and countries, have belonged to the ground, have tilled, and sown, and reaped in weariness and much toil. When we think of the world, it should not be as a world of shopmen, or priests, or gentlemen, but as a

* Geijer.

world of weary, begrimed, toilsome workers in the old mother Earth.

This is the rich part of Sweden. From these provinces she begins to export her wheat, though, but a few years ago, she never raised enough for her own consumption. This prosperity is partly due to improved agriculture, and partly to the fact that the wheat is so much less used for distilling.

Sweden, owing to the bad system of culture, has always had a difficulty in supporting her population on her own grains. In ancient times, many a king has been immolated or murdered after a bad harvest. It was this cause undoubtedly, which sent off so many of her sons in the early piratical expedition of the Vikings.

One of our drivers to-day was the owner of the horses, and a wealthy Bonder. He was a Secretary of the Parish-meeting, and my companion always addressed him by his title. We were both much struck with the number of drunken people we had met, both in Carlskrona and the neighborhood—more than I had seen in all the rest of Sweden. Our driver explained it from the influence of the sailors at the city, and from the fact that there were no local laws to prevent it, as in Kalmar and other places. The tax fixed by government could not in this region quite put an end to distilling, though it had much checked it.

"Does Herr Socken Skrifvaren know of much emigration to America from these parts?" said my companion.

"Many hundreds from my village," he answered. "Fools!

they could do much better at home. Sweden wants every one now. But it is this cursed *Läseri* (Methodism) !"

"Why, how is that? What have *Läsarne* to do with it?"

"They turn every one upside down," he answered. "They make disturbances and break the law, and then, Herr Resande (traveller) knows, they must be punished; and so they go to carry on their accursed doings in America. *Förbanna dem!* Damn them!"

"You see," said my companion, "no one believes in *Läsarne* here."

"But will Herr Socken Skrifvaren tell us, if these men are really immoral?" I asked. He was obliged to own that they were not, so far as he knew—though he had heard they had night-dances naked together, and certainly they did not believe in the holy Church!

My companion then inquired for me, of his opinions of his pastor. His replies were substantially the same which we hear everywhere, and fully justified the *Läsarne.* A selfish, grasping, worldly man, who had gone into his profession for the purpose of getting a comfortable living—so he, in effect, pictured his spiritual guide. This fact and the Methodism he did not put together at all; and we did not press him on the conclusion.

CHAPTER XXXVI.

CASTLE L——.

I HAVE just been over Castle L——, the property of a gentleman whom I have been visiting. The family resides in the summer at a country-seat among the trees, a few miles distant, and our host, Count X., has driven us over to see the old castle. All this part of Sweden is a perfectly level plain, sprinkled with innumerable boulders and small stones, which have been brought here from some distance. The castle is built in the midst of this plain, begirt with a moat and some pleasant old gardens, and a few large trees, carefully planted and guarded. The building is a turreted brick structure, with somewhat of the pointed Gothic in the style, built around three sides of a square. It has been burned and rebuilt three times, and the Count showed us yet in the doors the bullet-holes from the last attack, made, if I understood correctly, by an assault of the Danes in the Middle Ages.

With all the antique appearance of the outside, the rooms within are light, cheerful, modern apartments. The floors are the parquette flooring of different woods, with rugs or pieces of rich carpet in the centre.

The ornaments, bas-reliefs and small objects of art are graceful and pleasing. The paintings are principally portraits. One of the saloons is crowded with them, making a history of its walls. The family is an old Swedish family of distinction, and below each picture are names loaded with historic titles. My companion, who is familiar with the detail of Swedish annals, calls up something about each; and the Count, who at first courteously said nothing of the paintings, is drawn out to speak of the old faces. One had been killed at Pultowa; others had the costume which they wore in a glorious imprisonment in Siberia; others belonged to the unforgotten days of Gustavus Adolphus; another—a lady's face, blooming with exquisite beauty—was the face of the renowned beauty at the court of one of the Gustafs.

Some of the fair faces of the past were beautifully preserved, the coloring of the portraits as fresh and life-like as on the cheek of its original. Courtly or historic anecdotes of each were related by the Count, and the hour with the old paintings was an hour with the old Swedish history.

In one of the large saloons was a full length portrait of one of the present young princes. The most noticeable thing about the furniture of the rooms was the draping of the doors from one drawing-room to another, so that the hard angular character of the door-way was relieved. We visited the library and study—little snug, practical-looking rooms, where Count X. experiments in natural science. He showed me there a secret seal of a society of Free-Masons, bearing date *Röda Rosen*, 1802—founded by B——, of Hesse. He had obtained it direct from reliable parties; and it bore out all that the worst enemies of the Masons have ever said of them. It was an exceedingly lecherous and coarse representation.

The Masons are making great progress at this time with the nobility of Sweden. The princes themselves are said to have joined the society.

In one room, was shown us, preserved in a glass case, an antique drinking-horn set with silver in the style of the ancient horns of the first Norse period, preserved in the Museums, together with an ivory or bone whistle. A curious legend is connected with this, which I will relate as it was related to me. The book of visitors to this precious relic was handed me, and I put my name in it—the first American's that had been written there.

We drove back in an easy little brougham with two powerful horses. The count's place is one of the most unpromising situations in Sweden, in the midst of this vast plain—on one side, the débris of a torrent of stones which have been scattered over all this country, and on the other, a desert of sand which previously had been encroaching steadily on his cultivated land. The stones he has made into walls, and has cleared where it could be done; the sand he has resisted by plantations of pines. The work which he has done in his life-time, in sowing or planting forests where had been barrens, and giving shade and valuable wood to his posterity, is wonderful. We rode mile after mile through forests of pines, and over hills with well-grown beeches and oaks, all of which he himself had had set out. On one estate, there were 75 Tunland cultivated when he came, now there are 950. He has planted over 4,000 acres with valuable trees.

The estate is the largest, I suppose, in Southern Sweden. It contains three or four churches and a number of schools which were built or are the property of Count X. He himself is a historic character in Sweden. He was in high public service under King Charles XIII., preceding Bernadotte; had a share in the Revolution, was minister under Bernadotte, and, I think, was once in the cabinet of the present king. But for some cause, he suddenly left public life many years since, and has devoted himself ever since to the care and improvement of his vast estate, and to the pursuits of natural sciences. He has been frequently recalled by the voice of the nation and of the king to the public councils, but he has held himself in retirement. His title is strictly higher than count—*Excellenz*, which corresponds perhaps to duke.

The approach to the villa is through quite formal avenues, of beech, I think, bringing us first in sight of the high-peaked brick barns, inlaid with wooden beams, like the timber-houses of England. On one side is a garden and a thick grove of trees, with pleasant walks along a clear little stream—all laid out by the proprietor. The villa has the usual arrangement of three or four separate little houses, each hardly two stories high. The guests in one, the servants in another, and the family in a third. An especial servant has charge of us and our apartments.

Several guests and their families—officers and noblemen—are visiting the house, together with some very agreeable ladies. The old nobleman is a complete host—a very courteous and dignified gentleman, but adapting himself to every one wonderfully, and giving you the impression of great sincerity and character. He speaks English, French or German, as the words come most readily to him.

The style of living is generous and simple, much like an English country gentleman's, or that of our American families of wealth, whose property is mostly in the country. With less extravagance of wines perhaps, but with a certain greater ease and quietude of house-keeping—a result of the training of the servants. I understood that there were fifty or sixty of these on the place, but probably only a small part are house-servants. These are all under the charge of an *Inspector*, who keeps the business-accounts of the estate.

The meals are much more English-like than is customary in Sweden, and are served by two servants in liveries. Breakfast is taken together at nine, and not in the bed-rooms as in Germany.

The family and guests are thoroughly well-bred, simple, lively and unconscious, entering into a stranger's objects with much sympathy, and making the home genial by their kindness and informality. It is noticeable that they always talk with each other in the language which the guest uses at the time.

We were sitting out at twilight under the beech trees, and one of the ladies said in English, "We find the American-English much faciler to understand than the English we usually hear. We have observed it before."

I said it might be that our habits of public speaking in

America gave us greater distinctness of enunciation. The English considered us finical in this.

"We get most charming sensations of America from Mistress Bremer," said one. "Oh, those forests primeval!—but she must paint *en beau!* Surely there cannot be so many wonderful personages in any one country! Are you so musical as she thinks?"

I thought American taste was improving each year, and asked what music was best liked in Sweden. "Oh, ever the German! Some play the Italian, and it is easier indeed; but for most, the classical German is the favorite. It suits our serious Norrland-nature."

I spoke of the interest I had felt in the old superstitions, and of my impressions of the Swedish character, as connected with them.

They allowed that they were true generally—that a great proportion of educated people did still believe them. "But you should hear our legend—the legend of the whistle and horn which you saw in the castle!" said one of the ladies. "No one is permitted to cast a doubt on that! Tell it, F——!" After a little struggle, a young girl was induced to relate it in French.

THE LEGEND.

There was once a terrible giant in V——, who lived in the mountain, way up at the west there. While he lived there, some pious Christians built a church near the sea, at ——. It was fifty miles off, but the giant could not help hearing the singing of the holy nuns, and it grieved him. Every morning and evening when he listened to the chantings, he became more angry, until at length he took up a great stone, as large as our house there, and threw it with all his might at the church. But it broke in two without reaching it, and one piece fell not far from here."

"You passed it this morning," interrupted one. "It was the large boulder near the village."

For a long time, no one observed anything especial about this stone, and it was not suspected that the wicked mountain-folk—the little *Trolls*—came there. But at last, stories got about, that the elves were in the habit of raising this stone on golden pillars and dancing under it. *Fru Cisela,* a grand lady, lived then in Castle L——, and she heard of this, and became possessed with a great desire to know something of the wicked elves ; so she promised gold and jewels to any one of her huntsmen who should visit this giant's stone when the Trolls were there. The Trolls, you know, always dance on Christmas morn, between cock-crowing and daybreak. At first, no one ventured to go, but finally a brave young huntsman volunteered, and on the Christmas eve rode forth to the stone. When he came near by, he heard the noise of music and dancing, and he saw the great rock raised up on golden pillars, and bright lights underneath. And there were a host of beautiful little fairies, dancing and singing and drinking, as if mad ; they wound about among each other, and flew and whirled like the leaves in a whirlwind ; and there was one of them who was the most beautiful creature ever seen. She had a diamond-crown, and a little whistle in her hand ; it was the queen of the elves. When she saw the bold huntsman, she ran towards him and welcomed him, and he was so charmed with her, that he hardly knew what he was doing. She then told her servants to offer him drink, and they brought him a horn, full of some not very pleasant-looking drink. He was just tasting it, when his good angel whispered to him that he would forget everything which he had been, and become only an elf, if he tasted. So he dashed the drink on the ground, snatched the whistle from the queen, and spurred his horse away. Where the drops fell on his horse from the horn, the hide was burnt. The elves followed him close, shrieking and crying fearfully. He crossed himself often, and the horse flew like the wind, so that the elves did not quite reach him. When he came near the castle, the portcullis was down, and the Lady and her guards stood waiting for him. They knew if he could only get over the moat, the Trolls could not injure him. At length, he sprung upon the bridge, was over, and it was drawn up. Then there stood on the other side, the wicked elves, moaning and crying piteously, "Give us our horn and our whistle! Oh! give them to us!" And the queen of the elves came forward, and offered countless gold and diamonds to the Lady Cisela, if she would give up the horn and whistle. But the Lady replied, "Thou wicked imp! thou shalt never have again thy horn and whistle! They shall remain here, and thou mayst cry, till ye all come to judgment at doomsday!" Then the queen said that if they kept those elfin things, they must guard them carefully, for when they should be taken away, then should the castle be burned down. And Lady Cisela answered, "Begone, ye goblins! In the name of *Jesu*, begone!" and at that word they all vanished into the air, and were never seen any more—though sometimes now, the servants think they hear them round the castle. The horn and whistle were kept and exhibited; but in a few days, the bold huntsman who got them, and his horse beside, died very suddenly.

The horn and whistle were in the castle a good many years, until the Danes attacked it and carried them both off to Denmark—then it was that the castle burned down the first time. So the things were brought back, and as they were visited and touched by so many people, they became a little injured, and were sent away to be mended—when suddenly the castle burned down again. A third time, a hundred years later, people forgot the elfin queen's warning, and sent away the relics for some reason or other, and again the building was burned. The family that owned them—the Ulftands—died out; and now they are in grandfather's family and kept in a glass case, so that nobody can touch them! So there you have my long goblin story!"

"Bravo! Good! Good!" we all answered.

I found afterwards a long-printed narration of the legend. The story is placed in 1490, I think. The relics are genuine antiquities, all scholars allow.

THE TROLLS.

My friends gave me many curious facts of these little people, as the peasants believe them. There are such a number of superstitions about them, that some scholars have thought that the primeval inhabitants of Sweden might, possibly, in some of the deep forests, have survived till modern times.

The boulders and rocking-stones, so common on the plains of Sweden, are always attributed to the Trolls. Usually, it is their hatred to Christianity which has led them to throw these at some church. There are a number of families which still derive their descent from the mingling of the children of men with these creatures. Many of the Trolls are seen on the uninhabited rocks and islets which abound on the coast of Sweden, whither they were driven by the early Christians.

"Some sailors belonging to Bohuslän," says Thorpe, "when once driven on a desert shore, by a storm, found a giant sitting on a stone by a fire. He was old and blind, and rejoiced at hearing the Northmen, because he was himself from their country. He requested one of them to approach and give him his hand, "that I may know," said he, "whether there is yet strength in the hands of the Northmen." The old man, being blind, was not sensible that they took a great boat-hook, which they heated in the fire and held out to him. He squeezed the hook as if it had been wax, shook his head, and said, "I find the Northmen now have but little strength in their hands compared with those of old."

A noble family in Sweden, the *Trolle,* derive their name from a bold deed of one of their ancestors, who struck off a Troll queen's head that offered him magic drink in her horn. The horn was long preserved in the Cathedral of Wexiö.

It is supposed that the offspring of the Trolls are countless, but that they die when it thunders.

CHAPTER XXXVII.

TABLE-TALK.

We rode to-day over parts of the count's estate, and visited the schools and churches. He has the "patron's right" with regard to the clergymen; the peasants tell him they would not wish him to give this up to them; they like his selections. One of the churches was built on the banks of a lake, in very tasteful style.

We were in a little industrial school, managed by Countess X., where the children of the *Torpare*—the poor tenants, who do so many days' labor in the year for their rent—come for instruction. There were classes in weaving, sewing, and in out-door garden-work. As we entered, the eternal catechism was being droned over. I made some remark on the Swedish method of religious instruction as we were driving away. The count shrugged his shoulders, and said something about its being impracticable to go against the current of your day in such matters, and the subject dropped. These day-labor tenants seem a wretched class—as miserable as our Irish shanty-population at home. We passed their cabins, set down amid this drift of boulders and stones, and girded with a few acres of the most hopeless land for tillage which can be found in barren Scandinavia. They are frequently tenants of tenants, and pay, by a listless doing of jobs here and there, for their wretched tenements and grounds.

The old *Höferi*, which used to prevail in Scania, in which the peasants were bound to work like serfs, is now entirely abolished.

I was asking our host his opinion of the famous jury-system among the Bonders, of which I have spoken so much. He believed it excellent as a means of education in legal matters, but had no confidence whatever in the jury in any country—not even in England, where he had personally seen its workings.

He told me of an instance lately in an adjoining county, where these jurymen had unanimously voted against the judge, and so carried the day. It was in a singular case. A congregation found its pulpit vacant, and summoned in one or two candidates to preach. One of these preachers in his sermon held out certain pecuniary inducements for accepting him. This was considered a fit cause of legal complaint, and he was called before the *Ting*, and condemned thus by the jury. What the punishment was, I did not hear.

In driving through one of the Count's woods, the forest-master met us, riding in top-boots on a hunter. He was an old soldier, I believe. His manner, as that of all the followers, was very appropriate towards the old nobleman—manly, but full of regard and respectful feeling. He took us to a beautiful point of view; and showed with pride the multitude of trees he himself had set out.

DINNER.

The same customs prevail here of handing out to dinner, as elsewhere, in formal companies. The conversation is very lively ; wine is scarcely drunk ; the dishes are much the same as I have hitherto described. While at table, the mail came, and with it the Stockholm paper, containing a long article on the latest news from *Kansas!* which was eagerly read to me—every one wishing full information on a struggle in which they began to feel the deepest interest. The action of the House of Representatives in refusing supplies to the army, was read from the same journal. Here the military men at table were very inquisitive, and fearful for the stability of our institutions. I put the defence on the strong constitutional ground, so often shown forth in English history, of holding the purse-strings against the oppression of one part of the government.

Everywhere in Sweden is the deepest interest in these questions.

Mention was made of Lallerstedt's new work, "La Scandinavie, ses espérances et ses craintes"—a book written in French by a Swede, strongly on the French stand-point, attacking Bernadotte for his separation from Napoleon, and urging the union of Sweden with the allies in the Russian War. The designs of Russia on the Northern coasts of Norway are very vividly pictured ; and the great loss in giving up Finland, in the disastrous years of 1809 and '10. The writer urges that a vigorous campaign, pressed with the superior generalship of Bernadotte on the flank of the Russians through Finland, would have made Napoleon's invasion of Russia certain to succeed, and would have established Sweden in its original unity, as master of Finland, Sweden, and Norway. The present union of Sweden and Norway, he considers of very little advantage to the former country—Norway having most of the benefits with very little of the burdens, while Finland was an integral part of the Swedish kingdom.

The Count had figured historically in these scenes, and so far as he expressed his opinion, agreed with the view of most persons outside of both France and Sweden—that Bernadotte's policy was justified by the results. The French Empire was an accidental, temporary thing ; but the relations with the great Powers would probably be permanent and beneficial, both to Bernadotte's family and to Sweden.

It was objected by some one at table, that these late papers of Schinkel (the published Correspondence of Carl Johan, issued under his own supervision) proved the King thoroughly selfish in his policy.

"You see from them, he had his dynasty, not Sweden's interests, at heart. It is very plain that his ambition was to win the imperial crown of France, not to make Sweden a powerful kingdom."

"And yet," answered another gentleman, "see what he did make of Sweden. He found her plundered and despoiled, and just on the verge of utter destruction, and he made her at least respectable, and gave her Norway."

"But," replied the first, "these very papers of Schinkel

show that he had everything his own way, when he had the conference with the Czar at Abo. Alexander was prepared to yield Finland, if he pressed it."

"Still, he could never have held it," was the answer. "What an eternal bone of strife would Finland have been to us! Where would have been the natural boundary for us to defend?"

* * * * * * *

"It is true," said a lady next me in English, "we have not in Sweden a so great admiration as formerly for King Charles John. He seems so self-looking—how call you?—no: *selfish.*"

"But a remarkable man! A wonderful man in many respects," said the Count in German. "He was by nature an orator and a true citizen-king. He liked to speak, and he liked the people. Still, it was very difficult for us to get on with him. At one time, it would be, with a fiery enthusiasm, '*Moi—je suis Républicain!* No such measure must be proposed to me.' At another, when some parties had offended him—'*Les Rebelles!* They should be shot!' He had great executive and strategic talent. Schinkel shows clearly that the plan of the campaign, even to the great closing in Leipsic, was the King's."

A story was told here of Bernadotte, which has been in print, though it is not common.

He was commandant of a town in Hanover, and happened to be present at a public dinner. An English officer was at the table, who had served in India. Bernadotte and the Englishman were recalling the campaigns, and at length the officer related an adventure which had laid him under lasting obligations to the French. He was attacking a redoubt, where he was struck down and just on the point of being murdered by some of the native troops, when a French officer sprung from the hostile defences, dispersed the assailants at the risk of his life, rescued him, and had him tended afterwards with the greatest kindness. He was never able to thank his deliverer, as circumstances called the French officer immediately to another point.

Bernadotte listened with increasing emotion, and at the close, unable to restrain himself, rose, threw his arms around the neck of the Englishman, saying, "*Ah! mon frère! c'était moi!* It was I! I had that good fortune!" And he related to the astonished company that he had had the opportunity to do the little service to an English officer in India, but he had never met him till this day.

All were deeply affected at the coincidence, and the most fraternal feelings were the result between the French and English officers.

After retiring to his quarters, the *Aide* of Bernadotte said to him, "Are you not mistaken, *mon Général?* You were not in India on that year; you were, you remember, in so and so!"

"I know it, *mon cher.* I never saw the man before or heard the story. But it was *some* Frenchman; and we must keep up the glory of the great nation, you understand! It would not do to let such an opportunity escape!"

* * * * * *

Another gentleman, an old statesman, familiar with the court of Gustavus IV., gave some droll stories of the trouble they had with the King in his country palace, at Drottningholm, near Stockholm.

There was a forlorn arbor in the grounds, where, after dinner, the courtiers sat in sombre silence, and took their coffee. It was looked upon as an abode of sorrowful spirits, as the King liked no merriment or conversation in his presence. On the Sundays, the crowd always pressed into the neighborhood of this arbor, and stared at the distinguished party. At first, the King would swear and send out a servant ; then, as party after party came to gape and look, he dispatched others—ministers and gentlemen ; but it was like keeping away a crowd from some wonderful shop-window in a city street. Wave after wave of population came pouring in, and was only diverted by the rods of the ushers and the requests of the gentlemen of the court. At length, the King, with a fearful "*Sacrament!*" rushed out himself, small stick in hand, to keep back the vulgar mass, to their immense amazement and amusement ; and the ministers were obliged to send for the guards to protect the arbor.

Bernadotte, on the other hand, liked nothing better, they said, than to sit in these gardens and be stared at. He never had any guards, and talked sociably with every one.

The dethroning of Gustavus IV., in 1809, was vividly described by some who had taken part in it. The whole country had become so thoroughly disgusted with him and his insane efforts to set Sweden in opposition to France and all Europe, that a conspiracy among the nobles was necessary to avert a revolution. The nation had already lost Finland through his folly, and feared even for the existence of Sweden as an independent government, if Gustavus was allowed to go on in his reckless measures. The plans of the noblemen opposed to the king were well arranged ; the guards had been bribed or removed, and all seemed certain; when on the 13th of March, they rushed in on him in his apartments, and Baron Adlercreutz demanded his sword. The king is said to have drawn it with fury, and for a moment there was danger of bloodshed. When disarmed, there was still another moment of terrible suspense, when the king, by a *ruse*, escaped through a secret door, and rushed out in the court-yard, to arouse those of his guards who were yet faithful. By good chance, a powerful life-guardsman of their own party met him just as he was bursting forth. Gustavus had still another weapon, and drew it upon him ; but the soldier first threw his arms around him, and thus holding him helpless, bore him within the palace before any outcry was aroused. Here he was confined, and afterwards transferred to Drottningholm. A regent was appointed, and in May, when the Diet met, he and his posterity were declared incapable of wearing the crown, and Charles XIII. was called to the throne.

The Swedish people have never forgiven this monarch the disgraceful loss of Finland, nor the treachery in which his admiral, Cronstedt, gave up the Swedish fleet, and the almost impregnable fortress of Sveaborg, to the Russian army.

I was much interested to find that the count and other

gentlemen who had figured in those events, did not hold Cronstedt for the thorough villain and traitor which the majority of Swedes regard him to be. They considered him weak; but they said the Russians, during the siege of Sveaborg, managed to introduce Stockholm papers and forged letters, announcing the complete prostration of Sweden under the French emperor, and declaring that the only hope was to yield everything to the Russians, and secure at least their assistance; so that the admiral was utterly deceived and mistaken.

They stated also that Cronstedt never received any marked honors or pay afterwards from the Russians, but lived in retirement and disgrace.

Late disclosures show that the secret articles of the treaty of Tilsit, in 1807, gave up Finland to Russia, and that Denmark was to be compelled to make over her fleet to France, and to join in the confederation against England.

* * * * * * *

In speaking of the question we had been at first discussing, I mentioned a conversation I had lately had with one of the most cultivated men in Sweden—a man of long experience in public affairs, who said, *I sincerely wish Sweden could have been put for three years under Napoleon's rule!*"

They did not share my surprise at the sentiment. The admiration for the French and for the Great Emperor, was very deeply fixed in many Swedish minds.

I told Count X. that, to me, coming from a public man, it seemed the most earnest confession I had yet heard of the backwardness of Sweden in all good organization.

They would prefer temporary foreign conquest under an intelligent despot, to the present antiquated, awkward, slow machinery of government.

* * * * * *

"There is not such a *furore* for the French in society as there used to be," said a lady near me. "Of course, we must take the *modes* from them; but in reading and such things, we go now to England and America."

"Your health!" said the Count, drinking and rising. "You see we have not the English custom of drinking alone, without the ladies. Have you in America?"

* * * * * *

As I have said before, the impression one gets of the ladies of the upper classes in Sweden is delightful. We are too apt, perhaps, in theory to decry the advantages of wealth, though we overvalue them in fact. There are certain great benefits possible from it, and yet, by a happy providence, they are all attainable in modern days without extravagant means. I wrote at the time these words, and they seem still true.

"Wealth (with rank) produces a kind of *repose*—a habit of security and home-feeling, and a screened delicacy, which is truly something worth. It gives the habit of using the best, and the custom of luxury (which is not of much value), and more self or circumstance-trust, so that the bearer has a calmness and dignity as of one controlling, not controlled. It does not give, as of course, taste, or quickness, or education; but it shields, it quiets the storms which beat about the young growth, and takes away the coarse necessities, which *may* wear off a little of the delicacy of the soul.

"One would suppose that a connection with a noble historic past would pledge the inheritor to as noble action in the present; and as we of New England feel yet the earnest presence and heroic purpose of our national forefathers, so to the individual a cloud of witnesses, of generous and wise men, consecrated by history, of his own blood and family, would be an impulse in the struggle for good. It does not, however, anywhere appear to be the fact. Even as, in America, many of the direct descendants of the Pilgrims and the Revolutionary heroes, are among those most recreant to liberty, so, the world over, has the mantle of the past taken the place of its spirit, with those nearest bound by blood to its heroism.

"That nature is the nearest complete which has the delicate touch, the sheltered fineness, and the sweet calmness of good circumstances, with the robust habit of exertion, and the use to unpleasant realities of poverty; and such natures we believe to be found especially in America."

As I went to the guest-house at night, in the still moonlight, the wonderful repose of the old place seemed heightened by the monotonous chant of the night-watchman, patrolling in some part of the estate—

"Hör väcktaren ropa!
Klockan elfva slagen!"

"Hear the watchman cry!
Eleven o'clock is striking!"

Sleep is pleasant after such days, and Swedish beds are good.

CHAPTER XXXVIII.

SOUTH-SWEDEN.

THE post-stations through Scania are so uncertain that we were obliged to send *Förbud*, or a messenger on horseback to order horses. If a mail happens to go through at the right time, one can always send one's orders by it very cheaply. In this case, there was an addition of half the expense to every station. We posted, the day after leaving Count X.'s, about 70 miles south, over a flat, barren country, through moors with occasional patches of buckwheat and potatoes surrounding the sparse farm-houses—the stormy sea here and there visible on our left when we reached a higher ground.

A depressing, monotonous ride. It proved fortunate that we had ordered the horses, as a party of gentry, with four carriages, had engaged ten horses at each station. They passed us at one station, in very elegant travelling carriages—the gentlemen themselves, in some of them, sitting on the box. It was evening when, in the rain and mud, we reached Ystad, and were lodged in a kind of parlor at the principal hotel, the bedrooms being full.

The hotels in South Sweden are certainly much better

than in the north—though still poor enough. Ystad is a well-built, busy, little commercial town, on the southeastern coast of Sweden.

A MODERN ESTATE.

We stopped the next day at Baron V.'s, to whom we had introductions. He is known as a nobleman who has deeply interested himself for the peasants, having written a book for them dedicated to a Bonder, and striven in various ways to improve their condition. The rumor is that his efforts have not been met with much gratitude. The wealthy freehold Bonders who live near him, do not like to have their modern extravagant habits criticised, and have resented his advice. They claim that they have the right to their silks and champagne as much as the gentry.

The property of the baron is very pretty and new-looking —a great contrast to the quiet old place we had just left, with the settled air of antiquity about it. This is such as an American would lay out if he were suddenly placed in Sweden, with sufficient means :—a new brick and stone villa—the two usual separate houses here added as wings, so that the house surrounded three sides of a square ; a garden carefully laid out with new walks, among many young trees, planted in the last ten years ; and new brick stables and barns, with high-pointed roofs, constructed on the best modern principles. The only thing ancient was a small grove of old trees, which had been religiously preserved. The whole estate was enclosed from the bare, treeless plain, with thick shrubbery. The house had the same modern air: handsome rooms, opening into each other on the ground floor—a rich library of modern works—many engravings from the best living German and French artists, and a thousand tokens scattered about, expressed the life of to-day. Our host was a travelled gentleman of considerable culture.

He describes the Bonders in South Sweden as a class rapidly improving in means, and with increasing desires to raise themselves. He thinks many of them are losing too much of their old simplicity, and are aping the classes above them. They are generally in favor, he adds, of the new measures for education, and for building railroads.

I asked him about the Bonder to whom he had dedicated his book. He replied that he was a most remarkable man —a person of much integrity and simplicity, and yet of talent. He had been member of Parliament, and had done very much for his class. He was greatly respected through all South Sweden.

We rode out afterwards in the neighboring country, and visited some of the schools which he or the peasantry had opened. We passed, also, a new church, which the peasants were just building. He pointed out to us a number of fine properties belonging to the Bonders. "You see that large house with the high roof—that belongs to Eric S——, a rich old fellow and proud. He likes our preacher—who, by the way, is a son of the famous Tegnèr—but he will not come there. He says he won't worship where there is some one who can look down on him.

"There's another good *Gut* (farm)!" said he, in German.

"That man there is spoiling his son. He thinks he must send him to the University, though he is hardly bright enough for the plough. If the *Bauer* would only first get a little common sense, before talking of the Universities !"

"But they must come up !" I said. "You can't keep them down !"

"No : we do not wish to. But let them improve rationally. They need not complain ; they are the aristocracy. They have the power now."

The agriculture in this part of Sweden is very good. The fields are generally under-drained ; the crops looks full, and the grain-stacks at the barns are immense. This increasing wealth among the farmers, is all from improved culture of the soil. They still want, and are ready for, improved machinery—especially for reaping and mowing.

The baron desired much a list of English and American books, adapted for the people, which he might translate.

I gave him all I could think of. It is a pity that those excellent early tales of Miss Sedgwick, designed for working people, should now be out of print. The "Temperance Tales," too, would be very useful in Sweden—though, from all appearances, the country is no worse in respect of intemperance, than most others.

We were hospitably entertained at the baron's—the guest-house, with three comfortable warmed rooms being allotted us, and a footman to attend to our wants. Very delicate fruit—grapes and apricots and plums—were brought in at the edge of evening, from the conservatories. We supped at 8 o'clock on a bountiful meal, and separated for the night, with many cordial expressions and farewells, as we were to start away early the next morning.

MALMÖ.

On our way to this city, we visited the estates of some wealthy Bonders—men living as rich farmers would with us, plainly, but very comfortably, with many working people about them.

Not far from Malmö, we passed one of the large *tumuli*, where the old warriors, in the times of the Vikings, were laid, and perhaps where Kelt and Finn far back in the past have also burned or buried their dead. This hallowed spot is now used for a porter-cellar, and public gardens are laid out around it !

At Malmö, we merely stopped to change horses and go to a book-shop, before starting for Lund. Among the books for sale here, I found an English copy of *Dred*, almost at the same time in which it appeared in America. The new (English) Leipsic edition of American authors—Hawthorne, Emerson, Curtis and others—was also here. Malmö is the capital of this province.

LUND.

An easy ride over a paved road of an hour and a half, brought us to the old University City. Of Lund, Geijer says : "In the Sound, every summer of the ninth century saw the fleet of the Islesmen, which drew an ample freight of fish from the teeming coasts, or brought back meal, wheat and honey from the then celebrated Scanian fair, which was held in the autumn. About the same time, Lund is mentioned as a place of considerable trade, surrounded with a wooden barrier, where gold or other property gained by piracy was stored up for security, although itself a mark for the attacks of the sea-robbers, who swarmed everywhere in these streets."

Before the cession of this province, in 1658, to Sweden, the town was the Metropolitan See of Denmark.

It has a quaint, picturesque aspect. The prominent object is the old cathedral, an imposing and irregular structure, founded in the eleventh or twelfth century. There are visible in it traces both of the Byzantine and the Gothic school—perhaps even of three ages of architecture. Professor Brunius is at this time repairing and enlarging the building, with great skill, apparently. Beneath it, in a kind of crypt—used once as the scene of mysterious funeral rites, and for the last ceremonial of catholicism—our friends showed us two columns, with a human figure carved on each, one of a man, and the other of a woman, with a child. The tradition is this : The holy Saint Lawrence was walking through the wilderness, and praying that he might be able to build a grand church to his God, when a giant met him and promised to grant his prayer, on condition of the holy man's bestowing on him his two eyes, and the sun and moon. The saint appears to have had no reluctance in promising, and the giant went to work. At length, when he had nearly completed his labors, the holy father bethought him that he had these rather difficult wages to pay. He became alarmed, and knew not what to do. He wandered out alone in the forest ; and there, while in pious meditation, he heard a giantess quieting her child, saying—

"Hush! baby, hush!
Finn, thy father, comes home to-morrow,
Then with the sun and moon shalt thou play,
And with the old saint's eyes!"

By this, he learned the giant's name, and of course at once had power over him.

The giant and his wife found that they were betrayed, and went to the crypt and seized each a pillar, to destroy the church. St. Lawrence saw them, and, in the very act, made the sign of the cross over them, saying, "Remain there in stone till the Day of Doom!" And there they are still shown, each embracing a pillar.

The legend is an imitation of one of the old Eddaic stories. A Swedenborgian friend who visited them with me, said that they were mythical representations—of which the old church is full. The beastly and earthly passions attempting to shake the temple of faith and purity, changed and rendered lifeless by the power of the cross, the symbol of Divine Love.

* * * * * *

Lund is especially famous for its university, founded in 1668. Puffendorf was professor here, and Linnæus a pupil. It ranks perhaps second to Upsala. The property belonging to it is large, being in great part the old estates and rents belonging to the Catholic Chapter of Lund, transferred to it by the King. With this—consisting of four parishes, thirty prebends, and nine hundred pieces of land—it meets nearly all its own expenses. The professors are paid in natural products. Salaries, *paid in grain*, vary from the value of one hundred and twenty dollars to eight hundred dollars. The *Privat-docent*, or tutor, is paid by his pupils. The theological professors have a parish. Even the lay-professors have sometimes parishes given them, though they must of course take orders. It is not uncommon for a lay-professor* to be appointed bishop, as a reward for distinguished talents or character.

One of my best friends in Sweden, recently appointed bishop, was formerly in a political office, and, if I mistake not, a lawyer. Tegnèr, Professor of Greek Literature, in Lund, and Agard, of Botany, were both made bishops.

The examination for the entry of students is said to be strict. The course for theology is ordinarily two years, and for other branches, three. The theological student has an additional examination to pass before the consistory, when leaving the university, before he can enter on his profession.

THE "NATIONS."

This division of the students occurs here, as in Upsala. It is obligatory, and no young man can be matriculated in the university, without being a member of the "Nation"

* An instance is related of an officer coming in boots and spurs to the Swedish court, to thank his Majesty for being appointed a bishop!

from his own province. Each *Nation* has its rooms, library, reading-room, means of amusement and of study. Here is a very large, handsome building, with concert-hall, restaurant, and a number of reading-rooms, which belong to the Nations, combined.

There are four degrees in these voluntary bodies—*seniores, juniores, recentiores,* and *novitii.* To pass from one to the other, an examination is necessary before the class above. The Nation chooses among the professors its own Inspector, or general superintendent, who signs its acts and approves its decisions, and represents it with the academic consistory ; it also chooses from its own *séniores,* its *curator,* who is a kind of secretary and treasurer. Every student intending to pass his examination before the faculty, must first bring a certificate from his Nation of his conduct and studies. This body has a certain jurisdiction over its members, and even the power of expulsion, which is considered worse than expulsion from the university.*

It is said that many of the students live on one hundred and twenty dollars a year, without difficulty.

* * * * * *

I made the acquaintance of some very intellectual and accomplished men, among the professors here. We had an evening at Prof. B——'s, the most distinguished theological scholar of the university, and eminent, also, as a preacher. There is something wonderfully intellectual and ideal in the expression of his face, and he impresses one as a

* Marmier—Les Universités Suédoises. (Les Lettres sur le Nord.)

profound and scholastic mind. Yet I was disappointed, that a man of such world-wide culture should cling so closely to the political idea of the Church. I have met no theologian in Sweden so despotic and ecclesiastical in his theory. He listened to my rather frank expositions of the American system, with much respect, though apparently not so much caring to discuss them, as to get exactly our stand-point. In the course of the conversation, my friend spoke of the evils which all Sweden feels, in the mode of paying the pastor's salary—that is, the collecting it by fixed rates and little taxes among the parishioners, thereby encouraging a covetous and pecuniary relation alone between pastor and people. He suggested that it would be better for the Government, or for the parish-meeting, to determine the amount and raise it.

Prof. —— at once objected—"Nothing must be done which would weaken the legal claim of the Church to those rates and salaries. It was the Church's property."

I had understood he was engaged in reforming the liturgy of the Swedish Church, and it did not occur to me that, in this age, it could be but in one direction. I asked about the formula for the "Forgiving of Sins," and we compared it with that of the Norwegian liturgy. In the latter, the pastor, by virtue of his authority, declares the sins forgiven. In the Swedish, the absolution is more distinctly conditioned on the inner repentance, though still "declared" by the clergyman. It appears that a quibbling controversy has arisen in regard to this Absolution, and that this learned Protestant scholar, instead of seeking to wipe the whole declaration from the Swedish Prayer-book, as unworthy of a rational age, is striving to make it stronger—to establish that there is some mysterious, God-given, official power in the man of cassock and white bands, to heal the fearful diseases of the human soul, by *proclaiming* them healed! I may be doing him injustice, but such his position seemed to me; and I at once felt myself so far out even of the atmosphere of such ideas, that I listened to him in confused silence.

Our conversation on æsthetic and liturgical forms was more satisfactory. I told him that I felt on the æsthetical side of religious expression, men were almost necessarily one-sided. Historical associations, circumstances, climate, temperament, and other causes, make some classes of minds sensitive to a certain kind of religious and æsthetic impressions, while to another kind they are utterly obtuse or opposed.

This had struck me especially, comparing America and Sweden. Here, I found a ceremonial—a use of garments, colors, and forms, and tones, which, by the side of our bare and simple New England mode, seemed Popish and Romanistic—even as the Bavarian ceremonial probably seemed to him, going from Sweden. Yet, I could not doubt the essential spirit of worship in each and all.

He allowed the truth of this; but said, this was not true of the historic idea of a Church. Each country and people must have that for a full religious life; they must be connected to the past by direct spiritual bonds. The Church was mysteriously transmitted from age to age through its ordinances and divinely-blessed ministers, even as a State is. We had not this in America, and must, if we had not felt already, yet feel the ill effects of the want of it.

The existence of sects with us struck him in the same mournful light as I have before described among the scholars and clergymen.

We spoke of Bunsen, whom I felt to be one of the most enlightened and comprehensive theologians of the day. He did not like him, and spoke of the excessive individualism of his "*Signs of the Times*" with severity.

Our conversation, lasting for a considerable time, was very interesting, and I left him with a high respect for his courtesy of manner and his culture, though differing utterly from his theories.

* * * * * *

I have alluded to my Swedenborgian friend, Dr. K.—a most genial, agreeable person—a believer also in "Spiritualism" (so-called). It is a remarkable thing, that one meets with so few Swedenborgians in Sweden. The superstitious, dreamy temperament of the Swedes would seem to be just the atmosphere for such visions to flourish in; still the Revelation has now far more followers in England and America, than in its own country.

I have repeatedly read the prophetic and figurative parts of Swedenborg's writings. The profound convictions of his followers almost force one to look again, at what can inspire such an undoubted faith. But never have I been able to finish the perusal of his mystical visions; there is something incredibly dreary in them. That he was a great man, a man of vast erudition—though his Latin is sometimes wretched—and of much science, there can be no doubt. That he believed in the reality of his own visions, is probably equally true.

His theology, or rather Christology, as usually given by his followers, seems to me entirely consistent with the Apostolic standards, and to have within it, a life-giving truth, which is not, however, Swedenborg's more than it is Augustin's or Paul's—the MANIFESTATION of God in Christ to men. His followers, I have generally found very simple, earnest, religious people.

We had a very pleasant dinner with Dr. K. and some other agreeable friends, at Baron Gyllenkrok's. The Baron is an enthusiastic naturalist, and a well-known friend of the poor. His "Ragged School," near Lund, was probably the first of the kind in Sweden.

He believes, with many now in different lands, that it is bad and wasteful policy to be expending such sums on the punishment and imprisonment of children, when they could as easily, and at half the expense, be reformed. He has, accordingly, collected the subscriptions for a building and a farm, where the boys of the prisons, the outcast, homeless lads of the cities, all those growing up under Christianity in Sweden, yet outside of religion and civilization, should find occupation, training, and a home. The enterprise has worked well. The Swedish people is not one that recognizes its obligation towards that class of its society, as much as some other nations; still Baron Gyllenkrok has succeeded in collecting considerable sums for his institution. We found the building a large, comfortable structure, with a fine garden, and fields about it. Some of the boys were working in the garden as we drove up, and they ran to the baron's carriage, presenting their cheeks for him to stroke, and kissing his hand. The first room which we entered was a work-shop for basket-weaving. That and the garden and farm-labor are the principal industrial occupations. We visited, besides, the school-room and dormitories, and hospital-chamoer—all very neat and comfortable. It is strange, with all the Swedish manufacture of iron, that they have not arrived at the great improvement of iron bedsteads for their public institutions.

One especial means of reformation employed in this school, is *music*, and with the best effects. While we were there, the boys were called together to sing and play for us. One led, on a small organ, and the others sang; afterwards there was an accompaniment of violin and flute, with very good singing in parts.

Some of the songs were very touching, and our friends could not, several times, refrain their tears. One gentleman in our party, as he afterwards told the Baron, had once been as destitute as any of these little outcasts; he had known what it was to be on the verge of starvation, and had seen his father, a laboring man, return home at night, almost fainting, and shedding tears, because he had nothing with which to feed his starving children. Of course, such an education had given him an undying sympathy for the poor and degraded, and fitted him for the post he so well fills, of reformer and friend of the poor.

One pale boy, of not a bad expression of countenance, who sang well, the warm-hearted Baron frequently caressed, saying, "Poor boy! Six weeks on bread and water, and only ten years old!" This had been his sentence, it appears, for some crime of poverty, until the Baron had begged his release, and was now trying the effect of good fare and kindness.

After a certain time spent here, the lads are scattered abroad through families in the country; and thus far, the results have been here, as almost everywhere in similar enterprises, exceedingly fortunate.

The Truth is dawning on this age, that vice and crime can be checked by other means than punishment; that prison-bars and penal restraints for the young, are a disgrace on our Christianity, and show we have lazily neglected the prevention, and must now employ cruelty.

Sweden would never be disgraced by such a number of prisoners in her large cities, if she had more such reformatory schools.

There is one especial danger, however, in all such institutions. The managers are tempted to keep the reformed and improved children together, for the sake of showing to the doubtful and worldly what can be done with this miserable class. They come to have their model wicked-reformed children, who listen year after year to the tale of their former wickedness and their present piety, until they arrive at a condition, if possible, worse than their first sensualism and bold sinfulness—a conscious, canting, hypocritical state. Besides, this class of children are never improved by being kept in contact. They want most, the individual influences of a home, not of an asylum. The object should be everywhere to scatter them about through a country, placing them in kind, religious families.

The Baron's school had performed one thing in which the Swedish charitable institutions are usually shamefully deficient—the publishing of a succinct *Report* of expenses, receipts, and the various statistics of a reformatory institution.

At parting, the old Baron gave me a medallion of his head. He seemed really affected on bidding us good-bye, feeling it was hardly probable we should ever meet again.

When the kind old man dies at last—and may the day be far distant!—there will be many to mourn him in Sweden, but the sincerest tears, dropped on his grave, will be from the children of the friendless and the poor.

CHAPTER XXXIX.

THE CONSTITUTION OF THE SWEDISH CHURCH.

THE Swedish church is even more than united to the State. The two are, as it were, parts of one whole, so that, in communal matters, it is difficult to distinguish the one from the other.

All public actions are celebrated with churchly ceremonies :—the crowning of the king, the opening of Parliament, the sitting of the general court, the giving of university degrees, and the consecration of schools. The whole school system is under the care and guidance of the Church. The religious instruction in all schools is always Lutheran, and every academic term is opened with a theological examination. All office-holders must belong to the Lutheran church ; all garrisons, hospitals, and asylums,—all forces of the nation, by land or by sea, must have Lutheran chaplains, and shall hold daily religious exercises.

In Sweden, it is the parish, not the commune, which has the local government. The clergyman is, in fact, the governor of his little district, and a council (Sockenstämma) composed of the free-holders, members of the church, manage with him all the worldly affairs. Baptism and confirmation are made indispensable to holding office, or even to civil rights ; and the punishments of the church have the weight of legal penalties. The government and the church intertwine and become one in a manner so minute as to be indescribable, except in the details which can only be given in a traveller's journal.

The Swedish church cannot be called an Episcopal church, nor altogether a Presbyterian or Congregational. The best authorities* describe it as originally Episcopal in form, but now more nearly approaching the latter churches. Greater freedom exists within it than within the Norwegian. It holds, in the main, the congregational right of selecting its own clergymen, though the field of choice is limited by the consistory. It is estimated that two-thirds of all the pastors of Sweden are thus chosen ; the other third being appointed by patrons or by the king.

The church does not culminate in synods, but is rather a union of free local communities, presided over each by its own parish council. This council is founded on a feature of government which existed before the time of Christianity ; the division of the country into petty provinces, each with its centre of religious worship. It is a body having charge, through its committees, of the schools, the relief of the poor, the morals of the parish, the repairs of the church, the distribution of the church funds, and objects of a similar character.

Its principal committee,—composed of the pastor, vicar, and from four to eight elders, occupies itself especially with

* Prof. A. C. Knös, and Schubert.

the neglect of, or offences against, the church ordinances, such as absence from communion or severance of the marriage tie. This body originated in 1612 with the clergy themselves, and was caused by the difficulty of treating of moral offences of a delicate nature before the whole parish council. At one time, it had come to manage also the usual business affairs of the parish, but these have now been transferred to another committee, (Socken nämnd), and it retains its more churchly character.

Above the separate churches are the assistant of the bishop (prost), the consistories, and the bishop. The members of the consistories are the bishop, prost, and others, both lay and clerical, chosen in part by the king, and in part by the churches. The bishop is chosen by the king from those candidates presented by the diocese. He is considered a representative of the parishes, and, in the form of ordaining the clergy, it is distinctly provided that his authority proceeds from the trust of the churches, and nowhere is any apostolical succession claimed for him or his order. Both in the nomination of the clergy from the people, their duties, which are communal, not national, and in their support—from their parishes—it is attempted to be shown that the clergy, though associated with, are not servants of, the State.

The only bodies corresponding to the Presbyterian synods, are the synods of the dioceses, which act upon practical questions concerning the churches and the clergy.

The real synod, and highest authority for the church—next to the king, who, though not the head bishop, exercises many Episcopal rights,—is the *House of Clergy*, in the Swedish Parliament.

This is made up of the archbishop, who is *ex officio* president, and the bishops—twelve in number—together with the leading pastor of Stockholm, and forty-four deputies of the pastors or rectors, with a few deputies of the chaplains. Besides these, there are one or two members from each of the universities at Upsala and Lund, and two from the Academy of Sciences at Stockholm. The chaplains, being of the poorer class of the clergy, can only afford to send a few deputies, so that the whole number of members of the House is only about sixty-two. These sixty-two form one-fourth of the whole representation of the Swedish Parliament, though having a constituency of only about 2,700. They can block, by their resistance, any measure of importance, as changes in the Constitution require a majority of every house.

Though the church has a strong congregational character, the House of Clergy is very much under the royal influence. One-third of the livings are either in the gift of the crown, or of patrons who are closely connected with the government. The archbishop is appointed by the king from candidates proposed. The bishops, as has already been mentioned, are selected by the same authority, under certain conditions, and the remainder of the clergy are naturally much influenced by the wishes of the government, holding as it does the highest patronage in its hands. The king, also, has the power of absolute veto on all bills which affect the change or the forming of ecclesiastical laws.

The rectors alone are chosen as members by the congregation, from the three proposed by the consistory.

With this powerful royal influence, it is not strange that the House of Clergy has been the great hindrance to progress in Sweden. Through the clergy, the crown can also control the House of Peasants, so that full half the Parliament can generally be relied on as opposing any efforts at radical reform. It is a remarkable fact that in the Swedish Parliament, the liberal bodies are the Houses of Nobles and of Citizens.

The legislation of this clerical assembly has been such as might be expected. There are laws and punishments in the Swedish code against blasphemy, against the mocking of God's word and the sacraments, the falling away from pure evangelical doctrine, the spreading of erroneous doctrines, the violating the Sabbath, the despising of the sermon and the holy communion. It is only a few years since, that the law was repealed which forbade the attending any other church than the Evangelical Lutheran, by a Swedish subject, on penalty of about five riks-dollars.

So late as March, 1855, a law was passed aimed at the Baptists, which made it a misdemeanor, punishable with a fine of one hundred and fifty-five riks-dollars, for a layman to celebrate any of the sacraments, *i. e.*, to baptize or administer the Lord's Supper.

In 1853, an artist was condemned to six months' banishment, because he had renounced the Lutheran faith.

No Jews are allowed either to vote or sit in Parliament; and, before 1854, they were permitted to reside only in few towns of the whole kingdom.

The attendance of clergymen on Parliament is a great evil to their parishes, and I am convinced is one among many causes which have so weakened the spiritual power of the Swedish church. It seems to me quite right that a clergyman should occasionally have a part in legislation and in political life ; but thus to create a formal clerical diet, is not only injurious to the people, but gives to one small body an altogether undue and dangerous weight in the commonwealth. It originated when the priest was the only enlightened man of the parish, and all public affairs needed his assistance. That time has passed by in Sweden, as elsewhere.

This whole parliamentary system of apportioning a representation to the clergy, is one of the strong-holds which still support the almost incredible bigotry with which Sweden is now so painfully eminent. Where the Church is thus a power in the State, she gathers around her the worst vices of the world, rendered yet more dangerous by the cloak and ceremonial of Religion. Of course, there are beautiful exceptions to this among the Swedish pastors and bishops, instances of eminent piety and enlarged liberality ; I speak only in general of the tone and temper of the Church.

The Swedish writers who discuss this subject, seem to me generally to commit one great mistake—they confuse the Church with Religion. Of course, religion should now and evermore be united with all legislation and politics. The ideal of a State is a society and government inspired with Christianity. But the organized form—the Association, which, with its ceremonial, its wealth, its history and its men, is the means of imparting religious life to the world—

is quite another thing, and comes under the laws which affect human conduct, and is liable to no small share of the usual human temptations and dangers. It is not Religion, nor even organized religion ; it is only an implement, and a very imperfect one at the best.

Thus far, the experience of the world has shown that, wherever this spiritual organization is gifted with political power, and is placed in high official places, there will be formality, hypocrisy, bigotry, and spiritual lifelessness. The spiritual hope for Sweden lies now, we believe, in its despised dissent—the poor and ignorant *Läseri* (Methodism).

We believe it is no rash effort at foretelling, which should say that this century will see the disruption and convulsion of the Swedish State Church. The Baptists and Methodists are laboring in quiet, earnest way, on the great principles of Christianity ; and the very nature of these truths is to shatter hierarchies, and to tear open formalism and hypocrisy. They have thus far suffered persecution, banishment, and reproach ; but each day their cause grows stronger, and takes deeper hold of the hearts of the people. The upper classes, though hesitating to join the ignorant Läsare, are equally unsatisfied with the clergy and their teaching. The Swedish nature is one that cannot rest content with mere skepticism or with rationalism unlighted by religion. It is inclined to religious faith and consolation. It is, by temperament, almost superstitious. It will be long in taking to itself new supporters of its faith, or in adopting new means for imparting religious life, but when it does, it will be with a thorough renouncing of the old. The pro-sent clergy will become to the peasants as did the hierarchy of England to the Puritans of the Revolution. They will abhor and renounce them; and when the change comes, one of the great things done will be the utter sweeping away of the House of Clergy and all political powers belonging thereunto. The Church will be left to rest where it should, on the personal relations of pastor and people, on the affection of the one, and the abilities and self-sacrifice and piety of the other.

May the day soon draw near of such spiritual liberty to Sweden!

CHAPTER XL.

THE SWEDISH PARLIAMENT.

THE Riksdag or Parliament is made up of four Houses: 1. That of Nobles; 2. Of Clergy; 3 Of Burgers or Citizens; and 4. Of Bonders or Peasants.

I. The *House of Nobles* consists of three ranks, counts, barons and gentlemen. The senior member alone of a noble family has a hereditary right to a seat. In 1850, there were more than 1,500 noble families in the kingdom, and 432 representatives of them in the Parliament.

The senior member will frequently give his seat to a junior member either of his own or another family. A proxy is sometimes sold by a poor noble, indirectly, to government. An instance is related—though I am unable to say on what authority—of the crown prince's buying a seat during the late discussions on parliamentary reform, and giving it to a friend to vote against the liberal party. The nobles of Sweden are entirely dependent on the king for what is their great ambition—promotion in the army and navy. The President of this house is appointed by the king.

II. The *House of Clergy* has been described in the previous chapter. It numbered, in 1850, 64 members, and represented 2,773 voters. As has been shown, it is greatly under the royal influence.

III. The *House of Citizens*. This is chosen by all those who are members of guilds or handicrafts in the cities, or who belong to the magistracy. Many residents of the towns with large properties, have no vote for this body, or for their own local government, because they are not members of guilds. Yet, by a strange inconsistency, they can be *elected to* a city office.

In 1850, this house had 56 members and represented 13,496 voters. Five members were iron-manufacturers, and represented 216 voters. The admission of these last is a concession of modern years to the demands for reform.

IV. The *House of Bonders* (or Peasants). The class here represented number seven-ninths of the whole people, or about 2,250,000 persons. The voters, or freeholders, among these in 1850, were about 202,608. The representatives, 111; or 1 to 1,825 voters, and 1 to 20,270 peasants. No scale to the population was ever proposed. The President and Secretary of this house are appointed by the King.

A motion was made, in 1851, in the House of Peasants, that they should elect their own Secretary. It was carried, and finally passed all four houses, but was vetoed by the King.

The pay of all the members who are elected, is settled by their constituents. In the rotten boroughs, a bargain is often made, and the cheapest are sent.

Every member of Parliament must have been confirmed, either in the Reformed or Lutheran Churches.

In 1845, the population of Sweden was 3,316,536, of which the four classes represented in Parliament numbered only 2,346,248—leaving about a million of persons* entirely unrepresented, many of them men of property and intelligence, as, for instance, most of the members of the professions of law and medicine, literary people, the officers of the army and navy, all persons engaged in public service, not belonging to any of the four classes, and all day-laborers, apprentices, and Jews.

SCALE OF PROPERTY.

Nobles (in 1850), 11,248; real estate (of which one-third is mortgaged to the Peasants and Burgers), $30,000,000. Clergy, 15,000; real estate, $400,000. Burgers, 70,000; real estate, $14,000,000. Peasants, 2,250,000; real estate, $68,000,000.

Each house has an equal vote—so that two classes, the Burgers and Clergy, numbering 85,000, and paying a tax of $145,000, have half the voice of the Parliament, while the Peasants, with only one vote, pay a tax of $2,500,000; and of the unrepresented million, 70,000 persons of fortune and education pay a tax of $800,000, or nearly six times as much as the two classes mentioned above!

The first business of each house is the appointment of committees. These are appointed by electors, chosen by ballot for the purpose. The House of Peasants alone has the power of choosing the committees directly. The first is

* Hon. F. Schroeder—Dispatches to the Home Department.

the *Committee on the Constitution.* This, composed of six members from each house, has charge of all matters of constitutional law. It can indict the royal ministers before the Superior Court, and report on the proceedings of the Cabinet. The second, the *Committee on Finance;* the third, on *Taxes;* the fourth, on *Banks;* fifth, on *Statute-Law;* sixth, on general *Grievances and Order.*

After these appointments, thirty days are set apart for the reception of motions and petitions, and what is called the *Relation* or Report.

All reform-bills or fundamental changes in the constitution, must pass all four houses, and be carried over to another session, before they can be finally passed.

One of the most extraordinary features in this remarkable Constitution, is the deciding of questions, at the end of the session, by referring them to what are called "Reinforced Committees." These are made up of twenty or thirty members from each house, chosen by vote. They decide all questions by ballot, and, in order to secure a decision, the following singular means are employed. After depositing the ballots, one is taken out at hazard, to be reserved as a casting vote. If, without the reserved ballot, a majority of one should be the result, the ballot is destroyed unexamined, and a decision is thus often obtained, as fortune may direct. "Many vexed questions," says Mr. Schroeder, "after long debates, have thus been settled by a game of chance. Many changes of tariff thus, and, I regret to say, the game has not always been a lucky one for American interests."

The session of Parliament cannot last beyond three

months, though it may be prolonged, by informing the King, for one month longer, if the business be not completed. There have been instances of the Parliaments sitting nearly three years.

No member can be prosecuted or arraigned for words spoken in the Parliament, except with the consent of five-sixths of his house. The Parliament usually meets once in five years.

THE ROYAL POWERS.

As has been already mentioned, the King has power of absolute veto in cases of constitutional changes.

With reference to the increase or laying of duties or taxes, he has no power, even in the recesses of the Parliament. He has liberty only to reduce them.

The executive government of the kingdom is in the hands of the King and his Council of State, composed of ten members. The King himself chooses these—the only conditions being that they should be born Swedes, of pure character, and professing the Lutheran faith.

The King has the power of making treaties and declaring war, after consulting with an extraordinary Council of State. He is also the commander-in-chief of the forces by land and sea. Strict provisions are made in the constitution against his assailing the rights or interfering with the liberty of conscience of any individual Swede.

The King has the power of pardon, though, by a singular provision, it is left to the guilty person to accept it or not, as he may prefer (Art. 25).

The High Chancellor of Justice, the ambassadors and principal officials of the kingdom, the bishops, the curates of the royal parishes, and the burgomasters, are all appointed by the crown.

No requisition of men or money can be made for purposes of war, without the full consent of the Parliament.

GENERAL LAWS.

The liberty of the Press is one of the fundamental provisions of the Swedish Constitution, and has been further guarded by subsequent acts.*†

* A trial by jury is provided in Sweden for any one accused of abusing the liberty of the press. Thirteen persons are presented for jurymen, of whom the judge names five, the prosecuting officer four, and the accused four. The latter is allowed to challenge two—thus reducing the thirteen to eleven, and leaving only seven nominated by the court and public prosecutor.

† *Free Press in Sweden.*—Galignani's Messenger, of Paris, of 25th December, 1856, contains the following news summary:

"The liberty of the press has just achieved a triumph in Sweden. The four Chambers of the Diet have unanimously rejected a bill of last session, which erases from the constitution and places in the rank of ordinary laws that which guarantees the liberty of the press. In the Chamber of Nobles, one of the ministers (M. de Gripenstedt) made a sort of apology for presenting the bill, saying, 'Ministers are men, and as such are liable to commit errors.' The rejection took place almost without discussion, in the Chamber of the Clergy and of the Burgers. In the Chamber of Peasants, fifty members spoke against the measure. The last speaker, in concluding, said: 'The

In an elective kingdom, like this of Sweden, the right of election of the king, in case of the extinction of the royal line, is naturally left with the Parliament.

Careful provision is made for the impeachment of the Council of State, if it is discovered that they have either counselled the King to unconstitutional measures, or have themselves transgressed the laws of the kingdom, or neglected, when informed of them, the infractions of such laws.

REGENCY.

No two hostile countries, placed in unexpected union, could be more jealous and cautious in all their provisions towards each other, than are Sweden and Norway.

In case of the absence of the King, it is provided that there shall be a Regency at Stockholm, composed of ten Swedes and ten Norwegians. The Swedish members are, *ex officio*, the members of the King's Cabinet—that is, the Ministers of Justice and Foreign Affairs, and eight ordinary Councillors of State. The Norwegian are, the Norwegian Minister of State, two Councillors of State, always resident in Stockholm, and seven Councillors, summoned from Norway for the occasion. The Swedish Minister of Justice and the Norwegian Minister of State draw lots for the First Presidency, and then each presides in rotation for eight

liberty of the press is the tongue of the nation, and the wish now is to cut it out. Will you allow that to be done?' 'No! no! a thousand times no! God preserve us from it!' was the cry of all the others."

days. The President votes with the other nineteen, and, in a tie, has a second casting vote—thus giving a decision to each kingdom every alternate week. In Norwegian matters, the Norwegian language is used ; in Swedish matters, the Swedish language. Subjects affecting the interests of both kingdoms, shall be propounded by the Minister of Foreign Affairs, a Swede, and then drawn up by the Prime Ministers of each kingdom in their own language. No member of the royal family can be admitted to this council—not even the Crown Prince, who has a seat in the Cabinet.*

* "Those who take an interest in the affairs of the north of Europe have not, perhaps, passed unnoticed the fact published in the Swedish official journal of the appointment of a mixed commission of six Swedes and six Norwegians, to meet at Christiania, under the presidency of the Viceroy, for the better determination of the act of union between the two countries. It is worthy of remark that, though the sister kingdoms have been upwards of forty years under the same ruler, their mutual obligations, in the event of war, are still undefined. It is in order to supply this important omission, and to obviate any discussion that might arise in the hour of action, and prevent any fatal indecision at a time of common peril, that this commission has been named. It will be their duty to prepare the draught of a law fixing the military contingent to be furnished by each country in the event of their independence being threatened. They will also have to determine the forces to be maintained in time of peace, the reserves to be raised in time of war, the number of ships to be manned ; and, after providing for the defence of the two kingdoms, they will be called upon to decide in what proportion the expenses of the war are to be borne by each. Of course, due regard will be taken to make a fair allotment of those obligations according to the respective populations. At all events, the labors of the com-

The absurdities and awkwardnesses of the Swedish Constitution are so evident on the face of it, that they hardly seem to need detailing. The great wonder is, that an instrument so unpractical and cumbersome and unjust in its provisions, should have existed thus long in a country as intelligent and enlightened as Sweden. There is the less need here of enlarging on them, as my whole journey has been a commentary on their injurious effects.

Here is a constitution which creates four independent deliberative and legislative bodies, with a separate array of officers and order of business. Many important measures, to become laws, must pass three out of the four, and some must pass the whole four. How easy for one chamber to delay before taking up a bill, or to cumber it with amendments; how natural that the *esprit du corps* of each house should affect it in considering public measures, and hold it from meeting the wishes of the people; how many separate interests to conciliate, how many classes to manage, how many ceremonies and necessary business-arrangements, how much jealousy and rivalry and class-feeling, before even a simple measure of public interest could become a law! We see something of the difficulty in America, even with two houses: what would it be with four?

Then, in addition, one of these houses represents an interest which should not be represented on the political field—the clergy—which, if it be represented, will probably become the

mission must lead to a closer union of the two countries, and to a considerable increase of the common force."—*English paper*, *January*, 1857.

most impracticable, narrow, and illiberal interest of them all.

Beside this, the Constitution is unjust in only granting one-fourth representation to what makes up at least seven-ninths of the whole population—the class of farmers: a class which, in wealth and in its payments for the support of government, is by far the most important interest.

But, worst of all, this Constitution, through its arbitrary conditions, shuts out nearly a million of persons, many of whom would be the best qualified of any classes for the control of public affairs. Why this objection at least has not long ago been removed, is utterly incomprehensible.

The King, also, in this division of houses, is given an altogether undue weight, through his influence and power over two at least of the chambers.

What wonder that a country under such a government should be conspicuous in Europe, as almost the last to adopt modern improvements*—railroads, stage-coaches, telegraphs and popular schools! What wonder that the bigotry and narrowness of its legislation should be the object of scoffing, even in the Roman Catholic countries! In what Protestant country but in Sweden, at this day, could a man be punished or fined for his religious opinions?†

* There is not yet constructed a single railroad of any considerable length in Sweden.

† The following information has reached this country since the above was written. The bill for establishing greater religious liberty, which the king, on opening the Diet, announced, has been published in the official gazette in Stockholm, on Nov. 27, 1856. It sadly dis-

Where else could a law be still upheld, forbidding a commercial house from having a branch-house, or preventing a foreigner from transacting business except through an attorney?

All this is the more astonishing to a traveller, when he

appoints the friends of religious liberty. It leaves the provision of the Constitution, according to which only Lutherans are eligible for a public office, unchanged. It proposes a heavy fine for every one who explains publicly heretical doctrines in any other place except a church which does not belong to the State Church, and likewise for every one who persuades others to apostatize from the true Lutheran Church. A legal suit for contravention to this law can, however, only be commenced on order given by a royal chancellor of justice. The children of parents belonging to the Swedish church are considered as members of this church, and must be raised in her doctrines, even if the parents, after the birth of the children, should embrace another creed. The royal decree of 1726, which forbids all particular religious meetings, besides the public divine worship in the parish church, is repealed, but it is again provided, that every religious meeting, even the prayer-meetings of a family, if not presided over by the local clergy, must be open for the inspection of public officers, who have the right to dissolve them. The only concession made is the abolition of the punishment of exile, and the permission to secede from the State-Church. But even this trifle meets with a strong opposition. The whole conservative party declares itself against it. It has become known that, on account of this law, three ministers, who are considered as leaders of the conservative party, have tendered to the king their resignation. The conservative papers, in particular the *Monthly Review* of Mr. Crusenstalpe, alarm the country with the cry that the Swedish Church is in danger. The liberal party, on the other hand, makes great efforts to secure the passage of the bill, and circulates everywhere petitions, declaring that if the law is not adopted, the signers reflects on the public opinion upon this matter, which everywhere encounters him. Excepting a few among the clergymen, I hardly met with a man, peasant, citizen or noble, who seemed contented with the Constitution. Many projects of reform—as hinted at in different parts of my journey—have been put forward, but thus far with little effect. It is the opinion of enlightened Swedes, that nothing but the fear of revolution will force the government and the Parliament to measures of thorough reform.

With all these objections to the Swedish Constitution, there is one advantage from it in the history of the past, which is to be fairly and fully allowed. It gave an early and, for the times, fair representation to the class of peasants. Never having suffered under the oppressions of feudalism, this class have from the beginning taken such a position, as no other peasantry in Europe have attained. They have held it through the whole history of Sweden, and now, the masses of Sweden are far above the similar classes in continental Europe, in habits of government, and in the understanding of and love for their rights and liberties. With the improvement of schools, the introduction of railways and modern inventions, and a new Parliamentary system, this class will be prepared for what in numbers and wealth they could claim—the general government of Sweden.

will leave the state church in order to make the execution of the law impossible. They are of opinion that no ministry will dare to send thousands of Swedes into exile for having seceded from the church.—*Independent.*

CHAPTER XLI.

THE RACES IN SWEDEN.

IF one examines the museums of antiquity and the craniological collections in Sweden, he will find traces of what may be called the earliest *substratum* of the population; a race, which, in an unknown age of the past, was forced from the great plateau of Central Asia down among the forests and rivers of Europe. A people which perhaps first penetrated the primeval wilderness of Germany, and spread its tribes to France and Switzerland, long before the existence in Europe of the Celts, the Germans or the Goths, whom Latin historians describe.

By some mode, either reaching it in boats, or crossing to it on the ice, this great tribe gained a lodgment in the uninhabited plain of Southern Sweden, and among the savage forests of Scandinavia.

Their settlements or encampments reached as far north as Halland and West Gothland. They were solely a hunting and fishing people, and never engaged in agriculture. Their civilization, to judge from their implements, was scarcely beyond that of the South Sea Islanders. No metals were known to them; and bone and stone, the latter often not even polished or hewn, were their chief materials. The making of pottery was understood among them, and they made use of vases and lamps of clay. Their ornaments were often the teeth of dogs or of wild animals. Flint arrow-heads, precisely like those discovered in our American mounds, were everywhere in use among them. This savage race—the Indians of Europe—have left no trace in nearly all the lands which they invaded and inhabited, except their graves. No myths, or names, or superstitions, or early customs have come down from them. They buried their dead in mounds of loose stones; they hunted and fished, and finally in continental Europe became extinct, while in Scandinavia they were pressed back to the bleak polar regions—this is all that is known of their life. They are distinguished as having round or short skulls (*brachy-cephalic*), receding frontal bones, the nose with its roots deep sunk in the sockets, and projecting under-jaw. They belonged to the great TSCHUDIC family, and were kindred to the Finns, the Hungarians, and the Turks. Their modern descendants in Scandinavia are divided into the two branches of which mention has already been made—the Quanes and Finns.

The next invading tribe* which swept over Northern Europe, was of a far higher culture than the Tschudes. They came too from Asia, but of different stock. They brought with them a few of the arts of agriculture, the knowledge of bronze as a metal of use, a fine taste and

* There is some slight evidence of Phœnician settlement on the Swedish islands, not however worthy of much consideration here.

conception of beauty, superior to that of the Germanic tribes who followed them—our own ancestors—and a more imaginative mythology. They spread over much of Europe,* even to Ireland and Scotland, reaching England, it is supposed, about 600 B. C.† The names which they gave to the mountains on the continent still exist. In Scandinavia they have left a few words in the ancient Norse, a few myths among the superstitions of the people, and innumerable relics in their tombs. They are the CELTS, or more properly, following the Greek orthography from which they get their name, the KELTS. They do not appear to have penetrated farther North in Sweden than Bohuslän.‡ Unlike the preceding tribe, they burned their dead, though often using the old tombs of the Tschudic Finns. Their bronze is the very best admixture, and worked into all the implements of chase and war and common agriculture, beside manifold forms of grace and beauty for ornaments.

The museums of Sweden and Denmark have a vast quantity of the relics of this race, manifesting often a high degree of taste and refinement. The Kelts are distinguished by craniologists as having long skulls, and therefore nearer the Teutonic tribes than are the Tschudic Finns. Their language is only one branch of the great family in which the Germanic languages are included.

By what sudden and overwhelming attack from a ruder tribe this race was overborne in Sweden, or precisely in

* Bunsen's Philosophy of History. † Dr. Max Müller.

‡ Weinhold—Alt Nordisches Leben.

what year, is uncertain. Chronologists give 400 B. C., as the date of the great invasion of the Teutonic tribes ; and the Keltic remains show often token of a violent and unexpected destruction. By a singular evidence, confirming the testimony from the Scandinavian burial mounds, we are certain that our ancestors came forth from the great plateau of Asia while yet possessing some knowledge of agriculture. It is now well known that many of the words in our family of languages—the Indo-European—describing crops and processes of tilling the ground, come directly from the ancient Sanscrit. The Teutons were acquainted also with the use of iron, though still employing the bronze and the stone implements of the races who occupied the land before them. We have yet a word in English, which is a relic from our barbarous Norse fathers, as direct as the stone weapons in the Scandinavian museums—*hammer*, the old Norse word for the stone which they broke, and afterwards for the *stone*-implement which they used to break it, before the iron was employed for the purpose.

The Teutonic tribes who settled Scandinavia may be classed, accepting Dr. WEINHOLD'S division, into the *Dano-Gothic* and the *Norwegio-Gothic*. The former made their habitations in the Danish Islands and the neighborhood ; the latter crossed to Sweden and Norway. The Norwegian emigration might have crossed direct to the southern coast ; or, after passing over Sweden, have penetrated the North of Norway from the coast of the Arctic Sea, escaping thus the formidable barrier of the mountains which separate the two countries. The Swedish portion made two especial settlements, one near Gottenburg on the Götha, who were called the *West Goths;* the other on the Motala, near Norrköping, called *East Goths.* Still another Teutonic tribe, probably at a later period,* settled the central and northern provinces of Sweden, making their centres of worship and trade, Sigtuna and Upsala. These are the *Suiones,* or Swedes, who have given their name to the country, and whose kingdom was called Suithiod.

From both these great branches of the Teutonic family—the Danish and the Norwegian Northmen—our own race, the Anglo-Norman, is descended. Even at the present time, the natives of Sweden, Denmark, and Norway are able to understand each other's languages, though they cannot speak any but their own. In these early times, however, the language was the same, and even later, when the solitary little Republic of Iceland, protected from wars and favored by a climate which led to an in-door, intellectual life, had become the centre of an original and vigorous oral and written literature, it was the boast of her skalds, that the Norse tongue was the only language for warriors and poets from the North Cape over Sweden, Denmark, Normandy, and the English Islands to the western coast of Ireland.

The colony, from its superior cultivation, may be said to have given the language to the mother-country. At this day, the two languages, Danish and Swedish, are only idioms derived from the original Norse, while alone in

* Geijer.

Iceland are its pure remains to be found. The Icelander of this day can read the Eddas, but to the Danes, Swedes, and Norwegians they are almost as much a closed book as to an Englishman. The modern Norse, and its offshoots, are far below the ancient Icelandic* in richness and completeness.

This is one of the instances brought forward by philosophical writers,† to show how colonization will sometimes settle a language and preserve it in its richness, while the original language in the mother country may degenerate.

Of the appearance of our earliest ancestors, we have abundant evidence. The most imposing in size were probably the Norwegian, and as a natural consequence, these had a profound contempt for all the other Scandinavians. Some Arabian writers, who saw the Northmen later, as Værangians at the Court of Constantinople, describe their "forms to be like palm-trees." The king was frequently chosen for his weight of body. It is related of Hialmter and Ölver, two heroes, that one always needed two seats and the other three, on the drinking bench. Sörli, son of the Upland King, could break down a strong horse in half a day, by his weight alone. The skeletons found in the tombs show powerful, though by no means gigantic, bodies.

The hands and feet were small. The small handles of

* It is said that the old Norse has one hundred and fifty words to express the *sea* in its different appearances!

† Bunsen.

the weapons, preserved in Northern museums, excite astonishment even now. This delicacy was thought a sign of noble blood.

The color was blonde. Gods and goddesses had the light hair and pure color. The elves were fair ; only the dwarfs were dark. *Baldur*, the god of beauty and love, was blonde ; the divine women, Iduna and Gerda, had the whitest arms, and Gerda fills air and sea with her brilliancy.* The thralls were black. Disgracefully as the Americo-Norman has yielded to his prejudice against color, he comes ethnologically by it. The old Norse curse was "Be a black slave !" Hagny, the spouse of King Hiör Halfson, brought forth black and ugly twins. Fearing the wrath of her lord, she exchanged them with the new-born twins of a servant maid, which were fair. As they grew up, the latter began to show their slavish cowardice, while the others, though thralls, bore themselves like the free-born. At length, the queen disclosed it to the father, but he would have nothing to do with the "hell-skins," and left them in slavery.

An equal sign of the genuine Northman was his eye, which must be bright and sparkling, "with a quick play, like the serpent's."†

Siegfried, to escape his pursuers, disguised himself as a miller's maid ; but his eyes betrayed him, and he escaped by saying that he was an imprisoned Valkyria from the gods.

"Thou hast a noble man's eyes !" said Sterlingson to the

* Dr. Weinhold. † Ibid.

defeated Hrafa, who, disguised as a peasant, sought hospitality at his fireside.

The nose was high and straight. A small, distorted nose was the sign of serfdom. The hair was yellow and golden, and, on the women of beauty, very long. Jarl Thorgnyr, of Jutland, sits on the hill where his wife is buried, when a swallow, flying over, drops a human hair, long as a man and of golden brilliancy. The Jarl is entranced, and swears he must win her whose it had been. He discovers it is Ingegerd's, the daughter of the Russian king.

The men wore the beard full and long, but only seldom the moustache. Of a celebrated Bonder, it is related that his beard fell over his knees when he sat.

THE RUNES.

The earliest written language of the Teutonic tribes in Scandinavia—the Runic—was evidently obtained by them through the Phœnicians and Greeks, and derived from Eastern Asia.* Like the original Hebrew, each letter was an idæogram; it represented not a sound, but a thought, or an object, the word for which began with the letter in question. Though, by the abstract and sensual tendency of the German mind, thus early made a language of hieroglyphics, it was not confined to any one class. All who were educated used it. The Runic has left few important traces of itself;

* (Dr. Weinhold—Bunsen.) The only exception to this origin of the Runes, is the letter B.

and when, after the trading and plundering expeditions of the early Vikings, the people began to come in contact with the less cumbersome and difficult alphabet of the Latin races, the latter easily prevailed over the Runes. So that, except burial inscriptions and a few historical notations, the Runic language has given nothing to the world, while all the ancient sagas and chronicles have been rendered and handed down in the Roman alphabet. The Runic stones prevail most between the tenth and twelfth centuries, and disappear after the thirteenth. The Runes yielded first* in the churches, and among the monks and priests, to the Roman letters; and the change was undoubtedly one of the most fortunate circumstances for the improved culture of the Scandinavian races. Owing to the mystery attached in early times to writing, the Runes were, from a remote age, looked on as something magical or mysterious. Each letter was thought to have a peculiar supernatural power. There were runes of love; runes of medicine; runes of victory; of life and of death.

In an old Swedish ballad we hear—

"The first stroke she struck on the gold-harp,
So sweetly did it sound,
The wild deer, both in wood and wold,
Forgot to leap and bound,
Ye practise the runes so well.

"The third stroke she struck on the gold-harp,
So sweetly did it play,

* Dr. Legis—Die Runen.

The little fish in the flood below,
Forgot to swim away,
Ye practise the runes so well."*

By runes, Odin compelled the Vala to awake from the dead, in the realms of Hela. "By runes, he could vanquish armies, destroy the edge of weapons, raise or lay tempests on land or sea, put out fires, fill the hearts of men with terrors, or tranquillize the heart in sorrow."†

The runes even yet survive in Sweden, in calendars and business-notations among the peasantry.

* Howitt's Northern Europe. † Ibid.

III.

Denmark.

CHAPTER XLII.

COPENHAGEN.

Copenhagen is only an hour or two from Malmö by steamboat. I find the Danish capital a most agreeable old city, impressing one as it is always described, as a centre of much cultivation and intelligence. The manners of the people are exceedingly pleasant and courteous. Hospitality is given in the most simple and refined mode, and the table-companies show the sparkling wit and grace for which the Danes are so distinguished. It is surprising how generally education is distributed. The landlord of my hotel, for instance—the *Löven,* a second-rate house, though a most comfortable one—is a cultivated gentleman, speaking foreign languages, and interested in the scholarship and politics of the day. The schools are on a much better footing than either the Swedish or Norwegian schools. Then the facilities for study here, for the investigation of Northern antiquities and language, and for the pursuits of art, are remarkable. The collection of old Norse remains, of gold, bronze, iron, amber, pottery and bone, gathered from the thousands of tombs and tumuli over Denmark, Sweden and Norway, is excellent—worth alone a journey to Copenhagen to investigate. The arrangement—made by an enthusiast in the science, Prof. Thomson, is most clear and philosophical, and is said to have been imitated in the British Museum and all succeeding collections. Whether the professor's theory of the different "ages" of the different materials should be altogether accepted, is quite another question. I was shown also over the Royal Library by the librarian, and had the pleasure of seeing some of the old Icelandic MSS. Still, to be honest, I must own that books, as antiquities—that is, in the evidences they show of manual skill and labor—do not interest me as do other objects of antiquity, those especially more intimately associated with the life of a young people.

There is evidently much very pleasant sociality in the open air here, such as we see in the German cities. The parks and gardens around the city are thronged with cheerful groups of people. Time passes here with the intelligent agreeable society you meet, most easily.

It is an unfortunate time, however, for an American to visit the Danish capital. I cannot but feel a species of well-bred constraint among people which I never met with in Sweden. America is just now detested (during the disa greement on the Sound-Dues), as a quarrelsome bully, who is trying to wrest an ancient estate from a weak neighbor; and the Danish press foment this feeling by the most exaggerated stories of our coarse social manners and our corrupt politics, and by repeating many "ower true" accounts of the disgraceful tyranny and servitude in our Southern States. One gentleman I have met—who said he was probably commercially more interested in the Sound-

Dues question than any house in Denmark—allowed that we had complete justice ; that we were under no obligations to recognize the old arbitrary dues and restrictions established in feudal times by other powers, in treaties of which we were never parties. I told him that I was sure, so far as it was a question of money, it was a matter of no importance to the American government ; what we objected to was *the principle.* If the Danish government chose to put the same tax every year on our merchantmen, as compensation for her building light-houses and providing other securities on the coast, I was certain, though it might be considered exorbitant, the United States would never think it a fit subject for a national protest. But we were determined never to submit to anything like an arbitrary restriction on the liberty of the seas. We were the first to object to the traditional tribute to the Barbary powers, and had gone to war on the question. We had resisted, in a similar way, the asserted English "right of search ;" and we intended to do so to the end, and for my part, I believed it was to be one of the good services of the American people to the world, that they would break up the ancient traditional exactions and injustices which had cramped the free intercourse of nations.

In my experience thus far of the Danes, they impress me as very different from the other Norse-peoples. There is a more polished fineness and grace among them, more wit and humor and sparkle ; but they seem by no means to have the coarse power and independence of the Norwegians, or the half-chivalric courage and ardor of the Swedes. There appears something more petty and weak and dependent in them; the natural effect, probably, of a small State, pressed and overborne by neighboring great powers. Gossip seemed to be more prevalent in Copenhagen than in the northern cities of their brethren, and small interests more to occupy the public mind.

Among the most characteristic institutions of the country, are the *Courts of Conciliation* and the *Cloisters for noble ladies.*

These admirable Courts of Compromise, whose constitution I have already described, were established first by the Danish government, in 1755, in the West Indies, and afterwards in 1795, in Denmark itself. They have proved thoroughly successful here. In 1843, the number of cases brought before these courts was 31,338, of which 21,512 were settled, 299 postponed, and 9,527 referred to courts of law, where only 2,817 were prosecuted.

The fact that they have been established, and so often employed, reflects honor on both the nation and its government.

THE DANISH CLOISTERS.

These extraordinary institutions, the relics of medieval times, are designed alone for the ladies of the nobility. They are not merely interesting historically, but they contain in their management a new commercial assurance principle, which, it is remarkable, has not yet been applied in England or America.

The cloisters were formerly Catholic convents with large

properties, which, after the Reformation, in place of being appropriated to purposes of education, or confiscated to the Crown, as was done in so many European countries, were made the bases of what may be called "Maiden Assurance Companies" for the families of the nobles. That is, a Danish gentleman, at the birth of a daughter, for instance, deposits $2,000 in the funds of one of these cloisters, and registers his daughter's name as a member. She is to receive four per cent. interest, or eighty dollars per annum, till she is married, or till she dies; in either of these cases, the fund deposited goes into the general fund of the Cloisters.

If she remains single, she enters with the eighteen names above her, as the places become vacant by marriage or death, into what is called the "third class," where she receives two hundred and fifty dollars per annum, and rooms and appointments free in the cloisters; still later, with nineteen others, when the places become still further vacant by marriage or death, she rises into the "second class," where the income is five hundred dollars, with similar privileges. The highest, or "third class," composed also of twenty members, enjoys one thousand dollars income.

If a young lady, who has merely been receiving the interest, and has advanced to no class, should be married and become a widow in needy circumstances, the sum of five hundred dollars is allotted to her. If the sum has not been otherwise appropriated, a dower of one thousand dollars can be given from the surplus funds of the cloisters, to her on her marriage.

These cloisters had all, in the beginning, properties of greater or less amount, but these have been immensely increased by this assurance system, which varies in the different institutions. Taking any number of young girls, the probabilities are so much greater both of their marrying or dying than of living single, that the chance makes a fair basis for an assurance company, while, on the other hand, any father would gladly risk that small amount of deposit, if he could insure his daughter against poverty or dependence, in case she remained single after his death ; at the same time, receiving for her share a fair per centage, previous to her marriage, if she did marry, and possibly also a dower amounting to half his deposit. One of the especial evils of modern society, is the uncertain dependent position of single ladies in the educated classes. By such a society as this, such persons would be held in secure and comfortable circumstances, and would be living, in fact, on the assurance profits derived from those who, in other directions, had been more fortunate than they.

The members need not live in a building owned by the society, or make any public announcement of membership. It might be simply a kind of life-assurance, only designed for women alone, and with the addition, that the stock-holders who derived the most benefit, were maiden ladies. The Danish experiment by no means proves that such a society would be commercially profitable elsewhere. But on the face of it, it seems a reasonable scheme for any civilized country.

The most prominent of these cloisters in Denmark, are

1, that of Vallö in Seland, founded by Queen Sophia Madeline, in 1737. The Abbess or Principal must be connected with the Royal Family, and the Deaconess must be the widow of some official in the first rank of nobility. The first has $3,500 salary, the second $1,800, with residence and appointments in the institution. It is designed alone for the families of the nobility and the functionaries of government. Capital, besides forests and other landed property, in 1851, 1,840,000 riks dollars. 2. The Cloister of Vemmeltofte, founded in 1735. Capital, 945,600 riks dollars. 3. That of Gisselfeld, in Seland, founded in 1799. 4. Roeskilde, date 1699. Capital, 234,214 riks dollars. 5. Odense, 1717. Capital, 78,000 riks dollars. 6. Stövringgaard, 1735. Capital, 167,180 riks dollars.

THORWALDSEN'S MUSEUM.

The charm and attraction which, to the lovers of art, surround the Danish capital, which alone draw multitudes hither, come from one man's genius—Thorwaldsen.

I find nothing in modern plastic art nearly so graceful or so attractive as his sculpture. I have long known the casts of his best works ; but they give really no fair conception of his genius. The exquisite severity and purity of outline, the gentle shadowing and change of surface, expressing the most delicate sentiments, and, as it were, the fullness of exuberant life in the marble, are lost in the plaster. The cast is more shrunken, stiff, and even harder, and, except in the expression of very strong action and vigor, does not fully convey the ideal. This is contrary to my own impression, which has always been that the cast often left an effect on the feeling as distinct and pleasing as the original.

I wrote these words under the fresh impression of his works. They express still their effect on my own mind:

"There are feelings in the life of the soul which are the most exquisite, joyous and radiant that ever visit man. All other joys are poor and commonplace by their side. The memory alone of them is sweeter than all after pleasures. They belong to the fresh morning of life—to its bloom, and hope, and cheeriness. They are spirits who, with the fragrance and beauty of a happier sphere, come once to us in that early morning, and come not again. It is not given, except to poets, to utter the exceeding *joy* which they bring into human life. All that is most delicate and luxurious and cheerful in Nature, become their fitting expression. The song of thrushes and nightingales, the fragrance of roses and apple-blossoms, the richness of summer flowers, the sparkle of waves, the glimmer of moonlight, the radiances of spring-sunshine, all the sweetness and gaiety of the outward world, are their language. How even the poor and ignorant long to express this overflowing joy! It comes forth in music, in songs, in the merry dance. Words cannot give it. It is too subtle for language. The *grace* of life, the luxury and the unspeakable deliciousness of youth and love, have no verbal medium fine enough to convey them.

It seems to me Thorwaldsen, like the Greeks, has been able to utter these evanescent and most delicate sentiments,

The joyfulness and gracefulness of youth, the exquisite pleasures of love, the gaiety and frolic and blitheness of the morning of life, are his subjects. In his frolicsome children, and the lithe springing forms of his youths, in the sweetness of maidens and the luxury of womanly beauty, in classic scenes, revived with a feeling and naturalness which no other modern has shown, we feel the *joy* of life uttered. It is the very pleasure of radiant love and tender passion. We see that here is a touch which can trace the most delicate and beautiful sentiments and never slur them.

The bloom and grace of the first affection, the sweetness of youth, the luxury and *abandon* of a happy heart, the thrill of impassioned love, are drawn and made alive on the cold marble-slab. It is wonderful! That which words are too earthly to give; which comes up in never-to-be-forgotten memories, or in insatiable longings with every fragrant breath of spring and sweet melody of music; which alone once felt can make henceforth the meanest life beautiful, and of which the slightest traces and associations are more delicious than all succeeding enjoyments—this the Northern artist has been able to utter in the difficult language of sculpture, and to leave its enduring expression in the hard stone! Such a man has given a Spring to the world; he is a poet of its happiness.

I think, as I walk about the city and see his thoughts, in saloons, in poor men's houses, in cellars and taverns, that in future, long after their petty princes and statesmen are forgotten, this great heart will be cherished by the people, and perhaps, in far distant ages, the only thing which will preserve the memory of the Danish capital, will be that it was the home of THORWALDSEN."

The Museum of his works is, on the whole, well arranged—each important statue has a little apartment for itself, the light coming from above, and the walls being lined with suitable *bas-reliefs*. These *reliefs* are to me among the most precious of his works, and yet those of which the casts give the feeblest impression. It is very difficult, however, to get a good light for them in private houses. They demand, I think, a strong side-light.

Certainly, of all the representations of Christ, either in painting or sculpture, Thorwaldsen's is the most effective. It is known now through the world. That attitude of benignant and merciful dignity, of a noble pity and condescension, are made familiar in thousands of copies—yet it is not satisfactory. The original, however, is much more so than the casts. The giant size, perhaps, lessens the impression of weakness which the traditional face of Christ always leaves; and, standing in its niche in a church (the *Frue Kirke*), overlooking the row of apostles and the worshippers, with the strong lights and shadows from above on its features, one can sometimes realize faintly the ineffable grandeur and nobleness of that life of Suffering and Love, of which this is the feeble representation.

It is a remarkable thing, and shows the genius of Thorwaldsen, that he who has, above all modern artists, best restored the spirit of classicism, could not read a word of Greek or Latin, and could not write his own language correctly!

An interesting life has appeared of him, by *Thiele*, going rather too much into detail, but showing clearly the struggles and difficulties of the great artist. Poverty, dependence, and disappointment were some of the nurturing circumstances which surrounded the growth of his genius. He was the son of a maker of figure-heads for ships, an Icelander, though he himself was born in Denmark. While he was struggling with fortune at Rome, and just beginning to win his first chaplets, the father died in an almshouse in Denmark—an event for which Thorwaldsen, though by no means at fault, never ceased to reproach himself, and, most of all, his titled friends, who had promised to assist the old man. The first great work which made Thorwaldsen known to the world, was his *Jason*,* which yet ranks as among his best. An English gentleman bought it.

His life shows many of the peculiarities of genius. He was sometimes for a long period—even a whole year—under the most gloomy fits of depression, and utterly unable to labor, and then again he would throw off his most exquisite works with incredible rapidity.

* It is related by *Thiele* that a Danish lady of rank, who had encouraged the young artist when laboring at this statue, was revisiting his studio years after, with a company of friends, when he had become a great man, and, as they passed a cast of Jason, she said, patronizingly, "Thorwaldsen! that is my child, you know!" The artist, who remembered probably the years of suffering and trial and disappointment, before this work came forth, looked by no means pleased, and said bluntly, "Well, madam, you had very few pains of labor for it!"

He lived to win the praise of all Europe, as the greatest modern sculptor, and to return to his fatherland, to receive the highest honors and most cordial welcome from his countrymen.

CHAPTER XLIII.

THE SCANDINAVIAN MYTHOLOGY.

To every student of the religious beliefs of the world, the mythology of the Scandinavians must be deeply interesting. I regret that I can only treat it cursorily.

The tendency of the modern mind, it seems to me, on subjects of this nature, is to refine too much. A consistent and profound philosophy is assumed too often as the basis for ancient mythologies, as though every fancy and trick and dream of the religious imagination must have its deep spiritual meaning, and this alone is to be sought for. The early men and women were simple, child-like, imaginative beings, who clothed a thousand fancies and childish beliefs in bodily forms. Sometimes great natural laws were thus embodied ; sometimes profound moral truths, but they were nearly all accidental, and the fruit of poetic instinct rather than logical reflection. Under all these pictures and modes of presentation of different nations are, of course, great natural laws, showing the effect of climate, temperament, and history, on the religious imagination. These are legitimate objects of study. All philosophical conclusions beyond these, seem to me doubtful, though still interesting speculations.

The mythology of the Northmen, even as their early pagan customs and their language, reveals probably an oriental origin. Here, as in the Persian, is a contest forever being waged between Matter and Spirit, Darkness and Light, Evil and Good, ending at length in the complete triumph of Love and Goodness over the evil powers.

In the beginning, were two worlds, the Fire World * and the Mist World ; † from the one came forth poisonous frost vapors ; from the other, life-giving fire. The meeting of these two in the Abyss ‡ brings forth the first chaotic world-mass.§ Of the Abyss the Edda says, "It was Time's morning when Ymir lived. There was no sand, no sea, no cooling billows; Earth there was none; no lofty Heaven. Only the Gulph of Ginunga."‖ This matter produces of itself the evil powers, the Frost-giants, and Mountain-giants. At the same time arises an animal power, which cherishes and refines the mass of matter, until a high creative Divine Power unfolds itself, which creates in three forms, *Spirit*, *Will*, and *Holiness*.¶ They soon blend together in the All-Father, the *Spirit*—ODINN.

Henceforth, despite the power of Spirit, there is a continual struggle between the Beings of light—the Æsir, and the powers of chaos and darkness—the Giants and Dwarfs. These latter dwell in the frozen North, in mountains, in desolate places, and send forth the winter, the night, tempests, and diseases. The Sun and Moon, which

* Muspelheim. † Niflheim. ‡ Ginunga-gap.

§ Pennock's Translation of Keyser. ‖ Howitt's Translation.

¶ Odinn.—Vili.—Vè.

are the sparks of the Fire-World, are continually hunted by these powers—the Jötun wolves—and have no rest. The Æsir protect the green and living Earth, which they visit on the bridge of the rainbow: The Dwarfs—the agents of evil—they confine in useful labors within the mines and caverns of the world.

The power which creates man, again appears in a three-fold form—*Spirit*, *Light*, and *Fire*.*

The Ash-tree, Yggdrasill, is one of the grand mystical figures of the Northern Mythology. The best students of the Eddas suppose it to represent Universal Nature. It has three roots, one from the Abyss, one from the source of the evil and chaotic powers, and one from the homes of the spirits of light. It is represented as forever suffering. "The Ash Yggdrasill endures more hardships than than any one knows; The hart bites off its branches, its trunk decays, and the Dragon of Death gnaws at its root." Yet the tree is forever green with the sprinkling of the celestial Fountain. The higher powers support and preserve the material Nature.

By this Fountain are three dread beings, who, in the Northern Mythology, as in the Grecian, lie back of the present order of things—beyond and above even the spirits of light, the Æsir—they are the three Goddesses of Time and Fate,† the *Past*, the *Present*, and the *Future*; the Nornir, the allotters of Birth and of Death. All Nature, the decrees of the Æsir, the lives of men, the existence

* Odinn,—Haenir,—Lódurr,—Pennock.

† Urdier, Verdandi and Skuld.

of the Gods, are under their control. The whole cosmogony is of Time, and perishes with it.

Of the particular personalities of the Gods in this Mythology, it is not necessary here to speak. They seem often the embodiment alone of the powers of Nature: and sometimes of its abstract qualities, and their history is a continuation of the dire struggle between the powers of good and of evil, the representation of which runs through the whole mythology. The Heaven of the Northmen is one of the most sensual pictures of the celestial abodes which mythology has given us, and at the same time, most characteristic of the race. The hero who had fallen in battle, was taken by the invisible maidens to the halls of Valhalla. If he had died in his bed of sickness or of old age, there was no entrance for him to those abodes. There, in the splendid banqueting rooms, he found the warriors and sea-kings and heroes of his country assembled, feasting on boiled pork and mead and wine, served by beautiful maidens. Each day, the company goes forth to fight each other, and after the glowing excitement of the combat (than which the Northman knew no more heavenly emotion), the ghastly wounds are instantaneously cured, the hewn limbs restored, the hacked armor rebrightened, and the brave heroes return for the other enjoyment of their Heaven—wassail and wine.

This was the popular belief. But behind all this, the Eddas draw a picture which redeems the Northern superstition from its sensuality, and places the Scandinavian mythology among the most robust, if not the most moral of human mythologies. We have seen, in the theory of creation and the history of the gods, the solemn, dark conception of a mighty struggle going on between the Powers of Good and of Evil. Through it all runs also a warning of a final mighty contest between these powers, which is to end in fearful destruction—the age so poetically known in the Eddas as the "Twilight of the Gods."

The human mind usually cannot bear to imagine the annihilation of itself. It holds on to the present order of things. Its heaven, its gods, *itself*, will at least survive the final wreck of matter. Not so with the vigorous and really moral imagination of the Scandinavian Northman. In his faith, there was to come a fearful destruction and conflagration of heaven and earth, of men and gods, of the world below and Valhalla above—a day of awful wrath, whose description vies in terror with the fearful pictures in the vision of the Apostle of the final judgment.

The growing wickedness of earth shows its approach. The Voluspà says of the seeress :

"There saw she wade
In the heavy streams,
Men—foul perjurers,
And murderers,
And they who others' wives
Seduce to sin.

"Brothers slay brothers;
Sisters' children
Shed each other's blood.
Hard is the world:
Sensual sin grows huge.

There are sword-ages, axe-ages,
Earth-cleaving cold;
Storm-ages, murder-ages,
Till the world falls dead,
And men no longer spare
Or pity one another."*

It is a time of snows and winter, and tempest and darkness. The sun and moon are swallowed up, and heaven is sprinkled with blood. The bright stars vanish, the earth trembles, and the mountains are shaken from their base. But these sons of the North, even in the last convulsions of matter, are not those who call upon the mountains to cover them. They die in armor. In the fearful chaos and destruction, each god and spirit buckles on his armor, and hastens on to the great battle-field—the vast plains of Vigrid. The giant powers of evil are abroad. The Wolf, which fills the space between earth and heaven with its jaws, comes forth. The mighty Serpent, who had supported the world, rocks the ocean in his writhings, and blows out venom over air and sea. Over the lurid ocean sails the ship made of dead men's nails, carrying the weird Frost Giants. In the final battle, all the great powers of evil, and the historical gods, are destroyed, and the earth is burned up. Of Valhalla, we hear no more.

A new earth comes forth, eternally green and fair. Baldur, the god of purity and love, survives, and with him a few of the purer gods. A new race of men is born. All evil ceases, and sorrow and trouble come no more.

* Howitt's Translation.

"In Gimlé, the lofty,
There shall the hosts
Of the virtuous dwell,
And through all ages
Taste of deep gladness."

The close, so grand and so mysterious, pointing to the vague idea which always was behind the mythology, of an unnamable Spirit, we give in the words of the Voluspà, the ancient poem of the Edda.*†

"Then shall the MIGHTY ONE come from above: He who ruleth over all; whose name man dares not to utter.

"He cometh in his power to the great judgment-seat; he will appease all strife, and will establish a holy peace, which shall endure eternally. But the foul Dragon, the venom-spotted Nidhöggu (the Dragon of Death and Dark-

* Pennock's Keyser.

† Of him another passage of the Edda:

"Then one is born
Higher than all;
He becomes strong
With the strengths of earth.
The mightiest King,
Men call him;
Fast knit in peace
With all powers.

"Then comes Another,
Yet more mighty;
But HIM dare I not
Venture to name.
Few farther may look
Than to where Odinn
To meet the wolf goes."

ness), flees away over the plains and sinks out of sight, bearing death upon his wings."

So closes this robust prophecy—the restoration, the superintending Spirit, not appearing so distinct and certain as the destruction and ruin. Here again the tone is vigorous and moral to the last; the instincts of the bards seeing clearly the wickedness and the sensuality, but not discerning so clearly the redemption of nature. The Eddas prepared not unnaturally for the Evangelists.

APPENDIX.

I.—STATISTICS OF NORWAY.

(*From Mr. Sundt's Notes.*)

Province.	Number of Preachers.		Population to every Preacher.		
Year	1815	1855	1815	1845	1855
Christiania	164	168	2263	3376	—
Christiansand	64	74	2283	2978	—
Bergen	68	69	2348	3248	—
Trondjem	62	67	2260	3080	—
Tromsoe	47	51	1627	2166	—
Total	407	429	2190	3097	(3473)

Year.	Marriages.	Legitimate Children.	Illegitimate Children.	Percentage of Illegit. Births to Legitimate.	Percentage of Illegit. Births to Marriages.
1801–5	33,917	118,496	7,452	6.3	21.9
1806–10	31,389	115,905	8,072	7.0	25.7
1811–15	37,129	116,369	8,308	7.1	22.4
1816–20	41,583	142,371	12,136	8.5	29.2
1821–25	44,081	157,984	12,670	8.0	28.7
1826–30	42,558	167,284	12,614	7.5	29.6
1831–35	42,233	169,252	12,111	7.2	28.7
1836–40	40,681	159,606	12,017	7.5	29.5
1841–45	50,590	179,670	15,731	8.8	31.1
1846–50	52,506	193,408	17,479	9.0	33.3
1851–55	56,499	213,004	21,590	10.1	

POPULATION IN NORWAY.	TO EVERY 10,000 PERSONS BET. 20 AND 30 YEARS.		
Between 20 and 30 years of age.	Years.	Marriages.	Illegit. Children Living.
Year, 1801........ 136,959	1801—1810........	477	113
" 1815........ 160,090	1811—1820........	492	128
" 1825........ 175,482	1821—1830........	494	144
" 1835........ 172,348	1831—1840........	481	140
" 1845........ 239,266	1841—1850........	431	139

COMPARISON OF PUBLIC AND PRIVATE STATISTICS.

Report of Percentage of Illegitimate Births to Marriages, 1851–'2.		
District.	Official Report.	Private Report.
Group 1.—District around Christiania,......	39.4 per ct.	37.4 per ct.
" 2.—Upper Romerike, Osterdal, Hedemark, and Gudbrandsdal,......	66.3 "	65.3 "
" 3.—Valders, Hadeland, Kongsberg,...	36.0 "	33.5 "
" 4.—Drammen, Jarlsberg, Lauvik, Lower Thelemark,..............	25.7 "	25.4 "
	42.2 "	39.7 "
" 5.—Upper Thelemark and District near Christiansand,.................	16.3 "	14.1 "
" 6.—Mandal, Lister, and Dalecarlia,...	11.6 "	11.4 "
" 7.—Stavanger and region near by,...	20.2 "	17.4 "

Report of Proportion of Illegal Connections Producing Children, to Legal Marriages*, 1851–'52.				
Districts.	MALES.		FEMALES.	
	Class 1. Freeholders.	Class 2. Laborers.	Class 1. Freeholders.	Class 2. Laborers.
Group 1,........................	21	45	9	52
" 2,........................	26	85	12	92 (!)
" 3,........................	19	42	12	46
" 4,........................	12	32	4	35
" 5,........................	10	17	4	21
" 6,........................	6	20	4	23
" 7,........................	11	23	5	28

* This is, more strictly, *births*—but the proportion is made in order to show the relation of illegal to legal connections.

The Schools and Morals.

Districts.	Number of School-Children* for each Teacher in the County School.		Proportion of Children from 7 to 15 who have entirely neglected the School. Average both years.	Proportion to marriages of Illegitimate Births.—City and county.
Year,	1837	1840	1837—1840	
Group† 1,	95	89	5.5	39.4
" 2,	109	103	9.5	66.3
" 3,	93	91	7.8	36.0
" 4,	79	80	6.3	25.7
" 5,	61	59	5.4	16.3
" 6,	65	63	1.8	11.6
" 7,	77	77	3.6	20.2

Expenses for Schools (except board of teachers) to each person in Christiania Province.

	Skillings.
Group 1,	7.4
" 2,	7.1
" 3,	7.5
" 4,	9.2

Christiansand Province.

Group 5,	10.2
" 6,	7.0
" 7,	5.6

Percentage of Illegal Connections to Marriages.

Men.	Women.
45	52
85	92
42	46
32	35

Christiansand Province.

Men.	Women.
17	21
20	23
23	28

It will be observed in these statistics that Norway, in respect of sexual morality, has been steadily retrograding, since the beginning of this century. In the four years preceding 1855, *every tenth child* born in the whole country was illegitimate! and in the four years preceding 1850, the number of unlawful connections between the sexes amounted to *one third* of the whole number of marriages.

It will also be observed in the succeeding statistics that the immorality keeps very even pace with the want of religious opportunities, and that the most vice prevails where are the fewest preachers to the population. The singular custom of the *Fria* is observed in many districts of Norway; and I am informed by the statistician, Mr. SUNDT, from whom these facts are obtained, that the proportion of unlawful births is in almost precise relation to the extent of this custom, as is certainly to be expected.

* The most of these children do not attend school over eight weeks in the year.

† The names in the Groups have already been given.

It is also to be noted, that where the least money is expended for schools, in proportion to the population, there is the lowest state of sexual morality.

In the counties of Upper Romerike, Osterdal, Hedemark, and Gudbrandsdal, the number of school-children to each teacher, in 1840, was 103; the proportion of non-attendants on schools was more than nine per cent. The expenses of schools in these districts are about seven cents for each person. The population in the whole province to each preacher is larger than in any other province.

In the same counties, to every 100 marriages there are 92 illegal *liaisons*, bearing children, among the women, and 85 among the men of the laboring class. Among the freeholders, the proportion with the men is only 26 per cent., and with the women 12 per cent.

It is doubtful whether any district in Europe will show among the laboring class an equal immorality.

The two great causes, which can be reached by effort, we believe to be the want of thorough popular education, and the formalism of Church, which has lost its practical hold of the morals of the peasants.

II.—POPULATION AND FURTHER STATISTICS OF NORWAY.

In the year 1845, the population amounted to 1,328,471; to this must be added 1,145, who ramble about without having a fixed abode in any place, so that the whole population amounts to 1,329,616. The whole kingdom has 5,752 (Norsk) square miles, consequently about 220 to each square mile. In Norrland there are only about 81, and Finnmark only 33 to each square mile.

The first register of the inhabitants of the country was made in 1769, and then the population was only 723,141 in the whole kingdom.

ARMY.

A standing army was formed first in the year 1628, consisting of 6,243 soldiers. The Norwegian army now amounts to 23,484 soldiers. The artillery makes up one-tenth of the whole army, and the horsemen one-twelfth. The fortresses of the kindgdom are 13, besides some few sconces. The expenses were, in the year 1848, 747,000 dollars.

THE FLEET.

Frigates,	3
Corvettes,	5
Brigs,	1
Schooners,	5
Small Steamers,	5
Gun-Boats,	123

All seafaring Norwegians, from sixteen to thirty years of age, and, with certain exceptions, all men in maritime districts, are bound to serve five years on national vessels, if called upon. The number thus bound at the present time is 47,000.

Budget for 1851—$407,464. The system is very enlightened and progressive. One proof is the readiness with which Mr Maury's proposition for the keeping accurate logs of winds, currents, etc., on the high seas was accepted; and his invitation to a Meteorological Conference at once complied with.

INCOME OF THE KINGDOM.

In 1848, 4,696,600 specie dollars; for this they are chiefly indebted to the great revenues of Kongsberg's silver-works.

EXPENSES.

In 1848, 2,523,700 sp., of which 105,050 sp. are paid annually to the Royal Family in Sweden, and to the maintenance of the Royal Palace in Christiania. The surplus in the public treasury, at the close of 1847, was 2,172,900 sp.

EXPORTS.

In respect to exports, the city of Bergen surpasses the other Norwegian cities, its export being estimated at about 1,700,000 sp., yearly; Drammen's 650,000 sp.; Trondhjem's not fully 500,000 sp.; and Christiania's only 350,000 sp. Next to those cities come Sarpsborg, Christiansand, and Tromsoe. The articles of export are principally fishes, pickled herrings, train-oil, iron, copper, iron in bars, timber, anchovies, and window-glass.

IMPORTS.

In the year 1844, the import of provisions, of corn to Christiania was 195,000 tons; to Drammen, 115,000 tons; to Christiansand, 50,000 tons; to Stavanger, 79,000; and to Trondhjem, 88,000 tons. The articles of import are: corn, coffee, sugar, brandy, wine, tobacco. salt, butter, hemp, sole-leather, sail-cloth, cotton, etc.

MINES.

The most important branch of mining is the production of iron, Norway having nineteen iron-works; and the whole production for the years 1841–'45 was: iron in bars, 24,753 skippund. Next are the copper-works, of which there are nine. The production for the years 1841–'45 was 3,894 sk., yearly. The most important copper-works are: Róraas, opened 1644, and Alten, opened 1826. Kongsberg's silver mine is an important work. It was discovered in 1623. For a very long series of years, there was only loss in working it; but since 1832, it has been very profitable, giving, in the year 1846, 16,079¾ marks of massive and solid silver. About one million species is the annual income of the Norwegian mines.

MANUFACTURES.

For want of native manufactories, Norway imports manufactures. In the year 1846, there were imported of cotton, 888,638 pounds; of stuffs of cotton, 826,414 pounds; of silk wares, 12,560 pounds. The glass-making is nearly a failure; only three glass-works are now in operation. Of paper-mills there are only seven, so that paper must be imported; soap-houses are increasing, and the making of salt is considerable—Valló salt mine alone produces, yearly, 25,000 tons of salt. Of sugar refineries, the whole kingdom has only one in Trondhjem.

AGRICULTURE.

Every farm has an average of 5½ acres of land, and the number of farms is about 112,930.

HEALTH.

In 1845, 1,123 persons were infected with leprosy, mostly on the western coast, from Stavanger to Finnmarken. Lazarettos in Bergen, and one in Molde, have been erected.

III.—*An Abstract of the Report in regard to the working of the Copper Mine at Alten, in the five years from* 1850 to 1855, *inclusively.*

A TABULAR SURVEY OF EXPENSES AND PRODUCTION.

YEARS.	*Disbursements.*						*Production.*	
	SALARIES.		MATERIALS.		TOTAL AMOUNT.		ORE.	COPPER.
	Species.	Skip'd	Species.	Skip'd	Species.	Skip'd	Pounds.	Pounds.
1851	32,030	70	14,430	49	46,460	119	4,307,724	253,502
1852	32,345	23	12,480	12	44,825	35	5,107,168	243,238
1853	33,743	118	14,472	32	48,216	30	5,188,128	276,030
1854	38,302	104	16,544	101	54,847	85	5,422,560	285,889
1855	36,902	87	20,850	108	57,753	75	4,370,320	231,974
Total	173,325	42	78,778	62	252,103	104	24,393,600	1,292,915

A Norwegian species (sp.) is about the same as an American dollar. The Norwegian or Danish weight called a skippund (skd.) amounts to 352 pounds.

The works consist of twelve larger or less mines and a few pits, driven at indeterminate times. No new discovery of any importance has been made in the last five years.

In the year 1855, the copper works supported the following population:

WORKMEN IN THE MINES AND FOUNDRY (FURNACE):—Men, 218; Women, 145; Children, 124; Administrator, 1; Bookkeepers, 2; Physician, 1; Victuallers and assistants, 3; Controller of the foundry, 1; People for ascending and descending, 6; Keeper of storehouses, 1; Teachers, 3; Blacksmiths, 8; Bricklayers, 2; Carpenters, 2; Baker and Brewer, 1; Shoemakers, 4; Tailors, 2; Sailors, 3; Grooms and Drivers, 14; Persons settled at the work and by it nourished, but not in certain employment, 47; Children not capable of working, 266; Old and sickly persons, 5.

Of the above-named, there were in the year 1855, 439 Quanes, 273 Norwegians, 94 Swedes, 25 Englishmen, 17 Finns (Laplanders), 5 Russians, and 1 German, adults and children inclusive.

IV.—TERRACED BEACHES.—*See p.* 90.

IT is an interesting fact, in connection with the ancient terraced beaches on the coast of Norway, that Dr. Kane discovered similar traces of a secular elevation of the American continent, as far North as 81°.

He supposes the elevation to have commenced at some point north of 76°. In one place, the elevation reached the height of 480 feet.

He speaks also of a depression of Southern Greenland, corresponding to the depression of Southern Scandinavia.

V.—RESUMÉ OF STATISTICS OF SWEDEN.

Population in Sweden, 1854,	3,606,987
Males,	1,750,136
Females,	1,856,851
Population in Stockholm,	95,950

Number of Prisons in Sweden, 53; including 17 Cell-prisons, containing 1,257 light, and 62 dark cells.

Number of prisoners in Sweden,	15,472
Males,	12,141
Females,	3,331
Number of prisoners in Stockholm,	4,857

Receipts for prisons and prisoners, 1854, 1,115,641 Rdr., inclusive of 882,890 Rdr. appropriated by the Diet. Expenses for same, during 1854, 1,113,068 Rdr.

Children born in Sweden, 1850,	110,399
Males,	56,590
Females,	53,809
Children, dead,	68,514
Males,	35,595
Females,	32,919
Increase of born over dead children,	41,885
Males,	20,995
Females,	20,890

Children born in Stockholm, 1850, 3,190; including 1,424 illegitimate children. Children born in other cities, 1850, 7,805; including 1,538 illegitimate. Children born in the country, 99,404; including 7,358 illegitimate.

Proportion of illegitimate to legitimate children: at Stockholm, 1 to 2.25; in the other cities, 1 to 5.03; in the country, 1 to 1,434.

Stillborn children in 1850, 3,652.

Value of Imports from the United States, 1854,... 3,250,000 Rdr.

Tobacco,	1,120,137	"
Rice,	23,143	"
Sugar,	432,515	"
Cotton,	7,960,731	"

Value of Exports, during same year, to the United States:

Iron,	107,576	"
Steel,	3,609	"

Vessels arrived to Sweden from other countries, 10,648 of 418,615 tons. Vessels cleared from Sweden for other countries, 10,574 of 422,168 tons.

Custom-House—duties paid during 1854:

	Imported Goods.	Exported.	Total Rdr.
At Stockholm,	2,086,466	31,805	2,118,271
At Gefle,	73,577	6,035	79,612
At Gothenbourgh,	2,321,066	23,400	2,344,466
At Norrköping,	294,029	5,743	299,772

Cotton Spinning Factories, 1854: 14 consuming 8,204,270 lbs. cotton, producing to the value of 4,188,664 Rdr.

Clothing Manufactories 109, producing goods to the value of 4,986,454 Rdr.

Silk Manufactories 13, making goods to the value of 911,770 Rdr.

Norrköping has 86 clothing factories, producing, in 1854, goods to the value of 4,053,117 Rdr.

Number of pupils in the common schools, Stockholm, 1854,	16,101
Boys,	7,913
Girls,	8.188

Number of Teachers, 34; amount of their salaries, 11,261 Rdr. The income of these schools was, during that year, 24,298 Rdr., and their expenses, 16,353 Rdr.

VI.—STATISTICS OF CHARITY OF STOCKHOLM.

Houses for receiving poor children and institutes of education are eight. The largest of these houses contained, in the year 1853, 741 children; and the number adopted from such houses was, in January, 1854, 2,629. The expenses were, in 1853, about $23,850.

The Free Mason's house for receiving children assisted in educating 292 children. Their expenses are about $4,780. Marbeekska Institution for the education of poor girls, contained 26. The expenses, 4,102 Rix. This Institution has, within the last few years, been enlarged, so that it can contain double the number of children.

The youngest of those institutions is the Kronprincess Louisa for sick children. A home, a school, and also a hospital, are united with that Institution. The school was opened with fifty-eight pupils. In the home for children, were received during the last year, twelve girls. The Institution has a lady superintendent, and the committee consists of three gentlemen and two ladies. Their income, from the 31st of October, 1851, was 51,313 Rdr. banko, besides the 500 Rdr. banko which the King gave. That sum of 51,313 banko was obtained partly in gifts, and partly in yearly subscriptions. Their expenses, in order to get the Institution in perfect order, amounted to 44,330 Riks. There is also another branch attached to this Institution—a crèche for poor women.

The income of the city of Stockholm amounted, in the year 1850, to 356,440 Riks dollars, and the expenses were 423,905 Rix.

CRIMINAL STATISTICS.

Offences of all Kinds.	Persons found Guilty.
39,105 in 1845	33,026 in 1845
38,814 " 1846	32,401 " 1846
38,444 " 1847	31,092 " 1847
36,607 " 1848	30,121 " 1848
34,600 " 1849	28,743 " 1849

PROF. A. C. KNÖS.

Taking the whole population at 3,316,536 persons for 1845, the number of the guilty, in 1845, is 1 to 92; 1846, 1 to 102; 1847, 1 to 106; 1848, 1 to 110; 1849, 1 to 115.

In these cases, however, are reckoned all offences against the most minute police laws. It is claimed by intelligent Swedes that Laing, in his severe strictures on Swedish immorality, based on the public statistical tables, has committed the error of confusing many of these arbitrary police offences with real offences against virtue.

VII.

English view of King Oscar's speech before the Diet of 1856-57 :

"A Swedish Board of Works is to be established—the King has declared; and forthwith, a plan is to be submitted to the Houses for the construction of grand trunk railways, to draw the opposite ports of the United Kingdom together. Nor does the government limit its present promises to the construction of railways. The establishment of railways is to inaugurate, to use the King's words, 'a law still more closely in harmony than the last with the wise principle of Free Trade.' And, then, would a people enjoying the use of railways, free to trade, under liberal enactments—would a people so circumstanced remain content to live in a state of religious slavery? The question has been wisely answered by the Swedish Government. To that persecution of Catholics which has so long disgraced Sweden, is to succeed 'an enlightened tolerance for the creed of others, based upon neighborly love.' 'It is right,' exclaims King Oscar, 'that the people, whose great monarch Gustavus Adolphus fought for freedom of thought and conscience, and which freedom he sealed with his blood—it is right that such a people should follow his example.' These are sentiments that do honor to Bernadotte's son.

A long time has elapsed since a speech equally important to that of King Oscar has been pronounced from a throne. Railways are to be suddenly thrown open; a department of public works is to be established; freedom is to become the governing principle of commerce; Catholic emancipation is to be declared; unmarried women are to enjoy the rights of majority at twenty-five years of age; a statistical department is to be organized; and all during one session! If Sweden has held back somewhat doggedly from the general progress of Western Europe—it must be confessed, that our new allies appear determined to make up, by vigorous action in the present, for the years they have lost."—(*Sat. Review.*)

VIII.—CONSTITUTION OF SWEDEN.

From a French translation prepared for the use of Bernadotte.

SECTION 1.

The kingdom of Sweden shall be ruled by a king; it shall be a hereditary monarchy, according to the order of succession of the male descendants of the king deceased, who shall be appointed by the States.

SECTION 2.

The king shall always be of the pure evangelical doctrine as laid down in the confession of Augsburgh and assumed by virtue of the Decree of the Synod of Upsala of the year 1593.

SECTION 9.

There shall be kept a record of all the deliberations that will take place before the king in the State Council. The actual members of that Council shall indispensably express and explain their opinions, and have them recorded; they shall be responsible for their advice, and the final consequence of the same will be determined by §§ 106 and 107, but the decision reserved to the king only.

SECTION 12.

It belongs to the king to form treaties and alliances with foreign powers, after having consulted on the subject with the minister of foreign affairs and some other member of the State Council.

SECTION 13.

If the king will undertake a war, or make peace, he shall assemble, for an extraordinary State Council, all the members of the Council of State, representing to them the motives and circumstances to be taken into consideration, and asking their advice, which each of them shall give privately, in order to be entered in the Journal of Records, with the responsibility determined by §107. The king hereafter shall have the power to take and execute such resolution as he may deem most beneficial to the kingdom.

SECTION 14.

The king shall have the supreme command of the army and navy of the kingdom.

SECTION 15.

The objects relative to the military command, that is to say, such as are under the immediate care of the king in his quality as chief commander of the army and navy, will be decided by the king when he rules the kingdom himself in presence of that chief of the military department to whose province it belongs. Whenever such objects are introduced for discussion, that officer is bound upon his own responsibility to declare his opinion on the undertakings made by the king, and if his opinion disagree with the resolution of the king, to have his representations and counsels consigned to an official report certified by the king's signature. If the above mentioned officer discovers that those undertakings are of a hazardous nature, or founded upon precarious and insufficient means of execution, he shall, with the consent of the king, assemble a council of war consisting of two or more military officers of superior rank, that are present, and have the advices of said council entered upon record.

SECTION 16.

The king shall enforce and favor justice and truth; prevent and obstruct violence and wrong; neither shall he injure nor permit any one else to injure any one's honor or personal liberty and welfare, unless he be convicted by law and and condemned, nor shall he seize anything, or permit that any one's property, either real or personal, may be seized without process or judgment according to the rules prescribed by the laws and statutes of Sweden, neither shall he injure the peace of anybody in his premises nor permit him to be troubled; nor shall he banish any man from one place to another; nor force the liberty of conscience of any man or permit it to be forced (strained,) but protect every one in the free exercise of his religion, as long as it is harmless to the peace of the public and causes no scandal. The king shall order judgment to be rendered by the proper tribunal.

SECTION 21.

The king shall have two votes in the decision of matters in which he thinks proper to assist in the supreme tribunal. All lawful demands may be communicated to the king, and his votes concerning the same shall be collected and counted even if he has not joined the deliberations in the Supreme Court.

SECTION 25.

In criminal cases it is the king who shall pardon, modify capital punishment, and restitute honor as well as the property confiscated in favor of the crown. The Supreme Court, however, is to be heard for the petitions on that subject, and the king will render his resolution in the State Council. It will depend, hereafter, upon the culprit whether he will accept the pardon granted to him by the king, or suffer the penalty to which he had been condemned.

SECTION 29.

The Archbishop and the Bishops shall be chosen as heretofore, and the king shall appoint for those places one of the three candidates proposed.

SECTION 30.

The king, according to the custom heretofore observed, shall make appointments for the royal parsonages. As to the parsonages called consistorial, the parishes shall be maintained according to their election law.

SECTION 31.

The citizens of the towns shall continue to enjoy the right of proposing for the office of mayor three capable men; of whom one is to be chosen by the king. In the same manner it shall be proceeded as to the offices of councillors and the secretary of the municipality of Stockholm.

SECTION 36.

Those who occupy offices of the administration of either higher or lower rank, likewise, all the employés and functionaries, except those mentioned in §35, cannot, without preliminary proceedings and judgment, be dismissed by the king, nor can they be appointed or transferred to other offices unless at their own request.

SECTION 39.

If the king will undertake a journey in a foreign land, he shall communicate his object to the State Council when fully assembled, and he shall hear the advice on that subject in manner described in § 9.

If, subsequently, the king, after having resolved to travel, accomplishes this design, he will not occupy himself with the government of the kingdom, and will not exercise the royal prerogative while travelling abroad, but the State Council will conduct, during the king's absence, the government in his name, with all the rights that the present form of government attributes to the king; however, the State Council can never accord titles of nobility, nor promote to the rank of count or baron, or distribute orders of knighthood; likewise can all the vacant charges only be temporarily conducted by those who will have been constituted for the same by the State Council. Whatsoever there is to be observed, if the king remains longer than twelve months out of the kingdom, is stated in § 91.

SECTION 42.

If the misfortune should happen, that all the male members of the royal family which are invested with the right of succession to the kingdom are extinct, the State Council will likewise conduct the government with royal power and authority, until the States assembled have elected a new dynasty and the king elect have taken the reins of Government. In each of the cases mentioned in the four preceding sections, all the members of the Council shall be present in the State Council and give their opinions.

SECTION 49.

The States of the kingdom, by virtue of the present fundamental laws, shall assemble after the lapse of five years since the last session of parliament. During the recess of every such session the States shall fix the day on which they have to meet again, and record precisely the time of the convocation, together with the necessary instructions respecting the election of deputies. The king, however, will be at liberty to convoke, before that time, the States of the kingdom to an extraordinary parliamentary session.

SECTION 52.

The king shall nominate the Marshal of the Diet, the speakers of the order of the bourgeoisie and that of the peasants; also the secretary of the order of the peasants. The Archbishop shall always be the speaker of the order of the clergy.

SECTION 73

There cannot in future any new tax demand for men, money, or food, be ordained, levied or exacted without the free will and consent of the States, according to the forms prescribed as above.

SECTION 74.

The king shall not have the right of exacting any other contribution to a war that might occur than a quota of victuals that may be required by some county for the maintenance of soldiers during their march, when the different cities or villages through which that march takes place are unable to furnish the necessary provisions. For such contribution, however, there is cash to be paid without delay to those who furnish said provisions by the treasurer, according to the terms established for the public markets, and with a rise of one half of their amount. Said contribution may not be exacted for soldiers cantoned in some place, or employed during the war-operations; these men shall be supplied by the depots established to that end.

SECTION 76.

Without the consent of the States of the kingdom, the king cannot raise loans in the kingdom or in a foreign country, nor encumber the State with a new debt.

SECTION 79.

No change of the coin in the kingdom, concerning the title or weight either to increase or diminish it, shall take place without the consent of the States of the kingdom; however the right of the king to have money coined remains inviolated.

SECTION 80.

The national military establishments for the army and navy shall be sustained in accordance with the contracts with the provinces and cities; also the institution called the assessment (repartition) shall remain inviolated as to their foundations, until the king and the States deem it necessary to make alterations. No new levy of men in the country shall take place unless both the king and the States consent to issue a decree for that purpose.

SECTION 85.

As fundamental laws are to be considered the present form of government, the regulation to assemble the Diets, the Succession Act, and the edict concerning the general freedom of the press, which laws are to be unanimously established during the session of this Diet, by the States and the king, according to the principles laid down in the present form of government.

SECTION 86.

By freedom of the press is understood the right of every Swede to publish writings without meeting with any obstacle on the part of the public authority; without being thereafter prosecuted for their contents, except before a legal tribunal, and unless said contents be contrary to the laws tending to maintain the public peace, and stay the progress of general information. All the acts and documents relative to any cause whatsoever, with exception of the acts which are drawn up in the Council of State and before the king, in diplomatic affairs and matters of the military command, can be published by the press without reserve. There shall not be printed any records or documents concerning the bank and public debt which contain objects that must be kept secret.

SECTION 93.

When the king dies, and the successor to the throne is a minor, the Council shall convoke the States. The publication for the purpose shall take place within the space of fifteen days after the death of the king, in the churches of the capital, and immediately afterwards, in the remainder of the kingdom. It is for the States, without taking into consideration the testament of the king deceased, concerning the administration of the kingdom, to constitute one or more tutors (guardians,) who shall preside in his name and in accordance with the present constitution, until the king becomes of age.

SECTION 96.

The States of the kingdom shall appoint at each diet a man distinguished for his learning in the laws and his integrity, who in the capacity of their attorney, and according to their instructions, shall watch that the judges and employés comply with the respective rules and regulations, and who shall prosecute, before the proper tribunals and in due form of law, such as in the excercise of their duties commit illegalities by being partial, showing regard for individuals, or otherwise, and who neglect the faithful performance of their duties. Such attorney shall, nevertheless, be subject entirely to the same obligations which are prescribed by the code and proceedings to be observed by the public prosecutors.

SECTION 108.

For the better maintaining the freedom of the press, the States shall nominate at each diet six men famous for their intelligence and learning, with the procurator of justice, who will preside in their assemblies. These mandatories, of whom two besides the proctor of justice are to be lawyers, shall have the following functions: If an author or a printer personally delivers to them a manuscript intended for the press, and asks their opinion on the law relative to the freedom of the press in case of a prosecution, then the proctor of justice and at least three mandatories, one of whom to be a lawyer, shall give their opinion in writing. If they declare that the manuscript may be printed, the author and printer shall not be liable to any responsibility, but the said mandatories shall be held responsible. These mandatories are to be elected by the States through the medium of six electors chosen by each order who have to vote collectively. If in the interval of the diets one of those mandatories should fail (be missing) then the others shall nominate a qualified person to fill the vacancy.

SECTION 109.

The parliament shall not continue longer than three months from the day when the king will have given to the States or their committee, information respecting the condition of the public finances and the necessities of the State. If, however, by this time the States of the kingdom have not closed the business of the diet, they have to inform the king and demand that the diet may be extended to a time not longer than one month, which to refuse or prevent the king shall not have the power. If, contrary to expectation, it might happen that at the expiration of the term of said prolongation the States of the kingdom have not settled the condition of the national expenditures, or if they have been engaged in fixing upon the amount of a new subsidy, then shall the king dissolve the States, and the previous subsidy shall continue until the next diet. If the total amount of the subsidy be determined and the States cannot agree upon the repartition, then in accordance with the report of the sum which has been fixed upon and that which had been assessed on the preceding diet, shall the articles fixed upon in the last edict of subsidy be raised or lessened (diminished) in equal proportion, and the States shall commission their deputies to the bank and public debt to draw up and dispatch, according to this principle, a new edict of subsidy.

SECTION 110.

No deputy to the diet can be prosecuted by law nor deprived of his liberty for his actions and discourses in the assemblies of the orders of the kingdom or in the State Committees, unless the order to which he belongs have given permission by a formal decision that has been acceded to by five-sixths of the members of the order who were present when the opinions were given in general assembly. Neither can a deputy be sent away from the seat of parliament. If any individual or body, whether civil, military, or a party of what name soever, either of their own accord or in consequence of an order, undertake to commit violence upon the States of the kingdom or their committees, or a deputy in particular, or undertake to injure the freedom of their deliberations and decisions, that shall be considered as treason, and it will depend upon the States to order the prosecution by law for such offences.

SECTION 111.

If, however, a deputy during the session of the diet, on his way to or his return from the diet, be distured by words or deeds, after having given information as to his destination, such a case will be regarded and punished as an offence against the public safety.

SECTION 112.

No employé nor functionary shall improperly, and by authority of his office, exert his influence upon the elections of deputies. If any one is doing so he shall forfeit his place.

SECTION 113.

The mandatories charged with the assessments, and with the application of the dispositions concerning the subsidies, shall not be liable to any responsibility for their assessments.

SECTION 114.

The king will maintain all the States of the kingdom in the enjoyment of their privileges, advantages, rights and liberties.

In witness whereof we have agreed to confirm, accept and sanction this act, signing and affixing thereto our names and seals. Given at Stockholm on the sixth day of June in the year of grace 1809.

On the part of the Order of the Nobility,
M. ANKARSVARD, *h. t. Marshal of the Diet.*
On the part of the Order of the Clergy,
IAC. AX. LINDBLOM, *Speaker.*
On the part of the Order of the Bourgeoisie,
H. N. SCHVAN, *h. t. Speaker*
On the part of the Order of the Peasants,
LARS OLSSON, *h. t. Speaker.*

All that is herein prescribed, we will not only ourselves accept as the inviolable fundamental law, but we command and order all those who owe faith, respect and obedience to us and our successors, as well as to the kingdom, to acknowledge the present (actual) form of government, to observe it, and to conform and submit themselves to the same. In testimony whereof we have signed and confirmed this act by our own hand, and have avowedly hereto affixed our royal seal· Dated in our residence at Stockholm on the sixth day of the month of June, in the year of grace 1809.

CHARLES.

www.ingramcontent.com/pod-product-compliance
Lightning Source LLC
LaVergne TN
LVHW021313110826
845150LV00003B/563
9781425558406